Grace Upon Grace

GRACE

Nine Decades of Stories

UPON

from a Farm Boy, Midshipman,

GRACE

Officer, and Evangelist

JIM WILSON

COMMUNITY CHRISTIAN MINISTRIES
MOSCOW, IDAHO

Published by Community Christian Ministries
P.O. Box 9754, Moscow, Idaho 83843
208.883.0997 | www.ccmbooks.org

Cover design: Samuel Dickison
Interior design: Valerie Anne Bost
Back cover author photo: Mark LaMoreaux, lamoreauxphoto.com
Author photo on page x: Eizabeth Dickson, elizabethalisonphotography.com
"Giant Torii from Itsukushima Shrine in Miyajima," photo in Chapter 27: Flickr user Ankur P
(https://flickr.com/photos/ankurp/35110677474). Used under a Creative Commons 2.0 Generic
license (https://creativecommons.org/licenses/by/2.0/legalcode). Cropped and color edited.
Thanks to the author's family for contributing many photos...and for leaving their social
media accounts unguarded so we could pilfer many more.

Printed in the United States of America.

20 21 22 23 24 25 26 27 28   9 8 7 6 5 4 3 2 1

To Lisa Just, my brains and my memory,
without whom this book would not have been written.

"And the things you have heard me say
in the presence of many witnesses
entrust to reliable people
who will also be qualified to teach others."

2 Timothy 2:2

CONTENTS

"For from his fullness we have all received, grace upon grace."
—John 1:16

Some want to live within the sound
Of church or chapel bell;
I want to run a rescue shop
Within a yard of hell.
—C.T. Studd

INTRODUCTION

One of God's great gifts to me has been the privilege of being a son of Jim Wilson. There are countless ways I could talk about this, and any number of directions I could go, but I want to limit what I say to the fact that this is the introduction to my father's autobiography. I have to limit myself in this way lest we find my introduction turning into a book of its own.

As the subtitle puts it, we have here nine decades of stories from a farm boy, midshipman, officer, and evangelist. My father did plenty of other things also, but as you read this book, you should see that this subtitle really does capture the shape of the basic narrative. My father has roots deep in the Nebraska soil; he took to the Navy and to the sea as only a Nebraskan can, was indelibly shaped by that, and after his conversion at the Naval Academy (and down to the present), his central drive has been that of sharing the gospel with others.

There is no such thing as not having an opportunity to share the gospel. A number of years ago, when he had to have quadruple bypass surgery, I had the privilege of driving him to Spokane a number of times and accompanying him to his various appointments. Part of that responsibility of mine was to serve as a coolie, carrying a cardboard box filled with evangelistic literature. At various times when he has been hospitalized, he has taken this as clear guidance from God to set up a book table in his hospital room.

Many of the stories contained in this book I have heard many times, both when I was growing up and also in my adult life as I have heard my father recount all the ways God has been good to him—grace upon grace. That phrase comes from John 1:16. "For from his fullness we have all received, grace upon grace" (John 1:16,

ESV). The Greek is χάριν ἀντὶ χάριτος (*charin anti charitos*), but the *anti* there does not mean *against*, but rather *instead of*. God led off with grace, and then when He replaced that grace, it was with more grace. The context is talking about Moses (grace) and then Christ (more grace).

This is the pattern that God loves to follow, and this is why, when we see the new covenant replacing the old covenant—grace for grace, grace upon grace, more grace instead of previous grace—we are seeing the heart of God. "And with great power gave the apostles witness of the resurrection of the Lord Jesus: and great grace was upon them all" (Acts 4:33, KJV). The members of our family have been witnesses of, and recipients of, great grace. This book is my father's thanksgiving, and in this introduction, I would like to add the thanksgiving of the entire family.

As a pattern that He loves to follow, God pours out grace in the lives of His people, and so it is fully appropriate for someone who has experienced a lifetime of "great grace" to use the phrase *grace upon grace*. As I remember my father as a young oak, and as I see him now in his deep autumn, I can actually see nothing but the glorious gospel reality that grace is *cumulative*.

Even though I have heard a number of these stories repeatedly, they were a delight to read through again. Some were new, and some details were new, and all of them point to the faithfulness of God. Our family has been wonderfully blessed to have been led by a man whose great characteristic was the ability to believe the text in front of him, whatever it said.

The stories are great as stories, and I trust you will enjoy them that way, and be edified by them as well. But growing up in this household was like growing up in the book of Acts. By this I don't mean miracles (although some of the things that happened were indeed pretty weird), but I do mean growing up with the abiding sense of God's presence. He was always there, in the story, as an active presence. He was not the dead backdrop, or the painted scenery, in front of which we little Christians were to live our lives. No, His presence as an active agent was constantly expected, and while He was there, He *did* things. He answered prayers. He led and directed. He *provided*.

Our prayer is that as a result of reading this testimony of God's faithfulness, you will be encouraged in the belief that *God is good, all the time.*

Douglas Wilson
November 2019

Jim, Bessie, and Douglas, 1953

PREFACE

You are about to read a narrative of my life. It includes real events, fuzzy memories, perhaps a bit of fiction (entirely accidental), both good and bad examples, and some preaching. I will recount events that may strain your credulity, but they are not fabrications.

This book is about more than just my life on Earth. It is about the grace of God throughout my life: forgiveness, obedience, and every other provision that had nothing to do with me. In certain places, grace is the obvious explanation for the outcome. Yet everything else was grace-caused as well. My life is a testimony of the goodness, faithfulness, and forgiveness of God.

My life is made up of my hundreds of friends; my wife, Bessie; my children, Douglas, Evan, Heather, and Gordon; their wives and husband; their fifteen children; and their children's children (thirty-four at the last count); my parents; my five brothers; and all of their descendants.

I was hesitant to write a book about myself. "These chapters are so brazenly egotistic," as John Buchan put it, that my first thought was not to write them. But with the recommendation of Doug and his wife, Nancy, and with Gordon's encouragement, I am writing.

As you read about my life, you will hopefully notice two things: God is looking after me and using me, and most of my stories are about other people. My life is full of other people for the sake of other people. Many years ago, I decided to seek to love whoever was in front of me at any given moment.

I have a fairly good memory for names. In my ninety-two years, I have encountered thousands of people. Some of those encounters were neutral, some very positive, and some negative. The neutral ones I have forgotten. Names have been changed or left out when I describe any negative encounters.

The most important thing in my life is my relationship to God and my fellowship with Him. The second is my relationship and fellowship with Bessie, our children, our grandchildren, and now our great-grand-children. The third is evangelism. The fourth was my professional life as a naval officer. I have not written separately on evangelism here because it has happened in every year over the last seventy-two years, and these stories are intertwined with the rest of my story.*

In the 1930s and 1940s, there were two single-picture cartoons at the bottom of the funny papers. One was of a couple with a teen-age daughter and son. The other was of a bachelors' boarding house. One of the bachelors in that cartoon was a pompous old man named Major Hoople. Major Hoople was known for telling of his heroic exploits in the Boer War.† Over the years, if Bessie ever thought I was bragging too much in public, she would say two words: *Major Hoople*. No one else knew what she was talking about, but I knew. Bessie is not here, so you have my permission to write these words in the margin for me: *Major Hoople*.

Hebrews 13:7 says, "Remember your leaders, who spoke the word of God to you. Consider the outcome of their way of life *and imitate their faith*." I have been speaking the word of God for seventy-two years. Here is an opportunity to consider the outcome of my way of life and *imitate my faith*. The apostle Paul said it this way:

> *Therefore I exhort you, be imitators of me.* For this reason I have sent
> to you Timothy, who is my beloved and faithful child in the Lord,

* I have written three books on evangelism: *Principles of War, Weapons & Tactics*, and *Taking Men Alive*.
† The Boer War (1899–1902) was fought between the Boers and the British in South Africa.

and *he will remind you of my ways which are in Christ,* just as I teach everywhere in every church. (1 Cor. 4:16–17)

Whether, then, you eat or drink or whatever you do, do all to the glory of God. Give no offense either to Jews or to Greeks or to the church of God; just as I also please all men in all things, not seeking my own profit but the profit of the many, so that they may be saved. *Be imitators of me, just as I also am of Christ.* (1 Cor. 10:31–11:1)

The quotations on grace from the Scriptures at the head of each chapter do not necessarily relate directly to the chapter content. Each is inspired writing about something that happened to someone else centuries ago. But as a Christian, I have seen the grace of God in my life in many of the ways these verses talk about. I am not Paul or Timothy or Titus—but I need the same grace that they received from God the Father and the Lord Jesus Christ. When you read these verses, may you be overwhelmed with the One who gives grace, peace, and mercy—the Father, Jesus Christ, and the Holy Spirit.

Thanks to Lisa Just for putting this book together and doing much research digging through my old letters, files, and photos; to my daughter, Heather, for typing up many, many pages of handwritten manuscript; and to my son Doug for his work in editing the finished book.

A special thanks to my longtime friends Clay and Clara Buckingham, Graham and Libby Gutsche, Mike and Carol Heath, and Ray and Shanon Jones. You have been a great blessing to me.

"For from his fullness we have all received, grace upon grace" (John 1:16 ESV). Most of this grace I did not recognize when it came. I recognize it now as I turn my attention to write the story of my life. If it were not for grace, I would not be here. I would have died at least three times. I would not have been saved, married Bessie, or been the

means of other people being saved and growing in the Lord. I thank
God the Father for sending His Son that we might be saved. And I
hope that this book will direct others to the Father.

I thank God also for Psalm 91 (ESV):

> He who dwells in the shelter of the Most High
>   will abide in the shadow of the Almighty.
> I will say to the LORD, "My refuge and my fortress,
>   my God, in whom I trust."

> For he will deliver you from the snare of the fowler
>   and from the deadly pestilence.
> He will cover you with his pinions,
>   and under his wings you will find refuge;
>   his faithfulness is a shield and buckler.
> You will not fear the terror of the night,
>   nor the arrow that flies by day,
> nor the pestilence that stalks in darkness,
>   nor the destruction that wastes at noonday.

> A thousand may fall at your side,
>   ten thousand at your right hand,
>   but it will not come near you.
> You will only look with your eyes
>   and see the recompense of the wicked.

> Because you have made the LORD your dwelling place—
>   the Most High, who is my refuge—
> no evil shall be allowed to befall you,
>   no plague come near your tent.

For he will command his angels concerning you
    to guard you in all your ways.
On their hands they will bear you up,
    lest you strike your foot against a stone.
You will tread on the lion and the adder;
    the young lion and the serpent you will trample underfoot.

"Because he holds fast to me in love, I will deliver him;
    I will protect him, because he knows my name.
When he calls to me, I will answer him;
    I will be with him in trouble;
    I will rescue him and honor him.
With long life I will satisfy him
    and show him my salvation."

Jim (in the washtub) and his brother Leonard Lorraine, circa 1929

CHAPTER 1

THE NORTH ROOM

The boundary lines have fallen for me in pleasant places; surely I
have a delightful inheritance. (Ps. 16:6)

I "wrote" this last night (July 21, 2006); I'm putting it on paper now.
I wasn't sleeping—at least, I don't think I was. I had been asleep and
wasn't awake enough to open my eyes. I'm sure it wasn't a dream, because there were no pictures, still or moving. Dreams, however real
they seem at the time, give themselves away because of the erratic
aberrations from reality that do not stand up in the daylight. There
were none of those.

I was thinking of a place. My thoughts did not seem to have a
starting point, as if I had been awake for a while and then decided
to think.

The place is a room, the North Room, in a farmhouse in Nebraska.
It has always been a place of awe for me, and I am not easily awed.
Some places are constructed to cause awe or worship. St. Paul's
Cathedral causes awe for God in me in an indirect way. I am first
awed at the brilliance of Christopher Wren and secondarily at the
God who made him. It is the same with the Daibutsu in Kamakura.
Writing doesn't reach me, at least in terms of awe, whether it is of
Shardik or Aslan or the Ring of Power or the appearance of Pan in
The Wind in Willows. The North Room does.

The North Room, I think, is a living room, although living does
not take place there. The living is in the kitchen and dining rooms.
In my memory, it was always closed off like a holy place. It was cool
in the summer (probably cold in the winter). I do not recall the lights

1

ever being on in the North Room, whether kerosene lamps or electric lights. It was always pleasantly dark; dark in a nice, cool, comfortable way. For me it would have been sacrilege to turn on the lights.

One hundred years ago, when my aunt and mother were born in that house, there was no North Room. As the farm prospered and the family got bigger, the house was made into a proper residence with additional rooms, including the North Room and a veranda on the east side overlooking a lovely, large front yard with a front gate opening onto the road. All of these seemed holy; none of them were used.

In my childhood we played together there, my brothers, my cousins, and I. It was a wonderful place to play. It never occurred to us to be rowdy or wild in the North Room.

The furniture I do not recall, other than the bookcase, and of the books, I recall B.M. Bower's *The Flying U Ranch* and *Chip of the Flying U*, which has to prove the place really was not holy in a God-directed way.

Men make churches, shrines, and temples that cause people to worship because of their grandeur. All of these will end like the boast of Ozymandias: "Nothing beside remains."* Other places, like the North Room, which seem to be sacred although they are not consecrated, will end in decay even faster. "'This is what the Lord says: Heaven is my throne and the earth is my footstool. Where is the house you will build for me? Where will my resting place be? Has not my hand made all these things, and so they came into being?' declares the Lord. 'This is the one I esteem: he who is humble and contrite in spirit, and trembles at my word'" (Isa. 66:1–2).

It has now been thirteen years since I first wrote these paragraphs. It has been ten years since the house was lived in. Raccoons

* Percy Bysshe Shelley, "Ozymandias."

have attacked it. It is all decaying fast. The living things, the trees and bushes, are taking over. One of these years, the house, the North Room, and all the trees will be deliberately removed, and that portion of the southeast quarter of Section 33 of Platte County, Nebraska, will be cornfields.

Leonard and Jim, circa 1931

CHAPTER 2

EARLY EVIDENCE OF GRACE & MEMORIES FROM ELM STREET (1927–1936)

He who had set me apart before I was born . . . who called me by

his grace . . . . (Gal. 1:15)

I was born on October 6, 1927, in a farmhouse nine miles northwest of Monroe, Nebraska. It was the home of my Uncle Evan Lloyd and my Aunt Annabelle.*

My parents got together in this way. My father had been living up in Lemmon, South Dakota, (right on the North Dakota border) with his parents. He rode a horse down to Iowa and got a job working on a farm. The farmer's wife had been to teacher's college with my mother. She called up my mother and said, "We've got a live one working for us—come on over!" My parents were married in 1924 in Council Bluffs, Iowa, right across the Missouri River from Omaha. Shortly afterward, they moved to Faulkton, South Dakota, in order to farm. Leonard Lorraine, my older brother, was born there in 1925. But Mom got homesick for Nebraska, so my parents moved back in a covered hay wagon when Mom was pregnant with me. You don't normally think of covered wagons having rubber tires, but ours did.

---

* Many of the details in chapters 2–6 come courtesy of my older brother, Leonard Lorraine, who wrote down stories I would otherwise have forgotten. He went by Lorraine when we were younger, but switched to Leonard in later years.

In 1929, we moved to 2503 Elm Street in South Omaha—near where my father worked in the Armour meat packing plant. Immediately behind our backyard was a retaining wall, and above that was Plattner's lumberyard. Most of the yard was abandoned to weeds and an old cement mixer. For us and the neighbor kids, it was our own private park.

I was ill for the first three years of my life. At age two, I caught scarlet fever from my cousin. I was put in a quarantine ward of the hospital known as the pest house. While there I contracted small pox and diphtheria. It was by the grace of God that I lived. There is no other adequate explanation. As a result of these illnesses, I did not learn to talk until I was three and a half years old.

My earliest memories include lying on the couch with a hard rubber toy car which I used to knock a ball to the floor. The ball was red, and the car was blue. I also remember sitting on my grandfather's lap on the front porch. He had a large white mustache. My grandmother had died before I was born. I remember from her photo that she had a very dark complexion and dark, almost black, eyes. Leonard (my father) and his twin sister, Leona, were the youngest of their nine children. My father's oldest sister, Rhoda, was married and had two children before my father was even born.

One day, when we were still preschool, my friend Ralph Wolfe and I decided to leave home. My mother saw us walking across the Bancroft Street Bridge, about three blocks away. She caught us and took us home. Then she took about twenty feet of clothesline, tied one end around my waist, and attached the other end to the house. I was confined to an eighteen-foot half circle in the backyard. Much later, Mom told me that when my father came home he was not pleased with her for tying me up.

There was a corner grocery store called Raznowski's on 25th and Bancroft Streets, a block away from our home. One time when Lorraine was in first grade, Mom sent the two of us to the store to buy a dozen eggs.* The eggs were not in a carton; they were loose in a brown paper bag. On the return trip, I asked Lorraine for the privilege of carrying the eggs. He gave them to me. A few steps later, I tripped and fell and broke all of the eggs. I have no recollection of the consequences other than how awful I felt for losing the eggs.

The normal way home from school was past the pickle factory. They kept a barrel outside on the corner where they would dump the day's discards. Sometimes we could find a great plump (and good) dill pickle floating on the top. If there were a few pickles, they would be shared out and eaten on the way home. Sometimes, however, we had the challenge of how to get a larger amount home safely for the family.

A few blocks from home in the opposite direction of Raznowski's was the Hinky Dinky corner grocery. The barbershop next to it always had a puzzle in the window. Lorraine enjoyed matching wits with the barber on the puzzles. Once he won three half-pound boxes of chocolate by guessing the number of beans in a jar.

In the first grade, I was walking home past another corner grocery at 24th and Oak with Ralph Wolfe when he volunteered to teach me how to steal a cookie.

I was interested. Ralph said that his mother had given him money to buy a pound of hamburger on the way home. Here is how his scheme would work. We would go into the store, and he would give his order for the hamburger. When the owner went into the back

* Eggs were 10¢ a dozen.

room to grind the meat, Ralph would zip over to the glass door that covered the cookie bin, open the door, take out two cookies, and give one of them to me.

It worked according to plan. I only lived two blocks away. The cookies were chocolate with marshmallow on top and a chocolate coating over the marshmallow. I ate my cookie in the first block. Then I realized my mother would ask me where I got the chocolate. So in the second block, I industriously licked and scrubbed my face to remove all evidence. She did not ask. Sixteen years later, after I was saved, I went back to 24th and Oak to pay for the cookie. The store was not there, so I gave the money to the Lord.

I had my first day of school in 1932. Lorraine opened the door of the kindergarten classroom and shoved me in. I cried.

School and I did not fare well together the first six years. I spent one year in kindergarten, one and a half years in first grade, one year in second grade, one and a half in third grade, and one year in fourth grade. (At the same time, Lorraine skipped half of his third grade year and another half in sixth grade.) Everything seemed impossible to me. Once in second grade, I had to turn in a paper. It was impossible. I couldn't finish it. I put it on the teacher's desk, hurried out of the room, and ran around the school to a sidewalk behind a bank of the playground so I could not be seen. It did not work. A little girl walked over to where I was hiding and told me the teacher wanted to see me. I have no memory of what happened to that impossible paper.

Sometimes we would walk to Hanscom Park for the playground there. Mom would open a box of corn flakes, take out the cereal, and give us the wax paper that had held the flakes. We would sit on this waxed paper to go down the slide. That made us slide a lot faster.

Aunt Myrtle and Uncle Shirley lived across the street from this park. Uncle Shirley was missing one finger. He had at least two

stories about how he had lost it: 1) A cow had bitten it off. 2) Aunt
Myrtle had bitten it off. They had three children: LaVerne, Veronica,
and Kenneth. LaVerne was killed in a fight while he was in the Navy.
After the family moved to Seattle, Kenneth left home to come back
to Omaha. He was sixteen. He rode freight trains the whole way and
arrived at our house on Elm Street in the middle of a rainy night. He
did not want to wake us up, so he stayed the night in the coal shed.

Our house was heated by a coal-burning stove in the living room.
We burned big blocks of anthracite, the ash of which was big clin-
kers. The house had electricity and indoor plumbing.

During Prohibition, I went with my father visiting some of his
friends. He gave me a taste of homemade beer and told me not to
tell my mother. When she was sixteen, she had signed a pledge not
to drink. I did tell her.

One day, I told the other kids that I knew how to stop cars. I had
seen policemen do it by standing in the middle of the street with
their arms outstretched. I walked into the middle of the street and
held out my arms. Sure enough, the next car stopped. However, the
car was driven by my father. I got spanked in the middle of the street.

In 1935, my father drove into a wall at the end of a dead-end
street. It was foggy. There were no signs and no lights. He broke his
legs, his ribs, and his jaw. He was thirty-five years old. He had had
perfect teeth. He had never even had a cavity. He lost all his teeth in
the accident and had a limp the rest of his life. He sued the city for
$10,000 for failing to have streetlights or signage, and he eventually
won, although the lawyers got almost all of the money.

Because of his injuries, my father lost his job at the packing plant.
It was the middle of the Depression. After he was well, he got a job as
a watchman on a WPA* project a few blocks from our home.

---

* Works Progress Administration, the largest of the American New Deal agencies.

CHAPTER 3
THE FARMHOUSE (1936)

But we believe that we will be saved through the grace
of the Lord Jesus . . . . (Acts 15:11)

In the spring of 1936, we moved to 4366 Crown Point Avenue, a
small farm on the north edge of North Omaha. It was a little house
and one outbuilding on an acre of ground. The lot and house faced
south, with a few trees in the front yard. East of the lot, the hill went
sharply upward. We were separated from our neighbors to the west
by a row of poplar trees. Our acre ran to Kansas Avenue a block
away—but as the other end of a row of potato plants, it seemed over
the horizon. Here is one of Lorraine's memories of moving in:

> On our first day in our new home (March 19, I believe, a Friday),
> it was expedition time. Dad and Jim and I "walked off to see the
> Wizard." It was really the hardware man up at 42nd and Ames (about
> a mile or more away) in a small retail community there. A new world
> was opening, for Dad bought several garden implements and many
> packets of seeds. We were all loaded down for the return trip, because
> Dad also got a heavy bag of seed potatoes. Dad had arranged to have
> our garden area plowed. We spent the weekend getting part of it ready
> for an early garden and planted that part. That was the beginning of
> several years of heavy garden experiences.

We had a cow, chickens, and the garden. We planted all kinds of
stuff. I still remember finding parsnips that had been in the ground
all winter. They tasted very good.

9

I continued the third grade at Belvedere, seven blocks up over the hill. I was a fat little kid. For some reason, I was a favorite among the teachers.

One time there was a performance at the school that all the parents came to see. My classmates all had soft clown hats. They were to go onto the stage, each doing a somersault. I was the last to go on, but instead of a soft clown hat, I was given a long, stiff dunce cap. When I went to do my somersault, my forehead just skidded across the stage. The place broke up.

The outbuilding became home for the chickens, and we would let them out of their fenced area to roam about once they got bigger. Putting them back in was a task. Chickens do not herd well. At some point, Lorraine discovered that when the cow bellowed, the chickens all panicked and headed for the shed. With this new incentive, we all worked on our bellowing. Out came a bellow, and chickens from everywhere scrambled for the roost, half-flying, half-running.

Then came the potato bugs. Adult potato bugs are a striped hard-shell beetle. Their offspring, however, are squishy red blobs of varying sizes (depending on how many leaves they have eaten). The adults had laid their eggs in our potato plants. No pesticide had been developed against them yet, so we threw ourselves into the job of ridding the field of the bugs by hand—turning our fingers orange in the process. Our task was to pick a million bugs off the bottom of potato plant leaves, at a rate of 1¢ for every hundred bugs. The special equipment we used for this was a glass Mason jar with a little kerosene in the bottom.

By Sunday, May 17, we still hadn't won the potato bug war— but as things turned out, it wasn't going to matter. It started out a beautiful spring day. Then a dark cloud came over the hill to the west. We hurried to get the chickens in as the wind picked up. There was no time to get the cow from the neighbor's pasture where we kept her during the day. The first rain began to fall, and we all got in the house. Hail bounced off the ground and the roof, and the wind screamed; the poplars to the west were bending at the waist. The darkness outside was almost complete. Our parents hustled us all into the southeast bedroom and closed the door. All we could do was listen. We heard the hail thunder; we heard windows breaking; and water began to run under the bedroom door.

Then it was over. Mom and Dad kept us in the bedroom while they cleaned up the broken glass. The hail had shattered all the windows in the house except those on the east side (the leeward side). The poplars were stripped of their leaves, many of which were plastered across the walls inside our house. Two of the poplars had been snapped off. We went outside with our winter coats on, for the temperature had dropped mightily, and it was easy to see why. It looked like a snowstorm had hit, but it was hail everywhere—the ditches were drifted full. In some places, the hail was knee-deep. The garden was gone, and the trees were bare of leaves and bark. But the chickens were all right.

It was cold, but the sun was out, and the hail melted so fast that there was a flash flood. Lorraine and I were sent to check on the cow which was in a community pasture near the creek. People were standing in their yards, in the road, surveying the damage. Many inches of hail were still on the ground. As we passed along, the strongest rumor was that most of the cattle had washed down the creek and that hail had killed the others. We wondered whether we would find her.

The pasture was a mess; the creek was high and roaring. Cattle were huddled in little groups among downed trees and branches. In one of those groups, with eyes wide and rolling, our cow stood covered with cuts and looking ready to run—if she had any idea where it might do any good to run to. She wasn't sure she was glad to see us, but she came along anyway.

Later we learned that we had suffered an eighty-four-mile-an-hour wind in addition to the hail. Four cows had been lost down the creek, and others had broken through the fence in a panic and were founds some distance away.

My brother Everett was born at home on June 11. We older four were introduced to him in the morning. Harold's question was, "Is it a doll?" That month, we had another windstorm (maybe a tornado) where all but two of the row of Lombardy poplars west of the house were snapped off.

Then we had a plague of grasshoppers. They ate everything, and everything ate them. The grasshoppers went to sleep at night on the top of chest-high weeds. Lorraine and I would go out early in the morning each with an empty mason jar. We would place our jars over the tops of the weeds and snap off the stems. We would get a hundred grasshoppers inside the jar. We fed them to the chickens. Some would get swallowed whole and would be still kicking inside the chicken's grub bag. Sometimes we saw a grasshopper leg sticking out of the feathers.

The last windstorm of that summer had quite a different appearance from the other storms. There were no clouds in the sky. We could see a dark brown-black mass building over the horizon in the northwest. *Dust.* It was carried straight though Omaha at 120 miles per hour. That was the end of our little farm.

SEATTLE (1936–1937)

Thus says the LORD: "The people who survived the sword found grace in the wilderness; when Israel sought for rest, the Lord appeared to him from far away." (Jer. 31:1–2)

My father's twin, Leona, and his older sister, Myrtle, had been urging us to come west where they believed there would be better opportunities for us. So we sold everything, invested in a 1928 LaSalle, packed in Mom and Dad, five kids, clothes, and linens, and in early August we left Crown Point.

Our first stop was Faulkton, South Dakota, to see friends that Dad had met while farming there in 1926. The drinking water was so foul-tasting that the kids were offered coffee. I don't know how I survived because I did not drink the coffee or the water.

Our next stop was Bismarck, North Dakota, where one of Dad's brothers lived. His name was Jesse James Wilson. Guess who he was named after. Yes, that's right. He and his wife Elberta had many children, eighteen I think. They had a bunkhouse for the overflow of kids. Three of us cousins slept in the bunkhouse.

We then went on to Lemmon, South Dakota, where my father's brother Clarence lived. He was a sheep rancher. My brother Leonard wrote in his diary, "Uncle Clarence, for this was his territory, didn't follow roads. In this kind of country, he just cut across." There were no trees, but rounded hills that stretched on forever. I can remember a very large boulder that a glacier had deposited on top of a grass-covered hill.

From there, we drove to Aunt Florence's home in Sturgis. We were fascinated with Uncle Essel's radio, complete with earphones. The real attraction was the cool homemade root beer that Aunt Florence brought up out of a cave. The girls, Gloria and Joan, were the same age as Leonard and me. The boys, Wayne and Ronald, were younger.*

"These days were to be the last with family until we got to Seattle," Leonard wrote. "In that great distance in between, there were cowboys, mountains, rivers and lakes, apple orchards and big trees . . . . a long way east of Miles City, we saw our first cowboys—at some distance ahead on slopes that appeared unfit for man or beast . . . . They were close enough to the highway that I think we waved at them. At Miles City, the Yellowstone River became our companion for many, many miles, although we were going in opposite directions. We stopped along there in the first of three cabin camp stops. The next day was memorable for lots of reasons. Along that beautiful stream [the Yellowstone River] we had a flat tire."

Flat tires were a normal occurrence on the trip. We built small stone houses with river rocks while our father fixed the flat. "Dad was wrestling with the tire . . . and that was going to take a long time . . . . So we kids . . . built our own monument there between the road and the river. All of us gathered rocks and built a cairn, a pile of rocks in the rough shape of a pyramid. We were reluctant to leave off our building when Dad was ready to roll again. But people would know we had come that way. We had left our mark on the face of that part of the world."

That was the first day we saw real mountains, and lots of them. We spent the night in Deer Lodge. Although it was August, the nights were cool.

* The summer before my senior year at Navy, I hitchhiked west and visited them. That was thirteen or fourteen years later. The next time that I saw Joan was at a family reunion a few years ago. She looked like her mother looked the last time I saw her, in 1949.

The next morning, we passed through Missoula and went up, and up, and up. This was Lookout Pass, the Idaho-Montana border. There were no interstate freeways at that time. It was a scary drive. "Someone had forgotten to put a railing on the outside edge of the road," Leonard wrote. "There was just space out there, and it seemed to go down forever. It may not have been a drop of thousands of feet, but what's the difference after several hundred? It was the scariest mountain ride I've ever been on. I don't know how Dad must have felt. We were in the outer lane, with the usual mountain curves, and an eight-year-old car loaded with the large family and all our worldly goods—and no railing." However, my father said he never had to shift gears, up or down, because of the mountain grade. Shortly afterward, we saw "perhaps the greatest beauty on the trip, Lake Coeur d'Alene, a blue jewel of great size set in a necklace of mountains and trees." Then it was on to tumbleweeds and the barren plateau of eastern Washington.

Aunt Myrtle, Uncle Shirley, Aunt Leona, Uncle Ed, and Uncle Lester all lived in Seattle. We had lots of cousins there. For six months we lived in Seattle at three different cousins' houses.

My father was very strong and was a fast perfectionist.[†] He was relatively silent. He used no profanity but did use slang like "doggone it." However, we kids were not allowed to use that kind of slang, and I grew up without it.

Our father did not allow fighting (or arguing loudly). Lorraine and I were fighting one time in the dining room when our father came in from the kitchen with his razor strop.[‡] He did not say anything. Lorraine and I were whipped with the razor strop.

[†] Perfectionists want things done right and in order. It usually takes a long time to get it "right." A fast perfectionist does things right in a short time.

[‡] Before there were safety razors or electric razors, men shaved with a very keen-edge straight blade. They kept it sharp daily by the use of two three-inch-wide leather bands called strops. The other function of the strop was to spank boys.

A similar event took place earlier in the summer when we still lived in North Omaha. I was eight years old. We were in the front yard. Dad came around from the back of the house. He didn't say a word. He walked over the beech tree, took out his jack knife, and cut a switch. We got switched on the back of our bare legs.

The most important thing that happened during those six months in Seattle was going to church and Sunday school at the Church of the Open Door, pastored by a man named E.W. Kenyon. I was very much awakened spiritually. I could have been led to the Lord at that time. It gave me a hunger for God that was not satisfied until my conversion some years later. At Christmastime, we were given pocket-size American Standard 1901 New Testaments. I learned a hymn called "Where the Gates Swing Outward Never." I had known no other hymns. I can still sing one verse of it, though I have not sung it in church since. I also learned a Sunday School song: "She went away singing and came back bringing others to the water that was not in the well."*

In the March 1937, we returned to Nebraska in the LaSalle for Dad's suit against the city of Omaha over his 1935 accident. Along the way, we got into the middle of a caravan of gypsies. My father was dark-complexioned. Each time we came to a town, the town marshal would move the caravan through town. We got moved with it every time.

* "Jesus Gave Her Water" (author unknown).

CHAPTER 5

MILLARD, NEBRASKA (1937–1938)

For the law was given through Moses; grace and truth came
through Jesus Christ. (John 1:17)

Back in Nebraska, we stayed with cousins in Omaha for two weeks, then moved into a whitewashed chicken house at Aunt Rhoda and Uncle Cal's, at 52nd and C in South Omaha. It was low-cost housing and a gardening opportunity.

The main line of the Union Pacific was immediately next to the property. Freight trains and the streamliner passenger trains went by. The *City of Los Angeles* and the *City of San Francisco* passed us daily. We would wave at the engineers from our garden, close by the right-of-way.

The garden was very big that summer. Dad bought each of us three older boys a hoe and our own whetstone. Our hoes were very sharp and were kept sharp.

At the end of the summer, we moved into Millard, a town of 300 people five miles west of Omaha, where we lived in an apartment attached to a commercial garage. On the other side of us lived the Paul family, who owned a general store on the north side of their house. We had so much produce from the garden at 52nd and C that we transported it in the back seat of the LaSalle back to the Millard apartment, where Mom canned everything. On one trip the back seat was filled to the roof with sweet corn, on another with watermelons. Mom canned hundreds of jars of everything in the apartment, even tomatoes, watermelon rinds (pickled),* wild plums, crabapples, pears, beans, and wild berries. We ate the canned stuff all winter.

Dad went around to every house that had a vacant lot next to it and promised that we would keep the weeds down if he could use it for a garden. Many people agreed.

While in Millard, we owned a blue roan milk cow which we kept in a common pasture.† She did not like the pasture and would jump fences to where the grass was greener—except it wasn't grass—it was someone else's clover or sweet corn. We always caught the cow, but we had to do it more than once.

We were very poor, but we did not know it until 1937 when we were put on welfare. (It was called "relief" at the time.) There were no preservatives in store bread, and it would get moldy in a day or two. We had a 1928 La Salle with a straight-eight engine. My father would go to the bakery and buy all their day-old bread for 10¢. He filled up the back seat of the La Salle with the bread. We fed the moldy bread to the chickens and ate the non-moldy bread ourselves. This is one of many reasons I think Mom was brave. We boys thought all of it was an adventure.

That Christmas, because we were "poor people," we were overwhelmed with toys from the townspeople. Before Christmas, we stopped for gas at a service station. Dad went inside. Pretty soon an attendant came out of the station wheeling a bicycle and began to put air in its tires. We were amazed at the bicycle. It had twin headlights, a built-in horn, and a luggage rack. It was beautiful. We all coveted that bike. It never occurred to us that Dad had bought it. It was our Christmas present!

* Food was a precious commodity during the Depression. Mom pickled the watermelon rinds to make them edible.

† I am not sure of the breed, but that was its color.

On this Christmas bike, with some help from Dad, we learned to ride. There was a short dirt road half a block from the apartment which we used like a private track for practicing our riding and tricks. Dad rode the bike to his night job at the Cudahy ice plant in Ralston, five miles east, and we rode it in the daytime. When the bike was not in use, we wrestled it up the few stairs to our apartment off the garage and kept it in the front room. Lorraine loved the bike and spent much time tearing around, doing tricks, etc.

In the spring, we planted peas, beans, and tomatoes in the empty lots my Dad had gotten permission to cultivate. We set out twenty-one boxes of tomato plants, one hundred plants to a box. We dug holes two feet apart, put water in each hole, and plopped each plant into the mud at the bottom of the hole. Shortly after we got them all planted, the radio reported that there would be a freezing rain that night. To save the plants from the ice, Dad, Lorraine, and I took empty mason jars and put one over each of the tiny plants. We did this on our hands and knees in the freezing rain. When we ran out of mason jars, we got newspapers, spread one sheet over each plant, and put a plop of mud on each corner to hold it down. We saved all of the plants.

Soon after, we moved to a white house with a blue spruce in the yard. Lorraine rode his bike to school from there, just a few blocks. We continued to hoe all the lots Dad had arranged for us to garden. In the spring of the following year, we moved to a farm a mile north and four and a quarter miles west. Then Lorraine *really* used the bike to go to and from school. Here is his account of those rides:

There were no school buses. I had gravel road all the way. In the early months, I walked a large part of the highest hill, particularly in rain and snow. From the top, it was easy for a while—down and across about a mile of valley. The hill coming out of the valley was a tall one. Reaching its peak at night on the way home after basketball games enabled me to see a light burning on the western horizon—home, two miles away. After Mom learned that I looked for it, I'm sure she made sure it was there to be seen. There were still all those hills, but I had been reassured that home was right where I thought it would be.

I came home at three different times: right after school, or after basketball practice, or after basketball games. The night rides [after basketball were] lonely, and going downhill required good night vision and some faith in the smoothness of a track on a gravel road.

Riding a bicycle for five miles on every winter school morning and every afternoon or evening in Nebraska had its share of the very cold times, particularly for feet and hands. The feet were at least moving, but the hands were just clamped on those handlebars. My grandparents had some awareness of long cold rides on the Nebraska prairies, and one day I received a very unusual gift—cowhide gauntlets. The flared cuff went halfway to my elbow. The hand was just like a mitten—a thumb but no fingers. The exterior was red and white steer hide . . . . The gauntlets were cloth lined, and it was possible to wear gloves or mittens inside them, which I did. The flared cuffs covered the break between mitten and jacket or coat sleeve. I was a little uncertain about wearing the first time, afraid of the reactions of my schoolmates toward something so flamboyant. And boy, were they noticed, but they also worked. Through two winters we were inseparable and the envy of all the other kids.

One of my classmates lived a quarter mile west of us. His sister and my brothers were the student body in that one-room schoolhouse in the valley to the west. Robert Godsey rode one of their work horses to school. He had found a place near the school to keep the horse.

Near the end of winter when the roads became clear and solid and basketball season was over, he thought it might be great to ride a bike, particularly downhill. He had never had much to do with bikes. I had never had much to do with horses. He suggested we swap going home and see whether we like it.

While the other kids had made fun of his horse, it was "Hi ho, Silver!" for me, provided I could stay on. [Robert] had a little difficulty getting the rhythm of pumping, but I probably took some time, too, to learn the rhythm of the horse. Watching him working that bicycle, even on the level, assured me that I had the better of the deal. And when I just sat there going up that first hill, I knew it. Godsey walked and pushed the bike most of the way. But when we got to the top, and he straddled that bike and kicked off with both feet and a yell, it was what he had come for. He was halfway across that mile-wide valley before I caught him. We both liked the bargain and traded whenever we were to go home about the same time.

I rode that same bike over the same hills to go to church on Sunday. I wasn't aware of the hills like Lorraine was, but I was very mindful of the loose gravel and the wind.

All those garden plots my dad had started meant there was a lot of hoeing to be done. There was one day I did not want to hoe. I hoed one of the tomato patches for a while, then laid down in the dirt in the sunshine and pretended to be asleep. Someone came to check on me and found me sleeping. Everyone thought it was funny. I couldn't tell them I was faking it. They would not believe me! Dad already had a nickname for me—"Alibi Jim."

One day Lorraine and I were sitting in the alley behind our houses with Richie Paul. I was resting against a brick wall while Lorraine and Richie sat on the other side of the alley. Richie thought it was great fun to throw clods of dirt against the wall over my head so that the dirt would fall into my hair and down my neck. I returned the compliment. He got mad and came after me fighting. He was bigger than I was, so Lorraine got up and took him on. Richie was losing, or thought he was, so he sank his teeth in the top of Lorraine's left shoulder. That stopped the fight. The next day Richie brought a nickel to Lorraine as an apology. In 1985, at the family reunion at the Big Haus in Moscow, Idaho, when Lorraine was almost sixty (he always went by Leonard by that point), I asked him if I could see his shoulder. He showed me the teeth marks.

My mother often made navy bean soup. She would let the beans soak all night. She made homemade bread all the time, both to sell and to feed us. The loaves were enormous. She cut the bread an inch thick, and the slice would cover a dinner plate. We would cover the bread with soup, then cover that with ketchup. It was great stuff. When Mom baked bread, she would take extra dough, fry it in bacon grease, and coat it with sugar. That was great, too.

My mother, Lillian, was a force to be reckoned with. Her most threatening words to me were, "I'll skin you alive!" I don't think I ever got skinned alive, but I did have the anticipation.

My mother must have been in her mid-forties at the time, and a couple of my brothers challenged her to a race to the barn and back. She beat them both.

Dad worked for the Cudahy Packing Plant (a meat-packing plant) as a night watchman at their ice plant in Ralston. Refrigeration was not advanced in the 1930s. We did not have a refrigerator; we had an icebox. The iceman would deliver a cube of ice to our home. Cudahy had its own lake that froze over every winter, so they provided their own ice. One night, Dad took Lorraine and me to stay overnight with him. We mostly slept, but I did make the rounds with him once.

The next day, we went to 52nd and C where we had lived the previous summer. On the Union Pacific right of way, there was a lone

Lillian Wilson with her sons—Top, 1964; Bottom, circa 1975

giant cottonwood tree. It was to be our heat and cooking fuel for the winter. Dad felled the tree with a long crosscut saw (there were no chain saws), and we trimmed the trunk with our axes. We transported it back to Millard in pieces in the back seat of the LaSalle. Pickup trucks had been invented, but they were tiny.

That summer, we kids set up a roadside vegetable stand at the corner of Highway 6 into town. On the fourth of July, we did not set it up. (I entertained myself that day putting firecrackers in tiger lilies to blow them up.) We found out later that a semi truck had failed to make the curve that day and had turned over in the spot where we normally set up the stand.

That year, I started fourth grade at Millard School. My brother Floyd was in third grade but in the same schoolroom. One thing stood out to me from that school year: I was made to sit in the corner for something somebody else had done. I felt very indignant about being accused when I was innocent.

While we were in the house with the spruce tree, I still had the spiritual hunger left over from Seattle. I equated this hunger with church attendance. I did not know what grace was, but I was looking for it. St. Paul's Lutheran Church was one block from that house. I got up every Sunday, got dressed, and went to Sunday school and church. There was nothing there that would meet my needs, but I kept going anyway. When we moved five miles west of Millard in the fall, I would get up on Sunday and ride my bike the five miles to church. It was a waste of time. My memory is mostly of peddling against the wind in loose gravel.

When I finally quit riding my bike to church, I decided I would be good without God. In a limited way, I succeeded. For the next ten years, I did not swear, use slang, drink, smoke, or date. I did not know any other way to be godly. However, I *was* self-righteous, I was very proud, and I lied. I lied to my high school teachers about assignments.

I made up stories in letters to Leonard and my girlfriend, Marjory Mahoney. I made the National Honor Society my senior year because I had lied my way into good grades. I do not think I ever confessed the lies to my teachers who put me up for the society.

We lived in two different houses five miles west of Millard. Neither had electricity or indoor plumbing. We studied by kerosene lamps. When Everett needed to go to the bathroom, one of the three older brothers would have to take him to the outhouse. None of us would volunteer. He always picked me because I would sing to him.

That winter, we heated and cooked with corncobs. They burned fast and hot. In those days before combines, corn was picked by hand and put into corncribs. Late in the fall, a corn sheller was hired. That machine made a lot of noise. The shelled corn fell onto a track, and the cobs were spit out into a pile on the ground. It was our daily chore to bring in ten bushels of cobs from the pile to keep us warm through the night and to cook breakfast with.

The country school was a quarter mile away. It had been closed for lack of students; after all the farmer kids grew up, there were no children in the district until we moved there. It was reopened for the three Wilson boys (Floyd, Harold, and me) and a girl named Ethel Godsey. The school board hired a teacher for us named Miss Smith. She was nineteen and had done one year of Normal School (Teachers' College) in Fremont. I explained to Miss Smith that I was two years younger than my older brother but four years behind him in school. She told me that there was no one between me and the eighth grade, and she would give me all the subjects as fast as I could take them. For the first time, I got interested in school. I went through the material for the fifth and sixth grades and was passed into the seventh grade in one year. This was the grace of God, and it changed my life. If it had not been for that nineteen-year-old schoolteacher, I would not have made it to the Naval Academy.

It was a very severe winter, but I do not recall school ever being cancelled because of the weather. Even though we only had to walk a quarter mile, our fingers and toes got frozen on the way. We were in pain when they thawed out. At the time, we thought we had chilblains, but I now think it was frostbite. I had to carry Harold home when the snow was deep. Since I was the oldest student in the school, it was my job to run up the flag in the morning and take it down after school. I remember how frozen the rope was.

At home, the four oldest slept in one bed in a very cold room. There were other rooms off a hallway upstairs which we did not use. One night, I walked down to the other end of the hallway, put a sheet over my head, and waited for Floyd to come upstairs. When he got to the top of the stairs, I began making eerie sounds and moving toward him. He fled in panic. Mom came up the stairs a moment later. She was not pleased with me.

Another time, I was the one to get scared. Mom and Dad had gone into Millard and left Lorraine and me to babysit the other three boys. They were in bed. Lorraine and I sat in the warm kitchen. The rest of the house was shut off. Lorraine fell asleep. I thought I heard a door open in the living room and other noises coming from the same location. I was too afraid to move or wake up Lorraine. I just sat there scared until Mom and Dad got home. They inspected the living room but saw no evidence. They thought I must have heard a rat.

In 1939, after I had been passed into the seventh grade, we moved to another farmhouse a few miles south, which meant a change of schools. The new schoolhouse was a square brick building. I was afraid that I would be behind the other kids, but I was ahead of them. I hit the books—spelling, geography, history, and English grammar.

My mother shared the opinion of Fat Broad in the cartoon strip B.C.—namely, that there was no such thing as an innocent snake. I had orders to kill every snake I found. They were mostly bull snakes. I generally used an axe. One noon hour at school, I found a bull snake in a rabbit's nest with three young rabbits already swallowed. I did not have an axe, but I killed it somehow.

The following summer, I got hired by a neighboring farmer for a salary of 75¢ a week. We lived on the corner of a county road and US 6 between Millard and Gretna, Nebraska. Just north of highway 6, the county road was crawling with chintz bugs. It looked as if the road was moving sideways from the grass on the west into the grass on the east. The farmer lived on the east side of the road. He was trying to save his wheat. This is what he did. (I helped.) He plowed a furrow on the wheat side of the road with the steep edge of the furrow next to the wheat. Then every twenty feet or so, he dug a post hole in the furrow. At the top of the steep edge, he painted a two-inch wide band of creosote. The chintz bugs would fall or crawl into the furrow and climb up the other side. When they reached the creosote, they would crawl along the band until they came to the posthole. They would fall into the hole. The farmer would move from posthole to posthole with a flamethrower and burn up the bugs.

His wife would come out to the field in the middle of each morning with a great big lunch. At noon, we would go to the farmhouse for an even bigger lunch. In the middle of the afternoon, we ate another big lunch. I only worked for him for one week, but I never got my 75¢—just the lunches.

Jim, 8th grade

CHAPTER 6

PAPILLION

Give ear, O Lord, to my prayer; listen to my plea for grace.

(Psalm 86:6)

Before school started, we moved to Papillion, a small town and county seat closer to Omaha. I was entering the eighth grade. Lorraine, who now went by Leonard, was entering the eleventh, Floyd the sixth, Harold the fourth, and Everett kindergarten or first grade.

The main street of Papillion went north and south. It is now 84th Street in Omaha, but at that time, it was several miles southwest of Omaha.

Leonard was immediately elected president of the eleventh grade. Since I was now an eager student, the teacher liked me, and my classmates didn't (although my eagerness may not have been the reason). They nicknamed me "Suction" because of the pull I had with the teacher. The name stuck. The next year, in ninth grade, Mr. Sweeney, the general science teacher, heard one of the students call me "Suction." He stopped the class to explain that there was really no such thing as suction; it was vacuum. From that time on, I was "Vacuum."

Although I was a better student than before, I was still not a good student. I frittered away time. I would shoot baskets into the lighting fixtures with wadded-up paper balls.

Off and on during eighth and ninth grades, I was involved in another school tradition called "He got chose." That simply meant that one of the boys in the class was "chose" to beat me up. This happened three or four times. None of them succeeded in beating me. My father did not know what to do about it. Leonard had no problems like that. It may have been my attitude that caused it.

Two very pretty girls sat to my right in the eighth-grade class-room. Both of them wore bright red lipstick. The principal's son sat immediately behind me. One Friday morning, in order to get the girls' attention, he used his dividers and compass to punch me in the rear end. I turned around and told him to quit. He laughed and continued to do it. So I turned around again and gave him a straight punch right in the mouth. He jumped up, and we squared off. Just then, the teacher walked in. We both sat down and said we would meet each other in the park at lunchtime.

The fight took up the entire lunch hour. Near the park, a pipeline was being laid to bring natural gas up from Texas. The pipe-layers were off for lunch and gathered around laying bets on the outcome of our fight. I can still remember how much my face and my stomach hurt. After school, we met up and went at it again.

On Monday, I got called to the principal's office. That had never happened to me before. I was scared. I cried. That was the last time tears have come down my cheeks. (I have welled up since then, from a hymn or poetry, but not enough to cry.) However, the principal said that his son told him he had gotten a black eye while playing kick the can.

There was a Mexican family in town. Their son, Casey Coronado, was not very big, but he was all solid muscle. A group of us were sit-ting on a bench at the south end of Main Street. Casey and a friend stood in the middle of the street calling me names. I don't remember getting angry. I do remember getting up, walking over, and punching him in the mouth. Casey didn't flinch. I turned around, walked back, and sat down. I remember how much my hand hurt. There was an obsequious kid there. He ran over to Casey and then back to me. He was not a peacemaker, just a gossip.

I asked Leonard for advice, since he didn't get into fights. He asked me if the other kids fought fair. I told him that they did not. He said that I shouldn't fight fair, either. That made sense to me. Shortly after that, I was walking home from the free movie with a bunch of kids when they "chose" a tenth grader to fight me. I knocked him down. When he was on his knees, I remembered Leonard's advice and hit him in the face. Then another big kid proceeded to beat me up for not fighting fair.

A third time, Leonard and I were walking home at night when a Model A Ford came down the street. It left the street, crossed the sidewalk in front of us, and stopped. Two drunk kids, one of them eighteen years old, got out and offered Leonard a drink from a half-gallon bottle of beer. Leonard said, "No, thank you." Then he offered a drink to me. I said something like, "I wouldn't touch the filthy stuff." He was not pleased with my remark and told his friend to hold Leonard while he beat me up pretty bad. I remember getting one punch to his stomach, which got him madder. Dad spoke to his father about it.

From the eighth grade on, I became a reader. I read westerns (especially Zane Grey), Agatha Christie, *Falcons of France*, *Mutiny on the Bounty*, *Men Against the Sea*, and *Pitcairn Island*. I made cartoon strips of WWI dogfights on small pieces of paper, taped them together into a long strip, and unrolled them in a small homemade movie box. I had an album of every kind of warplane. It was not a neat book, but it was packed.

In ninth grade, I got a job at Ehler's grocery stocking shelves and candling eggs.* I became an expert at candling eggs. I would put two

---

* Eggs brought in by the famers had to be tested for freshness. We would put a light bulb inside a small metal box with holes in the sides. That way, we could see inside the egg to see if it was rotten or had a baby chicken inside. Those eggs were put aside, and the farmer would not be paid for them.

eggs in each hand, then flip them over in my hands and put another two in for inspection. I can still shift two eggs in each hand. I saved the rotten ones to throw as "hand grenades" at fence posts in the alley. One time I was ready to throw an egg when it exploded over my head. I stunk so bad I had to go home via the back alleys. Another time, I was slicing bologna with an electric slicer. I was not paying attention and ran my right forefinger into the slicer. I still have that scar.

I worked with my father in the summer of '42 digging ditches and mowing on the right-of-way of the Union Pacific in Millard. Dad got whatever jobs he could, and most of them involved horses, since he had the animals and equipment. We had two teams and two Fresno scrapers, a large, horse-drawn shovel. Dad had a team of grays, and I had a pair of mules. The front of the scraper was a blade to make it dig into the dirt easier. (Sometimes Dad would plow the area first to loosen the sod and make it easier to dig in.) We would lift the handles to make the scraper dig in. When the scraper was full, we pressed down on the handles; that would lift it up from the ground.

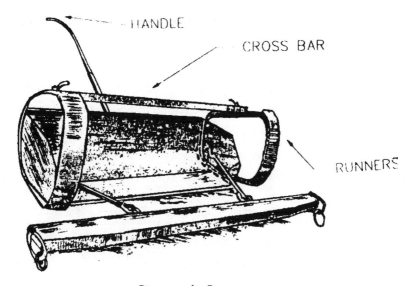

Diagram of a Fresno scraper

Then we would go over a steep bank and lift the handles again to dump the dirt on the other side. I would go around the bank instead of over it. My father asked me why. I told him it was too much for the mules. He said, "Give me those mules." He said one word to them, and over the bank they went.

One summer, Dad got a job digging basements for a new subdivision being built west of Omaha. It was an upscale district with beautiful trees. On weekends, other family members would help. Getting paid by the basement meant the faster you went through, the more money you got for the limited time. Dad would get the basement started and the pattern of movement set, and then one of us boys would continue with the rough work. Dad could see we weren't getting done fast enough, so eventually he hired men with a front-loader on a tractor to sculpt the corners. He would dig the main hole first, and they did the squaring off.

Before there were combines, all field corn was husked by hand and hauled from the field to a corncrib where it would be shelled later. The huskers wore gloves that each had two thumbs. When the fingers and palm were worn through, the gloves were put on the other hand. Over the right-hand glove, the husker wore a leather strap with a metal hook at the heel of the hand. On the right side of the wagon was a backboard several feet above the ground. The husker would stand on the board; as the wagon was drawn by the horses down a corn row, he would grab an ear of corn with his left hand and hook the husk with his right. That would leave the ear bare; he would grab it with his right hand, snap it off, and throw the husked ear into the wagon in the same movement.

When Dad was a young man, he had a reputation for being the fastest corn husker around. Many years later, I met someone who knew of his reputation. Dad heard that farmers were paying 6¢ a bushel for husking corn. He hired himself out to a farmer to husk.

He picked a hundred shelled bushels the first day. That was $6. One Saturday, he took me with him. He would take two rows, and I would take one. We worked all day. At the end of the day, we had picked only ninety bushels. I had slowed him down by ten bushels.

The United States entered World War II on December 7, 1941. I had turned fourteen the October before. Leonard was elected president of the senior class of '42. Because so many men were going off to the war, jobs were opening up. Leonard was offered a job at the Union Pacific Headquarters. It was to start May 1, more than a month before school ended. However, high school officials agreed to let him out of the rest of his classes and finals, and he still graduated as valedictorian at age sixteen.

Leonard started at Union Pacific as the office boy to the general auditor. Almost immediately, he was promoted to office assistant for William Jeffers, president of the Union Pacific, when the previous assistant joined the army. That did not last, because President Roosevelt tagged Jeffers to head up all wartime transportation. The Japanese had captured the places that were the source of our nation's raw rubber. Roosevelt wanted Jeffers to develop an artificial rubber supply—immediately. Within a few days of receiving the president's call, Jeffers left the railroad and Omaha to become the "rubber czar." Leonard himself joined the Navy as soon as he turned seventeen in January 1943 and went off to boot camp at the Great Lakes Naval Training Center.

Tenth grade was very quiet. I read *The Scottish Chiefs* by Jane Porter and got interested in history of Scotland. I also kept up with the war.

In tenth-grade woodworking shop, I decided to make a toboggan. I had no one to teach me how to curve the wood at the front. When I did not succeed, I cut up a country milk can and used the metal as the front. It was a good job. I named it *Corsair* after the inverted gullwing navy fighter plane F4U. I painted *CORSAIR* across the front with the front silhouette of an F4U.

We spent three years there in Papillion; then in the spring of my tenth grade, we moved to a ten-acre place at 45th and Harrison on the edge of South Omaha. We had five milk cows and lots of pigs. Almost everything on the farm was pregnant, including Mom, the cows, and one large Berkshire sow.

It was 1943, in the middle of the war. People everywhere were growing victory gardens. Dad would hire himself and his team of horses to plow ground for the victory gardens. He charged based on the size of the lot. I went with him on one of the jobs. It was on a fairly large lot. The team was a large black stallion and a mare that was sick. When Dad realized that the mare was ill, he took her out of the harness and let the stallion pull the plow alone. When the job was finished, the owner did not want to pay for the size of the plot, insisting that Dad had not measured it properly and that the lot was not as big as my father said it was. I was taller than my father, so Dad suggested that I step it off. The measurement was different than the previous one, in Dad's favor. Although my legs were longer than his, my stride was shorter.

When that was settled, we put the plow in the wagon, hooked up the team, and started home. We were a few hundred yards from home when the mare collapsed in the harness. The stallion began to rear. We (mostly Dad) struggled to control the stallion and somehow got them unhooked. As soon as it was done, my father collapsed into the ditch. The horses had already gone home. I ran to the house, got Mom, and headed back. We met Dad walking home.

My father had experienced a massive heart attack. He was forty-three years old, and there was no such thing as heart surgery in those days. The doctor said to him, "You have just smoked your last cigarette." My father had rolled his own cigarettes all his life. He quit smoking. He was bed-ridden for several months. When he began to recover, he would shoot rats near the barn from his bedroom window.

Floyd, Harold, and Everett were going to a local school. It was decided that I should finish tenth grade in Papillion. So in the morning, I would milk the five cows, slop the hogs, change clothes, walk a mile and a half to catch the school bus to Papillion, and return in the afternoon. On the way to the bus, I would throw rocks to see if I could hit the insulators on top of the electric poles. I continued to do this until I finally hit one. I thought I had better stop.

On the school bus, there were three high school girls who would spend their time giggling. One day they handed me a note. It said, "What is a w-h-o-r-e.?" I had no idea what a whore was. I read their question out loud, only I pronounced the 'wh' together as in "where" or 'when.' We were the only four on the bus besides the driver. The girls were greatly embarrassed when I read the question aloud. I was none the wiser. When I got to school, I looked up the word.

Another job my father and I had was mowing the right of way for the Missouri Pacific Railroad with horse-drawn mowers. While Dad was in bed recovering, I continued the job alone. One day the weeds were very high, and I could not see the tracks. When I got to the end of the track, I went to turn the mower. I did not realize that both wheels were between the tracks. The horses turned, but the wheels could not. It snapped the tongue off the mower. I had to leave it there and take the team home. Dad's twin sister Leona and other assorted relatives were in town because of his heart attack. Aunt Florence's son, Melvin, helped me retrieve the mower.

Dad had taught me how to load a hayrack (a wagon used to carry hay). I would rake the hay into windrows with a fifteen-foot rake. I had to stack the hay much wider than the hayrack itself. I did this by pitching hay so that it hung over the sides of the rack, then pitching more into the middle to hold down what was hanging over. I did that with the next layer, and the next. It took me a long while to load the rack, but I got it all home. Floyd and Harold helped unload it into the haymow* of the barn.

That year, Floyd contracted mastoiditis, then polio. He was very sick, but not paralyzed. Mother was at home pregnant, her husband was in bed, one son was off in the navy, one was working, one was sick, and two others were still in elementary school. On top of that, we had ten acres and pregnant cows and sows to take care of. She was a wonderful woman.

My brother Ken was born 20 May 1943 when the relatives were there.

The Berkshire sow labored with many little red pigs but could not deliver all of them. We called the vet. He helped deliver a few more, but not all, so the sow died. I have no idea what we did with the piglets, but we did save them. We called the rendering works to take away the dead sow. It was several days before the truck arrived. By that time, the pig carcass was in advanced state of decay. I could tell that the man did not want to take it. He said that his truck was broken, and he left. I hooked a horse up to the pig, dragged it to the lower part our corral, and buried it there.

The same spring, our outhouse got filled up. I dug another hole about fifty feet away. I think I dug it six feet deep. I hooked a horse to the outhouse, dragged it over the new hole, got it in place, and we were back in business!

I started eleventh grade at Omaha South High School. South Omaha was the home of first- and second-generation immigrants from Eastern Europe. South High was not a major school for college prep. I wanted to go to college, so with a few others I was put into 2nd year algebra. Dad was still in bed and could not work.

---

* Hay loft

CHAPTER 7
THE STOCKYARDS

Now the law came to increase the trespass, but where sin increased,
grace abounded all the more. (Rom. 5:20)

I turned sixteen on Oct. 6, 1943. After school the next day, I walked
to the chute house at the Union Stockyards of Omaha and asked for
a job. Fergy, the foreman, asked me how old I was.

"Sixteen."

"When did you turn sixteen?"

"Yesterday."

"I thought so."

I got the job. For the next two school years, I worked from 3:30
to 11:30 p.m. five days a week, all day Saturday, and Sunday evenings
too. (That was the busiest day of the week.) The trucks were lined up
for a mile waiting to be unloaded. In the summers of 1944 and 1945,
I worked all night, six p.m. to six a.m. My pay was 62¢ an hour. I gave
the paychecks to Mom. She gave me 35¢ for my evening meal each
day. That would get me a hot beef sandwich or a hamburger steak.

The work included driving cattle, stacking hay, shoveling manure, cleaning the hog yards with fire hoses, and goofing off. All of us
teenage boys had a supper break. We used to cross the railroad tracks
on the O Street Bridge to get to the restaurant we ate at. For a while,
there was a stationary railroad car filled with loose grain underneath
the bridge. We would jump off the bridge to land in the wheat. Then
we returned to the bridge to do it again. Once, Hobby Bryant was on
the railing when a city bus filled with people was crossing the bridge.

When the bus came abreast of him, Hobby turned toward it and yelled "Goodbye, everybody!" and jumped off the bridge. The driver stopped the bus abruptly, thinking that someone had just committed suicide. We all got in trouble for that.

Because the cattle needed to be fed once they were unloaded, box-cars filled with ninety-pound bales of prairie hay would arrive at the yards. This hay had to be stacked in giant hay barns. Each of us had a hay hook to lift the bales. The bales were high and wide and long. To get the hay to the roof, we would stair-step the bales and throw a bale to the guy on the next step. At the top next to the roof, there was a loose bale. When it was pulled out, it revealed a long tunnel framed by the roof and the bales on each side and underneath. We would all crawl into the tunnel and pull the loose bale back into place. At the end of the tunnel was an amphitheater made of baled hay. We could all disappear into the theater to have wrestling matches and other contests. It was soundproof because of the thick walls of hay. We could yell as loud as we liked, and nobody knew we were there.

One Saturday we were pitching manure in the sheep barns. All the cattle, sheep, and pigs were butchered by Saturday, so the barns were empty. Suddenly we heard a high-pitched "Baaa!" It came from a newborn lamb whose mother had been taken away by the packers. We all wanted to keep the lamb. The rest of the kids lived in the city. I was the only one who lived in the country.

I went out into the cattle yards where I found one lone cow. It was howling because it had not been milked. I got a cone-shaped red fire bucket and milked the cow. I diluted the milk with water. I put my right hand in the milk with my little finger sticking up. Then with my left hand I pushed the lamb's face into the milk where it could suck my finger and get fed.

I did not know how I was going to get the lamb home, because animals were not allowed on city buses. I found a paper grocery sack and put the lamb into it. I got aboard the bus pretending I was carrying groceries. But just as I was putting my token into the receptacle, my grocery bag suddenly went "Baaa!" The driver let me keep it. I named the lamb Mary Ann. She thought my mother was her mother. She followed her everywhere. When my mother was hanging up clothes, she would jump in and out of the clothes basket. A few months later, we found Mary Ann dead, cause unknown.

On Friday nights, we would clean the hog yards with fire hoses. Two of us were on each hose. Each team had a section of the yard to clean. It generally ended up with a water fight.

When we were unloading cattle cars, each of us was assigned the cattle from one car. A different rancher owned the cattle in each car, so it was important that they be kept separate from each other. There were long, wide gates in the cattle alleys to keep the cattle apart. Being kids, sometimes we tried to mix the cattle so that we could take time separating them. When the kid ahead of me would open the gate to let my cattle move, I would whoop and holler to scare them into a run so that they could get by the kid and into his load of cattle before he could shut the next gate. Sometimes he would get it shut just in time to catch mine running smack into his closed gate.

Black Angus were more easily spooked than Herefords or short horns. One rainy night, we were driving cattle through six inches of sloppy manure. I had a load of Black Angus. When the gate was opened, I yelled and whipped the Angus nearest to me. It worked; they took off at a dead run. Their back feet went backward in the slippery muck, and my mouth was wide open. My mouth got filled with runny cow manure. I could not do anything about it except spit.

One night we were told to leave the chute house and go to the motor truck division. We were on a high second level. One of the guys grabbed my cap and threw it down to the main level into the cow manure. I politely snatched his cap and threw it to the same place. He got angry and wanted to fight. He was one of the running backs on the South High Football team. I remember thinking, "The best defense is a good offense." So I threw the first punch and got in two or three more before he recovered. That was my last fight. I think it scared the other guys off.

Another time, a calf fell between the railroad car and the unloading chute. It was loose on the railroad tracks. We all got into the chase. We finally cornered it between two rows of cars. My plan was to station myself at the other end and hold out my canvas whip like a clothesline. When the calf was chased toward me, I would wrap the whip around its neck and throw it to the ground. The calf was running fast. When it hit my whip, the calf was not the one that got thrown to the ground. It flung me into a railroad car. I got several stitches in my head.

After a while, there was an opening for the position of dead checker. The job paid 67¢ an hour instead of 62¢. I wanted the pay increase, but I did not have the seniority to get the job. However, no one else wanted it, so I got it.

Here is why the job was not desired. If a cow decided to lie down in the railroad car, it would not be able to get up because the other twenty cows would trample it to death. When the car was unloaded, the dead cow would need to be identified with that car and be removed. I would put a rope around its horns and get ten guys to drag it out. If the cow had been dead for several days, the stench was awful.

Sometimes the cow would not be dead. When we started pulling on it, it would jump to its feet, crazy mad, and we would all have to climb high fences. One time Ole Johnson, the foreman, came along and found us all perched on top of the fence. When he asked, I told him we had a mad cow.

He scoffed. "If I had a bucket, I would milk it." He climbed over the fence, and the cow charged him. Ole Johnson was a tall, skinny guy. It was great to see him fly up onto the fence. The next day, a man went into the pen to give the cow water and was killed by the cow.

Sheep came in double-decker cars. If there was a dead sheep, I would have to crawl into the car on my hands and knees through the sheep manure to pull it out. If a sheep had been dead for several days, I often had to crawl back out and vomit before I could retrieve the carcass. I earned those extra 5¢ an hour!

Meanwhile, Floyd and Harold ended up doing most of the animal chores at home because of my schedule. I did very little homework my junior and senior years—only what I could do during schooltime.

I mentioned earlier that I grew up living a moral life with no slang, no profanity, no smoking, drinking, or running around. That was true. But I had no trouble lying. If I was given six algebra problems for homework, I would report to the teacher that I had done four, when in reality I had not done any. I could also lose my temper (not in fights, just at home).

How did I make the honor society? I lied, and I faked knowing more than I knew. When the history teacher asked where gunpowder was first used in Europe, I raised my hand and said it was in the Hundred Years' War at the Battle of Crecy. How I knew that I don't know, but Miss Guiter was impressed. I took first- and second-semester chemistry in the same semester. I memorized the periodic table. Mrs. Wehr was impressed. Dr. Kunzel, our English teacher, was blind, so all the answers were oral, and I was an auditory learner.

Mr. Sheetz, my algebra teacher, said that he would give us extra credit if we solved the Spanish Prisoner problem. I made several attempts with no success. A few days ago, I found out that the Spanish Prisoner problem was a trick problem that purportedly could not be solved. It was given to me in 1944. Naval Engineer Lt. J.G. Kaplan had solved it in 1927. Mathematicians had not been able solve it for quite some time.

$$x^2 + y = 7$$
$$x + y^2 = 11$$

Don't waste your time.

Dr. Kunzel gave us credit for how many books or magazine articles we read. I inflated my numbers. Dr. Kunzel was also the debate coach. I went out for the debate team but never debated because of my work schedule.

My education in the facts of life was a long metamorphosis with zero instruction. The two years in the Omaha Stock Yards were years of hearing very gross language and tales of gross conduct. I did not participate in the talk. I had no idea that there was such a thing as a homosexual—I had barely figured out heterosexual. Looking back, I can think of at least four men who were homosexual. They made different kinds of advances on me. I was too dumb, naïve, and innocent to know what they were doing. But God protected me.

After Dad got back on his feet, he went to the horse barn and bought several horses. Two of them were off the range and had never been broken. Dad hired a bronco rider to break one of them. We cleared everything out of the yard to give the horse plenty of room to buck. The rider mounted, and the horse began to buck. Then we realized that we had not taken down the clothesline! Nothing bad happened.

I asked Dad if I could break the other horse. Dad said no. He did not want me to get hurt. I kept asking him. One day, there was two feet of snow in the yard. He said I could break him. We held the horse while I saddled him. I got on, and he began to buck. He had a hard time because of the two feet of snow. I kept whipping him to keep him going. Finally, he was sweating so much that he got tired and quit bucking. I rode him for a while and then took him to the barn. I was very pleased with myself for having broken him.

I had a female Dalmatian dog named Sally. She had run away, so I took my horse to go look for her. I saddled and mounted him. He did not buck. I walked him out of the yard to the road, where I got him to trot. I was very pleased with this, so I urged him into a lope and then into a run.

Suddenly the horse stopped. I did not stop. I flew over his head and landed hard. The horse went back to the barn. I walked home embarrassed. My father was amused.

One time, my father was taking several horses to the horse barn to sell. The horse barn was a separate part of the stockyards. We had no truck, so I walked with the horses behind a wagon that he was driving. My mother was in the wagon leading the horses. It must have been Sunday evening, because L Street (which ran east-west) was lined up for miles with trucks full of cattle headed for the Omaha stockyards.

Dad was approaching L Street from the south. He needed to get in line with the trucks. As we were waiting to break into the line, a car came up behind the wagon and honked its horn. This scared the horses being led. They ran up alongside the right side of the wagon and then beside the team. This spooked the team into a run and then into a runaway. Dad could not control the team. It was on a dead run headed for the line of trucks. Dad told Mom to jump to safety. She did it, but she jumped facing the wagon, thinking she'd be able to land running. Somehow the runaway team got through the line of trucks. Mom ended up with stitches in her head.

CHAPTER 8

THE NAVY

So too at the present time there is a remnant, chosen by grace.

(Rom. 11:5)

On Dad's forty-fourth birthday, October 3, 1944, Leonard's destroyer escort, the *USS Shelton* (DE-407), was sunk by a Japanese submarine forty miles from Morotai, a month before the U.S. invasion of the Philippines. It remained afloat for eleven hours. The crew abandoned ship by jumping to another ship that came alongside. Leonard received thirty days' survivor's leave.

Leonard gave me two books, one of which was a novel about a sailor who won a Secretary of the Navy appointment to the Naval Academy. I made up my mind that I would go to the Naval Academy, and that was the route I would take to get there.

On 7 May 1945, I went into the Navy Recruiting Office to enlist. While I was in the office, Germany surrendered. On 28 May, I graduated from South High School and found out that I had two scholarships, one to the University of Nebraska and one to the University of Omaha. I could not take them because I had already enlisted in the regular Navy. I stood fifth academically in my class—but remember that part of this was lying and bluffing my way to that standing.

The Navy did not call me to active duty until September 1945. Japan had surrendered in August, so the war was completely over by the time I arrived at boot camp.

While I was still in the stockyards my senior year, one of my friends enlisted in the Navy. He went off to boot camp. A few weeks later, he was back in the stockyards. We asked him why. He said he did not like the Navy, so he had deliberately peed on his bunk so that they would think he had wet his bed in his sleep and would kick him out. That is exactly what they did. I actually think that's what really happened, and he lied to us that he done it deliberately.

I had taken the Navy physical on May 7, 1945. They asked two questions that I remember well: 1) Have you urinated in your sleep anytime in the last five years? 2) Do you have flat feet? I answered both in the negative; both of those answers were lies.

I knew that I had flat feet before I enlisted. In the physical exam, I stood with my feet consciously arched. The doctor did not notice what I was doing, so I passed the physical. A year later, I had another physical examination before entering the Naval Academy. I tried the same thing. The doctor saw what I was doing and stepped on my foot. He looked at my foot and said, "Maybe I can slide a dime under there." He passed me with the flat fleet. However, those feet caught up with me eleven years later. At sea, I found that I was tired in the morning even when I had had enough sleep. I could not find a reason for this. The Navy doctor thought it must be the flat feet and fitted me with orthotics which I wore for the next sixty years.

When I enlisted, I was seventy-one and a half inches tall and 154 pounds. My height increased over the first few years to seventy-four inches. Don't ask me how; it may have been having enough to eat all the time.

Before I was called to active duty, I heard that the Navy was short of radio technicians. They developed a test called the Eddy test, named after Captain Eddy. Anyone who passed it could go to boot camp as Seaman First Class instead of Seaman Apprentice and was guaranteed radio technician school after boot camp. I consulted my high-school physics teacher. He said, "Remember E=IR." I passed the test and went to boot camp with an entire company of radio technicians.

In boot camp, I saw a poster for the Naval Academy Prep School. I applied and was interviewed by a group of naval officers who selected me for NAPS. After boot camp, I went home for Christmas, then left for the Great Lakes Naval Training Center. In January 1946, I was put on a troop train to Virginia. On the train, I got into a blackjack card game, won the deal, and went away with lots of money (maybe $20). That was the last time I won anything.

At home in the 1930s, we had listened to lots of radio. As kids it was *Little Orphan Annie*; *Jack Armstrong, the All-American Boy*; *Fibber McGee and Molly*; *Amos and Andy*; and *The Jack Benny Program*. No one on the radio spoke with a southern accent except one singer, Dinah Shore. I did not know it was a southern accent. I just knew it was a woman speaking.

The troop train ran from the Great Lakes training school to the Naval Academy Prep School in Virginia. When we got off the troop train in Norfolk, all the men in the train station were talking like Dinah Shore. I did not know any man would talk like that. I thought all those men must be effeminate. Later I learned that a third of the United States talks that way.

NAPS was located at a former Navy Seabee base in the swamps at Camp Peary, Virginia. The school was hard. I had to study, and I did not know how to study.

When I was boot camp and in NAPS, Leonard was a quartermaster 1/C on the *USS Bremerton* in Tsingtao, China. We had both read *Beau Geste*,* so we corresponded with each other in narrative poetry as if we were in the French Foreign Legion in the Sahara desert. He

* An adventure novel by P.C. Wren

In boot camp, 1945

was Beau, and I was Digby. I recall seeing a fragment of our poetry somewhere in recent years.

Casco Bay, Maine
1 Oct. 1945

Dear Jim:

Sitting up in the conning tower, listening to the radio, really some beautiful music. We call this the red room of the *U.S.S. Bremerton* because we turn on all the red battle lights in here and it makes it look so cozy, even though it gives you plenty of light either to read or write by.

Well, the time has come, the walrus said. Going to Philly tomorrow, at least we're leaving in the morning for Philly and get into Philly sometime Wednesday afternoon. Reason for taking so long, Philly is so far up the Delaware.

We're supposed to be R.F.S. or Ready For Sea by midnite on the 6th of Nov. 1945. Then we're going "elsewhere." Afraid I might miss you in "Frisco." . . .

Leonard

I encouraged Leonard to apply for the Academy. The admiral said that he would recommend Leonard for the Academy. He applied but flunked the physical exam because of a heart murmur from the rheumatic fever he'd had in boot camp.

The sidewalks at NAPS were wooden on two-by-tens in the swamp. It was a rainy, cold winter. We had two pot-bellied stoves in every barracks, one on each end. We had to set a watch to keep the fire going all night. The difficulty was that the fine bituminous coal was kept in open bins in the rain. If a shovelful of coal was dropped on the fire, it would put the fire out. It was not a strange thing to see a sailor chopping up a wooden sidewalk with a fire axe in the middle of the night. As the months went by, chairs and tables began to disappear. By springtime, we were all sitting on the floor around the stoves to study.

I snored. At NAPS, I kept waking up with shoes in my bunk. The other students would throw their shoes at me during the night. One night, the officer of the day came through the barracks. He woke me up because the other guys were swearing at me.[*]

A few weeks after my arrival at NAPS, I received a letter addressed to Jim Wilson, Seaman First Class Radio Technician, Del Monte, California. I had never been to California, but that was my name and my rank. I read the letter. It had Bible verses in it. I was not comfortable with that. I made fun of it. But my conscience bothered me, so I sent the letter back to the return address with an apology for opening it.

A few weeks later, a sailor came into our barracks and asked if there was a Jim Wilson there. I identified myself. He said he was Jim Wilson, Seaman First Class Radio Technician. He had just come from California. He had been in a radio technician school in the old Del Monte Hotel. The letter I had gotten was one of his. He had some of my mail. We became good friends.

I had several problems at that time. One of them was that because of my comparative morality, I thought I was better than other people. I did not know the meaning of the term *self-righteous*, but that is what I was. The other problem was that I was not happy, and I did not have any friends.

When I got to know Jim Wilson, I found out that he had a higher standard of morality than I had, and he lived it with less effort. He also had friends, and he was happy. Suddenly I did not feel superior. In fact, for the first time in my life, I felt inferior. To make matters worse, Jim was an athlete and a brain, *and* he was a Christian.

* However, my roommates of four years at the Naval Academy did not complain; neither did Bessie.

I did not like the impact of this comparison. I tried to find something that I was better at than he was. Astronomy was the answer. Two summers of spending all night in the stockyards had gotten me interested in the stars, and I had subscribed to *Star and Telescope* magazine. I decided to take Jim out one night and name the stars to him.

While I was naming them, he interrupted me and asked me if I was going to Heaven. I had not been asked that question before. I replied, "I don't know. I will wait and find out."

He asked, "Well, what do you think?"

"I think so."

"Why do you think so?"

I told him how good I was and how bad I wasn't and said that if I did not make it, Heaven was going to be thinly populated.

Jim laughed. I did not like that. I thought he was putting me down. He had asked me a serious question, and I gave an honest answer.

I retorted, "If you are so smart, do you know you are going to Heaven?"

He replied that he was, and I could not say he didn't know.

I asked him how he knew, and so he gave me his testimony.

I asked him where he got all this. He told me that it was from the New Testament.

One weekend, we went to his home in Tuckahoe, New York, and Jim took me to the Word of Life meeting at the Gospel Tabernacle in Times Square. The gospel made no impression on me. I had been hardened to doing good works as a means to reaching Heaven. I found a New Testament and began reading it every day looking for the answer. What I was reading did not make any sense to me.

On the entrance exam for the Academy, I got a 2.50 in math and a 2.50 in English. 2.50 was the passing grade. I got higher grades in other subjects. Of the 1,200 or so sailors in NAPS, only 330 of us passed the exam. The Academy accepted all 330. Meanwhile, the other Jim Wilson had gotten out of the Navy and gone to Columbia University.

While I was waiting to hear the results of the exam, I took leave and headed to Nebraska. It was my first venture into hitchhiking. I caught a ride out of D.C. headed toward the midway on the Pennsylvania turnpike. The driver, a woman, had a preschool boy who seemed like three boys. He insisted on playing with the car's cigarette lighter. She was trying to keep him from it with her right hand and drive with her left.

On the turnpike, I got a ride in a new Buick. It may have been a 1942 model, but it was new. (No cars had been made during the war.) We were moving at eighty miles per hour, faster than I had ever gone before, when a Greyhound bus passed us up as if we had been parked.

From Pittsburgh, I caught a ride to Columbus, Ohio. I asked the driver if he could let me off at Port Columbus, a Naval Air Station. From there I caught a ride on a C-47* to Olathe, Kansas. I did not think any traffic would go straight north, so I hitched a ride to Kansas City and from there rode with an Army sergeant who was driving a '36 Ford. He was taking a weekend from St. Louis to Duluth, Minnesota, many miles away.

There were no interstate freeways at that time. All highways went east-west or north-south. I have no idea how fast the sergeant was driving. All I know was the half-mile hollows felt like bumps in the road. I was too scared to stay in the car any longer. I got off east of Plattsmouth, Nebraska, in the middle of the night. It was pitch black. There were no lights visible at any farmhouse, there was tall corn on each side of me, and there were no cars. Absolute silence. The combination had an effect on me called *fright*. I still remember being scared of the dark and the silence.

---

* The Douglas C-47 Skytrain is a military transport vehicle that is still in use.

U. S. NAVAL TRAINING CENTER
Bainbridge, Maryland

NM28/P11-1/(A-1)   WWB/WPM/nl

3 June 1946

To: J. I. Wilson, S1c, USN.

Subj: Notification of passing Naval Academy En-
       trance Examinations, delivery of.

Ref: (a) BuPers Ser. 826-IR of 22 May, 1946.

1.   Notification that you have successfully
passed the entrance examinations to the U. S.
Naval Academy is delivered herewith.

2.   The Center Commander takes pleasure in con-
gratulating you on your success.

                               Wm. W. BEHRENS
                          Commodore, U. S. Navy
                            Center Commander.

Encl:

1. (HW) BuPers Ser.   Pers-826-IR of   22 May
        1946.

CHAPTER 9

THE NAVAL ACADEMY

> But by the grace of God I am what I am, and his grace toward me
> was not in vain. (1 Cor. 15:10)

When I arrived at the Academy in June 1946, I had to be discharged as an enlisted man and sworn in as a midshipman.

I got my new uniforms and was back in my room changing from my sailor uniform to my midshipman's uniform. Halfway through that process, I was in the state known as stark naked when the door opened and in walked a commander in full dress whites with a sword at his side. He spoke to me by name and asked me how I was doing. I was so scared I did not know whether to salute, stand at attention, or jump out the window.

Plebe summer was rough.* We had a full academic load plus boot camp all over again. At the end of the summer, the upper classes returned from cruise and leave, and the academic year started.

The entire brigade of midshipmen was required to attend church. It did not make any difference which denomination they chose or whether they went to the Naval Academy Chapel. We each had to make a decision, and we would march together to the church we had chosen.

It had been years since I had been to church. I remembered the rich experience in Seattle nine years before, so I wrote my mother to find out what denomination the Church of the Open Door was. She wrote back that it had changed its name to New Covenant Baptist Church.

---

* Freshman year at the Naval Academy is known as plebe year.

That did it. I was now a Baptist and marched to Sunday school and church at College Avenue Baptist Church. I was not a Christian.

I was reading the New Testament every day. It still did not make any sense. I think I was reading it just to be able to say I had read the New Testament. In January, a classmate named Caryll Whipple saw me reading it and invited me to a Bible study. I was eager to attend because I thought I might be able to understand the Bible. Then he told me that it met at 5:45 in the morning. Suddenly I did *not* want to attend! I made the excuse that I did not wake up that early and that my roommate would kill me if an alarm clock went off before reveille. Caryll told me that he would wake me up.

The group met in the janitor's broom closet. In it were three or four midshipmen all like that other Jim Wilson. They knew they were going to Heaven. When I found that out, I insisted on attending. Then I discovered that the group met seven days a week! With few exceptions, I was there for the next three and a half years until my graduation from the Academy. For the rest of plebe year, sometimes I would fake it and pretend I was a Christian, and sometimes I would argue with them.

Leonard was a perfectionist like my father. When we were kids, we would go out to play. Leonard would come back into the house neat. I would come back looking like Pig-Pen in the cartoon *Peanuts*. I bring this up because the Academy had perfectionist standards, and I was not a natural for those standards. I found it easy to get demerits. If I got "fried," it was ten demerits and three hours extra duty, or fifteen demerits and four hours. I don't remember the limit on demerits, but I was close to receiving an automatic expulsion from the Academy my plebe year. That meant I also spent a lot of hours marching with a rifle on my shoulder. Somehow I made it through.

I was not wild, but I gave the upper class a bad time. Ten minutes before evening meal formation, a plebe was assigned to call down the

At the Academy, 1946

corridor. He was also to read out the menu for the meal. There was a first classman named Riley who used to haze me a lot. One evening, the menu was cold cuts. In order to get back at Riley, I changed the menu to T-bone steak and strawberry shortcake.

Riley knew it wasn't true. He called back down the hall, "Come around tonight, Mr. Wilson." That meant I would have to sit on a "little green bench" and read out the definition of *time* or *color* from the dictionary. The problem was that the little green bench was imaginary. There was no bench. I had to squat and pretend it was there.

There was another first classman named Green who was very nice and never had plebes "come around." However, he loved to eat, so he was anticipating T-bone steak and strawberry shortcake! When he found out that supper was cold cuts, he got very angry and also had me come around.

I had not gone out for sports in high school because I had to work. So in the summer of my plebe year, I tried out for Navy football. My reactions were not fast enough. When the ball was snapped, all I could see were cleats running over the top of me. In the spring of 1947, I went out for crew in an eight-oared shell. I made it into the first boat of the plebe crew. I had the starboard oar in the bow. Since I weighed only 168 pounds, I had the form, but not the horsepower. Although I rowed for all four years at the Academy, I never made the varsity team.

I remember two crew races. One was on Lake Cayuga against the Cornell freshmen. We won in a two-mile race. The other was the national crew races in the Poughkeepsie Regatta on the Hudson River. Thirteen university crews rowed abreast in a three-mile race. Navy Varsity won their race, Navy JV came in second in their race, and the Navy Plebes (my crew) came in third in the freshman race.

One spring, Buck Walsh, the crew coach, was waiting for the ice to disappear from the Severn River so he could get his shells in the water.

The wake of the *USS Carpelotti*, 1947

The thaw finally came but was not complete. There was still a lot of floating ice. There was also a cold wind and white caps. The shells were taking on water. It finally became apparent to Buck that all the shells were going to be swamped. Our feet were laced in shoes attached to the shells. Buck was yelling through the megaphone, "Save your oars, save your oars." We swam to Hospital Point with our oars and with ice in the river. Then I had to run shoeless back to the Boat House at Hubbard Hall in my crew shorts and socks, carrying the oar.

After the Poughkeepsie regatta and two days of celebration in New York City, we boarded the *USS Carpelotti*, an APD,* to catch up with the Naval Academy cruise, which had visited Scandinavia and was by that time in Portsmouth, England. I got very seasick in the North Atlantic. We arrived in Plymouth on July 4, 1947. A few days later, we reached Portsmouth, where I caught up with my cruise ship, the *USS Wisconsin*, an Iowa-class battleship. This was for my youngster cruise. My class-mates had already been aboard for a month. I was met by a sailor who gave me a bucket of machine gray paint and pointed to a space that

* Auxiliary Personnel Destroyer

went eight decks straight down to a pump room. He told me to paint everything that wasn't moving.

"What if it is moving?"

"If it's moving slow, paint it."

I took a trip to London with a classmate. He knew two girls from Northern Ireland who worked in the laundry of the Russell Hotel. His plan was to buy a bottle of wine, make out with the girls on a park bench in Russell Square, and ply them with the wine. I did not drink, but I did invest in the purchase of the

The USS Wisconsin, 1947

wine. I figured out that after the girls got drunk, he was planning for us to take them off to bed. The girls got drunk. However, their drunkenness was the kind that was more hostile than friendly. They wanted to get rid of us. Although not yet a Christian, I went back to the ship grateful to God.

There was an afternoon Bible study on the 011 level (11 decks above the main deck) of the *Wisconsin* when we went back to sea. I went to it but was still unsaved. When I returned to the Academy for my youngster† year, I started attending the daily pre-reveille Bible study again.

---

† Sophomore

CHAPTER 10

A NEW SONG

Through him we have also obtained access by faith into the grace
in which we stand, and we rejoice in hope of the glory of God.

(Rom 5:2)

Back at the Academy youngster year, several of my classmates and I
got into the habit of racing toy cars powered by CO_2 cartridges. We
would attach a rubber band with a roofing tack in it to the back of
the car and pull the rubber band out behind the car. When we let go
of the tack, the rubber band would snap it against the CO_2 cartridge
and puncture it, and the car would be propelled down the corridor.
We would also race the cartridges without the cars by filling the
empty cartridges with match heads as propellant.

Then a classmate named Webb went into town, bought the ingredients for black powder,* and made some. We would fill a cartridge
with the black powder and attach a fuse, then shake around† to see
who would light the fuse. I won (or lost, as the case may be). I lit
the fuse. A long, solid white flame came out of the jet. The cartridge
moved slowly forward about four inches, turned left, and blew up.
No one was hurt.

There was a first classman who lived directly across the court
from me. I was in the second wing, and he was in the fourth. He had
given us a bad time when we were plebes. Someone came up with

---

* Sulfur, charcoal, and potassium nitrate

† *Shaking around* was a means of making a random choice by passing around dice
and having each person shake and roll them to see who rolled the highest numbers.

the idea of launching a CO_2 cartridge out of my upper window so it would have a trajectory into his window. We built a launching pad on my desk aimed out my window. On either side of my door was a closet and a shower. Half of us got into the closet, the other half in the shower, and we lit the fuse. The cartridge took off. Instead of going out the window it hit the frame and rocketed wildly around the room while we crouched in the closet and shower. That was the end of our experiments with rocket science.

In the middle of October, Navy was playing a big opponent in football. Franklin Field was not big enough for a large crowd, so our home games were held in Baltimore. I and two of my classmates were fixed up with three girls for a triple blind date. We were to meet the girls on the thirty-yard line after the game. I was miserable through that game, knowing that if I went on the date, I was going to be in trouble. The classmates I was with were not moral, and I assumed that the girls would be of a similar mind.

I don't remember whether I showed up and told them I was not going with them or just did not show up. In any case, I found myself wandering the streets of Baltimore alone. Any large city has an unsavory part. In Baltimore it is called The Block. Somehow I ended up there, and the available entertainment was not designed for Christians. What in the world does a Christian do on a Saturday night in Baltimore? I was not a Christian, but I wanted to *think* that I was. I had the following conversation with myself:

What would those pre-reveille Christians do?

They would probably go to church.

Whoever heard of a church being open on a Saturday night?

I bought a newspaper and looked at the hundreds of church advertisements in it. I found one that said, "Saturday night, church, corner of North Ave. and St. Paul." I flagged a cab for North Avenue and St. Paul Street. There were two large churches on opposite corners. One was the Seventh Baptist Church. It was locked. The other was Northminster Presbyterian. It was open, and there were many people inside. I went up to the balcony to look over the congregation. I spotted three blue uniforms about five rows from the front. I went down the aisle and told them to move over. They were John Bajus, Willard Peterson, and Jim Inskeep, all Naval Academy men, class of '49.

It was a Youth for Christ meeting and had not yet started. The director, Deak Ketcham, saw the four midshipmen sitting up front and decided to ask them for testimonies. I told him I had nothing to say. The other three quickly volunteered.

I remember what Jim Inskeep said: "I could not love my mother as much as I do if I did not love the Lord more than I love her."

In my mind, I rebelled. "That liar! That hypocrite!" But I knew that they were not hypocrites. These men lived the way they talked; I had seen it.

Well, they must be mistaken.

If they are mistaken, they are the three happiest mistaken men I know.

There was a third alternative: they might be right.

The speaker for the night was a man named Gregorio Tingson, a missionary from the Philippines. He spoke on the first four verses of Psalm 40:

> I waited patiently for the Lord; and he inclined unto me, and heard my cry. He brought me up also out of an horrible pit, out of the miry clay, and set my feet upon a rock, and established my goings. And he hath put a new song in my mouth, even praise unto our God: many shall see it, and fear, and shall trust in the Lord. Blessed is that man that maketh the Lord his trust, and respecteth not the proud, nor such as turn aside to lies. (KJV)

Verse 2 really hit me. I had always been proud of my goodness, but I knew that my willpower to stay moral had gone through some major tests, including earlier that very evening.

After the meeting, Pete took me to another room and introduced me to the Father. I had the joy that is described in 1 Peter 1:8–9: "Though you have not seen him, you love him; and even though you do not see him now, you believe in him and are filled with an *inexpressible and glorious joy*, for you are receiving the end result of your faith, the salvation of your souls."

On the bus back to the Academy, I wanted to *sing*. "Is anyone among you in trouble? Let them pray. Is anyone happy? Let them sing songs of praise" (James 5:13).

But I had a couple problems. First, I did not know any songs. Second, I realized that this good news was too good to keep to myself. I set about planning how to tell the 2,600 other midshipmen about the way of salvation. I was going to stand on the roof of Bancroft Hall and shout it out! My thinking had not proceeded very far when I realized the Navy would take a dim view of such action, send me to the hospital for mental evaluation, then ship me home to Nebraska. No more Navy for me!

Well, I had to tell someone, so I decided to tell my roommate, Dick Daykin. He needed the gospel. We would get into fights; we had already broken the window of our door three times in the first few weeks of our youngster year. But there was a problem with me telling him. Dick was a profane man, but I wasn't. Even though he didn't know that it made no sense to me, I would read my Bible every day, and he knew about that. He also knew I got up every morning to meet with a few fanatics, and he knew I tried to stay out of trouble. If I told him that I had just been forgiven for my sins, he would say, "What sins, Wilson? I've been trying to get you to sin all year." So I decided not to tell him, either.

Several weeks went by. Then Dick cornered me and demanded to know what had happened. He said I had been unbearably pleasant for the last three weeks. So I told him.

That was my conversion. I continued to grow in the Lord for the next three years. My youngster and second class years consisted of early morning Bible study, classes, crew, study hour, witnessing, and an occasional blind date.

The last three years at the Academy, I lived in the best rooms in Bancroft Hall. Around the hall is a moat with a heavy metal fence surrounding it. There was only one room that was not next to the moat. That was my room (room 2013) youngster year. If a midshipman did not want to enter through a doorway for whatever reason (late, drunk, etc.), he would come in via my window, crawl across my feet in my bed, and go out through my door.

One Saturday night in the winter of youngster year, there was a ball in Dahlgren Hall, the Armory. I was not dating, nor was my classmate Webb. We decided to hole up in his room on the zero deck* and study. His room was on the outside of the second wing. We bought four quarts of milk and a box of cheese crackers to help us through the night of study. We put the milk on his windowsill in the snow.

The officer of the day was a Lieutenant Commander Vaughan. He had a great reputation for frying midshipmen. He was also the officer representative for crew. He was walking back from the ball on the sidewalk outside the second wing and saw the four quarts of milk on the windowsill. He counted the number of windows to the end of the wing, and the next thing we knew, he was standing in our doorway. We stood at attention immediately. We knew we were going to be fried. Then he recognized me.

* The ground floor

"Mr. Wilson, do you have any milk on the windowsill?"

"Yes, sir."

We could see him pondering. He did not want to fry a member of his crew.

He finally said, "Drink it or pour it out."

We did not want to pour it out. He stood there and watched us drink four quarts of milk.

June week[†] of my youngster year, my girlfriend from Omaha came to visit me at the Academy. Her name was Marjory Mahoney. She was smart and funny but not a Christian. Later that summer while on leave in Omaha, I broke up with her because of that. I was heartbroken and shared my problem with Pete, who was now a first classman. He read me Matthew 10:37[‡], only he added *girlfriend* to the list. I did not know that *girlfriend* was not in the text.

My second class cruise was on the aircraft carrier *USS Coral Sea* (CVA-43) to the Mediterranean during

Jim and Marjory

---

† Now called Commissioning Week, June Week marked the graduation of the first classmen who had completed four years at the Academy. The week is celebrated with ceremonies and other events and traditions.

‡ "Anyone who loves their father or mother more than me is not worthy of me; anyone who loves their son or daughter more than me is not worthy of me."

the summer of '48. We stopped in Lisbon, Gibraltar, Nice, and Villefranche, where I dated a girl from the French Alps. Her mother was Auboine de Sezanne, a French countess. She had a pair of cufflinks shaped like the helm of a sailing ship with a small magnetic compass in the center. I admired them. Later I received them with a note attached in her imperfect English: "You are the only one who admired them. Don't lost them never." I wore them for the next eight years. They were stolen from me on a carrier in 1956.

One of my favorite things is a good, crispy, juicy apple. My custom my whole life has been to eat everything but the stem. The only exception to this was that summer on the *Coral Sea*. When I was a kid, any body of water was an invitation to throw or skip rocks. Here was the whole Mediterranean Sea, and no rocks to throw. I sacrificed the pleasure of eating the entire fruit and saved up my apple cores to chuck into the sea.

During that summer in the Mediterranean, we would conduct air operations. I was riding in a torpedo bomber, a TBM, with another midshipman. I was in the rear gunner's seat, and he was in the lower gunner's seat. The guns had been removed. The point of the exercise was for the TBMs to avoid being "shot down" by the F4Us (Corsairs). I remember watching the corsairs slide sideways across the sky. Our pilot was doing all kinds of evasive maneuvers. I got violently airsick. I motioned to my classmate to pass me a vomit bag. He looked around but could not find one. He handed me some rags. I held them in front of my mouth and vomited. The vomit did not go into the rags; it went past my nose and all over the concentric-circle gun sight. Later I had to clean it up.

We had a happy hour on the hangar deck that summer. I put together a skit on Robert Service's "The Shooting of Dan McGrew." I recited the poem, and classmates acted it out. Hammet played the kid hitting a "jag-time" tune, and Frank Young was "the lady known as Lou." We had no women on board, so we procured two grapefruits to give "her" a figure. It went well until "she" bent over and one of the grapefruits rolled out on the stage. I picked it up and threw it out to the audience. The place went wild.

The winter of second-class year, there was a blizzard in central Nebraska that cut off all communication with home. For two weeks, nothing got through. Planes had to drop hay to stranded cattle. At that time, I flunked the final exam in electrical engineering. The blizzard was not the primary cause, but it probably contributed to my lack of concentration. I was called up before a review board of the heads of academic courses. All of them were four-stripers.* I was scared. The alternatives were being discharged and dismissed from the Naval Academy; repeating the entire year in all subjects, which would put me in the class of '51; or being allowed to retake the exam. One Head of Department, Captain Seabring, knew me and thought well of me. He spoke up on my behalf, and I was retested.

In January 1949, I marched with the Brigade of Midshipmen in Truman's inauguration.

* Navy captains (the rank below admiral)

CHAPTER 11

WORD OF LIFE CAMP
AND HITCHHIKING

> And from there they sailed to Antioch, where they had been com-
> mended to the grace of God for the work that they had fulfilled.
> (Acts 14:26)

At the end of my second-class year, several other Christians from the classes of '49–'51 and I were counselors at the Word of Life Camp for high school kids on an island in Schroon Lake in upstate New York. During my week there, I heard great Bible teaching and evangelism from Tommie Titcombe,* who spoke on Psalm 91. I claimed the promises of that Psalm for my life, and it has been my favorite passage of Scripture ever since.

While at the camp, I read a copy of *China's Millions*†, which tells the story of the China Inland Mission. From then on, I longed to go to China as a missionary. There were two hindrances: I was in the Navy and couldn't leave; and it was 1949, and China was closed. No one went there for the next thirty years. However, this was a desire I would revisit some years later.

From camp, I hitchhiked west to visit my Aunt Florence near the Black Hills of South Dakota. Then I hitchhiked back home and went on the summer cruise to Cherbourg, France.

Hitchhiking was my normal method for travelling on leave. One Christmas, Cliff Colvin and I were hitchhiking together, he to Illinois,

---

* A missionary to Nigeria and subject of the biography *Tread Upon the Lion*
† By Hudson Taylor, originally published in 1890.

and I to Nebraska. We got stranded on the west side of Akron, Ohio, at 0100 in five-degree weather. We stood there until 0500. Every few minutes, Cliff would say something about not letting me ever talk him into this again.

On another trip across Iowa in the winter, the driver was going so fast that birds could not get out of the way. The car splattered many blackbirds across its windshield and grill.

One time, I was hitchhiking home by air with Russ Needlun. We caught a B25 with canvas bucket seats from Bellville, Illinois, to Colorado Springs. The plane's engines were very loud, and we were flying between thunderstorms. We rode from Colorado Springs to Denver with the assistant to the governor of Colorado. He took us through Denver and let us out next to a gas station on US 6.

It was late at night, and the station was closed. We left our suitcases next to the highway and stood on the lee side of the gas station to get out of the wind. We could see headlights for miles, so we had plenty of time to get to the highway and put up our thumbs.

Suddenly, we saw headlights coming up over the hill nearby. We did not understand, because we should have seen them miles away. We ran out just as the car pulled up. It was a Colorado state trooper. He had been going west, saw the suitcases, turned around, and came back.

We told him what we were doing. He told us it was against state law to hitchhike in Colorado. We told the trooper that we did not know that, and we would flag the next Trailways bus and pay our way. He said that we could not do that; we were on private property, and he could not allow us to stay there. I asked if he could give us a ride back into Denver to the bus terminal. He said it was against regulations for him to give rides. Russ suggested, "Maybe we could dig a hole, climb into it, and pull the hole in after us." He gave us a ride to the bus terminal.

One time between Lincoln and Omaha, I was picked up by a car with four University of Nebraska students in it. I was grateful and told them that when we stopped for gas the Cokes were on me. At the next stop, I bought six bottles of Coca Cola. The guys in the back seat told me not to open the bottles myself because they had a bottle opener. I handed them the bottles and got in the front seat.

It seemed like they were taking a long time to open the Cokes. Finally, they passed mine up to me. It was the funniest tasting Coca Cola I had ever had.

We were going downhill on a long grade when the driver said, "Look, no hands!" He had let go of the wheel. The guys in the back seat had poured half of each Coke out the window and replaced it with whiskey. I decided to get out of the car at Gretna.

At Christmas 1949, I went home to Nebraska, but I stayed so long that no train could get me back to the Naval Academy on time. I went to Offutt Air Force Base in Omaha to see if I could hitch a ride on military air. At Air Operations, I met an Air Force captain who was flying an empty C47 to Andrews Air Force Base in Maryland. He said I could have a ride. I was the first one to apply for a ride on the empty plane.

Before departure, thirteen Air Force women returning to Andrews came looking for a ride. They had been at Offutt Air Base looking for housing because Strategic Air Command was moving from Andrews to Offutt. The pilot had guaranteed me a ride, but, being a gentleman, I let the women go aboard before me. They had all taken seats and put on the parachutes in the seats. Parachutes were required for everyone. When I came aboard, there were none left.

The captain told the women that he had promised me the ride and since I had been the first to arrive, one of them would have to give her parachute to me and stay at Offutt. No one moved. He tried again. Still no movement. The captain finally gave up and said that he would break regulations and take me without a parachute. He invited me to sit in the radioman's seat in the cockpit.

The plane flew through solid fog for thirteen hours. On our approach to D.C., all the airfields were socked in with fog, and there was a traffic jam over Washington. I had the radioman's earphones, so I could hear the communication between the pilots and air control. Each plane was assigned a different arc to circle at a different altitude until a runway opened up.

Finally, the captain told the ground control that he only had ten minutes of fuel left. Washington National cleared us for an emergency landing with a ground control approach (that is, the airport would give instructions to the pilot on the approach, since he could not see the landing strip through the fog).

The voice on the other end of the radio said that he had our plane on radar. "If I lose you, turn back, gain altitude, and try again." We were descending per instructions when he lost us. We circled up and descended again.

Again we were lost on the screen and were told to gain altitude, circle, and restart the descent. Then the voice said, "If I lose you this time, climb to five thousand feet and wait for further instructions." He did not say what the next instructions would be, but landing did not appear to be in the plans. I imagined they would go something like this: "Direct the plane toward the Chesapeake Bay; have the crew and passengers bail out." I was the only one without a parachute.

Again we were lost. The captain said, "I am coming in anyway." We continued the descent blind. Suddenly, the runway lights blinked through the mist right in front of us, and we landed perfectly. I thanked the captain profusely.

CHAPTER 12

FIRST CLASS YEAR

We have different gifts, according to the grace given to each of us.
If your gift is prophesying, then prophesy in accordance with your
faith; if it is serving, then serve; if it is teaching, then teach; if it is
to encourage, then give encouragement; if it is giving, then give
generously; if it is to lead, do it diligently; if it is to show mercy, do
it cheerfully. (Rom. 12:6–8)

My first class year was very important to me. I was one of the leaders
in the Christian movement taking place at the Academy. We had
pre-reveille Bible study groups running in each of the six wings
of Bancroft Hall. We held a Christian meeting in the south end of
Memorial Hall every Sunday afternoon with a regular Bible teacher
from Washington Bible College, Willis Bishop. We also had guest
speakers there. The group was loosely affiliated with the Officers'
Christian Union (now the Officers' Christian Fellowship).

The first OCU Bible study in the United States was at the home
of Brigadier General Hayes Kroner at 1616 21st Street NW in
Washington, DC. General Kroner married an Englishwoman and
later moved to England and changed his name to H.K. Ashby de
Gray. At the time of OCU's incorporation in 1943, the men in the
Bible study realized that when the war was over, the British would
go home, the General would retire, the reserved men would get out
of the service, and the OCU would be no more. They began to pray
that God would raise up a witness at the service academies, and that

prayer was answered. In 1945, God sent two Christian plebes named John Bajus and Jim Inskeep to the Naval Academy as well as a math professor named Joseph Findlay Paydon. In 1946, Frank Watson entered West Point and began an OCU study there along with Clay Buckingham. Each of these men had a strong witness.

The OCU was run by an elected council. During my first class year, there were no OCU Council members on active duty; all members were reserves or students from the service academies. When I was commissioned on 1 June 1950, there were only thirty-five members of the OCU on active duty, and most of them were cadets and midshipmen. John Kirk, Morris Riddle, and Caryll Whipple were my classmates and partners in the ministry.

In the spring, I realized I was not going to make it into the varsity shell, so I dropped crew. This gave me more time for ministry and study.

Around that time, Corrie ten Boom came to Annapolis. Her travelling companion was her niece, Nollie. I remember escorting Nollie around the Academy Yard. Corrie was not yet famous. She gave me a copy of her first book, *A Prisoner and Yet*. It was probably the second Christian book I had ever read.

As June week approached, I planned an evangelistic banquet for the midshipmen, their girlfriends, and their families, figuring that many of them were not Christians. We held it at Barnes Restaurant in Annapolis. I invited Major Batt of the Cold Stream Guards, a famous regiment in the British Army, to be the speaker.

My parents were to arrive the same day as Major Batt. I knew that my father was not fond of the British, and I did not want things to become awkward. I met the major, showed him around the Academy, and explained to him that my father did not have a high view of the English.

My parents and I sat at the head table. Major Batt preached the gospel. After the banquet, the major asked my mother how long she had been a Christian.

"Oh," she said, "I've been a Christian all my life."

He said, "That's funny. Over in England, we become Christians when we're eighteen." Then he asked my father the same question.

My father replied, "To tell you the truth, Major, I am not a Christian."

OCU members. Back row: ?, Eric Nelson, Jim Wilson, ?, Caryll Whipple, ?, ?
Front row: ?, Jim Inskeep, ?, ?, Willard "Pete" Peterson, ?

CHAPTER 13

GOING HOME

So they remained for a long time, speaking boldly for the Lord,
who bore witness to the word of his grace, granting signs and wonders to be done by their hands. (Acts 14:3)

I was at the Naval Academy from 1946–1950. Meanwhile, life continued to be busy back at home. Here is an account written by my
brother Everett about home life while I was away.

We moved from South Omaha to Giltner in early February 1946—
Mom, 45, Dad, 46, Harold was almost 14, I almost 10 and Ken almost 3. Floyd was staying with Aunt Rhoda and Uncle Cal McGinnis
to finish his sophomore year at Omaha South.

The house was an improvement on the Omaha house, because
it had a cistern and a pump indoors. We had left our last indoor
bathroom in Papillion in 1943 and did not have another until we
moved to Hastings in 1950. Early on, the windmill was restored to
operation, so the windmill filled the cistern, not by hand pumping.
The forty acres we rented was named much later as the geographic
center of tornado activity in North America.

In many respects, life at home was not too far removed from pioneer days—what was big is that we usually could get away in the car.

A power outage then was not the disaster it is today. There were
no pipes to freeze. We could cook and keep warm without outside
help.

No furnaces; hand-fired stoves. In our Giltner house, clean corncobs were the fuel—lightweight, highly flammable, plentiful. For the

75

three years east of town it was my primary job to haul the corncobs in bushel baskets into the house. A lot more than one trip, because cobs burn fast.

My older brothers worked a lot harder and more profitably than I did. Floyd could harness a team, hitch a walking plow to it, and plow a small field when he was seventeen, after recovering from appendicitis, mastoid surgery, and polio in his early teens. Harold was a hired man at fifteen. He could also drive a loaded two-ton truck.

Harold was tiny for his age. His high school friends called him Peewee. On his sixteenth birthday he shyly announced that he was glad because he was now too old to spank—too old, but unfortunately not too big; Dad, with a twinkle in his eye, scooped him up, draped him bottom-up over his left arm, and gave him a birthday spanking, not hard, but loud. Harold did not think it was funny, but he realized that he had set himself up for it. From the way he looked at me, I knew that laughing would not be healthy for me right then.

In the winter, though we woke up in a bitterly cold house, we were toasty warm under Mom's hand-tied patchwork quilts. After Floyd joined us, Dad would knock on the wall separating their room from his as a signal to get up and get the fires going.

One bitter day, Harold was at the kitchen stove and I was at the dining room stove, racing to see which of us could make the thermometer hit ninety first. I won, because the kitchen had an outside door, and the dining room did not. Our parents were strict, but not predictably so. I don't know how close we were to burning down the house; I hope they knew . . . .

We raised chickens by the hundreds, and Dad began custom hauling* of grain and livestock—not bad for a man whose heart was a time bomb . . . .

---

* Hauling upon request for whoever hired.

But things were tight. Decades later Mom said that she grieved over not being able to do more for Leonard and Glenda's wedding, since Glenda's mother had died not long after we moved there. The wedding was in the Warren living room . . . I thought it was beautiful.

The next year, with Ken firmly in school, our Mother left her twenty-two-year run as a stay-at-home mom to return to teaching, which she continued until she was past seventy.

We got our first electric refrigerator in 1948 or 1949.

In 1950, Ken and I got to go with Mom and Dad to Annapolis for Jim's graduation from the Naval Academy. During June week, Jim got us in to eat with the Midshipmen. I don't remember the main course, but I remember the dessert: great serving bowls of strawberry ice cream, from which we could help ourselves.

We didn't see Washington, D.C. Dad had to change a flat on the freeway during rush hour on our way to Annapolis. That was enough of that.

The end of the week was packed. The ceremony was on Friday afternoon, after which we piled into the 1948 Straight-Eight Olds 98 and drove in considerable style back to our cold-water house, arriving on Sunday morning. Some of us even went to church and a Youth for Christ rally in Aurora Sunday afternoon. The next day we were at Hastings College for Leonard's graduation, the main reason we were in a hurry to get home.

Here is Leonard's account of life at home after he left the Navy:

When I returned from the Navy after World War II, the folks had moved out on to a 40-acre place near Giltner, Nebraska. There were 11 cows for milking, and I had never milked a cow before—except for a few squirts. This was for real, by the bucketful. However, there were five of us who could milk, Dad, Mom, Floyd, Harold, and I. I had to play student for a while, with sprained fingers in both hands. There was some satisfaction in it. But there was also the occasional kicked and spilled bucket, a whiplash of a tail across the face. And of course, it was a chore that never quit, every morning and every evening—and it was mostly cold weather. We also ran a separator to enable us to sell the cream.

There was, in addition to the milking, the need to feed the cows and to clean out the barn regularly. The last, of course, was not a wanted job, but a highly necessary one.

Sometime in that year, Dad was raising a lot of chickens. I know that when I got home we were taking a lot of eggs to market. Then we were picking up day-old chicks by the hundreds—a hundred at a time every week, and sometimes two hundred. These were to be raised as fryers, and the staggered arrival dates would allow us 10 to 12 weeks later to have 100 to 200 fryers ready for market each week. These, too, took a lot of care. Most of them would get a start in the kitchen at home and in a few days be put out under a brooder for a while. Feed, water and medicine were continual chores. The equipment had to be cleaned all of the time. There was a different feed for different aged chickens. And of course, there was the matter of cleaning out chicken houses.

I graduated on June 2, 1950. After graduation and commissioning, we drove to Nebraska on US 40. We drove straight from Friday June 2 to Sunday morning June 4.* Everyone wanted to go to bed, but I insisted that we go to church.

There was only one church in Giltner. It was a Methodist church. I was in uniform——I had no other clothes. The pastor, who was in his late sixties, was impressed that I had just graduated from the Naval

---

* On Monday, Leonard graduated summa cum laude from Hastings College after only three years there. He had gotten out of the Navy in 1946 as a first class quartermaster. In the fall of 1952, he was recalled to active duty and ordered to Astoria, Oregon.

Pers-3113-SHR-1
3 May 1950

From: Chief of Naval Personnel
To: Following Ensigns, USN
    Garrison E. MURPHY   533060/1100 USS MADDOX (DD-731)
    James I. WILSON   533283/1100 USS BRUSH (DD-745
    Frederick F. Duggan,Jr. 532762/1100 USS SAMUEL N. MOORE (DD-747)
    U.S. Naval Academy
    Annapolis, Md.
Via: Superintendent

Subj: Change of duty

1. Upon graduation, you will regard yourself detached from duty at the U.S. Naval Academy, Annapolis, Md.; will proceed to San Francisco, Calif., and report to the Commandant, Twelfth Naval District for transportation to the port in which the vessel indicated above may be and upon arrival report to the commanding officer of that vessel for duty.

2. You are hereby authorized to delay until 7 July 1950 in reporting at San Francisco, Calif., in compliance with these orders, such delay to count as advance leave. Keep the Bureau of Naval Personnel advised of your address.

3. Travel via government transportation is directed outside the United States. Class Two priority is certified for travel via government aircraft.

4. While traveling via air, 65 pounds baggage to accompany you is authorized, and an additional 50 pounds baggage is authorized as air cargo for shipment under the same class of priority as for yourself.

Copy to:
ComTwelve
ComCruDesPac
ComDesRonNINE
ComDesDiv 92
ComServPac(2)
CO,USS MADDOX(DD-731)
CO,USS BRUSH(DD-745)
CO,USS SAMUEL N. MOORE(DD-747)
Jacket copy
Pers-311s
    82212 (T&P 0750)
    3118-F
    3113
    311E
    321

certified a true copy
James Q. Philson

J. W. ROPER

Upon reporting, forward to BuPers copy of these orders. (Staff Corps Officers an additional copy to cognizant Bureau) via new Commanding Officer with all endorsements.

16590

1st endorsement
U. S. NAVAL ACADEMY
Annapolis, Maryland
2 JUNE 1950
1. Delivered; detached.

R. G. LEEDY
By direction

Jim's graduating class in review

Academy. He asked if I would say a few words about the Academy. I think I gave my testimony. At any rate, I said something Christian. It was a shock to the church.

After the service, I suggested that the pastor have a week of meetings in the church. He asked, "Why?" I replied that it looked like church attendance was poor. He agreed but added that he was too old to preach every night.

I said, "Leave it to me. I will find an evangelist."

His reply was, "No, sir. No evangelist in my church."

Then I suggested Rev. Rosehart, the Mennonite pastor fourteen miles away.

He replied that the Mennonite pastor was a good man but that he dwelt a lot on the Second Coming, and he himself did not believe the Lord was coming again, so we could not have him. He said, "That was a fine talk you gave this morning. Why don't you do it?"

I could see the restrictions that would be placed on me, so I declined.

Back home, I saw in the local newspaper that Stuart Hamblen was speaking that afternoon in the ballpark in Aurora, about fourteen miles away. Stuart Hamblen was the Johnny Cash of the day. He had written the song "(I Won't Go Huntin', Jake) But I'll Go Chasin' Women." He had been converted in the first Billy Graham tent meeting the previous November in Los Angeles. Two other converts from that same meeting were Olympic athlete Lou Zamperini and Jim Vaus, Mickey Cohen's wiretapper.

I told my brothers, "Let's go."

My twenty-year-old brother Floyd, his friend Marvin Ruebsman, fourteen-year-old Everett, and Rodney Campbell, a sixteen-year-old wild kid, decided to go with me. Eighteen-year-old Harold refused to go. He said he was not going to listen to some fanatic.

We arrived at the ballpark. I was in uniform and had my Bible. I was asked to give my testimony. I went up on the stage and left the other four in the bleachers. After Stuart finished preaching, he gave an invitation. We were all praying. When I looked up, Everett was the only one I could see in the bleachers. I left the stage, grabbed Everett, and took him behind the stage, where he received Christ. The other three had already received Christ. I taught them some choruses, and we sang all the way home.

Everett went into the house first and said, "Guess what, Mom? I'm saved!"

She replied, "Floyd, too?"

"Yes, Floyd too!"

About six p.m., Harold came into the house laughing. He had just returned from the pool hall. Rodney Campbell had stopped off there on his return from Aurora to let everyone know about his conversion. Harold said, "Guess what? Rodney Campbell says he's saved!" He thought that was the funniest thing he had ever heard.

Then his older brother said, "So am I," and his younger brother said, "Me, too."

Harold was very upset. It was bad enough having one fanatic in the family. Now there were three!

Harold and Floyd had both flunked out of the University of Nebraska for partying too much. Floyd had been in his second year and Harold in his first. While my parents were back in Annapolis, Harold, Ellis Warren, and Don Wilson had painted a '37 Chevy bright red at Don Wilson's farmhouse on a Sunday morning. Don Wilson's family was Mennonite. Later they took it high speed in loose gravel and rolled it seven times. No one was hurt.

After Floyd's conversion, Harold spent the next two days kicking things around the house.

On Monday, we all went to Leonard's graduation from Hastings College. On Tuesday night, there was a father-son dinner at the Methodist Church. My father had six sons, so we all went to it.

I left the dinner soon after it was over and walked home. When I got near the house, I saw a car parked in the yard. I was walking toward the house when a voice called out from the car. "We've got some questions about religion."

I had no idea who "we" was. I replied, "I've got a lot of answers, but I'm not giving any. Goodnight."

I took a few more steps and changed my mind. "I will tell you what. I will answer one question. I pick it."

There was silence. Then the voice said, "What's the question?"

"If you want to know how to be saved, I'll tell you. Otherwise, good night!"

"That's what we really want to know."

I got in the back seat and preached the gospel. Three eighteen-year-old boys received Christ—Ellis Warren, Don Wilson, and my brother Harold.*

On Saturday night, there was a free grade B movie in the park. After the movie, I was walking home when a Mrs. Dodson came up to me. She said that the whole town knew of the change in these seven kids. She had a twelve-year-old son named Kent who would swear at her and tell her to do it herself if she told him to do anything. She wanted to know if I would come home with her and talk to him. I did. Kent and I were sitting on the carpet when, in tears, he received Christ.

In the six days since my arrival back in town, eight boys between the ages of twelve and twenty had received Christ. On Sunday, I told the pastor I had changed my mind and would be glad to preach at the week of meetings.

* Forty years later, I got a call from McCall, Idaho. It was Don. He and his wife were going to be in Moscow and wanted to take me to dinner. He said that I had been the most important person in his life. He went to Grace Bible College in Omaha, then on Young Life Staff. Now he was farming with his six sons.

We took a week of praying and planning, then the meetings started. I had all eight of those guys testify, and I preached. There were converts every night.

On Tuesday, I heard a farmer across the road from our house swearing at his tractor. That evening in enumerating sins I included "cursing at tractors." At the invitation, the farmer came and knelt at the altar rail. The pastor was alarmed, went down to the farmer, and explained to him that this was just for teenagers. The farmer got up and went back to his seat.

I insisted on doing all of the personal evangelism. There were about thirty conversions over the course of the week. On the last night, six teenagers responded. They sat on chairs in a circle while I explained the gospel. An adult came down the aisle, took a chair, and sat outside the circle. It was my father.

Dad had an off-and-on drinking habit. I only saw it two times. Once during Prohibition, around 1931, he came home very drunk. We lived on Elm Street. Half a block away on 25th Street, there was a permanently-vacant house called the Brown House. Apparently there had been a prohibition party in the Brown House. I remember my father lying unconscious on the sofa.

In 1944, after Dad had recovered from his heart attack, he left home. My mother assumed he had gone off drinking and sent me looking for him. I went from bar to bar and found him drunk in a bar on 24th Street. He came home with me. I did not know how to drive, and he was drunk. Between the two of us, somehow we got the car home without being pulled over.

The drinking did not happen often, but it was often enough for my grandmother to encourage Mom to divorce Dad. On that last day of the revival meetings, my father received Christ. That ended his drinking. I had always looked up to him as my father, and I found out he was looking up to me for his Father. He wanted the answers I had.

When my thirty days' leave was up, I took the train to San Francisco to join my ship. I had promised Dawson Trotman I would attend the Navigator conference at Hume Lake, so I spent two days there on the way to my ship. Two hundred twenty-five men between the ages of eighteen and twenty-five attended the conference. I was sitting in a truck with Dawson and told him what had happened in Nebraska.

He got very upset. "You left thirty new babes in Nebraska? You should not be here!" He wanted me to return home to disciple the new converts.

I replied that I only had a thirty-day leave. I was in the Navy! There was a ship waiting for me in the Philippines, and I had no choice.

Dawson Trotman had me tell the story to the men. Then he said, "How many men will quit their jobs and go to Nebraska?"

Eleven men stood up, but he did not send any of the eleven. He sent another man, named Jim Hardie. He will come into this story again later.

CHAPTER 14

LIFE AS A NAVAL OFFICER

But Paul . . . departed, having been commended by the brothers to
the grace of the Lord. (Acts 15:40)

I returned to San Francisco, where I reported in and waited for
transportation to the western Pacific. While I was there, on June
26, 1950, North Korea crossed the 38th parallel and invaded the
Republic of Korea.

The following is a letter I wrote to my brother Lorraine from
Japan a month later:

24 July 1950
U.S.S. Brush (DD 745)
Sasebo, Kyushu, Japan

Dear Lorraine,

I really hit it right. A wonderful time at Hume Lake and at Aunt
Toots'. I reported in the seventh, Friday, got three shots, typhus, ty-
phoid and first cholera, and a cowpox vaccination, second cholera is
to be taken seven to ten days later but the corpsman said that was it.
They couldn't keep me that long. They moved the Seventh Fleet personnel up to priority one. Mine [had been] two . . . . Took off midnight
Tuesday from Fairfield in a Stratacruiser, landed at Hickam field 0710
Hawaii time. Priority one, we couldn't leave the field. Took off at noon
bucket seat; Johnson Island, Kwajalein, Guam, Okinawa and then
supposedly Manila. We had 37 hours flying time and about 60 alto-
gether. We went swimming at Guam. We crossed the date line at midnight and so lost Thursday the thirteenth. Okinawa was the long way
to Manila but it was the only thing I could get from Guam. We had a

one-hour stop in Okinawa during which I found out the "Valley"* was anchored in Buckner Bay. I tried to call and find out what else was there but everyone wanted to play dumb. The Air Force knew nothing. White Beach, "the biggest little port in the world," knew nothing. A big harbor but the NOB† is just a shack on the beach. I remembered the exec's letter was postmarked on the *Valley Forge*, so I unchecked my bags to find out myself. A two-hour ride across Okinawa brought me to White Beach.

The *Brush* was there. On the way out we passed the *Valley* and the *Rochester*, Struble's home. We had heard that the *Valley Forge* had been sunk, to which the Navy replied that she was right where she was supposed to be. This was where she was supposed to be. This was all Saturday. I arrived at my new home in time for dinner in the Wardroom (first one). A many page Op order (secret) came out at the same time. As Ass't Navigator I got to read it. We got underway Sunday morning, rendezvoused with Task Force 95, put the First Cavalry Division ashore and sent strike after strike with fighter sweeps across North Korea.

All this time we were cruising around the Sea of Japan tracking two typhoons that followed us up. We were hoping they would swing off to the right because we had a date in the Yellow Sea. The typhoons had merged and were still coming straight north. If the mail is censored, it is news to me. The storm was over Nagasaki when the Admiral decided to run through the Western Straight (Tsushima). It wasn't so bad. We were in the less dangerous side of the typhoon.

We kept our date in the Yellow Sea and now are refueling here in Sasebo. I've been aboard eight days. It's going to take a long time to become qualified. The skipper takes the con a lot. There are two new NROTC ensigns aboard who graduated this year. Cole was a math major at Oregon, and Reese was a finance major at UCLA. Also there

* *The USS Valley Forge*
† Naval Operating Base

are two 49'er ensigns and two other ensigns. I am also Ass't Combat Information Center officer. General Quarter I am Ass't Gunnery Liaison Officer in combat. I have all the 40mm and 20mm mounts and directors on my circuit and Air Defense. My job is to keep an Air summary plot and assign different mounts to different targets.

I stand deck and combat watches, one in three (one four hour watch on, two four hour watches off); GQ an hour after sunset and an hour before sunrise every day. The ship is in Readiness Condition three. Read the newspapers to find out where we are in the future.

How is Glenda? I've been praying that everything will go all right. Let me know. I have many people to write to so please excuse the incomplete sentences. I'm in a hurry.

I've had a terribly busy week. We've been operating with the *HMS Triumph* (carrier) and one can (destroyer), the *Camus* (D20). The *Juneau* and the *Toledo* are here along with another Limey carrier.

Let me know all kinds of news.

Love, Jim
Acts 27:25

Task Force 77 got underway for the Sea of Japan where it supported the landing of the First Cavalry Division in Pohang on 18 July.

On 19 July, we were returning to Sasebo and had to ride out a typhoon in the Tsushima Straits. My quarters were up forward one deck below the main deck. I had the junior officer of the deck watch on the bridge 0400 to 0800. We were to relieve the watch at 0345. I got up at 0330, got dressed, and went up to the interior of Mount 1 of our 5"/38[‡]. I opened the hatch to the main deck (with a wheel) and stepped out into the middle of the typhoon. It was pitch black. I shut the hatch and got hold of a rail on the outside of a bulkhead. I had walked one step along the rail when a wave came over the bow,

‡ A deck gun used by the U.S. Navy from 1934 to 2008

knocked me off my feet, and rolled me to the side of the ship. The web caught me and kept me from going overboard. I lost my brand-new officer's cap (six weeks old). I crawled back to the rail and was walking hand over hand along it when I ran my head into the housing of an intake blower. I went hand and over hand back to the hatch and returned to my room to change into a dry uniform. I called the bridge to tell them I would be late relieving the watch and found an interior way up to the bridge. I was late! In the Navy, there is no excuse for being late. It would only have been understandable if I had gone overboard.

The staging base for the Navy in the Korean War was the port of Sasebo on the island of Kyushu. I first arrived there on July 20, 1950, and was in and out for the next three years.

Photo taken from the deck of the USS Brush DD-745 showing the web that kept me from going overboard at 0340, July 19, 1950. (Photographer unknown.)

At sea, seven destroyers in the task force served as a bent-line screen, and one destroyer served as a plane guard. The carriers were the *USS Valley Forge* and *HMS Triumph*. My watch and battle station were in CIC*. When the carriers turned into the wind, the bent-line screen had to scramble to get ahead of them without colliding with each other. I became an expert on giving the course to the bridge.

Air operations were mostly run from the Sea of Japan, but we had one tour in the Yellow Sea. The Yellow Sea was filled with thousands of giant jellyfish, all touching each other. We steamed through a carpet of jellyfish.

6 September 1950
USS Brush

Dear Lorraine, Glenda and kids,

We pulled into port today after two weeks up front. Des Div 92 is being transferred from the Task Force to another Task Force of a different nature entirely. I'm going to have to do a lot of studying in the next few days. I've been transferred to the first deck division because we have now too many "O" division officers. I'm Ass't First Div. Officer, Ass't First Lieutenant. My first main job beside the War Diary is Inventory of all spare parts of torpedoes, 5"/38 20mm, 40mm and fire control and order everything that is on our allowance that we don't have. Second, I'm to write and have mimeographed a detailed gunnery doctrine for 20mm. I don't know of any in the Navy. If I do a good job at that, I may find myself writing doctrine for every piece of attack and defensive equipment on board. I am satisfied that we have the best skipper in the Pacific Fleet, the best Gunnery Officer (Mr. Burnside, a mustang†, a brain, received a

---

* Combat Information Center

† A mustang is an officer who has been promoted up through the ranks of enlisted men rather than attending an officers' candidate school.

commendation letter from Com Cru Des Pac* for the best "call fire, shore bombardment" in the destroyer fleet), the best communicator, a good navigator, the best A.S.W. Officer and a very good CIC officer. Mr. Fisher, the Exec, is misplaced; he has had seven years of work and [postgraduate] study in guided missiles, and he is here on a destroyer. He is not too good as an Executive Officer.

I'm writing with a 300-yen (83.5 cents) fountain pen. It is the best pen I've ever had.

In three days you will be 25 years old. How is your hair holding out? Old family man! In a month I'll be 23 myself, and I'm just starting my foreign duty . . . .

Scuse please for last letter! I'm getting more mail than I ever got in my life. Keep it up.

You wonder what the kids are getting out of the Bible Club. Where do you think I got my meager knowledge of the Word? I think that is the best possible thing they could be doing [even] if they got next to nothing from it. You didn't think Harold should go to camp. I know the folks are having a hard time of it. You said the folks didn't object to him going. They wanted him to go! Harold learned more in that one week at camp than he did in a semester at the University. Mom writes inspired letters. She said that she wished Harold would write to tell me about camp. I'm glad that you didn't have a chance to say anything about it. You sound a little skeptical of the results of my ministry of the saving grace of Christ. Enlighten me. What do you think of Ellis? He writes a terrific letter.

I just received a PVT message from the *Worcester*. Johnny Bajus, '49, is on it. I'll see him tomorrow afternoon.

We're on four hours' notice.

You're fed up with politics? I'm fed up with democrats. I'd be fed up with Republicans too if they were in a position to foul things

* Commander, Cruisers-Destroyers, Pacific Fleet

up. As it is they are just talking. I don't like Truman and a few select members of his cabinet.

Whatever you do, don't work too hard. I might take a course in Oriental History from Nebraska through USAFI. I would like to take more but I will see if I can get this in.

The Lord's ministry is looking up. I received a letter from Floyd too.

I would suggest instead of Personal History or O. Henry or Kenneth Roberts for daily reading, one of the Gospels, Acts, and letters to the young churches. I know you've read them. I've read them many times.

This letter is getting long. It may sound like I'm giving you a growl, but out here these letters are the only places I can express myself. If the Captain says the ship is made of gold, it's made of gold.

Deck watches are great. Every time I get wakened for a mid-watch I think there must be a better way to make a living. I conn the ship unless something happens, any ordinary turns, zigzag plans, I can handle and still keep station.

Yours in Him,

Jim

On 6 September, we left TF77 to join Task Group 95.2 for gun-fire support in the front line in Pohang Dong at the east end of the Pusan Perimeter. After twenty days on the front line, the *Brush* and the *Maddox* were sent north to the Chinese-Russian border to en-force the UN blockade.

I was in the first division, the deck division, for regular duty. When I was not on watch or at general quarters†, one of my regular assignments as a junior officer was correcting charts. Corrections came down from the Bureau of Navigation; we would take our charts

† General quarters—all crew at battle stations and on alert

out and make the corrections. One sailor was assigned to work with me; he was also one of the men at the same battle station as me. While we were correcting charts together, I talked to him about the Lord, and he received Christ. The next day, while correcting charts, he told me that he had a problem. I encouraged him to tell me about it. I thought I could help him.

He said, "I have two wives."

"What do you mean you have two wives?"

"My first wife is in Baton Rouge, and the second one is in Pearl Harbor."

"How did that happen?"

"I just never told the second one that I was already married."

"I'll have to think about that."

This was out of my league. I did not even have *one* wife. I was still praying about what to tell him when our ship hit a mine later that month, and he was killed. I realized that God has solutions to problems that I cannot solve.

The captain was to write personal letters to the dependents of those killed by the mine explosion. He delegated me to write the letters, and he signed them. The sailor's wife of record was the only who got a letter. The second one never heard a word.

CHAPTER 15

THE CHRISTIAN AND THE MILITARY

Grace to you and peace from God our Father and the Lord Jesus
Christ. (1 Cor. 1:3)

In 1943, at the age of fifteen, I was talking to the Methodist minister
about my eagerness to get into the war. I could hardly wait until I
was seventeen and old enough to join up. The pastor told me it was
wrong for a Christian to be in the military. I answered him with the
stanza from *The Battle Hymn of the Republic*: "Christ died to make
men holy; let us die to make men free."

His answer shook me. He said, "Die if you want to, but don't kill
to make men free."

I was convinced that he was right. The contradiction of being a
Christian military officer was clear, but it was not enough to stop me.
If I could not be both a naval officer and a Christian, then I would
just be a naval officer. I enlisted in 1945 and arrived at the Naval
Academy in June 1946.

When I became a Christian in October 1947, I was very happy,
but that decision left me in a quandary. I had been convinced earlier that a Christian should not be in the military, and now I was a
Christian and a naval officer.

I went to Pete Peterson with my problem. He pointed out that
we were not at war, so no killing was taking place. He told me not to
worry about it—it would work itself out.

I forgot about it and began to grow in my Christian life. This went
on for a year and a half.

Then another contradiction surfaced. It was August 1949, the summer before my senior year at the Naval Academy, and the fleet was returning from Cherbourg, France. I was on board a destroyer minelayer, the *USS Shea* (DM30), known to the crew as the "Dirty Thirty." It was about noon on a beautiful Saturday somewhere in the mid-Atlantic. I was thinking that I had had no opportunity to witness on the way over to Europe, so I was praying that God would give me an opening. I prayed something like this: "God, I had no witness on the ship going to France. Please give me an opportunity on this return trip."

I had no sooner prayed this when an ensign came out of the wardroom* and told my classmates that the captain had said at the end of the meal that he thought we should have "Divine Services" on the ship on Sunday. As soon as he said that, every one of the officers got up from the table saying, "Excuse me, Captain," and left the wardroom. Each one was afraid that the captain would appoint him to conduct the service. As the last officer left, the captain said, "If no one will lead the service, I guess we can't have one."

When I heard this, I told the ensign that I would be willing to do it.

The ensign said, "The captain is on the bridge; go tell him."

I went to the bridge and volunteered my services.

The captain was grateful. He had only two requirements: he would pick the hymns (he only knew two hymns, and he would sing the ones he knew), and, as captain, he should read the Scripture. I could let him know which Scriptures to read.

I had preached once the preceding spring, but I had not done anything this like this before. On Saturday afternoon, I prayed and studied. I decided not to preach the gospel, because that might

* The officers' mess hall

scare the captain, and I might not get another opportunity to preach. I decided that I would speak on how to go ashore and not get into trouble.

Sunday was a bright day with a calm sea. Chairs were set up on the 01 deck† aft of the number two smokestack. There were about ten sailors, the captain, the exec, the officer in charge of midshipmen, and the ensign.

The hymns were sung, the Scripture read. I realized I might not get another chance to preach the gospel no matter what I spoke on, so I did not preach what I had prepared. I preached on the second half of John 1:29: "The next day John saw Jesus coming toward him and said, 'Look, the Lamb of God, who takes away the sin of the world!' "

As I preached, the sailors were listening, but all the officers in the front row were looking at the deck. I knew I was going to be in trouble, so I spoke as fast as I could to get it over with.

When I finished, I gave an invitation: "If anyone wants to become a Christian, see me after the benediction." Seven of the ten sailors came to see me. One of them wanted to get back to the Lord. The other six wanted to be saved. It was noon, so I told them I would meet them by the number two main battery after lunch.

I had no idea how to lead anyone to Christ. After lunch, I told the sailors, "Believe on the Lord Jesus Christ and thou shalt be saved."

"How do we believe?"

I did not know what to tell them, so for a couple of hours I tried to get them into the kingdom without knowing what I was doing.

That sermon I had preached changed my life forever. It was answered prayer. Those six sailors received Christ that day, and that started me on a life of evangelism.

† The first deck above the main deck

About three p.m., a sophomore ROTC midshipman came to tell me that Lt. Cdr. Raney wanted to see me in his stateroom. He was the lieutenant commander in charge of the midshipmen.

I went in and stood at attention. The Lt. Cdr. did not say, "At ease." He said, "Mr. Wilson, what you said this morning has me interested. I would like to become a Christian." I did my best to preach the gospel to him.

As we approached Guantanamo Bay, Cuba, my classmates on the different ships in the fleet were looking forward to going to the officers' club in Guantanamo to drink. However, the officers were not eager for 691 midshipmen to overrun their club. They decided that each officer could host one midshipman. The midshipmen had to shake around to see which ones were to be invited. I said, "Leave me out. I have no desire to go to the club."

I was watching them shake the dice when a sailor came down from the bridge and told me that I was to be the captain's guest at the club that night.

My classmates went ashore in the officers' launch, and I rode in the captain's gig with the captain. We had a table to ourselves. The captain proceeded to get drunk on a rum mixture call *añejo*. I drank Coca-Cola. While we were at the table, the captain recounted his life to me and confessed all of his sins as if I were a priest at the confessional. It was the result of my preaching the preceding Sunday.

We spent several days in Guantanamo. One night, I was officer of the deck on the quarterdeck. It was a mid-watch (0000–0400), and sailors were coming back from liberty. The procedure is for the sailor to salute the officer of the deck and request permission to come aboard. The officer returns the salute; then the sailor salutes the flag on the fantail of the ship and comes aboard. I was returning salutes when Lt. Cdr. Raney came aboard. He was very drunk—shirttail out, cap in his hand, no necktie. He did not salute anything but staggered off to his room.

When we arrived in Norfolk, Lt. Cdr. Raney sought me out. I was in a passageway near the radio shack. The one-way conversation went something like this: "Mr. Wilson, you have been doing a lot of talking on this ship, but today I'm doing all the talking. Your conduct has been unsatisfactory. I should flunk you for leadership, but I am going to give you a passing grade. However, you should know that you will be lucky if you ever make it to lieutenant junior grade.* Take my advice and get out of the Navy as soon as you can." He gave me a barely passing grade and told me I was unfit to be a naval officer.

We had been back at the Academy for a few weeks when I was summoned by Lt. Law, the company officer for the 19th Company. He said, "Wilson, what did you do on cruise to get such an awful grade?" I don't know what I said, but he understood. He said, "If you want to resign your commission, I will forward it recommending approval." Resignations are not accepted after youngster year, and this was my first class year. I was not going to do it.

But things got worse. I was in the chaplain's office talking to the chaplain when the telephone rang, and he answered it. I could hear the other voice on the phone. I was the subject of the conversation. The question was what to do with Wilson.

A few days later, I was called to the office of the Assistant Commandant for another one-way conversation. The commandant informed me that on a ship at sea there were three subjects that an officer did not talk about: politics, religion, and women. (He was wrong on all three.) He told me very clearly that when I went to sea I should leave all this stuff (especially religion) ashore.

Two years earlier, I had been in a quandary about being a naval officer and a Christian because of killing people. Now I could

---

* The rank just above ensign. Midshipmen are promoted to the rank of ensign upon graduation from the Academy.

see that the Navy and Christianity were incompatible, not because of my pacifist convictions, but because the Navy could not tolerate Christians who lived it and talked it. I decided to take Lt. Law's advice and submit my resignation.

Having made my decision, I started looking at seminaries. My hardest course was Ordinates and Gunnery. Since I was going to go into the ministry, I would not need Ordinates and Gunnery, especially the working of the fire control computer, so I quit studying.

A few weeks later, my resignation came back from the Secretary of the Navy: *Disapproved.*

I did not know what to do. I was now flunking Ordinates and Gunnery. I decided to take a weekend in Washington, D.C. I had nothing in mind.

I stayed at Washington Bible College because it was inexpensive. My roommate there was a middle-aged man named Gene Scheele. He was speaking at a church Saturday evening. I went along. We were walking to the location when Mr. Scheele stopped at a newsstand to buy a paper. He led the newspaper boy to Christ. We continued our walk. He stopped for a shoeshine and led the shoeshine boy to Christ. I was impressed with his message, although I don't remember what it was he said.

Later that night after I had gone to bed, I noticed that Mr. Scheele was on his knees at his bed. I woke up the next morning and saw Mr. Scheele on his knees by his bed. For all I knew, he had been there all night.

Before I returned to the Academy, I asked him what he would be doing the next few weeks. He said he was going to Annapolis, where he would be teaching personal evangelism to Christian businessmen every night.

"What are you doing in the afternoons?"

"Nothing."

I asked him to be at the south end of Memorial Hall the next day at 3:30 p.m. and gave him directions on how to get there. I told him I could not be there myself because I was rowing crew. That evening, I went to the midshipmen in charge of the Bible studies in the six wings of Bancroft Hall. I told each of these Christians to have anyone they were witnessing to show up at the south end of Memorial Hall at 3:30 on Monday.

When I was returning from the fifth wing, I saw Frank Young's door open. Frank was a classmate from Omaha. We lived at opposite ends of the hall, so I seldom saw him. I stuck my head in his room. He met me with a blast of profanity. I asked him why the anger.

The U.S. Air Force was a brand-new institution, and there was no Air Force Academy yet. Therefore, Congress had determined that the Air Force was to get twenty-five percent of the Naval Academy graduates and twenty-five percent of the West Point graduates. However, more than twenty-five percent of the midshipmen wanted to go into the Air Force. (Texas was more attractive than the middle of the Mediterranean.) A drawing was held to determine who got to go. Frank had won on the drawing and gone into town and bought a new blue convertible to drive in Texas. He had also bought his Air Force uniforms. (Officers have to pay for their own uniforms.) He returned to the Academy to find out that someone had objected to the way the drawing was done, and the superintendent had ordered a new drawing. He had lost out on the redraw. That was why he was mad.

I told Frank I had an answer for his problem. He wanted to know what it was. I told him the answer would be at the south end of Memorial Hall at 3:30 on Monday.

The next afternoon when crew practice was finished, I returned to Memorial Hall. The meeting was over. I asked Frank about the Air Force.

He said, "Air Force, schmair force." He didn't care. He had just received Jesus Christ.*

In the week following the disapproval of my resignation, ten midshipmen came to Christ. Over the next month or two, I began to realize that this was the reason my resignation was disapproved, and I accepted the truth that God wanted me to be a missionary to the United States Navy. I graduated 660th in a class of 691, primarily due to the poor fitness report from Lt. Commander Raney on the summer cruise.

I decided to ask for a ship in the Western Pacific in order to help missionaries when my ship was in port. The USS Brush (DD-745), a Sumner-class destroyer with the Seventh Fleet, was in the Philippines, so I requested it.

I was commissioned on 2 June, 1950. Mom, Dad, Everett, and Kenneth came for my graduation and commissioning. After thirty days' graduation leave, I reported to San Francisco. While I was waiting for transportation to the Philippines, North Korea crossed the 38th parallel into South Korea, starting the Korean War.

My plane landed for fuel in Okinawa. We heard a rumor that the Seventh Fleet was in Buckner Bay on the east end of the island. We got off the plane to check it out. Sure enough, the Seventh Fleet was there in Japan instead of in the Philippines. I reported aboard the Brush on July 15, 1950. Task Force 77 got underway on July 16, supported the landing of the First Cavalry Division in Pohang on July 18, and rode out a typhoon in Tsushima Straits on July 19. There were two aircraft carriers in TF 77 — USS Valley Forge and HMS Triumph. Our destroyer division formed a bent-line screen for the carriers.

---

* Frank later made it into the Air Force, where he spent his entire career and retired as a colonel. I saw him again at our 50th class reunion, and we talked about how Gene had led him to the Lord.

I had come to the Far East, supposedly in peace time, to help missionaries. Instead, I found myself in a war.

My battle station was the Combat Information Center (CIC). I still had not solved the problem that I had been putting off—being a Christian in the military. I rationalized that I wasn't killing people; I was just handling combat information.

At the same time, the reserves were being called back into the Navy. A lieutenant came aboard at this time. The executive officer greeted him and said he had arrived at the right time because we were going to the front line, and we had no officer in charge of Gunnery Plot. That was to be his battle station.

The officer violently disagreed. He hadn't asked to come back into the Navy, and he was going to do what he knew how to do, and that was Combat Information Center. The exec told me that the lieutenant would replace me in CIC, and I would go to Gunnery Plot.

There were two ironic things about this move. 1) The fire control computer which I was now in charge of was the computer I had quit studying in Ordinates and Gunnery after I had submitted my resignation earlier in the year. 2) Not only was I one of the first of my classmates to join the war, I was now the only person on the ship actually pulling a trigger. I was professional on the outside but confused on the inside.

The *Brush* stayed with TF 77 for six or seven weeks. During those weeks, the North Koreans took all but the southeast corner of Korea (inside the Pusan Perimeter).

On 6 September, the *Brush* received orders to join Task Group 95.2 consisting of the *USS Helena* (CA-75) and the *USS Thomas* (DDR-833) and proceed to Pohang Dong for gunfire support on the front lines. We got underway on September 9 and rendezvoused with the *Helena* and the *Thomas* en route to Pohang that night. On the way, we went to forty degrees north to destroy patrol craft on the north side of an island called Mayan To. We fired 162 rounds of 5″/38 and 875 rounds of 40mm. We went back to Pohang Dong and commenced firing there at 0748 on September 12.

Gunnery Plot was one deck below the main deck and forward of the forward fire room. All sound-powered telephones went through this space. The main gyroscope was there along with the computer and the stable element, a repeater of the gyroscope connected to the 5″/38 batteries. There was a pistol grip with a trigger on the computer and another one on the stable element. We engaged in harassing fire, interdiction fire, and called fire on moving tanks.

I had two chief fire-control petty officers with me in Plot. One of them, Duffy Morris, had fought in both WWI and WWII. One day it was heavy weather, so I was firing from the stable element. The marine spotter called for concentrated bombardment of a troop concentration in a warehouse. He called for twenty-eight rounds of regular high explosive and two rounds of white phosphorus. When I pulled the trigger for the five rounds from the six guns, Duffy Morris said, "There you did it, you murderer," and laughed. I did not know how to take it.

At the end of the twenty days, the Maddox and the Brush were sent north to the Russian border to enforce the UN-declared blockade. We came across an abandoned junk and set it on fire. Returning from the Russian border, we were cruising along the North Korean coast near Tanchon. Late in the morning on September 26, we saw some railroad cars on the coast railroad. The commodore on the Maddox decided to close the range and destroy them with gunfire. We went to general quarters.

We were now far north of the front lines, so we had no Marine ashore spotting our fire. We had to spot our own. We had an optical range finder in the main battery director above the bridge. Lt. Burnside, the gunnery officer and my boss, would direct the fire from there. I was at my battle station in Gunnery Plot below the main deck.* Mr. Burnside called me on the sound-powered telephone and told me to come up to the optical range finder.

I said, "Sir, we are at general quarters." (It is a court-martial offense to leave your battle station when the ship is at general quarters.)

He replied, "This is an order. Get up here."

I was a new ensign, and Mr. Burnside was a mustang lieutenant. He had no sympathy for Naval Academy graduates, especially ensigns. I gave my phones to the senior chief fire controlman and left him in charge of Plot.

I reported to Mr. Burnside. He had no idea why he called me.

"When you think of it, sir, give me another call."

"No, you stay here."

I had nothing to do, so I looked through the optical range finder. I had been shooting at Korea for twenty days, but this was the first time I had seen it since we went to battle stations.

While I was up there, the ship continued closing the range to destroy the railroad cars. Then there was a deafening explosion. The ship heeled over to starboard, then took a heavy list to port. The *Brush* had struck an underwater mine on the port side, ripping her midships section and breaking her keel.

I requested to return to my battle station. Instead, Lt. Burnside told me to take charge in the director† while he reported to the captain, and he left.

I tried to call Gunnery Plot, but there was no answer. I tried to call anyone, anywhere on the ship. No answer.

The damage control and rescue team reached the site of the explosion. The mine had detonated immediately below Gunnery Plot

* When the ship was not at battle stations, I was in the deck division.

† The control tower for the main battery

and obliterated it. The senior chief was blown out of the room, and the telephone was embedded in his chest. He lived for two hours and then died. One sailor named Lynch was pulled out alive. He was a Christian. The rest of the men in Gunnery Plot had been killed immediately, some of them lost overboard.

The rescue party did not pull me out. They knew that was my battle station, and since we were at general quarters, I must have been there, so the word went around the ship very quickly that I was the only officer killed.

Meanwhile, I was still up in the director unaware of this, and I could not communicate. All of the ship's phone lines ran through Gunnery Plot, and they had been destroyed. After about an hour and a half, I yelled to the captain on the bridge to request permission to leave my temporary battle station. He yelled back, "Permission granted!"

I came down to the main deck to see a couple dozen men with third-degree burns laid out on the fantail and on the starboard main deck. It was a shock to the ship when I showed up still alive—without even a spot on my uniform.

Thirteen men were killed—some drowned in the forward fire room, five were killed instantly in Plot, and some were lost overboard. One other died later in hospital, and an additional thirty-one were injured.

The chief was the only one of the dead that they had been able to pull out onto the deck. The rest were either overboard or unreachable. The doctor said that if any of the bad burn cases found out that someone had died, we would lose another half dozen from shock. The decision was to get all the wounded into bunks below, then hold a funeral service for the chief. The executive officer came to me and said, "Mr. Wilson, we are going to bury the chief at sea. You are the Christian on the ship; you conduct the service."

I was twenty-two years old. I conducted the funeral for the man who died in place of me. I did not pronounce the chief in Heaven. Instead, I preached to the survivors. I told the crew that death could well be imminent for all of us.

After the service, we saw a ship hull-down on the horizon. We did not know who it was. The gunnery officer got a few of us together to fire the number three mount manually. Firing the two forward mounts at that point might have broken the ship in two. When we could see the hull number (144), I realized it was the light cruiser *USS Worcester*. I knew the number because John Bajus had been on it in the Mediterranean. We were only making about four knots, so we transferred all the wounded to the *Worcester*, which took them to the hospital in Yokosuka.

We were losing about two feet a day by the bow. The solution was to move all the anchor chain manually and drag it link by link back to the fantail. We did the same with the five-inch projectiles from the forward magazines.

During this operation, Mr. Burnside came up to me. "Wilson, have you figured out why I called you up to the Director?"

I replied, "No, sir."

"Well, that'll teach you to start a Bible study on this ship."

The captain was going to court-martial me for not being dead because I was not where I was supposed to be when we hit the mine. But Mr. Burnside told him that he had ordered me out of there.

"Why did you order him out?" the captain asked.

He said, "I don't know, sir."

Later, the captain spoke to me in the head.* "Mr. Wilson, that was Fate or something that took you out of the plotting room."

I answered, "Yes, sir. *Or Something.*"

---

* The captain's head was damaged, so he had to use the officers' head back aft.

The ship wasn't religious, but it was superstitious. The word went around that God had spared my life. People who didn't believe in miracles all believed that God had done this.

It took us eighty-four hours to get back to Sasebo making four knots on one screw. During those days, I set up a counseling place on the torpedo deck and met with sailors who wanted to talk. The most common question was, "Why did Joe have to die?"

"That's not the question you need to ask," I would tell them. "What you need to know is are *you* ready to die? We are a long way from home with a broken keel, and a heavy sea could crack it in half."

We got back to Sasebo and tied up to a tender.* We could now get the bodies out of the fire room and Plot. The people in the fire room were drowned, but the men in Plot were blown up. I had to go on the tender and identify the men because I was the only one who knew all of them well enough to identify them, even with a head or arms missing.

That first night back in port, another ensign and I went for a long walk. I do not remember our talk. I had a violent headache, and I don't get headaches.

Thirty days were spent patching up the *Brush* in Sasebo in the largest dry dock in the world, designed for two Yamato-Class battleships. Those ships were seventy-two thousand tons and had nine 18.1″ guns. The *Brush* was 220 tons. It looked like a toy boat in the massive dry dock.

During those thirty days, I had a lot of time to think. It would take a year to put the ship back together. By that time, the war would probably be over, and that would solve my problem. However, I knew it wouldn't really solve it; I would just be avoiding it again. I was in turmoil. This is where I stood:

* A boat or ship used to service other ships by transporting people and/or supplies to and from the shore or another ship

- I had tried to resign from the Navy because of my convictions about killing and the Navy's view of Christians.
- The resignation had been rejected.
- I came to the western Pacific in peacetime to help missionaries.
- The war started when I was in San Francisco, making me one of the first of my classmates to join the fighting.
- I rationalized that I was not killing anyone. Then we were sent to the front lines, and I was the only person on the ship pulling a trigger.
- When my battle station was blown up, I was delivered, and my team was killed.

Mentally, I was a pacifist, but I could not claim that I was a conscientious objector. No one would believe me. I was a Naval Academy graduate and had been regular Navy before that. It would have been branded cowardice under fire. I would have been court-martialed for refusing to obey orders in a time of war and sent off to Portsmouth.[†] I could not confide in the missionaries in Japan, either. They would say, "What are you doing in the Navy?" I couldn't tell anyone, so I didn't tell anyone. I realized God had put me in this position, and I had not yet learned why. I kept quiet and prayed for light.

As things stood, the war was over for me, and I would be home for Christmas. However, I thought I had better stay in the war until I learned what God was trying to teach me. While we were still in dry dock in October, I wrote a letter to the Bureau of Naval Personnel telling them that the *Brush* was out of action and asking for a transfer to any combatant vessel remaining in the forward area. I also wrote to my brother telling him of my request.

† The Navy prison

7 November 1950
USS Brush

Dear Lorraine, Glenda, Karen and Jeffrey,

I notice Navy has won a game and Nebraska a couple. I don't know how Giltner is making out.

We flooded the dock yesterday and made a sea trial today. A month and six days in dry-dock and many stitches. The *Brush* looks as good as new from the outside. The scars are painted over; in fact, the whole ship is painted ready for stateside duty. On the inside of the hole there is nothing in plot and chiefs' quarters. We'll put steam tables back in tomorrow. Forward Fire Room is still a wreck; there are a lot of sprung bulkheads and decks. We creaked and groaned and the bow had a funny vibration in it from 10 to 25 knots this afternoon.

The whole patch will have to come off, false keel and all, when we get back home. Scuttlebutt says Bremerton, and I think it is good dope. If so we may travel great circle and if so it will be rough, wet, and cold.

If I don't get orders within the next week I may be going home too. I would like to tell you all of my plans and visions for the Lord's work, but because I haven't received orders yet and because of the several serious setbacks I've had, I'm not sure that my plans and my way are His plans for me and His way for me.

If my request is approved, but late, I will have to turn right around and come back here. Right now I would like to come home but I'm so positive He wants me here I had to turn in my request. It is such an impossible request [that] I will know that if it is approved it is the Lord's will.

I'm picking up the language slowly.

Floyd pulled down the best school in the Navy right now. Fire Control Technicians spend years in school keeping up with computers and Radar Fire Control equipment.

I've heard that Ellis is going with Jim Hardie for training in "Navigator" mission work. I'm glad.

Sincerely in the bonds,

Jim

Psalm 68:11

The *Brush* left for the States early in December. The trip was harrowing. We bucked fifty-knot winds for ten days before reaching Midway Island. The motor whale boat, the ship's lifeboat, is usually on deck, but we rigged it over the side in case we needed to drop it fast to rescue a man overboard. We got up in the morning to discover that it had been carried away by waves during the night. We also lost our port bilge keel.* It was slapping the side like a willow switch as it was peeled off by the wind.

The Bureau of Naval Personnel does not often receive letters *asking* to be stationed in a combat zone. After an initial disapproval, they changed their minds and approved the request. I received orders to the *Brinkley Bass* while we were at Midway Island and got off the *Brush* at Pearl Harbor to fly back to Japan.

This was my fitness report:

Ensign WILSON has performed all duties assigned to him in a satisfactory manner. He has interest and enthusiasm for all he does and does each job to the best of his ability. His lack of experience is compensated for by his willingness to do the best he can. His work as Welfare and Recreation Officer was excellent. He has an aptitude for personnel work and it is believed he would excel in that field. His personal and military characteristics are excellent. Recommended for promotion when due. Capt. Sheffield.

* A stabilizing keel at the turn of the hull

SECOND ENDORSEMENT on LMS J. I. WILSON, 533283, USN ltr of 17 Oct 1950

From: Commander Destroyer Squadron NINE
To: Chief of Naval Personnel
Via: (1) AdComCruDesPac NavFE
        (2) ComCruDesPac

Subj: Change of duty; request for

1. Forwarded, recommending approval.

2. It is further recommended that ENS WILSON be transferred
to another destroyer in CruDesPac.

H. C. ALLAN JR.

Copy to:
CC, USS BRUSH

The Brush in the 1960s (U.S. Navy photo)

At Midway I also got the first of several visits to the gooney birds.*

I was detached from the *Brush* at Pearl Harbor on 11 December and reported to the 14th Naval District for transportation to the *Brinkley Bass*. At the office, I asked where the *Bass* was located. The response was, "East Coast."

I said, "The East Coast?!"

"Yes, the East Coast of Korea. That's the only East Coast we know out here."

I called my family to tell them I would not be home for Christmas.

The following is a letter I wrote to my brother Lorraine from Barbers Point, Hawaii:

16 December 1950

Dear Lorraine,

I don't know what to say only I figure I had better write. I didn't do any Christmas shopping as such—just stuff and junk I picked up. The doll was given to me by the director of the Shinwa Bank.

I have 45 minutes to throw the rest of my junk together and get to the Space Control. My plane won't leave until 1800 tonight. I was supposed to leave yesterday at 2200 only I found that my left drum had been perforated again and slightly infected. The doctor held me over one day. Technically I am not supposed to fly but I got to get over there. I don't want to spend a week on a AKA [cargo ship] or APA [personnel ship] or something else just as slow.

Although there is nothing I can do as such, I know Pete is one of the boys cut off up at Hamhung or whatever you call it and I feel kind of helpless over here. The boys are coming in every day by the

---

* A nickname for the Laysan albatross. After it was deserted following World War II, Midway Island quickly became overrun and is now home to an estimated one million gooney birds (http://articles.latimes.com/1990–08–19/news/mn-2698_1_midway-birds-gooneys).

dozens with their legs frozen up to their knees. I wish I was in the
infantry, not because I want to get any closer to killing people because I don't. I'm still a theoretical conscientious objector. The Lord
kept me alive for a purpose. He has given me a dozen reasons why
and none of them were so Wilson could go home.

That is one of the reasons I requested a transfer because I'm trying to find out whether it is right to kill people. His Word says it is
not right. Another reason is the job I started in Japan, and the first
reason is because I know He wants me to stay over here.

I know I don't have to defend myself to you for staying when I
wanted to come home so bad, but I thought you might explain it to
Dad. Maybe it doesn't need explaining.

Well, I'd better finish this and throw the rest of my junk together.

Waiting here I spent a few days with Stacey Woods, General
Secretary of the InterVarsity Christian Fellowship, and with Gwen
Wong, Regional Director. I was able to help a few kids at the
University of Hawaii. Isn't our Lord Wonderful! You should get to
know Stacey Woods, Chicago.

The only time I could have perforated that ear was when we were
hit [by the mine].

I'm going to be in transit, so Merry Christmas.

Jim

I had four days in Yokosuka, three of which were spent visiting
Tokyo. The last four hours before my train left in Yokohama I spent
with Bessie Dodds, a missionary I had been told to look up. She did
not know of my problem. However, she gave me an autographed
copy of *A Very Present Help* by Lt. General Sir William Dobbie, who
had been governor of Malta when it was the most-bombed place on
earth. I read the book on the thirty-six-hour train ride to Sasebo,

Kyushu. (I was in a sleeper, but the beds were only about five feet long, so I didn't do much sleeping.)

The answer to my prayers came through Bessie's book. General Dobbie was from a pacifist church. The fifth chapter of his book is entitled "Christianity and Military Service," and Dobbie wrote an appendix on pacifism to accompany that chapter:

> A common mistake today is to regard peace as the chief characteristic of Christianity, but it should be noted how the primacy of righteousness over peace is maintained throughout Scripture. *The wisdom that is from above is first pure, then peaceable* (Jas. 3:17). Melchizedek, King of Salem, was *first* King of Righteousness, and after that also King of Salem, which is King of Peace (Heb. 7:2). *Follow righteousness, faith, charity, peace* (II Tim. 2:22). *The kingdom of God is not meat and drink; but righteousness, and peace, and joy in the Holy Ghost* (Rom. 14:17). *If it be possible, as much as lieth in you, live peaceably with all men*, wrote St. Paul (Rom. 12:18), but he did not always find it possible, for he said, *When Peter was come to Antioch, I withstood him to his face, because he was to be blamed* (Gal. 2:11).
>
> We *must* live righteously; for that very reason we may not be able to live peaceably with all men. And in these days, when so many are working for peace and stability, it is well to recall the words found in Isaiah 32:17: *The work of righteousness shall be peace; and the effect of righteousness quietness and assurance for ever.* It is always wise to do what is right, rather than what is merely expedient.

The question of peace was dealt with by the Archbishop of Canterbury on the eighth of October, 1935, as follows:

> At the outset we must recognize, though it may seem a hard saying, that peace in itself is not an ideal. It is a state which results from the achievement of ideals. Of these

foremost are the ideals of a rule of reason, justice and law within and among the nations. These are ideals to be preserved for their own sake. In so far as they are realized, peace will follow. They are primary. Peace is secondary and derivative. There is, therefore, no intrinsic worth in mere peace if it means acquiescence in the violation of justice and the rule of law. Indeed, the pursuit of mere peace may defeat its own object, for assured peace in the state and between states can be secured only by the vindication and the establishment of justice and the rule of law . . . . Of course, if all persons acknowledged the principle of love and were amenable to its appeal, the difficulty would not arise. It arises precisely because in the world as it is there are persons who reject that principle, scorn that appeal and obey only the motive of self-will. If no attempt were made by the state to restrain—if need be by force—those who defy the rule of law, anarchy would follow, and the very basis on which the life of the community rests would be broken. I cannot believe that Christianity compels me to this conclusion.

It should be noted that the words *When a strong man armed keepeth his palace, his good are in peace* are the words of the Lord Himself, as also the injunction *He that hath no sword, let him sell his garment, and buy one* (Luke 11:21 and 22:36). In this connection it will not be out of place to quote from *Practical Christianity** of April, 1932:

A sister in a Jerusalem mission hospital tells of the wounded being brought in after local riots between Moslems and Jews, a ghastly array, but adds: "This was, of

* *Practical Christianity*—the bimonthly publication of the British OCU

course, before our troops arrived in Palestine." In a letter to The Times from Sir Flinders Petrie is this paragraph: "The impending raid on the prosperity of the country was averted only by the prompt action of our Air Force; a day's delay would have brought massacre." A lady missionary, traveling by river to Hong Kong, tells of having to lie for safety in the bottom of the boat because of frequent attacks by rioters from the shore, but on rounding one reach of the river they came in sight of a British gunboat, from whence onward safety and peace were happily assured to them. And, as regards the pacification of other nations, The Times correspondent might be quoted: "All is now quiet in Cyprus; a company of the King's Regiment was flown from Cairo, and arrived just in time to pacify a mob."

Pacifism in the present state of the world may be little less than a sacrifice of Christian principle to humanitarian settlement. The Christian attitude must be "Righteousness at any cost," not "Peace at any price," for the best way to preserve peace is to be strong in righteousness.[†]

My basic question was about the seeming inconsistency between Exodus 20, where God commands, "Thou shalt not kill," and Exodus 21, where the death penalty is required for murder. There was much killing in the rest of the Old Testament, a great deal of it clearly in the will of God. Were these contradictions, or was there something else I did not see?

In the Scripture, there is a precedence for Christian qualities. *A Very Present Help* helped me see this principle.

---

† Dobbie, William George Shedden. *A Very Present Help: A Testimony to the Faithfulness of God.* Zondervan, 1945, pp. 92–93.

The fruit of righteousness will be peace; the effect of righteousness will be quietness and confidence forever. (Isa. 32:17)

This Melchizedek was king of Salem and priest of God Most High. He met Abraham returning from the defeat of the kings and blessed him, and Abraham gave him a tenth of everything. *First,* his name means "king of righteousness"; then also, "king of Salem" means "king of peace." (Heb. 7:1–2)

But the wisdom that comes from heaven is *first of all pure*; then peace-loving, considerate, submissive, full of mercy and good fruit, impartial and sincere. (James 3:17)

Righteousness both precedes and causes God's kind of peace. God will not have peace at the expense of righteousness. This was the reason for the Flood, for the destruction of Sodom and Gomorrah, and for God allowing Israel to take possession of the Promised Land.

The LORD saw how great man's wickedness on the earth had become, and that every inclination of the thoughts of his heart was only evil all the time. (Gen. 5:6)

After the LORD your God has driven them out before you, do not say to yourself, "The LORD has brought me here to take possession of this land because of my righteousness." No, it is on account of the wickedness of these nations that the LORD is going to drive them out before you. It is not because of your righteousness or your integrity that you are going in to take possession of their land; but on account of the wickedness of these nations, the LORD your God will drive them out before you, to accomplish what he swore to your fathers, to Abraham, Isaac and Jacob. Understand, then, that it is not because of your righteousness that the LORD your God is giving you this good land to possess, for you are a stiff-necked people. (Deut. 9:4–6)

The *Brinkley Bass* off the San Francisco Naval Shipyard, April 7, 1954
(U.S. Navy photo)

On that train trip, I read Galatians, Ephesians, Philippians, and Colossians five times. When I arrived in Sasebo, I had complete peace about my participation in the war.

I spent Christmas alone in Sasebo, then caught a ride to the Sea of Japan on the cruiser *USS Manchester* (CL-83). On New Year's Day 1951, I came aboard the *Brinkley Bass* (DD-887) via a bos'ns chair on a high line from the *Manchester*. The fleet had been at sea for fifty-four days surrounding the evacuation of Hungnam, another Dunkirk. *

As soon as I came aboard, I heard the men talking about Riley. Riley was a seaman who had been home on emergency leave. He had become a Christian and a pacifist. When he returned to the ship, he refused to stand gun watches. The crew did not believe he was a pacifist. They thought that he just did not want to be in a 40mm gun tub

---

* The Hungnam evacuation took place from December 11–24. It was the greatest sealift operation since the invasion of Okinawa.

at 0400 in five-degree Fahrenheit weather. The exec had threatened him, and the gunnery officer had tried to convince him from the Bible. Nothing succeeded.

I sent for him. He came into my room thinking he was going to get another tongue lashing from another officer. I had him sit down.

"Riley, are you a Christian?"

"Yes, sir."

"So am I."

I told him what I had just learned. He was convinced.

I said, "Let's go see the captain."

Riley told the captain that he would be the best sailor on the ship.

The *Bass* was my home for the next thirty months, until 26 June 1953.

CHAPTER 16
LETTERS FROM HOME

Hastings, Nebr.

Sept 29, 1950

Dear Jim,

I just now rec' your letter to me and was sure glad to get it because you don't know how nervous I have been about you. Mom don't think so because I never write or let her know how I feel but your letter just about broke me down. It is noon and Kenny and Everett are home from School and Mom won't be home till about five o clock, so I am going to send before she gets home and won't know, so you see I'm a tough old man.

I pray for you every day, Jim, and I know God hears me. I have read Job but I have a little trouble with Harold. He thinks he knows a little too much. I told him this morning to believe as Jim does and he will do alright. Thanks a mill Jim for everything but I wasn't worried about finances Jim because I don't care about that any more, but don't tell Mom.

Love Dad

2 October 1950

Dear Jim,

Well, boy, the reason for the sudden letter is that Ellis* was down telling us about a news item in the *Omaha World-Herald* on Friday, September 29. It concerned the *USS Brush* hitting a mine and listed those of the Omaha

---

* Ellis Warren was Leonard's brother-in-law, one of the three eighteen-year-olds who had received Christ in the car in Giltner.

area killed or missing. Said that nine were killed and five were missing, besides several being wounded. Did not list the wounded, and we hope and pray that you are not among the wounded. The article further stated that the *Brush* made it back to a port in Japan under its own power, etc . . .

I can in a way imagine the time the First Lieutenant and his assistant (plus the shipfitters, boatswain's mates, etc.) had keeping the ship in a condition fit to make it back to a port in Japan. More fun, more loss of sleep, more strain, more tension, more everything leading to an experience that though dimming already will long remain in your memory. Well, in my frank opinion, you've had enough to last the rest of your life, come on home and get a little stateside liberty and leave, and then go on patrols all over the world, observing what makes things tick.

"Blessed are the peacemakers for they shall be called the children of God."

I have little doubt that in your moments of crisis you were a credit to the service of the Lord and the U.S. Navy (if you'll pardon the use of both in the same phrase).

Write when you get a chance, Jim, or we'll expect you when we see you.

Love,

Leonard, Glenda, Karen and Jeff

Oct 17, 1950

206 East Second Street

Hastings, Nebraska

Dear Jim,

If that last letter was such a surprise to you I am going to surprise you again, but you know they all go away and leave me alone all day and hide all the stationary so I have to write on this old tablet paper but it don't make no difference to me if it don't to you. Just so you get it is all I care.

Got your letter yesterday but the news in it made me too weak to answer at once but I have been thinking since. Oh I believe it was a miracle all right, but you know the Lord works in miraculous ways. Remember I ask you about that last summer if he took the Christian or non Christian in such cases, and you said undoubtedly the Christian. But I didn't think so entirely as we do not know and never will know what the Lord has in mind for us. All we can do is live and pray to the best of our ability.

We haven't heard from Floyd since he finished boots . . .

Harold got a car and had it just a month and a connecting rod went through the block so he has no car again. It is time for me to go to work. Mom said she would write some today if I would so I have kept my bargain, see what she does. Hoping to see you Christmas.

Love Dad.

CHAPTER 17

JAMES TAYLOR & THE BEANO BRUSH

But because of his great love for us, God, who is rich in mercy,
made us alive with Christ even when we were dead in transgressions—it is by grace you have been saved. (Eph. 2:4–5)

There was not much for the crew to do during the thirty days of
patching the port side of the ship.

When I first came aboard the *Brush*, I found that it was a low-mo-
rale ship. Its nickname was the "Mighty Beano." I asked how it got
that name. "There will *be no* liberty. There will *be no* ice cream. There
will *be no* . . ." Whatever might be fun, there would be none of that.

At the lowest point of morale, a new cook named James Taylor came
aboard. He was a second-class petty officer, a good cook, a good leader,
and a good dirty-story teller. James Taylor invented fast food (at least on
the *Brush*). He would station a sailor ten men down the chow line to ask
the men how they liked their eggs. When each man got to the counter,
his eggs would be ready as ordered. Between the cooking and the dirty
stories, James Taylor single-handedly raised the morale of the crew.

When we hit the mine, thirty-plus men suffered third-degree burns.
Taylor was one of them. He was selfless. He kept telling the corpsmen
to take care of the other men first. At the hospital, Taylor helped the
corpsmen. As a result of his conduct, he was awarded the Bronze Star.

Taylor reported back aboard near the end of our time in dry dock.
He was a hero, and he liked it. He ate up the attention. But when he
came back from the hospital, he found out all the men were talking
about *me*. He was jealous.

One day I was walking aft on the port side of the main deck. Taylor was in the midships passageway with a group of sailors listening to his stories. He spotted me. "Hey, Mr. Wilson, sir, I hear God saved your life! He saved mine too, and I got the Bronze Star. What did you get, sir?"

Of course, I did not get anything. I ignored him. He did this sort of thing every day. I continued to ignore him.

Finally, he said, "Mr. Wilson, why don't you answer me?"

"Taylor, I will talk with you anytime you want, without your little cheering section listening in."

"Sir, that's what I'd like to do." Then I wished I had not said that. I saw myself talking with him, and Taylor going off and telling the whole ship I'd tried to convert him.

We went into the storekeeper's office, a long room on the port side of the superstructure, and sat down at a desk near the hatch. At the far end of the room, the storekeeper (a chief petty officer) was working at his desk.

"All right Taylor, what do you want to talk about?"

"Mr. Wilson, I want to become a Christian."

I did not believe him. I thought, "Oh no." I was sure it was a trick, and he was going to tell the crew all about my attempts to convert him. To stall for time, I said, "Taylor, what kind of Christian do you want to be?"

"Mr. Wilson, I want to be an 'all the way' Christian."

Then I knew he meant it. I told him the Good News, and he believed. The chief petty officer at the other end of the room had listened in; he became a Christian at the same time.

The next day, Taylor stood in the midships passageway and told the sailors to gather round. They assembled, expecting a dirty story. Taylor pulled a New Testament from under his apron and told them about his conversion. It was like another bomb had gone off on the ship!

CHAPTER 18

BESSIE DODDS

I give thanks to my God always for you because of the grace of God
that was given you in Christ Jesus. (1 Cor. 1:4)

When I was a first classman at the Academy, I had read an article in
Practical Christianity, the British Officers' Christian Union magazine.
Later I read the same article in InterVarsity's *His* magazine. It was
written by Irene Webster-Smith, an Irish Quaker missionary with the
Japan Evangelistic Band. The article was about how God had used her
to lead Japanese war criminals to the Lord in Sugamo Prison.

Miss Webster-Smith had led to Christ a very bitter woman whose
husband was on death row in Sugamo Prison, having been convicted
of war crimes. The woman asked Sensei (Japanese for "teacher"), as
Irene was known, to take her place and visit her husband. Sensei
gave him a gospel of John and introduced him to the Father through
the Son. She told him that Jesus was given His name by God before
He was born, because He would save people from their sin.

When his wife came to see him, she found she had a new husband.
He led his cellmate to Christ. The prison kept changing his cellmates,
so the gospel spread through the prison as the prisoners told each
other the good news. Sensei continued to visit new prisoners.

I decided then that if I ever got to Japan, I would find Sensei.

About the same time, Dr. Paydon's wife, Sadie, and her sister
Lillian told me about another missionary, Bessie Dodds, and asked
me to look her up. They had known her in Edmonton and also
through InterVarsity. Bessie had been on the Canadian staff of

Bessie Dodds

Inter School Fellowship and was with Miss Webster-Smith the day
Japan surrendered.

When the *Brush* was seaworthy, we stopped in Yokosuka at the
south end of Tokyo Bay en route to the United States. While we were
there, I caught a train to Tokyo. At the Tokyo station, I found a young
man who spoke English and asked him if he knew any mission soci-
eties. I named a few, which he did not recognize. Then I mentioned
InterVarsity Christian Fellowship.

He said, "I'm a member of InterVarsity."

I told him I was looking for Irene Webster-Smith. He said to get a
ten-yen ticket, catch the train on track two, get off at the second stop
(Ochanomizu), walk back half a block, and I would find her.

I found her. Sensei told me stories until it was time to go back to
my ship. I told her I needed to look up two other missionaries, and I
mentioned that Bessie Dodds was one of them. Miss Webster-Smith
told me that Bessie had lived with her in Tokyo for fourteen months
while she was in language school, and that she was now running the
Kyoritsa Bible School for Women at the Women's Union Missionary
Society in Yokohama. If I would come to hear Sensei speak at the
Yokohama Chapel Center the next day, she could take me to meet
Bessie afterward.

The next day, Miss Webster-Smith and I arrived at the women's
mission, and Sensei introduced me to the three missionaries who
lived there. We made a tour of the girls' high school, then came back
to the mission house. I was the only man there. Miss Webster-Smith
was in her sixties, Mary Ballantyne in her forties, Bessie Dodds in
her thirties, and Maxine in her twenties.

Bessie had received Christ in 1935 in Edmonton, Alberta, at the
age of fifteen. At nineteen, she had gone to Prairie Bible Institute.
Afterward, she ministered in homestead country and taught high
school in both Toronto and Calgary. In 1948, she went to Japan to

reopen a women's Bible college that had closed in the war. She was a Bible teacher and a natural leader.

I was very impressed with Bessie. At the dinner table, I asked, "Bessie, how old are you?"

She replied, "Thirty-one. How old are you?"

"Twenty-three. Why didn't you wait for me?"

"I didn't know you were coming."

The other women were shocked.

During the two or three weeks we had in Yokosuka, I spent most of my free time in Tokyo. The Pocket Testament league was in Tokyo handing out Japanese copies of the Gospel of John at Shinjuku Train Station, and I joined them. The testaments came in packets of fifty. I had fifty copies in my left arm and fifty at my feet. I called out, *"Kore wa Seisho des."* "This is a holy book." In a very short time, I had handed out the fifty in my arm. I stooped down to get the other packet of fifty, and I could not get back up because of the crowd pressing in on me. I handed those fifty out to the hands over my head.

A few days later, Sensei invited me to her home for a meeting of the heads of several mission boards. She introduced me to Bob Pierce, Bob Finley, and David Morken that night. Dawson Trotman was the speaker. At the meeting, I sat on the floor in a corner in awe of these great Christian men. Dawson Trotman spoke of a "faithful man," one of his favorite expressions. "Do you want to know a 'faithful man'? Jim Wilson, stand up." I was embarrassed, as I should have been.

That was how I met David Morken. David had been a missionary to cannibals in Sumatra and in China after the war and had been under house arrest in Shanghai for fourteen months under the communists. He had just gotten out and come to Japan. David later performed my wedding, and we were close friends until he died fifty years later.

After I had enlisted in the Navy, I still supported my parents just as I had in my junior and senior years of high school. When I entered the Academy, I got paid $4 per month (two $2 bills) plebe year, $7 per month youngster year, $9 per month second class year, and $11 per month first class year. All the money was sent home. When I was commissioned at age twenty-two, I still did not know what money was.

Now I was receiving several hundred dollars a month, but I was at sea and had no place to spend it. I sent home $100 per month. I bought a ninety-six-piece set of china for my mother in Sasebo. The rest I saved. I had about $600 on the books when God spoke to me. I don't know how, but it was very clear to me: "I want your money."

"How much, Lord?"

"All of it."

I checked out the $600 and gave it to missions. I thought, "Now that the Lord is paid off, I can get back to saving money." By November 1950, I had saved another $600.

Then the orders came again: "I want your money!"

"How much, Lord?"

"All of it."

"God, how often is this going to happen?"

"How long will it take you to learn?"

I checked the $600 out of the bank. I did not know who to give it to, so I put it in the safe in my room.

Then came the meeting at Sensei's house and meeting David Morken. David asked me to have lunch with him. Over lunch the next day, he introduced me to Lou Zamperini.* Lou had been a wild kid. His brother found out he could run and got him onto his high school track team. Lou was the youngest entrant in the 1936 Olympics. He became famous for climbing a flagpole in Berlin and tearing down a

---

* For Lou's full story, see *Unbroken*, by Laura Hillenbrand, or Lou's autobiography, *Devil at My Heels*.

swastika as a souvenir. When WWII started, Lou joined the Army Air Corps and became a bombardier on a B-24 out of Hawaii. He was on a search and rescue mission for a plane that had disappeared when his own plane crashed into the Pacific. Lou, the captain, and one other officer survived the crash. They floated west on a life raft for forty-seven days. One of the men died on route. The other two were finally picked up by the Japanese. They had floated two thousand miles. They were put in Japanese prison camps and greatly mistreated for the next two and a half years. When he came home, Lou was voted as the man who had suffered the most in WWII and come out alive.

When Billy Graham held his now-famous crusade in Los Angeles, Lou and his wife were both converted. The bitterness he had had toward his captors was gone. God had forgiven him, and he forgave them. Lou had then returned to Japan to tell the Japanese guards who had imprisoned him that he had forgiven them. It was on that trip that I met him.

At lunch, Lou told David and me that his house in North Hollywood was being foreclosed. He was in Japan and did not have money to stop the foreclosure.

I asked him how much he needed. He said $600. I told him to come with me.

We caught a train to Yokosuka, went aboard the ship to my stateroom, and got the $600. I told him it was a gift.

Lou insisted on writing an IOU on a three-by-five card. I knew that it was a gift, so I used the three-by-five card to keep telephone numbers on. I left it in a phone booth in Tokyo. David Morken later found it and returned it to me.

Later, Lou had the money to return to me. I told him to give it to missions.

The mayor of Hiroshima had given Lou a rifle or machine gun recovered from the wreckage of the atomic blast. It was a twisted piece of metal. Lou didn't want to try taking it back on the plane and asked me to carry it back to the States on the *Brush.* *

When I received my change of orders at Midway, I was flown back to Japan to transfer to the *Brinkley Bass.* I arrived in Yokosuka on December 17. I had four days before my train was due to leave for Sasebo. Three of those days I spent with friends in Tokyo.

On the fourth day, I had four hours to kill until the train left. I called Bessie Dodds. She gave me instructions on how take the streetcar. She said she would meet me at the streetcar stop and walk me up to the mission. It was dark, and there were no streetlights, so I offered her my arm. She refused to take it. She was not going to be caught by Mary or the girls at the Bible school hanging on to some naval officer's arm!

I said, "Are you a lady, or aren't you? Take my arm, or I'm going to get back on the streetcar." She took my arm.

We had a Bible study together on Psalm 46. That was the night she gave me the autographed copy of *A Very Present Help.*

At the end of the visit, Bessie rode the streetcar with me back to the train station. On the way there, I told her that she was wonderful. Mary was returning from an errand, and she and Bessie rode back together on the same streetcar. Bessie told her, "That young man better not come often."

Bessie, circa 1942

---

* I left the *Brush* at Midway Island to join the *Brinkley Bass.* Meanwhile, Lou's souvenir went on to San Diego without me, where it stayed until I returned there six months later.

CHAPTER 19
OFFICER OF THE DECK

And God is able to make all grace abound to you, so that having all
sufficiency in all things at all times, you may abound in every good
work. (2 Cor. 9:8)

Much of life at sea (work and watches) is simply boring. Three kinds
of events will take you out of the boredom: a storm at sea, enemy fire
(or other battle conditions), and humor.

Before the Korean War, an ensign of the class of '49 was stationed
on the *USS Isbell*. The *Isbell* was the favorite destroyer of Admiral
Struble, Commander of the Seventh Fleet. Before fleets had helicop-
ters, destroyers were used as messengers. If the admiral needed to go
somewhere, he would call the *Isbell* to the flagship, and he and his
chief of staff, a captain, would transfer to the *Isbell*, which would leave
the fleet and proceed independently to the admiral's destination.

The *Isbell* was on such a mission. The new ensign had just been
qualified as an officer of the deck underway. His first watch was
a mid-watch on the bridge. During his watch, the officer of the
deck is virtually in command of the ship. However, this particular
officer only had to keep the ship on course and speed. Here he was
on his first watch with all this authority and nothing to do with it!
He wanted to give somebody an order. But there was nothing that
needed doing.

Finally, he realized that he could call the wardroom pantry and
order some coffee for the bridge. He rang the pantry, and no one answered. He rang the pantry several more times. No answer.

In his stateroom, the admiral heard the ringing and picked up the phone. The voice at the other end said, "Bring some coffee up to the bridge."

"What did you say?"

"You heard me. Bring some coffee up to the bridge!"

The admiral woke up his chief of staff and said, "They want some coffee on the bridge."

"What did you say, Admiral?"

"You heard me; they want some coffee on the bridge!"

The chief of staff got up, went to the pantry, and took the coffee up to the bridge. The poor ensign did not know what to do when a four-striper delivered his coffee.

Wonsan Harbor is a beautiful, round harbor on the east coast of North Korea. It is located where the east coast turns to the north. On the southwest corner of that harbor, near the city, is a small peninsula called Kalma Pando, the northern end of which is called Kalma Gak.

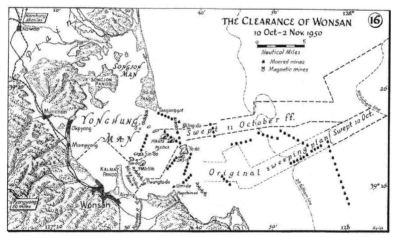

Wonsan Harbor during the Korean War (U.S. Navy image)

In a cave on Kalma Gak was a 75mm weapon. All the surrounding land was held by North Korea.

The U.S. Navy occupied Wonsan Harbor for two and a half years. The purpose of the occupation was to provide calm water for our carrier planes to ditch into if they were shot up over Korea. A single destroyer stationed in the harbor was the means of keeping it free. The destroyer was also tasked with picking up any pilots who ditched there. The *Brinkley Bass* had that duty in May 1951, March 1952, and March 1953 for two weeks each time.

The third time, we also had a minesweeper ship working in the harbor. Ships at sea must follow established traffic rules. When there is a collision, the ship that had the right of way is automatically not at fault. But minesweepers do whatever they want! They just go back and forth looking for mines.

One night I was officer of the deck. An ensign was with me as junior officer of the deck. I left him with the control and went inside. I was in the pilot house checking the chart when I glanced over at the radarscope to see the minesweeper on a steady bearing, closing the range. (That is Navy terminology for a collision course.) There was no time to call the captain. I yelled to the man on the engine order telegraph, "All back full!" He pulled the handles for both engines. The ship shuddered to a stop, then went backward at as full a speed as we could manage. That was an exciting few minutes.

Another time, we spotted a mine floating in the harbor about twelve feet from the side of the ship forward of the starboard beam. We were afraid to move forward or backward. Anything might set it off. Finally, a chief petty officer suggested that we use the fire hoses to roll the mine away. It worked. Afterward, the starboard lookout was questioned as to why he had not seen the mine. His reply was that he had seen it, but he also saw that it was not going to hit us, so he had not said anything.

I am fascinated with the effectiveness of Christian books in evangelism. It started in the spring of 1950 when Corrie ten Boom came to Annapolis. She gave me her first book, *A Prisoner and Yet*. I had only read one or two other Christian books.

Then in the spring of 1951, the *Brinkley Bass* stopped in Hong Kong. I was wandering through the streets of Kowloon and came across the Biola Bookstore. I went in. I was amazed. I did not know that there were that many Christian books in the world. I did not know what to buy, so the manager, a longtime missionary, suggested a few. I bought four or five biographies of famous Christians and a copy of *Hymns*, the InterVarsity hymnal.

I went back to the ship and read the first chapter of each book. I wanted to read the rest, but there was no time. I was the communications officer, which meant eight hours of work during the day, plus eight hours of watch duty. I spent four hours each night on watch (2000–2400, 2400–0400, or 0400–0800) and had another four hours in the daytime. The third eight hours I ate and slept. I prayed for some time to read the rest of the books and went to bed.

About 2200 (half an hour later), a sailor woke me up and told me the captain wanted to see me in the wardroom immediately. I jumped into my clothes and ran up to the radio shack (my duty station) to see who had fouled the ball, because I knew the captain had not called at that hour to give me a "well done."

The trouble was that the cryptograph machine had broken earlier that day. All incoming messages are encrypted, so the captain couldn't read any of them until we fixed the machine. It had taken until evening to fix it.

I reported to the captain in the wardroom. He was very angry. When he had come out of the evening movie, he had been given a stack of dispatches (with date and time stamp), including a very important message from eight a.m. He wanted to know why he was receiving it twelve hours later. His first words were, "Mr. Wilson you are in hack." That is Navy parlance for "You are under arrest in your room."

I said, "Aye-aye, sir."

"Do you have any excuse?"

"No, sir."

I explained the situation to the captain. He still put me in hack.

If this had happened the year before, I would have been devastated. But now I could recognize answered prayer when I saw it.

I was in hack for three days. That meant three days with no watches: that was twenty-four hours of free time. My meals were brought to the room. I did my communications work from there, caught up on my sleep, and read all of the books in the first two days. The third day I fasted and prayed. I learned that week that God answers prayer.

I learned something else, too. Example is the best means of teaching, and imitation is the best way of learning. I had wanted to continue growing in the Lord, but I had a problem. Who in the Navy could I imitate? From those books, I learned that I could imitate Christians who had lived and died a century earlier. I have been reading biographies ever since.

Sometime after that, a box of paperback Christian books arrived from Denver addressed to the chaplain of the USS Brinkley Bass. There was no chaplain on the ship, so the box was delivered to me. This happened twice. I went down the enlisted men's chow line and gave them books to read.

In the winter of '51, the *Brinkley Bass* was in the Sea of Japan. We were in a heavy sea with a temperature of five degrees Fahrenheit. Every drop of water that hit the steel ship immediately turned to ice. The problem was that there were many drops of water. As the bow plunged into a wave, the wave would wash over the ship and freeze. We woke up the next morning to find ourselves on a steaming iceberg. The five-inch guns had become ten- and twelve-inch guns. The ship was top-heavy with ice. The primary job for all hands that day was chipping ice.

It was summertime in the East China Sea, and I was on the *Brinkley Bass*. We had a sailor on board who was chronically seasick. He could not work or stand watches. One bright, sunny day, the sea was big with rolling waves but no wind and no whitecaps. It looked like rolling hills of water. The only motions available to us were going up a hill, going down a hill, or plowing through a hill.

The sailor's bunk was in the enlisted men's quarters aft, below the fantail. He had to vomit. He ran up the ladder to the main deck and rushed to the side of the ship to vomit overboard. As he leaned over, the ship rolled to port and pitched him overboard. Several men saw it and yelled, "Man overboard!"

There is a special maneuver that will take a ship right back to where a man went overboard. The ship went into that move and came back to the place, but the sailor was not there. He was a hundred yards to port treading water. Sometimes we could see him, and sometimes he was behind a wave. We put the motor whale boat in the water to retrieve him. By the time we got to him, he had been treading water in the rolling waves for twenty minutes. He was never seasick again.

CHAPTER 20

INTEGRITY

When he came and saw the grace of God, he was glad, and he
exhorted them all to remain faithful to the Lord with steadfast
purpose. (Acts 11:23)

On payday, the *Brinkley Bass* became a floating casino. There were
poker and blackjack games on the mess deck and everywhere else.
I spoke to the exec about it because it was against Navy regulations
to gamble aboard ship. He said that the captain had decided that
since the officers played penny-ante poker in the wardroom, the men
should be allowed to play poker on the mess deck. Except it was not
penny-ante poker. It was big stakes. The captain said it was OK. I let
it go.

I was the postal officer. I made out $1,500 money orders to be
sent home. One day a young sailor told me he had lost his whole
paycheck in a poker game. He had a wife at home who was expecting
money, and there wasn't any. I told the exec I was going to put everyone I found gambling on report. I added that I would be looking for
the card games.

One day I came across a poker game on the deck of the living
quarters back aft. The game was set up on a blanket on the deck with
chips stacked in front of each player. When the men saw me, they
said, "Mr. Wilson, we're not gambling, we're just playing for chips."

I said, "If that's the case, you won't mind this." I grabbed the blanket by its four corners and shook all the chips together.

In late April 1951, we were escorting a troop ship across the North Pacific to Muroran Ko in Hokkaido. We were at "darken ship." (No visible lights were allowed.) My room was back aft. At 0330, I was walking up the starboard deck to relieve the watch on the bridge when I noticed a light in the battery locker. I opened the door to see why the light was on. It was a crap game run by the ship's three card sharks. They had cleaned out the boots* earlier in the evening (it was payday), and now they were working each other over.

I was scared. I did not want to find myself in the North Pacific Ocean after having been hit on the head by a dog wrench. Though scared, I bent over and scooped up the $90 in the pot with one hand and the dice with the other. "I will see you in the morning," I said.

I took the watch on the bridge with $90 and the dice in my pockets. At 0800, I turned in the names of the men to the exec along with Exhibits A and B.

Later in the morning, two of the sailors came to me to apologize. I asked them why they had come. They said that the exec had told them I was angry and that they should apologize to me. I went back to the exec to ask him what he had done. He said he had told them that he was keeping $10 for Navy Relief and gave back $80.

In July, the ship was on its way back to the States at the end of a six-month tour. Unknown to me, the captain had decided to buy a case of Canadian Club whiskey in Yokosuka and not declare it at customs in the States. The commodore did the same. They agreed to let the rest of officers and the chiefs in on the plan. If everyone was guilty, then no one would snitch.

Soon there was so much whiskey on the ship that there was no place to keep it. A decision was made to empty the 40mm magazines, leave the ammunition in Yokosuka, and store the whiskey in

* The enlisted men

the magazines. Although I was one of the officers, I did not know anything about the plan. I must not have been trustworthy, or they knew that I did not drink and would not approve.

The gunnery officer determined that one case of Canadian Club was not enough for him, so he bought another twelve quarts, which he stashed in the safe in his room. Just before we left Yokosuka, the gunnery officer was called home on emergency leave. He realized his whiskey would arrive in the States without him to protect it. He asked the narcotics custodian if he would keep his twelve bottles in the narcotics safe.

When we arrived at Midway Island, I received orders from the captain to relieve the present officer as narcotics custodian according to Navy regulations. I read the responsible regulation and met with the lieutenant in the wardroom to inventory and transfer all of the ship's narcotics to my custody. Everything checked off on the inventory until we came to the whiskey. The inventory said four quarts, and there were sixteen. I brought the discrepancy to his attention. I was going to change the inventory to read sixteen quarts, at which time the bottles would become U.S. government whiskey.

He said, "No. Leave it at four quarts."

I said that I was going to sign for what was on the ship. I could sign for sixteen because there were sixteen there, but if I signed for four, then the other twelve were going over the side.

He said "No" to that also. "Sign for four."

I could not figure out what was wrong with him. Couldn't he count? I went to the exec and explained the difficulty. To my amazement, the exec said that the lieutenant was right. I could not change the inventory to sixteen, and I could not drop twelve over the side, and I would sign for four.

I told him I would write a letter to the captain. He reminded me that the letter would have to go by the chain of command. In other words, he wanted to see my letter. He read and initialed it, handed it back to me, and said, "Let's just say that the captain saw it."

I told him respectfully that I was going to put the letter in my record. It is probably still in the Navy archives somewhere.

We arrived in San Diego, and I took thirty days' leave in Nebraska. When I came back to the ship, the whiskey had all disappeared, and it was then that I found out what had happened.

While the ship was in San Diego, the marines arrested one of the sailors on his way into the Navy base because he had a half pint of Seagram's Seven Crown whiskey in his belt. He went before the captain at mast for having whiskey aboard a naval base. The captain gave him a summary court martial. The sailor asked me to be his defense council. I agreed.

In the meantime, I asked my roommate if he thought the kid was guilty. My roommate was the president of the court and the former narcotics custodian. He said that it was self-evident that the sailor was guilty. I kicked him off the court for deciding on the sailor's guilt before hearing the evidence. The sailor was acquitted. Why? Every officer on the court was guilty of the same offense.

As a midshipman, as a naval officer, and in Christian work, there have been occasions where personal integrity called for an unbending decision and action. In the Navy, I put my career on the line several times. Later, I left two Christian ministries because I was not willing to bend or compromise on moral issues.

CHAPTER 21
CONFESSION OF SIN

What then? Are we to sin because we are not under law but under
grace? By no means! (Rom. 6:15)

When we receive Christ, we are made completely clean. As Christians,
we confess any sins we commit. Also as Christians, we have a joy that
we never had before—because we are indwelt with the Holy Spirit,
and all our sins are gone. Do you have as much joy today as you had
the day you received Christ? To get back to that, confess the sins
you've committed since your conversion (or since the last time you
confessed). And from now on, confess the sins as you commit them.*

This was a lesson it took me several years to learn. I had become
a Christian in 1947. In 1950, my ship was in and out of the port of
Sasebo. I became acquainted with an Army sergeant who wanted to
start an orphanage there. He had raised money and deposited it in
the Shinwa Bank, then received orders to another station. I was stuck
in Sasebo with the *Brush*, so he asked me to take charge of the money. We went to the bank together, and he signed the funds over to me.

I discussed the matter of the orphanage with Mr. Sakata, president of sixty branches of the Shinwa Bank in Kyushu. We did not
know what to do with the money. I prayed about it.

In early 1951, my new ship, the *Brinkley Bass*, steamed into
Yokosuka, and I went to a missions meeting. At the meeting, I heard
of Doreen Shaw and Mabel Halversen, two women with World

* If a person is not a believer and confesses his sin, it is not forgiven. A nonbeliever
could not possibly confess all his sins, and even if he could it would not do him any
good. He needs to confess Jesus Christ as Lord, and all his sins will be gone. In order
for your sins to be forgiven, you've got to be a Christian first.

Missions to Children who had come to Japan to start an orphanage. They had been running into roadblocks everywhere while trying to open it.

I introduced myself to them and told them about Mr. Sakata and the money in Sasebo. I could tell that they were not open to the idea. I was a naval officer; they were missionaries—what did I know about such things? Nevertheless, I gave them the information for how to get the money.

Through my talks with Mr. Sakata, I had gotten to know the girl clerks at the Shinwa bank. When the ships were in Sasebo, the clerks had money-changing tables on the dock. The next time the *Brinkley Bass* steamed into port, all the bank clerks were on the wharf exchanging dollars into yen, and the girls recognized me. As I came off the ship, they ran up to me. "Your missionaries are here! Your missionaries are here!" Mabel Halverson and Doreen Shaw had opened the orphanage in Sasebo.

When my ship was in port, I would visit the orphanage. These two missionaries seemed to think (and they were right) that I was not very godly; I was a worldly naval officer. I wasn't as worldly as they thought, but I *was* worldly. They gave me a book called *The Calvary Road* by Roy Hession. I read it in the Sea of Japan and found out that they were right. I suddenly realized that I had been accumulating sin since my conversion three and a half years earlier. I had three and a half years of unconfessed sins on my conscience (not gross sins—just sins like complaining, anxiety, impatience, etc.). While I was still at sea, I cleaned house.

> Blessed is he whose transgression is forgiven,
> Whose sin is covered.
> Blessed is the man to whom the LORD does not impute iniquity,
> And in whose spirit there is no deceit.

When I kept silent, my bones grew old
Through my groaning all the day long.
For day and night Your hand was heavy upon me;
My vitality was turned into the drought of summer. Selah
I acknowledged my sin to You,
And my iniquity I have not hidden.
I said, "I will confess my transgressions to the LORD,"
And You forgave the iniquity of my sin.

(Psalm 32:1–5 NKJV)

If we confess our sins, He is faithful and just to forgive us our sins and to cleanse us from all unrighteousness. (1 John 1:9 NKJV)

Christians get disciplined, and it is not joyous when that happens. If you want to be back in the joy of the Lord, acknowledge your sin to God, and He will completely forgive you.

I had memorized 1 John 1:9 early in my Christian life, but I didn't really start to practice it until this point. It made a major difference in my life. Although I had been a Christian for several years, had memorized a lot of Scripture, and had decided to obey God, I had not kept short accounts with Him through confession of sin. The result was that I did not have the joy that I had possessed when I first received Christ. Nor was I able to be as obedient as I had decided to be. Although God's hand was upon me in protection, and His faithfulness was with me in using me in the lives of others, I still was not victorious. I confessed my three and a half years of accumulated sins to God. When I did that, my joy returned.*

Fifteen months later, in August 1952, after arriving in San Diego, my ship was ordered to the Puget Sound Naval Shipyard in

* In the years since, I have given away hundreds of copies of *The Calvary Road*. I teach on confession of sin and have written a booklet on this subject called *How to Maintain Joy*.

Bremerton. We were steaming north along the Pacific Coast en route to Puget Sound. I was the communications officer. The operations officer, Lt. Bill Pritchard, my boss, gave me an order to get something done. I put it off.

Late one morning, I ran into Mr. Pritchard outside the radio shack. He asked me if I had done the job.

I replied, "Yes, sir."

It was not done; I had lied.

I tried to explain to myself why I had told a lie. My explanation was, "I'm just used to saying, 'Yes, sir' to officers senior to me." Having justified it, I tried to hide the lie. "I will do the job right now." (It was a small job.) "He will not know the difference. After that, I'll confess my lie to God."

All this went through my head in a moment while I was still facing him in the passageway. I turned to go into the radio shack.

Just then, he said, "Are you sure it's done?"

"Yes, sir." This time I could not claim that I was just used to saying "Yes, sir." I turned again to go into the radio shack.

"Are you *sure* you're sure it's done?"

Any idiot would have realized that he *knew* the job wasn't done. But liars are dumber than idiots, and so I said, "Yes, sir."

I did the job, then went to my room and confessed to God that I had lied to Mr. Pritchard three times. I received no peace. So I confessed it again and again and again . . . but received no peace. Finally, I said, "God, I confessed my sin, and You haven't forgiven me, so I am just going to forget it."

Before I became a Christian, I was arrogant, and I lied regularly. Those are the two primary characteristics of Satan. Jesus spoke of Satan's lying in John 8:44: "You are of your father the devil, and your will is to do your father's desires. He was a murderer from the beginning, and does not stand in the truth, because there is no truth in him. When he lies, he speaks out of his own character, for he is a liar and the father of lies."

For some people, lying is easier than telling the truth, even when there is no advantage in lying. Many years ago, I was visiting the daughter of some friends of mine. She was not a Christian. The telephone rang, and she answered it. A few minutes later, she told the other person that she had just returned from a visit to a doctor. I asked her (after she hung up) why she lied (she had not been to the doctor). She replied that it was none of the other person's business what she had been doing, so she lied to them. She lied all the time.

Back in my stateroom, I got no peace after confessing my lies to God. I decided to forget that God was not going to forgive me. It was like trying to forget you have a left leg.

It was 1540 and time to relieve the watch on the bridge as officer of the deck for the first dog watch (1545–1800). We were steaming independently, so we had no formation to keep. I just had to keep the ship on course and speed. There was a moderate sea and a stiff breeze. I relieved the officer on duty and went out on the open bridge. Most of the bridge watch was inside the pilot house to stay out of the wind and the spray.

To help me forget my lies, I planned to work on my memory verse. I had memory cards in my pocket, so I stood out on the open bridge and reviewed my verses. It did not work. I got more miserable. I tried singing hymns. I sang into the gale. No one could hear me.

About an hour had passed with these two attempts when it seemed like the Lord said to me, "Wilson, don't you think you should tell Mr. Pritchard that you lied to him?"

"If I tell him I lied, the whole ship will know I am a liar, and who would hold the worship services on the ship? God, it would ruin my testimony! It would ruin *Your* testimony."

The reply was, "I suppose you think your testimony isn't ruined anyway? Where is your joy? Where is your peace?"

Apparently, God didn't care about His testimony. I knew I had to confess to Mr. Pritchard. I spent the rest of my watch trying to think of a nice-sounding synonym for *lie*. I couldn't think of any.

I got off duty at 6:00 p.m. and went to the wardroom. Mr. Pritchard was sitting on the couch reading *Look* magazine. I walked up to him and said, "Bill, I lied to you this morning."

He looked up and said, "I know it," and went back to reading his magazine.

I had peace with God. If I had not confessed, I would not be in the ministry today, and I certainly would not have written about it here.

CHAPTER 22

ENGAGEMENT

But he gives more grace . . . . (James 4:6)

While I was a senior at the Naval Academy, I went on a date with Virginia Bell, Billy Graham's sister-in-law. She was a Wheaton grad and a nursing student at Johns Hopkins. I thought, "If I had any sense, I'd date this woman again," but I never did. Years later, I heard Billy Graham speak at West Point. Afterward, I asked him if he had sister-in-law named Virginia. He said *yes*. I said I had dated her. He said he knew—she had mentioned dating a midshipman.

During the three weeks in Giltner, Nebraska, after my graduation in June 1950, I had become interested in a girl who was a junior at Wheaton College. Her home was in Giltner. I had been corresponding with her ever since. Then during a two-day Navigator's conference in California, I learned that I should not marry a woman who was not willing to be a submissive wife. At that time, it was only theoretical, but now after several months of our correspondence courting, I realized I should find out what she thought about that kind of thing. In October or November 1950, when I was still on the *Brush*, I wrote to her asking her opinion of Ephesians 5.* I got a long answer explaining that this passage was not about husband and wife but about Christ and the Church.

---

* "Wives, submit yourselves to your own husbands as you do to the Lord. For the husband is the head of the wife as Christ is the head of the church, his body, of which he is the Savior. Now as the church submits to Christ, so also wives should submit to their husbands in everything" (Eph. 5:22–24).

I have no idea whether I wrote to her about that or if I just quit corresponding. I do remember thinking that if this godly girl felt that way, maybe all of them did. If so, I would remain single. Then I remembered Bessie Dodds. I decided to write to her to see what she thought of Ephesians 5. I anticipated an even stronger answer, stronger in the "explain-it-away" sense. She was thirty-one, a single woman in an all-women missionary society, ministering to women along with other single women. I expected that her answer would be the same as the first girl's, only in spades.

I wrote the letter and got this answer:

January 2, 1951

221 Bluff

Yokohama, Japan

Dear Jim,

Your letter finally beat its way to my door landing slightly bewildered on account of I think it had been censored en route. However, it did arrive and I was glad to get it and read some of the meanderings of your mind.

You will find, I am afraid, that I am even whackier in letters than in person—why, I don't know. But if I write somebody and it is not necessary to be formal, I am inclined to be a bit silly. If you do not approve, it will have to be the end of a beautiful friendship. It is necessary for me to write letters that will inspire and support; in writing you I know you already pray for me, and support isn't in the question.

Because there are days of holiday I am mainly doing letters, so I was able to write to Emi* . . . and I hope I shall hear from her. I am also sending her a "Daily Light" recently published in Japanese.

* Emi was a young Japanese woman to whom I had witnessed while she was ill with tuberculosis.

Are you acquainted with it? If you are not, you should be! I know this would not reach you if I sent it via Japanese post, at least that is what I am told. Therefore, I shall try to prevail upon an Army friend to send it to you. They will probably conclude I have a boyfriend, but I shall assure them that it is for the upkeep of the morale in the armed forces.

Your letter was interesting Jim, as a couple of places I felt like nudging you to keep you awake, but apart from that it was almost like a visit with you. I shall be praying for the work in Sasebo and also on your ship.

The Lord gave me a grand verse for 1951. I asked Him to bring it to me in the course of my Scripture reading, and He did as I read Philippians. I was reading in my Weymouth translation . . . It is in the 4th chapter verses 6 and 7. "Do not be over anxious about anything, but by prayer and earnest pleading, together with thanksgiving, let your requests be unreservedly made known in the presence of God. And then the peace of God which transcends all our powers of thought will be a garrison to guard your hearts and minds in Christ Jesus."

Don't you think that is a wonderful promise for '51, Jim? I am certainly counting on needing that peacekeeping guard in my heart. I spent an hour earlier tonight trying to put in Japanese some of the thoughts that came to me from the verse. I hope to use it in a message sometime.

Now for some news—Christmas Day! We had four boys from the hospital. Three had seen Korean duty; one had been in a car accident in Japan. Two of them were in hospital robes . . . The one which touched our hearts was Mel, only 17, but he had seen a lot of action. He told us he felt he had been miraculously saved as an answer to prayer. In talking to four people I found it rather hard to mention spiritual things—when I did, the conversation would seem to end at that point. They seemed to enjoy sitting by the fire and talking, and we can only leave the results with the Lord. We wish that Mel especially would take advantage of our invitation to come again. He seemed more receptive. I was wishing some keen Christian fellows had been available but unfortunately they are scarce in this city . . . .

By the way, when I left you at the wicket and sobbed my way back to the street car, lo and behold, Mary and Mr. Jimbo our school principal were also waiting for a car. I was devoutly thankful it had not been 15 or 20 minutes earlier. Not that I don't like hanging on to your arm, James, but imagine trying to explain that to a senior missionary. When I told her what I was up to she was very cordial, which could have been otherwise had she seen me earlier. Mary has a funny idea that I am due to run away soon and only if the men are too old or too young does she feel at ease about me. It is funny she should feel that way, but at 45, 31 seems young!

I read Ephesians 5 as directed, a very familiar portion to me. I shall tell you my feelings on the matter gladly . . . . Does it surprise you to know that I'm 100% for Paul's exhortation? That is the great difficulty. At times I have thought I cared for somebody sufficiently that I could marry on those terms, but unfortunately, the men never proposed to me! Interested friends always claimed that I put spiritual qualification so high that I eliminated most everybody and when I did meet someone who was pious, I was inclined to idealize them beyond proportion and the whole thing was most unnatural, hence my unmarried state. I cannot, though, submit to someone who is not spiritually superior to me; does that sound proud? I do not mean to be. But if I see someone go against my God-given convictions, how could I ever bow meekly to such a one and do as I'm told? When you are young there is room for growing together in your thinking, but I would find it hard I know. On general living I could pass I guess, keeping a home and being a fairly decent tempered person, but if I had to drag or nag a husband in spiritual matters I would find obedience difficult. How is that for honesty? Mind you, if I meet someone who is spiritual and who returns the interest, I might not be too unwilling. One other qualification: good sense of humor is absolutely necessary or he could never stand me . . . . Now that is enough about me. But you will see I am just about hopeless.

Sometime I shall tell you what I think you should do—I shall be glad to pray for you for a sweet Christian wife who will obey you 100% (because your walk with the Lord will be real enough to warrant it).

So glad you enjoyed Dobbie's book—I think it is very fine and faces the facts of war very clearly. I so enjoyed hearing him speak a few years ago . . . .

I'm wondering where you are and how you are—one thing I know, Christ will be "a very present help" to you. Your love for Him is an inspiration, Jim. I pray that you will be daily conformed to his image . . . . I have many favorite hymns but this one is special—do you know it? I may have room for two verses—in fact, three.

May the mind of Christ my Savior
Live in me from day to day.
By His love and power controlling
All I do and say.

May the love of Jesus fill me
As the waters fill the sea.
Him exalting, self-abasing
This is victory.

May His beauty rest upon me
As I seek the lost to win.

And may they forget the channel
Seeing only Him.[*]

I'll make that the substance of my prayer for you tonight.

Goodnight—in Him,
Bessie

Bessie's letter was dated January 2, the day after I came aboard the *Brinkley Bass*. I had written my letter around Christmas from Sasebo after reading General Dobbie's book. The thing that stood out to me from the letter was that Bessie had agreed with Paul one hundred percent about Ephesians 5. I had received the answer from the Wheaton girl only a few days before that. (I had written to her in October or November, before I had met Bessie.) When I read Bessie's letter about the kind of man she would be willing to marry, I thought, "You've just met the man."

In February, we arrived in Yokosuka. I got off the ship, went into the city, bought an orchid corsage, and telephoned Bessie. I told her to get dressed up, because we were going to the Grand Hotel for dinner.

She said, "We are *not* going to the Grand Hotel."

I said, "I have a 'going out' gift for you."

"That makes no difference. We are not going out. You may come to the mission if you want to."

I went to the mission and gave her the corsage. We had a Bible study and prayer together.

Another thing I had learned at the Navigator conference was to never ask a woman to marry you without having told her that you love her. And never tell a woman you love her unless you are immediately prepared to ask her to marry you.

---

* Kate B. Wilkinson, "May the Mind of Christ, My Savior," public domain, 1925.

As we were praying, I was praying that she was praying the same thing I was praying.† I told her that I loved her.

She said, "You're crazy!"

That was not much encouragement, but I continued.

"Bessie, will you marry me?"

"Absolutely not."

Every time the ship arrived in Yokosuka, I would travel to the mission in Yokohama and propose to Bessie. I usually saw her several times each visit. She kept saying *no.* She was the principal of a Bible school, and I was a career naval officer. She was convinced that she should be submissive to her husband, and she could not imagine being submissive to me. Bessie was from Prairie Bible Institute in Canada, a very strict religious school (i.e. she was not worldly). I came from the United States Naval Academy, also a very strict school, but secular; therefore, I must be worldly. I was also eight and a half years younger than she was.

On one trip, I took Bessie to the GI Gospel Hour at the Tokyo Chapel Center. On the train back from Tokyo to Yokohama, she came up with (I think) fourteen places where we differed. I can remember five of the fourteen items:

She said, "I don't drink."

I said, "Neither do I."

She said, "I don't dance.

I said, "Neither do I." (I had quit eighteen months earlier.)

She said, "I don't smoke."

I said, "Neither do I."

She said, "I don't play cards."

I said, "Neither do I."

This kept up for another nine *don'ts*, with me saying, "Neither do I" to each one.

† She wasn't!

Finally, Bessie said, "I don't go to movies."

I said, "Neither do I," and then heard what I'd said. I *did* go to movies! At sea there was a movie every night in the wardroom. I said to myself, "Well, I don't anymore."

In March, after a handful of refused proposals, Bessie said, "Jim, you say that you are interested in missions and you wish to help. I want you to know that you are not helping; you are inhibiting the work. I want you to leave and promise me that you will never see me again." That was pretty strong, and Bessie was a strong woman.

I became melodramatic and promised I would never see her again. That was rough.

The ship had two more days in port. What was I going to do? The next day I decided to go to Tokyo with no particular object in mind. I was depressed. It must have shown in my countenance, because a sailor on the train recognized me from a Navigators conference in California and came over to sit beside me. His name was Byron Ryles. He asked me what the problem was, and I told him my trouble.

Byron's answer was, "Women! Forget 'em. Come with me." He was on his way to the Oriental Missionary Society compound to visit some missionary friends of his. I went along.

At the mission, I sat in a corner, depressed. Mildred Rice (the missionary's wife) asked Byron, "What's wrong with your friend?"

"He asked a missionary to marry him, and she said no."

Mildred came over to me. "What's her name?"

I replied, "Bessie Dodds."

"Bessie Dodds?! I know her. Don't believe her—go get her!"

That was encouraging—but I had just promised Bessie the night before that I would never see her again. Before my ship got under-way, I called Bessie. "Bessie, forever is a long time. How about changing it to six months?"

She replied, "OK. You ought to grow out of it in six months."

In late April, my ship was escorting a troop ship from the Northern Pacific to Hokkaido. I called Bessie on April 27 from an outside telephone booth in Muroran Ko. It was a poor connection with a lot of static and an unhappy Bessie on the other end of the line. I was firmly impressed that Bessie was really trying to get rid of me.

I called Bessie again from Kyushu; the lines were static again, and she was upset. On the afternoon of May 5, I got a U.S. Armed Forces telephone line with no static and called her again. The line was clear. Bessie said, "Jim, you promised not to see me, and you haven't, but you write letters and telephone me. I want you to stop until your ship leaves for the States in two and a half months."

I said OK. "But before I promise, I would like to know something. Why is God not answering your prayers about us the same way He is answering mine?"

"That's easy."

"What do you mean? Why is that easy?"

"Some things are so ridiculous you don't bother the Lord with them."

I replied, "*Sodesu ka?*" which is Japanese for, "Is that so?" "Bessie, I promise not to telephone or write to you for the next two and a half months on the condition that you pray about it."

She said, "That's a deal!"

That night, Bessie prayed about it and realized that I was the right man. I did not write to her from early May until I saw her on July 14, 1951, over two months later. During those two months, she wrote a love letter to me nearly every day but did not send them. I received them one at a time after we were engaged.

The *Brinkley Bass*'s first duty in Wonsan Harbor started on May 15, 1951. It was the first of three two-week visits to Wonsan. The captain of the destroyer we were relieving told our skipper that they had not been shot at during their two weeks, so he advised him just to drop anchor and shoot away at targets ashore. The skipper was wary about it. He decided to do it halfway. He anchored but would put the anchor on a pelican hook in case we needed to move fast. He had an empty barrel fastened to the chain as a buoy. We went to general quarters as a precaution. My battle station on the *Brush* had been in Gunnery Plot. On the *Bass*, the captain wanted me with him on the bridge, so I was also officer of the deck as my battle station.

The other destroyer had just left the harbor when the 3″ weapon in the cave at Kalma Gak opened fire on us. The shells were stitching up the water. The captain yelled, "Full speed ahead!"

"Captain, we're anchored."

He yelled, "Slip the hook, slip the hook!"

All the men were at gun stations. No one was at special sea detail to slip the hook.

I said, "Captain, I will do it." I had no idea what I was doing, but I grabbed a fire axe on the way down the ladder to hit the pelican hook. When I got there, others had arrived before me and done it. The buoy was thrown over the side as the anchor chain disappeared after the anchor, and we went full speed ahead.

When everything quieted down, we went back to the buoy to retrieve our anchor and chain. Someone had neglected to secure the buoy to the chain. Our starboard anchor and many fathoms of chain are still on the bottom of Wonsan Harbor.

Five days later, on May 20, the near miss of a 75mm shell exploded on contact with the water on our starboard side. The shrapnel killed one man and wounded seven others. An English Tokyo newspaper reported that one man had been killed on the *Brinkley Bass*. The man's name was not given. Bessie read it.

Sunday, May 27, 1951

Jim dear:

You may never read this unless God leads us together as man and wife. But I have to write just to relieve the pent-up feelings I have right now. I know you think I am reserved—I have to be, for otherwise I would be just the opposite.

How can I explain my feelings when I heard that your ship had been hit and that there were casualties? I knew you had said you have assurance of God's protection but oh my dear, for the moment I was stunned and I realized how much I did care and do care. I have prayed so much for you since, but I have also thought of you, remembering so many little things about you which are so dear. It would be no effort to go right into your arms and stay there. I still feel there are tremendous obstacles in the way of our being married, but I am not going to fight this feeling I have for you any more. I love you, it is ridiculous; perhaps it could be explained away, but the fact remains, I love you too. Right now, with another month of separation still ahead I wonder how I can go through it. His grace will be sufficient. But when we do meet again, I think it should be to test ourselves on some other things relating to our compatibility. Now that I want to be married to you it will be a matter of seeing God resolve the difficulty of our different fields of service. We have spoken so generally of this—my fault I know, for I just couldn't ever think of it fairly and squarely. . . .

If you were here right now, my resistance is at low ebb. I would be in your arms, happy thought!

Yours, completely,
Bessie

The following month, the *Bass was* again with TF77 and then assigned to the Formosa Patrol, then on to Hong Kong. En route to

Yokosuka early in July, I sent Bessie a message: "Standby for things to happen."

We were to arrive in Yokosuka on Friday, July 14, and leave for the States on July 18. That was only four days, so I decided to take my thirty-day annual leave in Japan. During those days, I planned to court Bessie, marry her, and pack her off to San Diego at the end of my leave.

However, I had to get permission from Commander Naval Forces Far East in Tokyo to take leave in Japan. I called Bessie to tell her that I had to go to Tokyo. I did not tell her why. She said to get off the train in Yokohama, and she would meet me at the station and drive me to Tokyo.

I got off the train, and she flew into my arms. That hadn't happened before. Then I got to COMNAVFE with my request, and they turned it down. The Lt. Commander said, "Show me your airplane ticket." I did not have one.

I was bummed. I really got out of fellowship. In no way did I think this was the will of God. (It was!) I still lost my joy.

That evening I asked Bessie to marry me. She said, "No." That was on Friday. I asked her again on Saturday. Again she said, "No."

I said, "Listen, Bessie, the ship leaves on Tuesday. I want the real answer tomorrow."

She said, "OK, but don't come in the morning."

On Sunday morning, I went to the Far Eastern Air Force Chapel. There I met a friend, Jack Philips. We had lunch and a Bible study together. It was a good time, but I had to get to Yokohama to see Bessie. When I got up to go, he objected. There was nothing more important than the two of us studying the Word! I told him I had an appointment with Bessie Dodds.

He said, "Bessie Dodds! If I could find a woman like Bessie, I would marry her tomorrow."

I said, "Well, Jack, that is what I'm going to find out if I can do."

When I arrived at the mission, I did not need to ask her again. She had decided to give me her real answer, and the answer was obvious. We had one day together engaged, and the ship left on July 18 for six months.

Before I left, Bessie wrote the following to her supporters:

NEWS LETTER No. 8.

"Ask of Me, and I shall give thee the heathen for thine inheritance and the uttermost parts of the earth for thy possession."

Dear Friends:
221 Bluff, Yokohama, Japan,

July 16, 1951.

You have not been overburdened with prayer letters from me, have you? I see my last one is dated January 22nd, and it was only the seventh letter written in my two and a half years in Japan.

When I last wrote I asked prayer for the Bible Training School which was to open in April. Before the war we had a well-equipped school that was completely destroyed during the war, so this was to be a new beginning. It was with some fear and trembling that we sent out information and application forms. The first week we had only two students, but we continued to ask the Lord to send others until finally we had six . . . . These students have lived in a small house left to the Mission by Kido Sensei who had served her Lord so faithfully in our work before her death. We realize now the imperative need for a dormitory for next spring and so once again Mary Ballantyne and I will be poring over plans and talking about things not exactly in our line! I know that you will pray that God will guide us in every detail . . . .

Since my last letter two girls have accepted the Lord Jesus at the Saturday Bible class. What a joy it is to kneel beside another woman who is aware of her sin and is asking the Lord to forgive her and make her His child. It is a joy and a privilege that I want to know increasingly. I am more than ever convinced of the power of the Word of God coupled with the working of the Holy Spirit in bringing conviction of sin and salvation to needy hearts. All our Lord asks of us is that we give out that Word, and I am constantly amazed at the way He uses our simple presentation of His gospel.

Since January, every Tuesday morning I teach the Gospel of Luke to the Judges of the Yokohama Court. Some fifteen judges and a few other officials gather for this class, and what a joy it has been to tell them of the Savior! They know English quite well but when they do not understand me the court interpreter makes the meaning clear. We have reached the eighth chapter, and I do believe the Lord is speaking to their hearts. Two are Christians already, but others have expressed a desire to "enter Christianity." In our country, certain things are understood by most people, but in Japan the groundwork must be carefully laid. I do not mean that they cannot be saved immediately on hearing the gospel, but I am finding it necessary to go into things that I have never considered carefully before that are implications of the gospel. Judge Miyamoto wrote me his impressions of our class as follows:

"At first I attended this class to learn English, but now I attend it to hear your kind preach and know the meaning of the scriptures. Now under your guidance I can understand almost all your saying and the outline of the scriptures and it is a very pleasant time for me when I hear you preach about Jesus Christ. As you know, I was being confined as a prisoner for nearly five years in Soviet territory until the last month of the year before last. I was completely bruised, mind and body by the mal-treatment of her country, but I was constantly longing for high things of spirit in my long and painful time of prison life. Now to my pleasure, my long desires are being full-filled at this Bible class . . . "

Please pray that Judge Miyamoto may soon experience the liberating power of the gospel. I know your prayers will do much for these men . . .

I am conscious of your prayer help. Thank you again for your faithfulness.

In His Joy,
BESSIE DODDS.

After my ship left port, Bessie wrote to tell her mission about the engagement.

221 Bluff, Yokohama, Japan
July 24, 1951

Dear Ellen*,

This will be a rather short note but I think it is necessary. I have written and already sent a letter to Mrs. Paddon† of this important matter but Mary and I feel that in the summer with the danger of letters not reaching people that I should also send word to you.

The matter? I became engaged on Sunday to Ensign Jim Wilson of the USN and promised to marry him next spring . . . . I met him in November just after the destroyer "the Brush" was hit and he was miraculously preserved. In February he proposed to me and I refused but definitely! Since that time it has been very difficult and had he not persisted I would not be writing this letter now. He was in Korean waters from April 1st to just this past Friday and we have had three

* Ellen Colson, secretary of the mission society
† The president of the mission society

days together. I could not say anything but "yes." He is requesting far east appointment and it is my desire to continue to do as much as I possibly can in the Lord's work here. His ship returned today to the US and may not be out again until Christmas . . . . A recent issue of *Christian Life and Times* carried an article about him when he was on the Brush. Many of the points in the article were twisted but it does honor the Lord. He was converted while at Annapolis through the witness of other Christians. I may add to you that I have fought this and even yet am pretty scared but I do have a peace about the situation up to the present . . . .

Ellen, I shall always remember your labor of love for the Lord and the kindness that you have shown me. I feel a bit like a renegade but the Lord knows I have sought His will above my own and even yet would be willing for this to end if it is not His perfect will for me. The wonderful thing is that Jim is so keen for the Lord and I do not feel I am stopping the mission work for he is an aggressive witness for the Lord . . . .

Ever in Him,
Bessie

45 Astor Place, Rm. 316
New York, 3, N.Y.
August 3, 1951

Dear Bessie:

Can't you picture the scene when your letter arrived? I was home on vacation and Elsie phoned to tell me of the day's mail. She said there were letters from Japan and wondered if she should just send them on to my home. However, I said she had better glance through as it was just about the time Mary Lou was to sail and I thought there might be something about plans for her, etc. Then came the distressing voice over the phone—"Oh! Some awful news from Japan!" I thought you were all dead! Then the truth came forth—"Bessie is engaged!"

We love you, Bessie, and do want the Lord's very best for you and want you to have every joy which is in His plan for you. We do not wonder that "Jim" fell in love with you—for we did, too. We just want you to go slowly and be sure that this is of Him. An "old maid" like myself can readily remind you of the seriousness of the step—I know you are realizing that fact and therefore you write that you are a "little scared." I wish you might have an opportunity of getting personally acquainted with Jim's family and background, etc. before you are married.

We know your devotion to the Lord and that only a companion who was an earnest Christian could have any attraction to you. We are anxious to see the article in *Christian Life* you mentioned—and will try to get hold of a copy . . . Do tell Jim to call on us if he comes to New York. Tell him not to be afraid of us! . . . .

Rest assured, Bessie dear, that we will be praying earnestly for you these momentous days. If this is of the Lord, He will give His peace and confidence—if it is not His will, these will be lacking and you will know that this is not His way for you, and will give strength to choose as He directs . . . .

Lovingly,
Ellen

Dear Ellen,

Vacation is over, we are unpacked, and Mary is back at school today. I am trying to sort things out mentally and get back into a schedule before our next term opens this coming Monday . . . .

I was very happy to hear of Mrs. Paddon's proposed visit to Japan . . . I am expecting to hear from her as I am still wondering about the official Board pronouncement concerning my engagement. I would like to see ahead into the next six months very much for myself, but the Lord has given peace that He will guide. Jim was able to fly to Canada and spend several days with my family. He saw my brother and sister reconciled after 19 months of not speaking to each other, and also had a wonderful time of dealing with my brother Jim about acceptance of Christ. They studied the gospel together, whereas my brother would not even read the Bible at my request. In all, they gave him a good reception into the family, and I am greatly encouraged to continue to pray for their salvation. It seemed a lovely seal on the step I have taken . . . I am still in love with him, and he speaks of wanting to swim the Pacific, so I guess he still is too!

Sincerely,
Bessie

221 Bluff, Yokohama,
October 26th, 1951.

My dear Ellen,

Well, the joyful occasion of welcoming Ms. Paddon and Miss Marstaller is a thing of the past, day before yesterday to be exact and so much has been done and said since then that my head is still in a whirl . . . .

We still have not had much time to talk personally about "me" but I was very embarrassed to learn that I had written such a short letter of explanation at the time of my engagement . . . Actually, the happy little details were weighted down with much agony and fears and headache of giving him up several times and having him reappear on the scene, happily confident that the Lord meant me for him. We have not had sufficient time together to have any understanding of the future and so much has to be done through letters. As you know, I am busy or should be, and he is extremely busy, and the ocean is very wide, and letters do not settle problems very quickly . . . . I am sure that in many of these things, too, Mrs. Paddon will be able to give me some helpful advice . . . . How I thank the Lord for the wisdom and aggressive ability she has . . . .

Love to all
In Him,
Bessie

During our six months apart, Mrs. Paddon, the president of the Women's Union Missionary Society (WUMS) that Bessie was affiliated with, arrived in Yokohama. She reminded Bessie that she had signed a statement that she would not get married during her first term on the field. Bessie had not signed such a statement and would not have done so if it had been required. We had decided that Bessie would still work at the mission after we were married as long as my ship was in the Far East. The president was grateful for that but insisted that we take precautions once we were married because Bessie might get pregnant, and she couldn't be pregnant and be headmistress at the same time. Bessie wrote to me to get my view of that.

I replied that we would not take precautions. If it was the will of God for her to be principal and pregnant, then she could do it. If it was the will of God to be principal only, then she would not get pregnant. If she could not be both, and she became pregnant, then it was God's will that she not be principal.

Meanwhile, I was on my way to San Diego. The *Brinkley Bass* spent a few days in Pearl Harbor en route. The ship arrived in San Diego on 6 April 1951, and I went to the *Brush* to retrieve Lou Zamperini's Hiroshima souvenir that I had left on board when I transferred to the *Brinkley Bass*. The *Brush* was back in full commission. I called Lou and told him I would bring the gun to him.

We met up on a Sunday morning. He said, "Where do you want to go to church?"

I said, "I'd like to go to Hollywood Presbyterian."

He said, "Why?"

"I hear it's a great gospel-preaching church."

"That is true. But," Lou said, "it's filled up with Presbyterians and Hollywood people, and I don't know who's who. I know them so well that I don't dare ask them if they're Christians." He went on, "I will take you to Hollywood Pres on the condition that anybody I introduce you to, you ask him if he's a Christian, and I'll listen to the answer."

We decided that if anyone answered, "Of course," we would assume he was not a Christian.

There were four hundred people in the adult Sunday School class that morning. Afterward, Lou introduced me to Jack Williams, the president of the class.

I said, "Glad to know you, Mr. Williams. Are you a Christian?"

He said, "Of course!" Lou and I looked at each other.

I started talking to Jack's wife. Jack turned to Lou. "Lou, that's the first person who ever dared ask me if I was a Christian!"

Lou said, "Let me be the second. Are you a Christian?"

"I don't know, Lou. What's a Christian?"

That happened several times. One guy said, "Of course," and as soon as Lou got out of earshot, he whispered in my ear, "As a matter of fact, I haven't been born again."

"Would you like to be?"

"Yes, but I'd have to admit I'm not already."

Christian churches are full of people who know the words, and their heart isn't there. When a person becomes a Christian, he is changed from the inside out. The Bible was written for believers. It says in the Bible that the natural man (that is, the unsaved, non-Christian person) doesn't understand the things of God. They are foolishness to him, because they are spiritually discerned. If the Bible doesn't make sense to you, it might be because you are not a believer.

After the weekend, I took my thirty-day annual leave and immediately headed to Edmonton to ask Bessie's oldest brother, Frarey, for permission to marry Bessie. I also met Bessie's siblings Jim and Molly. They lived on the same street a few blocks apart, but hadn't spoken to each other for years. Then I went home to Nebraska.

When I got back to San Diego, I used the rest of my time to memorize a lot more Scripture. It did not make me godly, but I thought it did. I became a strong Navigator. I was one of Dawson Trotman's "fair-haired boys."

Dawson Trotman, founder of the Navigators, had visited the Naval Academy during my first class year. On a Sunday afternoon, he spoke to about twenty Christian midshipmen in Memorial Hall. He was a dynamic speaker. At the end of his talk, he said he would like to speak with those of us who really meant business with the Lord. A few of us took him to the chaplain's office.

"How many of you want to sin?" he asked us.

None of us wanted to sin.

"I will teach you how not to sin." That sounded good to us. Dawson quoted Psalm 119: "Wherewithal shall a young man cleanse his way? By taking heed thereto according to thy word . . . . Thy word have I hid in mine heart, that I might not sin against thee" (Psalm 119:9, 11 KJV).

It was simple; all we had to do was hide the Word of God in our hearts.

Doug Cozart was assigned to disciple me. I was impressed. I had a Daily Light devotional book, and any verse I pulled out of it, he could quote, or he could give the reference if I read the verse.

Over the next fourteen months, I memorized the 108 verses of the Navigators' Topical Memory System. (I found out later that Bessie had also memorized them several years earlier.) I memorized three verses a week for the first year, and the following year five verses a week.

Then I began to get suspicious. I was still sinning. "How many verses do I have to have in my heart to not sin?" The problem was that I had been hiding the verses in my *head*, not in my heart. I was less like the Lord Jesus because of my arrogance about how much Scripture I knew.

When I graduated from the Naval Academy, I had bought a Scofield Bible. I wound up using it for less than a year; while I was at sea, I read a chapter from it along with the notes on the chapter and realized that the notes were not in accordance with the text. When I got to San Diego, I bought an Oxford King James Bible from the Christian Science Reading Room for $5. I used it until the mid-sixties. It had no notes or references.

Because of my experiences in the Korean War, the director of San Diego Youth for Christ asked me to speak to the kids from the Christian high school on a bus after school. Just before the event, the director called to tell me that he had accidentally double-booked me with some Dutch woman. It was Corrie ten Boom! We both spoke to the kids.

Corrie remembered me from Annapolis. After our talks, I told her that I was getting married in Japan. She said, "I'm going to Japan, too."

CHAPTER 23

COMMUNICATIONS OFFICER

But since you excel in everything—in faith, in speech, in knowledge, in complete earnestness and in the love we have kindled in
you—see that you also excel in this grace of giving. (2 Cor. 8:7)

In January 1952, the *Brinkley Bass* returned to the Korean War. It was
my third six-month tour. I was able to see Bessie a couple of times
that winter.

My second two-week tour in Wonsan Harbor was in March 1952.
We continued to pick up downed pilots in the harbor and later built
an airstrip on the island of Yo Do so they could land. Every afternoon at two o'clock, the North Koreans would wheel a 75mm out of
the mouth of the cave on the peninsula and shoot at us. This was the
same cannon we had lost a man to on March 20, 1951. Now, a year
later, we were back with the same skipper, the same ship, still getting
shot at.* We had been there for two weeks, and on April 1 we were to
be relieved. The captain was afraid we would get hit again before our
duty was over. All the officers knew that he was counting the days
until we were relieved on station.

Lee Ivey was the gunnery officer. Lee came to me a few days before our duty was over and said, "Jim, we are going to be relieved on
1 April. You know how anxious the captain is about it. Let's play an
April Fools' joke on him. You're the communications officer. How

---

* Cdr. Aaron Beyer, the skipper of the *Bass* for two Westpac tours six years before,
had been skipper of the destroyer *USS Raymond* in the battle off Samar. He received
the Navy Cross for that action. The battle is recounted in *The Last Stand of the Tin
Can Sailors*, by James D. Hornfischer.

about putting a bogus message from Commander Task Group 95.2 that says something is wrong with the ship that's to relieve us, and it has been delayed for two weeks. Then have a second message that says, '1234567 Zebra, April Fools.' Include these when you give the messages to the captain at breakfast. When the captain sees it with the other messages that came in during the night, we'll all say, 'April fool, Captain!' "

I made the phony messages and handed the message board to the captain at breakfast. He read the first message: "*USS Brinkley Bass*, copy to *USS Silverstein*. *Silverstein* has burned-out super heaters and is unable to relieve the *Bass*. *Bass* remain on station for two more weeks." The captain was so steamed he threw the board down in anger without reading the second message. All the other officers decided it was not wise to shout, "April Fool, Captain!" Guess who had to explain to him that it was a joke . . . .

Once he understood, the captain got an idea of his own. "Just to make your trouble a little bit worse, I want you to show the commodore this same message when he comes in for breakfast."

I showed it to the commodore. He didn't say anything, and just put the board back on the table.

The captain said, "Well, sir?"

The commodore said, "That's a bogus message."

"How do you know it's a bogus message?"

"The *Silverstein* is a destroyer escort, and destroyer escorts run on diesel. They don't have super-heaters." That made the captain look even more of a fool.

One of my duties as communications officer was to safeguard the cryptographic machine. Since we were in close to North Korea, if we were sunk, the machine could be retrieved by the North Koreans. In Sasebo, I procured a twenty-four-inch square magnesium bomb that sat on top of the cryptographic machine. If we were going to be captured or sunk, I was to set off the bomb, and it would melt the machine. Since Lee, as gunnery officer, was responsible for all explosives on the ship, I informed him that I had installed the magnesium bomb. He took me to see the captain about it.

The captain asked Lee about the bomb. Lee said, "Captain, if it goes off, it will burn a hole right through the bottom of the ship."

The captain said, "Get that thing off my ship!" Lee and I dropped it overboard.

CHAPTER 24

MARRIAGE

And God raised us up with Christ and seated us with him in the
heavenly realms in Christ Jesus, in order that in the coming ages he
might show the incomparable riches of his grace, expressed in his
kindness to us in Christ Jesus. (Eph. 2:6–7)

There was no one in sight to relieve Bessie as headmistress of the
school. The mission put pressure on her, so she felt very obligated to
them—so much so that she felt guilty about being in the will of God
by deciding to marry me.

I wrote a letter to the president asking her to relieve Bessie of all
obligations to the mission, whether they be legal, moral, or anything
else. I asked that if there was a financial obligation, would she let me
know how much it was? I got an answer from her stating that $800
would be fine.*

The president's answer arrived the day *after* we were married. I
don't know how I paid it off, but I managed to do it in a few weeks.
Bessie said, "I'm not worth it." Too late! (She realized later that she
more than worked it off over the years!)

The wedding was going to be in the Nasugbu Beach Chapel, an
American Nazarene chapel in Yokohama. Bessie wanted to know
when my ship would arrive in Yokosuka so she could set a date and
send out invitations. However, I was not allowed to tell her, because
all ship movements were classified. By faith, Bessie set Monday, April
7, 1952, as our wedding date.

* The equivalent of close to $8,000 in 2020.

Nasugbu Beach Chapel Center in Yokohama, circa 1950.

The last two weeks of March, we were in Wonson Harbor. We were relieved on station on April 1 and arrived in Yokosuka on April 4, a Friday. Bessie came to the ship and had dinner in the wardroom.

Commander Naval Forces Far East required all U.S. Navy personnel who wished to marry a Japanese citizen to get permission from him in writing before the marriage. The rule, of course, did not actually say "Japanese citizen." It said a "foreign national." Bessie was Canadian, which meant she was a foreign national. On Friday evening, we wrote the request letter. The wedding was planned for 1600 Monday, which meant that the letter would have to be walked through COMNAFE on Monday morning.

The rehearsal was on Saturday evening. I had duty on board on Saturday, so I missed it. My younger brother, Floyd, was a fire control technician stationed in Yokosuka. He was my best man. He made it to the rehearsal.

On Sunday evening, Bessie and I went to a chapel service in Tokyo. John and Eldora Schwab were there. They were missionaries with

TEAM.* They had been on the same ship with Bessie when she came to Japan in December 1948. When I was first showing an interest in her, Bessie had gone to Eldora for counsel. At the same time, I went to John for counsel. John was a very strong Navigator. He had a verse for everything. To him, you had to have a verse for guidance. "No verse, no guidance!" He asked me if I had a verse. I did not have one. He informed me that I did not have guidance from the Lord to pursue Bessie. Here it was fifteen months later, the night before our wedding, and John asked me again if I had a verse. I still did not have one. I know he was worried.

On Monday morning, the ship was to be given a communications exam, and I was the communications officer, so I was busy being tested. Bessie had to take the request letter to COMNAVFE in Tokyo on her own.

My crypto machine was broken. It looked like I was going to flunk the exam. The officer in charge of proctoring it asked the captain to cancel the exam until the crypto machine was repaired. I got off the ship and caught the train to Yokohama.

At the Yokohama station, I met Bessie, who had just returned from Tokyo with permission for us to marry.

Japan did not recognize religious weddings, only civil ceremonies, which meant we had to go to the American Consulate to get "officially" married.

When we arrived, the consulate staff was out to lunch. We went to the Grand Hotel for lunch and returned to the consulate. The official had never performed a wedding before. He was nervous. He said, "Put your left hand on the Bible and raise your right. Do you solemnly swear . . . ?"

I had strong convictions against swearing. I had refused to take oaths on several important occasions. But I thought if there was a

* The Evangelical Alliance Mission

time *not* to stand on one's convictions, this was it! I did not want to say no. So I "solemnly swore."

After this first wedding, Bessie asked me in the cab if I had a verse for our day. I did not have a verse, but I had been working on my Scripture memory. The verse that came out of my mouth was Romans 8:18. "For I reckon that the sufferings of this present time . . . ." Wrong verse!

Our church wedding was at four in the afternoon. It was a bilingual service with Japanese citizens, missionaries, and naval officers present. David Morken sang "The Love of God" and preached from Deuteronomy 11:18–21:

> Therefore you shall lay up these words of mine in your heart and in your soul, and bind them as a sign on your hand, and they shall be as frontlets between your eyes. You shall teach them to your children, speaking of them when you sit in your house, when you walk by the way, when you lie down, and when you rise up. And you shall write them on the doorposts of your house and on your gates, that your days and the days of your children may be multiplied in the land of which the LORD swore to your fathers to give them, like the days of the heavens above the earth.

The Japanese high school girls sang Psalm 121 in three-part harmony, with a descant.

The wedding was recorded on a reel-to-reel tape. The other side of the tape was blank. We decided to send it to friends and relatives in the States, so we recorded greetings on the blank side. We sang a duet to "Redeemed, how I love to proclaim it." We sent it off but got no comments.

Later, we found out that the singing was awful. It had been recorded on Japanese 50-cycle alternating current and played in the

United States and Canada on 60-cycle. It made our voices so funny that everyone who heard it was embarrassed for me.

The day after the wedding, I had duty and had to be back on board. When I woke up that morning, Bessie was sitting up reading a book——*The Christian's Secret of a Happy Life*, by Hannah Whitall Smith——and she was in the chapter on doubt!

After my duty was over, Bessie and I had Wednesday, Thursday, and Friday together in Tokyo at the Fairmont Hotel.

On Friday, we went to see Mildred and Roland Rice with the Oriental Missionary Society.* During the visit, the telephone rang. Rolly came back from the phone and said, "Some Dutch woman is lost here in Tokyo." It was Corrie ten Boom!

Saturday, the last day of our honeymoon, was spent at Bessie's mission house. Who should show up but Corrie, my brother Floyd, and two sailors from the *Brush*! That finished our honeymoon.

My ship went back to the war, and Bessie had Corrie for the rest of her time in Japan. Corrie told Bessie, "Too bad you got married; you could have been my travelling companion."

---

* Mildred was the one who had said, "Bessie Dodds! Don't believe her. Go get her."

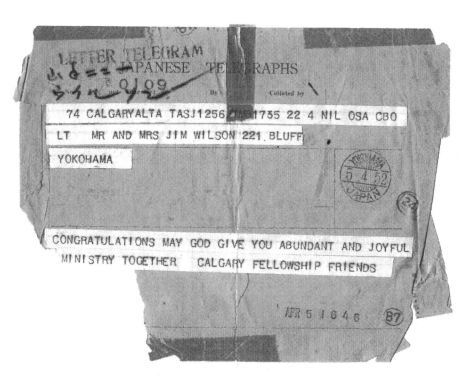

Congratulatory telegrams received after the wedding.

CHAPTER 25

MARRIED LIFE AND EVANGELISM IN THE NAVY

Likewise, husbands, live with your wives in an understanding way,
showing honor to the woman as the weaker vessel, since they are
heirs with you of the grace of life, so that your prayers may not be
hindered. (1 Pet. 3:7)

In July, my ship came into Sasebo, and Bessie traveled down from Yokohama to meet me. My friend Mr. Sakota, the president of sixty branches of the Shinwa Bank, offered us the use of the home of the former finance minister of Japan. We accepted. Although it was a nice large house, it was infected with fleas. We were eaten alive. We only stayed there one night.

We moved to a Western-style hotel. The room had a big bed and overstuffed furniture. The problem was that there was no room to walk. We stepped from the bed to the sofa. We stayed there one night.

Our last night was with friends of mine, Sergeant and Mrs. Butler. We slept on the couch. Then it was back to sea for me.

On June 18, 1952, I was promoted to Lieutenant Junior Grade. One month later, we left for the States, I on the *Bass* headed to San Diego, and Bessie on a Navy transport ship to San Francisco. Her ship was filled with Japanese brides. On arrival, the brides disembarked in alphabetical order. Since Bessie's name was now Wilson, she was the last passenger to leave the ship.

Dad and Mom met Bessie's ship in San Francisco and drove her to San Diego to collect me. We all went to Nebraska with Dad doing the driving. He was fifty-three years old. My mother was close to all six of her daughters-in-law. My Dad was closest to Bessie.

When we returned to San Diego, the ship headed north for Puget Sound. Leonard had been recalled to active duty and was stationed in Astoria, Oregon. He was a Quartermaster First Class. Bessie and I went down to see him and Glenda and the kids. Since he was a college graduate, I encouraged him to apply for Officer Candidate School in Newport, Rhode Island. He did and left for Newport soon after.

My ship was in dry dock, which made Bremerton, Washington, a nice honeymoon place. The workload was minor, and there were no watches.

Bessie and I became active in the Christian Servicemen's Center run by Ma and Pa Green. One day, I stopped by. Mrs. Green told me, "Jim, I met a wonderful Christian officer."

"What's his name?"

"I've forgotten it."

"What's he look like?" She told me that he was tall, a famous athlete, and stationed on a ship that began with "M."

I looked at the roster of ships in Bremerton. Half of them had names beginning with "M." I picked one off the list and went aboard. I think it was the *Montrose*. On the quarterdeck, I asked the officer who conducted the ship's worship services. He directed me to their hospital corpsman. I went to sickbay and told the corpsman I was looking for a tall naval officer who was a famous athlete. He said, "It must be Mr. Wade. He was quarterback for Vanderbilt."

I found Billy Wade sitting at the desk in his stateroom writing a letter. There was a Bible on the desk. I was so sure I had the right man that I started talking with him like we were old Christian friends. He interrupted me. "Jim, I don't know who you're looking for, but you've got the wrong man. But I'm interested; keep talking." Billy was religious but not saved. I spent a long time with him but did not think I had made the gospel clear.

When he got out of the Navy, Billy played for the LA Rams and the Chicago Bears. After Bessie and I moved to Annapolis, I would wonder about him when the Bears played the Colts. There was no Super Bowl in those days, but Billy was considered the top quarterback in professional football. If there had been a Super Bowl, he would have been there.

Ten or twelve years later, I got a letter from Chuck Morris in Memphis. He said that he had gone to hear Billy Wade speak. Billy had given his testimony, saying that he had received Christ in Bremerton after an officer named Jim Wilson had talked to him for six hours. Billy later came to Annapolis to see me, and we jogged together on Farragut Field.*

The *Isbell* was in the next dry dock over from the *Brinkley Bass*. Their galley was out of commission, so the officers ate with us on the *Bass*. There was an ensign on the *Isbell* named John Mighell who wanted to go into the Episcopal ministry. He did not believe in Hell. He thought it was selfish to receive Christ to keep from going to Hell.

I said, "You mean a person should receive Christ because he is a sinless sinner?" He liked that idea very much. That described him to his satisfaction. I went to the Christian bookstore and bought him a copy of Jonathan Edwards's *Sinners in the Hands of an Angry God*.

In the spring of 1953, we were back in San Diego. There was a knock on the door. It was John. In the doorway, the first thing he said was, "I believe in Hell." In the spring of 1956, I saw John again at the Episcopal Seminary when I was in Berkeley on an emergency leave to see Dad.

Sometimes I tried to play jokes, but they didn't always go over well. While we were in dry dock, I made a remark which I thought

---

* I did also find the athlete I was looking for; he was a basketball player stationed on the same ship as Billy Wade.

was funny. We were sending the torpedo men and radar men over to torpedo school on the beach. Mr. Jones, the operations officer, was older than I was, but he was a mustang. Back when he was in high school, he had tried for the Naval Academy and failed entrance exam, so he enlisted and came up through the ranks to be a lieutenant.

Both as an enlisted man and as an officer, he had spent almost all of his time in engineering. He didn't know anything about navigation, operations, or bridge watches. Then he found himself assigned to the *Bass* as an operations officer. Although I was junior to him, I had been a communications officer and a navigator and was a Naval Academy graduate—all things that made him think I knew much more than he did. I was not aware of this; I respected him and only knew him to be capable, competent, and senior to me.

Our TERI plotter (torpedo effective-range indicator) was so beaten up that you could hardly read the numbers on it. The guys came back from torpedo school and said the TERI plotters over there were just beautiful. The operations officer said that's the way it always was—the schools have the good equipment, and the operating ships have junk that doesn't work. He said, "The next time you go over to the school, just make a quick switch. Give him ours and bring back one of theirs." This tends to be standard operating procedure in the Navy.

Everything was shut down since we were in dry dock, and I was hanging around the combat information center with a bunch of radarmen. Mr. Jones came in and asked me to hand him the plotter to make the switch.

I said, "Yes, sir," reached under the DRT, and pulled it out.

He was standing behind me. I handed it up to him, and he said, "Boy, you can hardly read the numbers on this thing."

"Depends on where you got your education," I said.

Well, Mr. Jones didn't hear that, but everybody else whooped it up laughing and thought that was a very funny remark.

He said, "What did you say?"

He thought he had missed the joke, so I repeated it. Jones was a great big blond with a bright red face—red all of the time—and when he heard me say that, the blood just disappeared right out of his face like a thermometer going down. Whoops!

He came to my room that night. "Mr. Wilson, was that remark addressed to me this afternoon?"

"Yes, sir, but . . ."

"No *buts*. I know exactly what you meant." He thought I was making fun of him for coming up the ranks instead of going to the Naval Academy; he was very self-conscious about not being educated like the other officers. He told me that he was going to give me a bad fitness report; he did, but someone else changed the report later.

"Depends on where you got your education" was a smart remark I was in the habit of using. I hadn't meant to put Mr. Jones down; I was just being a smart aleck. But being a wise guy got me in trouble more than once.

In November 1952, Bessie and I took a train to Edmonton to see her siblings Jim, Molly, and Faye and Mrs. Mother (Bessie's "adopted" mother, her best friend's mother). Bessie was pregnant with Douglas, our first child. We went on to Calgary to visit her friends from when she was with ISCF in Alberta.

I was elected to the Officers' Christian Union Council in 1952 and went to my first council meeting in Philadelphia. On the train to Philadelphia from Calgary, we crossed the U.S.-Canada border in the middle of North Dakota. At the border, we found out that Bessie was not supposed to leave the States while she was waiting for her citizenship. Since she was married to a U.S. naval officer, she had been put on a fast track to American citizenship. Included in this fast track was a provision that she not leave the United States until the process was complete. We either did not know that, or we'd just completely forgotten it. They refused to let her back into the States. We did not bribe the official, but it took a lot of begging to get Bessie back in.

The OCU meeting was followed by the Army-Navy game. I had only been out of the Academy for two and a half years, so our tickets were in the end zone. I had left my glasses in Bremerton. Bessie did not understand the game, and I could not see it. Then we attended the Army-Navy Banquet and sat with Philip Howard, Joe and Mary Lou Bayly, and Dr. Fran Steele.[*]

We visited New York City, where I was invited to speak to the Women's Union Missionary Society Board (the mission Bessie had been with). From there I went alone to Newport to see Leonard, who was about to be commissioned. He was the commander of his class. I asked what he had requested for duty. He said he had asked for Guam. I encouraged him to ask for Japan. He told me before I left that he had changed his selection to Japan and received orders to Commander Naval Forces Far East in Yokosuka.

Dorothy Flaxman (Bessie's best friend) came up from Norfolk to meet "Bessie's husband." The first thing she did was grab my hand and inspect it. I asked her what she was doing. She said that Bessie had said that she would never marry a man with hair on his hands. I passed inspection.

Bessie was pregnant, and we realized that she could not handle the long train ride back across the continent to Seattle. We turned in

---

[*] Philip Howard (1923–2015), brother of Elisabeth Elliot, was a long-time missionary and Bible translator for native tribes in Northern Canada and also served as president of the Northern Canada Evangelical Mission. Joseph T. Bayly (1920–86) served as east coast staff director and later director of InterVarsity Christian Fellowship as well as editor of *His* magazine and president of David C. Cook Publishing Company. He authored several books including *The Gospel Blimp*. Francis R. Steele (1915–2004), was a specialist in Babylonian archeology and later served as home director for Arab World Ministries for forty years.

our train tickets and used the funds to buy her a plane ticket. I would hitchhike by military air. It took longer than expected.

Back in Bremerton, I was promoted from communications officer to navigator. Our primary means of navigation at sea was a sextant and celestial navigation. As navigator, I did not stand watches; I was on duty all of the time.

Repairs to the *Bass* were completed in the spring. On the return trip from Bremerton to San Diego, the captain wanted to go via the Santa Barbara Channel. This meant steaming through the channel at night. All I could think of was a photograph on the wall of Luce Hall at the Academy. It was a picture of seven destroyers up on a beach. There had been fog, and six of them followed the leader. The eighth destroyer in the squadron had turned away. Under the picture were these words: "The price of good navigation is constant vigilance."

On 18 April 1953, the *Bass* left San Diego for the Western Pacific. There was a scope on the sextant. However, I could not use the scope with my glasses on, and I could not find the right star with my glasses off. I would find the star and quickly take my glasses off and bring the sextant up to my eye before I lost the star. We had to shoot the stars at twilight because we needed the horizon. Once it was dark, we could see the stars but could not see the horizon. We needed three stars to get a fix. When we got a fix, it would look like the image on the left below. It should look like the image on the right.

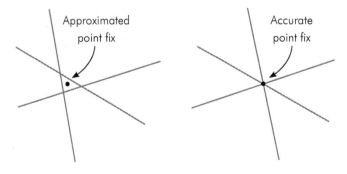

Approximated point fix

Accurate point fix

If we got a point fix, we knew exactly where we were. If it turned out to be a triangle, we did not know which two stars were right, because there were three points, so I would place our location in the middle of the triangle. Another officer saw how I was using the sextant, and he didn't see how I could possibly navigate that way. He followed me to the chart house to be sure I wasn't cheating. I did the math, and it turned out to be a perfect point fix.

In Pearl Harbor, the officers went to the Submarine Officers' Club, because it was the best club there. We swam in the pool and played volleyball. While we were there, I lost my Naval Academy class ring. We searched the volleyball court and swam around the bottom of the pool but could not find it. I left a note at the club, and the ship left for the Far East. I was sick about it.

I had received my class ring at the ring dance the spring of my second-class year. I had not thought of marriage, so I had the ring fitted for my left hand. When I got married, my wedding band went on the same finger as my class ring. They did not fit together, so when we were in Annapolis in December 1952, I had the wedding band curved to fit against the class ring.

At sea, Academy graduates are a small minority. There were usually only one or two Academy officers on any destroyer. On the *Brush*, the executive officer and I were the only ones. At the evening meal, officers remain standing until the captain comes in and sits down. The chairs were metal. As we grasped the backs of the chairs, our heavy rings would clang against the chairs. Because of this, Academy men were known as ring-knockers. I could not afford to pay the several hundred dollars for a new ring. Suddenly I was no longer a ring-knocker.

After being depressed about it for two weeks, I realized I was guilty of idolatry. That metal ring meant too much to me. I confessed my sin and thanked God that it was gone.

There was another problem, though. Now that the class ring was gone, I had a curved wedding band that looked odd on my hand. In 1956, I was in Okinawa visiting Bob and Jean Boardman, Navigator missionaries. Bob said, "What happened, Jim? Did a horse step on your finger?" I had the ring straightened in Tokyo.

In March 1958, I received a telephone call from the Bureau of Naval Personnel. We were living in Washington, D.C., at the time. The voice on the phone said, "Come down to BuPers and pick up your ring." It had been gone for almost five years. The class number on the ring was 1950. The "50" had been filed off. Someone had been pretending to be a ring knocker. The ring became my access to the military academies as a representative of the Officers' Christian Union; it told cadets and midshipmen that I was an alum.

CHAPTER 26

NAVAL POSTGRADUATE SCHOOL, MONTEREY

And when he wished to cross to Achaia, the brothers encouraged
him and wrote to the disciples to welcome him. When he arrived,
he greatly helped those who through grace had believed.

(Acts 18:27)

We traveled across the Pacific by the Great Circle from Hawaii, arrived in Tokyo Bay, and the *Bass* had its third tour in Wonsan Harbor
in May 1953.

In the middle of this trip, I received orders to the U.S. Naval
Postgraduate School in Monterey, California, for a one-year course
in command communications. I flew to San Francisco, caught a bus
to Monterey, and rented a house whose back fence bordered the park
of the old Hotel Del Monte, which was now the Postgraduate School.

Mom, Dad, Everett, Kenny, and Uncle Clyde* had come from
Nebraska to be with Bessie for Douglas's birth. They left California
before I returned. I arrived in San Diego ten days after Douglas was
born in the Balboa Naval Hospital. I did not know what to think; I
had left as a husband and came back as a father. I was twenty-five
years old.

I bought a car, a '48 Nash. For several reasons, I did not know
how to drive. From the day I had turned sixteen, I worked eight

---

* Uncle Clyde left home when my father was ten or eleven. He was not heard from
for more than forty years. He came to San Diego with my parents for Douglas's birth
but left before I got there. I never met him.

hours a day after school for two years and twelve hours a day for two summers. No time! My older brother was at sea, and my father was in bed. No one to teach me! Then I had one year as a sailor, four years as a midshipman (three of which I was not allowed inside a car), and after that I spent three years at sea.

I acquired a learner's permit and got an ensign friend of mine to drive with us to Monterey, where I earned my driver's license.

At the Postgraduate School, I was not a great student. If I had been going for a full master's degree, I probably would not have made it. But there were some good things about the year in Monterey. I took a correspondence course in strategy and tactics from the Naval War College. This is the course that got me entranced with the principles of war. It took me three years to complete the course. (I started it 1953 and finished in 1956.) Bessie, Douglas, and I got to establish our family life. We held the first OCU Conference the weekend of January 1, 1954, at Mount Hermon. I was asked to preach weekly at the new Seaside Baptist Church, which I did until graduation. Bessie became pregnant with Evan.

I had several dental appointments while in Monterey. The dentist did not show up for at least two of them. The dental technician (a corpsman) cleaned my teeth and took x-rays. I told him the gospel. When he went to the dark room, he wanted me to come along to continue telling him the good news.

One night, he telephoned and told me that he had orders for Kodiak, Alaska, and was leaving the next day. He wanted to know if he and his wife could come over. We had been taught at the Academy that naval officers should not have social relationships with enlisted men. I was caught between my Christianity and my Navy culture. Christianity won, but my culture made it awkward. They came over. He was about twenty, his wife was eighteen or nineteen, and their baby only a few months old.

Socially, I did not know what to do. I think I started to talk about the weather. The wife interrupted and said, "Mr. Wilson, my husband tells me you talk about God."

I shifted subjects to God and started with Genesis. This time, the Holy Spirit interrupted me. "Wilson, shut up, and let these people get saved."

I said, "Would you like to be saved?"

They looked at each other, then both of them got on their knees. The wife put the baby on the floor. Bessie came in, scooped up the baby, and took it to the kitchen. They both received Christ. I have not seen them since.

I invited Lou Zamperini to speak to the officers at the Postgraduate School and checked it out with the Protestant chaplain, a lieutenant commander. He gave it the OK. I wanted to put an invitation to the event in every student's mailbox. The invitation had a drawing of two men on a life raft. To get approval for this, I took an invitation to Rear Admiral Moosbrugger's office and left it with his flag lieutenant.*

When all this was well underway, I came home, and Bessie told me that the Protestant chaplain wanted me urgently. I checked in with him. He said that the Chief of Staff to the Admiral wanted to see me. We went to his office together. The chaplain pretended that he did not know anything about the Zamperini visit. Before the war, Zamperini was voted Catholic Youth of the Year. The senior chaplain, a captain, was Roman Catholic, and the Chief of Staff, also a captain, was Roman Catholic. I remember the Captain's soliloquy almost word for word:

"Mr. Wilson, this is not the CYO [Catholic Youth Organization], the Epworth League [a Methodist youth group], or the Jewish

* The Navy version of an *aide de camp*

Community Center. It is the United States Navy Postgraduate School. We have two capable and competent chaplains who are able to prose-lyte anyone who wants to be proselyted without the help of Lieutenant Junior Grade Wilson or this guy Zamperini. Furthermore, if anyone invites anyone to speak at the United States Postgraduate School, it will be Admiral Moosbrugger, not Lieutenant Junior Grade Wilson. The Admiral regrets that he cannot attend, but he hopes you have a good attendance."

The attendance was not big, but two officers from the USNA class of '48 were there and afterward started attending the OCU Bible study. They were Reuben Prichard, a Cutlass pilot,* and Curley Olds. I noticed that many of Curley's comments in the study were on the unbelieving side, but at the time I made no comment.

I received an invitation from a Baptist Church in Watsonville (near Santa Cruz) to be the speaker at an evangelistic banquet. I replied that I could not do it because it was on my Bible study night. Their answer was, "Bring the whole group. They can all testify." I checked it out with the OCU Bible study, and they agreed to come along.

A few days before the banquet, I ran into Curley in the library. I asked him what he was going to say at the banquet.

He replied, "I'm going to surprise you all. I am going to stand up and tell everyone that I am not a Christian."

I said, "You are not going to surprise me. But why did you join the Officers' Christian Union? To sign their membership card, you had to say you were a Christian."

"I liked the Bible study, and I thought I would not be welcome unless I was a member of the OCU, so I signed it. Since I'm not a Christian anyway, I didn't think another little lie would make a dif-ference." He continued, "Wanda and I have been married six years,

* On the ground, the Cutlass looked like a praying mantis. It was a dangerous plane that did not last.

and we have no children. We have checked everything. You say you are a Christian, and you say you believe in prayer. You want me to become a Christian. Pray me up a son, and I will believe."

I planned on replying, "Curley, you have it all wrong. God doesn't make deals. He doesn't do you favors so you'll believe."

Instead, I heard myself say, "Yes, sir."

He said, "I mean it."

I said, "*I* mean it."

I had no other explanation than that God had given me faith. I went home and told Bessie that God had given me faith to trust Him for a son for Curley and Wanda. We prayed and thanked God. We knew the prayer was heard and answered.

A few weeks went by. At refreshments after the Bible study, John Bajus came up to me. He had been talking with Curley. "Curley just told me that Wanda is pregnant. He said, 'Don't tell Jim. He has known it longer that I have.'"

That same evening, Curley came to me. "I know this is answered prayer, and I told you that I would become a Christian, but I am not going to become one."

The son turned out to be a girl. Wanda's mother was in a cult called Unity, and her mother insisted on Wanda naming the baby "Unity." Wanda replied, "Mother, you will not understand, but if we name it anything, it will be 'Jim Wilson.'" That girl should be thankful she was named Meredith!

Fourteen years later, in the spring of 1968, I ran into Curley with his thirteen-year-old daughter in the plaza near Tecumseh at the Naval Academy. He was still not a believer.

"Curley," I told him, "you have been going to church. You know and I know that all kinds of people are church members, but they have not believed in their heart or repented of their sins. I know you were raised in a Christian home, but that does not mean you are a

Christian. 'A mouse born in a biscuit box is not a biscuit.' You have done many wonderful things, but God does not grade on a curve."

New year's weekend 1953–4 was the end of a weeklong OCU Conference for officers and their wives at Mount Hermon in California. InterVarsity staff were having a conference there at the same time. We had no speaker, so we borrowed their speaker for our meetings. On Sunday morning, the two groups had worship together. The speaker was a German theology student from Fuller Seminary. He had a heavy accent. His text was Philippians 4:6–7. I had memorized those verses three years before. Because I knew the text, because I thought I knew what he was going to say, and because of his accent, I was prepared to be bored.

"Do not be anxious about anything, but in every situation, by prayer and petition, with thanksgiving, present your requests to God. And the peace of God, which transcends all understanding, will guard your hearts and your minds in Christ Jesus" (Phil. 4:6–7).

After he read the text, the seminary student asked the congregation several questions, to be answered with raised hands.

- How many of you make your requests known to God? (All our hands went up.)
- How many have your requests answered? (All hands again.)
- How many of you thank God when He answers? (All hands.)

Then he asked his last question:

- How many of you do not thank God until He answers?

We were stunned. We did not want to raise our hands. The text says make your request *with thanksgiving*. We are to thank God *before* He answers. "Now this is the confidence that we have in Him, that if we ask anything according to His will, He hears us. And if we know that He hears us, whatever we ask, we know that we have the petitions that we have asked of Him" (1 John 5:14–15). If we trust God to hear us, we can thank Him before the answer comes. This is how He tells us to pray in Philippians 4. I was blessed.

The camp closed, and everyone packed up and headed for home. Since I had set up the conference, I stayed behind to pay the bills. The weekend had been solid with pounding rains. As I walked back up to my cabin, I saw Roy Grayson leaning over the engine of his '48 Studebaker. He was trying to dry off the little puddles of water that had formed around each of the six spark plugs of the straight-six engine. His car would not start.

We finally decided to push the car out of the trees and onto the mountain road. His wife Carolyn and their children were in the car. When we had pushed it a car's length up the road, Roy jumped in, turned the wheel, and took off down the mountain out of gear. As I watched the car rush out of sight down the mountain with the engine still silent, I was glad he was a fighter pilot. I was also glad I was not in his car!

My car, a '48 Nash, was parked under the trees on the other side of the road. The starter was under the clutch. I got in the car and stepped on the starter. The engine turned over once but would not start. I prayed and stepped on the starter again. Nothing. I prayed and tried again. Still nothing. I kept trying. Every time I stepped on the starter, I prayed.

Soon the battery was dead, and no sound came when I stepped on the starter.

Bessie and Douglas (six months old) were in the cabin waiting. We had to get back to Monterey, and everyone else had already gone. I had no one to help push the car onto the road like we had done with Roy's. I prayed, "God what are you trying to teach me?"

The answer came back, "What did you learn this morning?"

"Make your requests with thanksgiving." I asked God to start the car and thanked Him for starting it. I stepped on the starter. There was no sound.

I confessed. "God, I was just plugging the formula." This time, I asked God again and really thanked Him. I stepped on the starter, and the engine roared into life.

Bessie and Douglas got into the car, and we drove down the mountain. At the bottom, I saw Roy's car parked on the side of the road. Roy was walking up the road toward us. I said, "Roy, I will give you a push."

"It's not necessary," Roy said. "My car is running."

"Guess how I got *mine* started!" I said.

"I know. You thanked God. It took me thirty minutes to think of it, too."

CHAPTER 27

THE NAVAL SECURITY GROUP

To me, though I am the very least of all the saints, this grace was
given, to preach to the Gentiles the unsearchable riches of Christ.

(Eph. 3:8)

Before the last trip to the Far East in 1953, I had to be reevaluated
at the Balboa Naval Hospital because of my corrected vision. I had
always wanted to go Naval Air. However, by the time I was a midshipman 2/C, my eyesight was so bad that I could not read what was
written on the blackboard. That meant no flight school, which I had
planned on since the eighth grade. I was issued Navy glasses and had
to forego Naval Air. Even though I was an unrestricted line officer
(1100), meaning I could be assigned to any type of duty, it was with a
waiver to be reevaluated at the Naval Hospital after three years.

After my evaluation at Balboa, it was recommended that I switch
to special duty because of my experience and graduate school study,
so I requested to be transferred to Communications Special Duty
(1610). I had no idea what that was.

My new designator came through while I was at the Naval
Postgraduate School. My orders were for shore duty in Japan on the
staff of Commander Naval Forces Far East in Yokosuka, in the office of the Chief of Staff for Communications. I thought that was a
special duty appointment, but it wasn't. I had been in that position
for about a year when the commanding officer of the communications facility in Yokosuka found out that I was a 1610. He fired off
something to Washington telling them that a 1610 officer was filling

a line officer's billet. I got immediate orders to Kamiseya, Japan, and our little family moved to Yokohama. Then I found out what Special Duty was. It was working with top-secret security information.

I wasn't supposed to tell anyone what I did there. The Naval Security Group was tasked with intelligence gathering and with keeping intelligence from our adversaries. We spent our time listening to and decrypting Chinese communications, mostly Morse code. The Russians had strung a cable underwater to the Kamchatka Peninsula. The Navy sent a submarine to interrupt the cable and record all the messages; it would return periodically to pick up the recordings for us to decrypt. That is what I did for the next year.

Because Bessie was pregnant, she and Douglas were not allowed to travel with me to my new duty station in Japan. Bessie did not have any family with her. She was staying in a motel in Oakland. One night there was a peeping Tom at the motel. She was alone and scared. Dick Mack and his wife Dorothy took her in. Dick worked in the high-energy lab in Berkeley. He was one of the founding members of OCU and had been at the conference over the New Years' holiday. Dick and Dottie took care of Douglas when our son Evan was born in the Oakland Naval Hospital on October 8, 1954.

According to regulations, Bessie should have been allowed to come to Japan shortly after I arrived, but she was not given permission until December.

It was nine years after the end of World War II, and there were still no cars in Japan. When I was first there, five years after the war, all transportation was by bicycle-pulled rickshaws. By 1954, there were new charcoal-burning taxicabs, but no private cars. When I received orders to Yokosuka in June, I shipped our '48 Nash ahead of me. Because stealing gasoline was commonplace, all cars shipped had to have locked gas caps. I got the car fitted with a locking cap and put the keys on my key ring. Sometime later, while driving at night

Bessie with Douglas, 1954

Jim with Evan, 1955

in Japan, I found that I had been driving around with the gas cap key in the ignition.

My brother Leonard was also still in the Navy. Back in 1953, he had received orders to the operation room for COMNAFE in Yokosuka. When he checked in, a captain asked him what his major had been in college. Leonard told him it was political science. The captain said that he belonged on the Truce Team and sent him to Panmunjom. Off he went.

The UN's chief negotiator with the North Koreans was Major General William K. Harrison. General Harrison was a Christian. Three and half years earlier, during my first class year, I had heard that there was a Christian major general in fellowship at Cherrydale Baptist Church. I asked him to come to the Naval Academy to speak to the Christian midshipmen. He said he would be glad to speak and asked what the uniform was. I replied that I was not accustomed to prescribing uniforms for generals! That was the start of a good friendship that lasted until he died in the 1990s.

Since I knew General Harrison, I wrote to tell him that my brother was on his team at Panmunjom. When the general got my letter, he went straight to Leonard's tent (Leonard was only an ensign) and said, "Wilson, you did not tell me that your brother was a friend of mine!"

The truce was signed while I was still in Monterey. Leonard was the messenger who carried the signed truce to Tokyo. Then he was stationed back in Yokosuka. He and his family were still there when I arrived.

On Halloween, I dressed myself up in a kimono that had been specially made for me. I painted my face white and painted my eyebrows and all the lines in my face with charcoal. I went to Leonard's house, knocked on the door, and scared all his kids. When the kids from the base came trick-or-treating, I scared them out of the house.

The day after I arrived in Japan, I attended the weekly OCU Bible study. A year earlier, I had spent one day in Yokosuka before returning to the States. I had looked up two Christian officers, introduced them to each other, and held a Bible study with them. I encouraged them to continue it. This OCU study was the result of that first one.

The study met in the home of Lt. Cdr. Dewhurst, a Navy dentist. There were about a dozen officers and wives seated in a circle with their Bibles. Outside the circle, in a second row, there was a man sitting by himself. He was barrel-chested, big biceps, crew cut, and was flipping through the pages of a *Life* magazine while the rest of us studied the Scriptures. I had no idea who he was.

The next day, I went to the BOQ* for lunch. When I walked into the dining room, I saw him sitting alone at a table. He asked me to have lunch with him.

His name was Ray Clemons. He was waiting for orders for his next duty station. I sat down, and he turned to me and said, "I will tell you what's wrong with you Christians."

I did not think he could be talking about me, because I had just arrived. I thought I would find out what was wrong with the rest of the Christians. I said, "Tell me."

He was quick to respond. "You tell this poor pagan five impossible things: You tell him that all men are sinners. That is impossible! I do not believe that. You tell him that all sinners go to Hell. That is impossible! I don't believe that. You tell him that God became a man. That is impossible! You tell him that this God-man died on a cross to save sinners. That is impossible! Then you tell him that this dead man came back to life. That is impossible!

---

* The Bachelor Officers' Quarters, where the unmarried officers lived. I stayed there until Bessie and the boys arrived in Japan.

"You follow this up by saying, 'If you believe this you're saved; if you do not believe it, you're lost. Do you believe it?' The poor pagan says, 'I don't know.' And the Christian replies, 'Make up your mind!'"

There was something missing in Ray's recital. What he had recounted was the gospel, but without any kind of love in it. He had never heard the gospel given in love. I made up my mind to love Ray into the kingdom. All my time off duty was spent with him. We met daily at six a.m. In August, he passed from death to life while reading Isaiah 53.

Then I found out why Ray was waiting for orders. He was awaiting a general court martial for twenty-one counts against the federal government, including grand theft and black-market sales.

2 November 1954

Dear Bessie, Doug, and Evan,

Last night I didn't write because it was 1230 before I got home. When I got home from work, Larry Britton was in the room and soon Ray came down and we talked about the Word. We skipped supper and went to OCU. The singing was good. There were 15 there including two chaplains.

Ray learned in that afternoon that the General Court Martial will be Thursday. He is going to plead guilty to every charge. It has been 10 months since he was apprehended. Most of the time he wasn't working. He had told very few people that he was waiting for a general court martial and so it shocked everyone last night as he told his testimony from start to finish. He gave God all of the glory. He knows that he wouldn't be a Christian now if it weren't for the trouble he got into. Harold was over at Leonard's all evening.* I left OCU early and went over there. To have more time with Harold I

* My brothers were both in the Navy at this time. Harold was stationed on a transport ship that traveled back and forth across the Pacific. We saw each other when his ship was in Japan.

offered to drive him to his ship in Yokohama. Ray wanted to come along and he drove while we talked. Harold is witnessing and reading the Word.

Jim

Ray pled guilty. He was given a $10,000 fine and was "dismissed from the Naval Service for the good of the Naval Service."

When Bessie finally arrived in Japan, she told Ray that she could not understand why the Navy had not let her come five months earlier. Ray told her that he was the reason: if Bessie had been in Japan, I would never have lived in the BOQ, and he would not have become a Christian.[†]

During those same months, in the Chief of Staff's office I had occasion to meet a lieutenant junior grade who worked at the Communication Facility. We crossed paths frequently on communication business. He was very arrogant. His favorite word was "stupid." He used it to describe everyone, from the admiral on down. One day, he heard me say something complimentary about my immediate superior, a commander whom he had already determined was stupid. That made *me* stupid.

One evening, we were talking in the BOQ about naval communications. Although he was smart and knew his business, he did not have the experience or the education that I had. He had only been in the Navy for eighteen months; I had been in for nine years, plus I had two years' experience as the communications officer on a destroyer and one year of graduate school in command communication. My present job was troubleshooter in communications for Commander Naval Forces Far East. I wasn't showing off, but it did not take him

† Seventeen years later, I received a letter and a gift from Ray. That letter first led me to consider Idaho as a place for future ministry.

long to find out that I knew far more about communications than he did.

By midnight, I realized that I had gotten out of his "stupid" book. As I headed off to my room, I turned around and said to him, "Vic, the next time I talk to you it will be about God."

I let him think about that for two days, then I got my Bible and went to his room. He told me to come in. He was standing in front of the mirror, tying his necktie. It looked like he was preparing to go out.

I said, "Vic, I came to talk to you about God. Unless you have other plans, I will stay."

"I had other plans, but I just changed them. Sit down."

I took the only chair in the room. Vic went to his closet to get a book, sat on his bunk, and opened the book. About two thirds of the way down the page was a paragraph underlined in red. When he had that in front of him, he said, "Shoot. Prove to me there's a God."

"No, Vic, I didn't come to prove God; I came to declare Him."

"Unless you prove to me that there is a God, there is no basis for a discussion."

"Nevertheless, I am not going to prove Him. Suppose there is God, an omnipotent God," I continued, "He made billions of stars, billions of people, billions of buttercups, and billions of raindrops, and you stand up in front of Him and say, 'Show me, God, and then I'll believe.' He doesn't have to show you—you are one of two billion! I am His representative; I don't have to show you, and I'm not going to show you."

Vic closed his book. He said, "OK. Well, what are you going to talk about, then?"

"I thought I'd start with the subject of sin."

"*Sin*? There's no such thing as sin! Sin where?"

"Well, since you asked, it's the sin in Vic Jensen that I'm concerned about."

He laughed again—it was a hollow laugh this time—and said, "There's no sin in me!" But he knew that there was, and he knew that I knew there was.

I said to him, "Are you telling me that you have no conscience? Have you ever felt guilty and known that everyone else knew it?" I could see the guilt in his face as he reflected on his conscience, and he changed the subject.

"What are you going to use for your authority?"

I said, "Well, I brought my Bible; I thought I'd use that."

Again, Vic objected: "You can't use that for an authority!"

"Why not?"

"For two reasons: First, the Bible is not allowed in intercollegiate debate. Second, I will not accept it as an authority, and I don't believe it."

"You are wrong on both counts. 1) This is not intercollegiate debate. It's war, and the rules are different. 2) I don't care if you do not believe that it is an authority. Of course you don't believe it! You have never read it. You don't have a clue what it is." (For the Bible says that faith comes by hearing and hearing by the Word of God.)

I went on, "Suppose I had a broadsword in my hand, and I said, 'Jensen, I'm going to chop off your head,' and you laugh at me and say, 'Wilson, you can't chop off my head, because I don't believe that's a sword.' Then it's *my* turn to laugh. Whether you *believe* it is a sword has nothing to do with it. If I sheath the sword and say, 'Well, he doesn't believe it's a sword, so I guess I can't chop off his head,' that only proves that *I* don't believe it's a sword! 'The Word of God is quick and powerful and sharper than any two-edged sword, dividing asunder between the soul and spirit, joints and marrow, discerning the thoughts and intents of the heart.' Vic, I'm going to have your head."

I continued, "What do you think the Bible is? Fiction?"

* Hebrews 4:12

"Yeah, fiction."

"Like *Terry and the Pirates* and *Pogo*?"*

"Yeah."

"Do you read *Pogo*?"

"Oh, yeah, I love *Pogo*."

"*Terry and the Pirates*?"

"Yeah, I read fiction all the time."

"Then you won't mind if I read you a few chapters of fiction."

I opened my Bible and read him the first eight chapters of the book of Romans. Then I went to bed.

A few days later, Vic came to my room and said, "Let's have some more of the book." I read him the first five chapters of Acts.

He came down to my room again. This time I gave him a Bible so he could follow along as I read. I read the next thirteen chapter of Acts, the resurrection accounts in the four gospels, and 1 Corinthians 15.

The next week, Vic received orders to a ship in the Atlantic fleet. When he got on the plane, I gave him a copy of *Peace with God* by Billy Graham. I have not been in contact with him since. I do not know if he got reaped, but I know he was plowed and planted in good ground. I am confident that I will see him in Heaven.†

As soon as I arrived in Japan, I had begun planning a weeklong OCU conference to be held at the Far Eastern Gospel Crusade compound near Yokohama in the fall of 1954. It was the first of six such conferences we held over the next three years. Delbert Keuhl, a former Army chaplain, was the speaker. He had parachuted into Sicily with the 101st Airborne Division.

---

* Cartoon characters

† See my book *Taking Men Alive* for more on this terminology of evangelism.

When the fall conference was over, we planned a spring conference. I asked the missionaries in the area who was the best Bible
teacher they knew. The answers all came back the same: Bill Pape.
I found Bill and on a train ride asked if he would teach the OCU
spring conference on the lordship of Christ. He was not sure about
doing it because his studies had all been in the Old Testament.

After the fall conference, I heard of a Christian Air Force optom-
etrist in Tokyo named Jim Blocksom. I went to visit him. I noticed
he had an Abingdon New Testament Commentary on his bookshelf.
When he was out of the room, I leafed through the commentary.
Every page was unbelieving.

We held the 1955 OCU spring conference in Oiso, Japan. Bill
Pape did give the conference, speaking on the lordship of Christ
from seven chapters of Isaiah. Moody Press published these lectures
as *The Lordship of Jesus Christ*.‡ Bill later became the local representative for the OCU in the Far East.

Jim Blocksom attended the conference. There was a nineteen-
year-old girl there named Alexa. She was the daughter of the head of
the Naval Hospital in Yokosuka and was a new Christian. I decided
to talk with her about the gospel. She did not need it, but I knew that
Jim Blocksom was listening to our conversation. I spoke to Alexa,
but I was really talking to Jim.

Jim had to take a short break from the conference to go to Tokyo
for a business appointment. When he returned, he had been converted. He resigned from the Air Force and went to seminary. Jim and
his family were missionaries in Japan for many years. Later I visited
Jim in Tokyo. I looked at his Abingdon Commentary again. Jim had
written "Rubbish" across each page.

---

‡ The book is currently in print with Community Christian Ministries; find it at
ccmbooks.org or on Amazon.

One of my responsibilities in Yokosuka was the charge of classi-fied documents. Every six months, they had to be inventoried with two officers signing off on the inventory. Some of the publications were in Tokyo. I made the first Tokyo inventory trip was while Bessie was still in Oakland expecting Evan. Since I need a second officer as a witness, I grabbed Ensign Bob Scarborough, a Navy vehicle, and a Japanese driver, and we headed for Tokyo.

On the way there, we passed a Buddhist priest in full regalia blessing the land of a peasant farmer. I commented how awful it was for the priest to take money from this peasant for a blessing that would do no good. Bob was offended at my judgmental comment and blasted me for my prejudice against Buddhism. That did not make it easy for me to preach the gospel to him, so I didn't.

Six months later, we had to make the trip again. I was careful about my comments this time. At lunch we went to see Sensei (Irene Webster-Smith), the woman who had taken me to meet Bessie four years earlier. The house where I first met Sensei had been replaced by a building several stories high, a student center. Sensei had built it by faith. She showed us the steel rods going up from the roof, ready for the next story. She was trusting God for more floors.*

This amazed Bob. He was so impressed with Miss Webster-Smith that he asked me when the Yokosuka Bible study was. I told him that it met that evening and that a Christian named Lou Long who lived in Bob's BOQ could take him to it. He came that night.

As soon as we got back to Yokosuka, Bob went to Lou's room and said, "Don't just lie there, let's study our lesson." A few weeks later, he received Christ.

When I got word that Bessie could be coming to Japan six weeks after Evan was born, I started looking for a Japanese house to rent,

---

* Many years later, when Sensei visited us in Annapolis, she told Bessie and me that she had prayed for our four children every day.

since it would be a while before we could get into the housing on base. I looked at many places, but nothing was right. One day, Ray Clemons and I found a house in Kamakura that seemed perfect. The price was right. It was so right that I found myself planning where each piece of furniture would go.

I stopped. "Ray, wait a minute—we haven't asked God if this is the right place."

"What for?" Ray asked me. "You like it, and you can afford it."

I replied "I know, but I am going to ask God that the owner would not rent it to me if it is not the right place."

We got on our knees on the tatami† and prayed for the landlord to turn us down if it was not the right place.

Ray said, "That's a stupid prayer, though. The landlord's not going to turn down American money!"

We went next door to the owner's house to sign the lease. The owner asked me to bring a can of coffee from the Navy base when I paid the rent.

I said, "No."

"Sugar."

"No."

"Cigarettes."

"No."

He wanted me to bring these things from the base each month so that he could sell them on the black market. When I refused, he refused to lease the house to me. I thanked God, but I was bummed because Bessie, Doug, and Evan were arriving the following week.

I decided I was not going to waste any more time looking for a house. God would have to provide the place. I was going to "seek first the kingdom."

† The mat floor

It was Saturday night, and Delbert Keuhl was speaking at the Serviceman's Center. I invited my brother Leonard and his wife Glenda.

The place was crowded. I sat down next to Dick Courtney, and he asked if I had found a house yet. I replied in the negative and added that I had quit looking. Dick told me that the TEAM (The Evangelical Alliance Mission) missionary house, right there in Yokosuka, was going to be empty.

I replied that I would not check on it. Then I prayed that if that were the house for us, God would have the director of TEAM ask me to live in it. Delbert Keuhl was the director.

After the meeting, Delbert asked me if I was on my way back to the States. Someone else answered him. "You must be thinking of Leonard. He is returning. Jim just arrived, and his wife is coming over next week."

Delbert was surprised. "Jim, do you have a house?"

"No."

"We would like you to live in the TEAM house, but it will not be available for two weeks."

When I got back to the BOQ, there was a message from Bessie. She was deeply disappointed—the Navy would not let her come for two more weeks.

Bessie still arrived a few days before the house was ready; we stayed in the Far Eastern Gospel Crusade Mission until it was ready. I had bought a giant stuffed panda bear for Douglas, who was eighteen months old. This gift was not the best, because the little missionary kids could not understand why Douglas got a panda bear, and they didn't.

The TEAM house in Yokosuka was a Quonset hut on top of Chuo hill. We lived there until we got base housing a few months later.

We celebrated Christmas 1954 in the Quonset hut. I got Bessie a pair of cufflinks for Christmas. On the cufflinks was a painted scene

A Quonset hut is a lightweight prefabricated structure of corrugated galvanized steel with a semicircular cross section. (U.S. Navy photo)

A torii is a symbolic gateway between the mundane and the sacred at the entrance of a Shinto shrine.

of Mt. Fuji with a Torii gate—an entrance to a Shinto shrine—in the foreground. When Bessie saw the Torii, she would not accept the gift. I threw the cufflinks over the back fence.

The Korean War had been over for over a year. COMNAVFE* got orders from the Bureau of Naval Personnel to reduce the enlisted staff of the communication facility by fifty percent. The chief of staff of communications called the commander of the facility into his office and informed him of the orders. The commander replied that it could not be done. That was passed back to BuPers. BuPers said to do it anyway. The response was again that it could not be done. This went back and forth for some time.

One day, I went to the communication facility and tracked the messages as they went from desk to desk. I found out that everything was being done twice. I made a schematic diagram of where every message went and why; then I made another diagram showing how every message could have the same actions with half the desks.

The chief of staff was a captain, and so was the commander of the facility. I was only a lieutenant junior grade. I was unwilling to show my research to the captains directly, so I took my charts to a lieutenant. They made sense to him.

I said, "Let's take them to Commander Bill." We did.

He was sold. "Let's take them to the chief of staff."

We did, all three of us. The chief was convinced. He called the commander of the facility and showed him the charts. The commander could see the reality of the reduction and backed down. The chief of staff sent a message to BuPers saying that he would comply with their orders.

Then came the awful part. "Mr. Wilson, this was your idea," the chief said. "You implement it." It was an impossible situation. As a

---

* Commander Naval Forces, Far East

lieutenant junior grade, I could not tell a lieutenant commander what to do. He wouldn't do it!

Shortly after this, in the winter of 1955, I received orders to Kamiseya. We moved to a Western-style house in Yokohama until quarters were available in Area X, the military housing. While there, Bessie and I decided to take over the teenage group at the Army chapel. The high-school kids were the children of colonels, Navy captains, chief petty officers, and master sergeants.

There were twin boys from the Decker family in the youth group. The Deckers were a Roman Catholic family. The boys had received Christ and were growing in the Lord. Because they were Catholic, they could not take communion unless they went to confession. I asked them what they confessed to the priest. They told me they had nothing to confess, because they had already confessed their sins directly to God.

"What do you tell the priest?"

"We tell him what he wants to hear."

"What is that?"

"We confess that we went to your Bible study."

Another of the kids in the youth group was a junior in high school named Tom Hemingway. His father was a mustang Marine captain. This boy was a football player and had been a Christian for two weeks when I met him. When we held an evangelistic banquet, I asked Tom to give his testimony.†

One evening we had Tom Hemingway over to our house so I could help him with his math homework. During the evening, Bessie

---

† That was the beginning of a dynamic testimony. Tom had three tours in Viet Nam—one with the British Marines, one with a Vietnamese regiment, and one with an American Marine regiment. Later he was the director at OCF's Spring Canyon Lodge and a speaker for the Promise Keepers. There's a talk by Tom on YouTube called "Hope" and an article about him by John Knubel at ocfusa.org. I recommend you check out both of those.

served us watermelon. Tom ate his watermelon down to the dark green part of the rind.

"Tom, you do not have to do that. We have more watermelon."

He said that he would eat more watermelon, but he would eat that down to the dark green, too.

Tom made it clear that he would never, ever wear a necktie and would not join the Marines. In the fall of '56, Tom received a football scholarship to the Citadel, the military college of South Carolina. He wore neckties and served as a Marine for the next twenty-one years.*

The work at Kamiseya was done in an underground tunnel. It was a twenty-four-hour-a-day operation. Hundreds of sailors worked there. When the watch changed, officers were relieved before enlisted men, so the officers left the tunnel while the incoming watch of sailors was entering it. Kamiseya was a saluting base, which meant we each returned the salutes of hundreds of sailors on our way out at the end of every watch.

The kids in the high-school group called us "Jim and Bessie." One of the girls was dating a sailor. He was about six five. In the youth group, he knew me as "Jim." One day when I was returning salutes with another officer, this tall sailor waved at me and said, "Hi, Jim!" My fellow officer looked at me with disdain. "Did he just call you Jim?" I had a private talk with the sailor later.

During the 0400 to 0800 watch in the morning, all work would suddenly die. I would go out the end of the tunnel to get some fresh air in the gravel yard. I'd get a broomstick, throw up a rock, and swing

* When I became the Academy staff member for the Officers' Christian Union in 1956, the Citadel was one of the academies I covered. I worked with Tom his five years there. When he was at Quantico, I had him and his bride, Sarah, come to Annapolis to minister to junior high kids. We stayed in close communication until he died. His son Matt won the silver medal in the high jump in the 2004 Athens Olympics.

as it came down. I can hit a ball, but it never occurred to me to go out for baseball or softball, because I can't run. I could not make the bases or chase a ball in the outfield fast enough to catch it. I followed the World Series; I was a Brooklyn fan in the National League and a Yankees fan in the American League.

When I was at the Naval Academy my senior year, it was dead week[†]. Finals were already over, and there was nothing to do until graduation, so my classmates decided to play a pickup game of softball. When I came up to bat, I did not expect to be able to hit the ball. My classmates didn't expect it, either.

A slow pitch came, and I hit a very long run. If there had been a fence, it would have been a home run. As it was, I only got to third base. One classmate told me that he could have circled the bases in the time it took me to get to third. Batting the gravel in the Kamiseya tunnel was great fun because I could hit ninety out of every hundred, and it didn't matter that I couldn't run.

One of the ensigns at Kamiseya was a recent graduate of Harvard. His name was Bob Sobel. We became good friends, and I talked with him very much about the gospel. One day, he told me that he was Jewish. He wanted to scare me off, and saying he was Jewish had worked with other Christians. When I did not back off, it took him a while to figure out why. Then he realized that in my view a Jew was just another type of person who needed the gospel.

One day we were working together and talking. Suddenly he dropped all the papers on the floor. He was physically shaking. He said, "You got me all shook up, you #$^&*!" and ran out of the room.[‡]

[†] The week between the end of classes and June week.

[‡] In 1957, Bob was in graduate school at Harvard studying architecture when John Stott had a mission there. I was in Boston and took him to the mission one night. The talks John Stott was giving later became the book *Basic Christianity*. Unfortunately, Bob did not respond to the gospel.

Most of the married officers at Kamiseya took their lunch to work. I did not, because I wanted to witness to the bachelor officers who ate lunch at the club. For dessert one day, I ordered a hot fudge sundae. While I was eating it, one of the officers said, "Jim, we do not think you should eat that sundae."

I asked, "Why do you think so?"

"We've been watching you a long time and have come to the conclusion that, in your book, if it's pleasant, it's sin. You are enjoying that sundae, and we don't want you in sin."

I smiled and quoted 1 Timothy 6:17: "'Command those who are rich in this present world not to be arrogant nor to put their hope in wealth, which is so uncertain, but to put their hope in God, who richly provides us with everything for our enjoyment.' He gives us richly all things to enjoy if they are received with thanksgiving. I thanked Him for this sundae, and I am enjoying it."

CHAPTER 28

COMMANDER CARRIER DIVISION 5

And with great power the apostles were giving their testimony to
the resurrection of the Lord Jesus, and great grace was upon them
all. (Acts 4:33)

In November 1955, I was informed that I would be sent as officer in charge of a twenty-man detachment on temporary duty to the staff of Commander Carrier Division 5 operating in the East China Sea. I did not want to go, because it would mean another six months away from my family.* The new duty also meant leaving the good witness we were having in Yokohama. So I prayed that my orders would be cancelled.

About the same time, I came across the story of the woman at the well in John 4. Two verses hit me hard: "Don't you have a saying, 'It's still four months until harvest'? I tell you, open your eyes and look at the fields! *They are ripe for harvest.* Even now the one who reaps draws a wage and harvests a crop for eternal life, so that the sower and the reaper may be glad together" (John 4:35–36).

Jesus speaks of the harvest being ripe right now. He sent the disciples to reap, to bear fruit for eternal life. That text was true then.

---

* Before Bessie and I were engaged, I was at sea. When we were engaged, I was in San Diego, and she was in Japan. After we were married, I was at sea, and she was in Yokohama. We came back to the States on two different ships. When Douglas was born, Bessie was in San Diego, and I was in the Sea of Japan. When Evan was born, Bessie was in Oakland, and I was in Japan. We had been together in Japan as a family for about a year when I got orders to Carrier Division 5.

Was it still true now? If so, there is a ripe harvest in any given society right now.

Matthew 9:37 also came to mind: "Then he said to his disciples, 'The harvest is plentiful but the workers are few.'" If this is true now, the harvest is not only ripe—it is great, and there are few harvesters. This means that more people want into the kingdom than there are Christians who want them in.

As I meditated on these things, my prayer gradually changed from wanting to stay in Japan to wanting to go to the 2,500 men and 250 officers on that aircraft carrier as soon as possible. I could be going to a large and ripe harvest. As I prayed, I began to imagine what it would be like if half of those officers were ripe for harvest. I would not have to plow or plant; that had already been done by their grandmothers. All I would have to do is to say, "Get on your knees," or, "Repent," or, "Receive Christ." What a harvest that would be!

Then I imagined that during my six months at sea I was able to witness to half of the officers. And six months later in my imagination I left the ship with no converts. How come? I witnessed to the wrong half. I did not witness to the ripe half. The thought scared me. I knew I was perfectly capable of witnessing to the wrong half. Suppose there were only ten who were ripe for harvest. It would be very easy to witness to the wrong ten out of two hundred and fifty. I was not willing for that to happen—but I had no idea how to recognize a ripe harvest.

I prayed for wisdom. God gave it to me through a missionary who was teaching from Acts 8–10.* Here it is in a nutshell. God led Philip to the Ethiopian and the Ethiopian to Philip. God led Ananias to Saul of Tarsus and Saul of Tarsus to Ananias. God led Cornelius to Peter and Peter to Cornelius. In each case, the Christians were

* See *Taking Men Alive* for more on this.

reluctant and would not have gone to the very ready unbeliever if they had been following their own witnessing schedules.

On November 18, 1955, I reported for duty on the staff of Commander Carrier Division 5 riding the USS Hancock in Yokosuka, Japan.[†] I looked up Ross Olson, USNA '55, the only Christian I knew on board, and told him what I had just learned. We decided to meet daily to pray that God would lead the ripe harvest to us because we weren't trustworthy enough to be led to the harvest. We met daily for several weeks and watched the harvest come in.

The ship got underway on Friday to go through the Inland Sea to Iwakuni, a Marine air station near the west end. We arrived on Saturday. I was the officer in charge of a team comprised of myself, a lieutenant junior grade, an ensign, a chief, and about twenty enlisted men. They were all radiomen, but special—CTS (communication technicians). They could listen and type in Russian or Chinese. From the East China Sea, we listened to Chinese radar stations along the coast. We had a direction finder so we knew which station we were hearing. We had consistent weather reports from them, all in code. They changed the code monthly. The code was simple substitution, so we always had it broken shortly after the change.

We tracked everything they tracked. I made a map of the coast of China with a clear plastic cover, and with a marker on the plastic I tracked everything their radar was picking up in the air. Once we saw objects moving directly east out of China headed across the Pacific between 30 and 35 degrees north. It took us a while, but we figured

† Two days after embarking on the Hancock, we pulled into Iwakumi. I called Bessie. She said, "I think I am pregnant." I was away from her most of the next six months. During this time, I wrote to Bessie every day. I have all the letters written from the Shangri-La, but cannot find my letters written from the Hancock and the Kearsarge. This time will have to rely on my memory.

out that they were U.S. weather balloons which had been launched in the United States east across the Atlantic.

We also tracked radio broadcasts of airplanes flying into Hong Kong. Most of this activity was benign. One time, however, I was tracking a plane flying from the East China Sea when I realized that it was one of our carrier planes—and it was flying over China. I raced up to the bridge and showed it to the admiral. He asked if I was sure. I told him I was dead sure. He told me to go to CIC and tell them to recall all planes.

"Admiral, they won't believe me."

"Tell them anyhow," he ordered.

I did it. The commander said he knew where all of his planes were. He did not believe that one of the carriers' aircraft was over China, but they did recall all the planes.

The carriers had been conducting air operations all day and figured their position by ded reckoning.* They had not gotten a navigational fix; they were two hundred miles closer to China than they thought they were. The Chinese knew where our planes were better than we did, and they inadvertently told us.

Bob Sobel had come aboard with me and wanted to go bicycling in the Japanese countryside on Sunday. I did not want to go. I was afraid that if I left the ship, I would miss the ripe harvest there, whoever it was. Ross and I had been praying for two days and were expecting an answer. I did not tell Bob that since he was not a Christian. I agreed to go, then prayed that the bicycling would be cancelled.

On Sunday morning, I went topside. It was raining very hard. I called Bob. He said, "We can't go."

I hung up the phone and praised God, then went down to the wardroom for breakfast. Almost everyone was sleeping in, since it

* *Ded* is short for *deduced*.

was Sunday. I walked into the wardroom alongside Joe Howard, the only USNA classmate I had on the ship. He was the assistant landing signal officer. We had been in the same 5″/38 gun mount on the USS Wisconsin together our youngster cruise; he was first loader on the starboard gun, and I was first loader on the port gun. On our first class cruise, we were on the USS Shea together.

We had breakfast together and talked. After breakfast, Joe went back to his room. I saw him at the chapel service later that morning. He had received Christ in his room. He joined our daily prayer group and evening Bible study.

In the study, Joe said, "Jim, I will live the life, but I will not tell anyone about it." He was too shy to tell the gospel and have it be known all over the ship that he was a Christian.

A few days later, Joe told me that he had seen a New Testament by the bunk of one of the AD[†] pilots. I asked him if he had talked with the pilot about the gospel.

Joe said, "I told you I would not talk to anyone."

"You won't talk to him, and I don't know him, so let's pray that God will lead him to us."

The next day, the executive officer decided to have the officers sit by their exact rank at the dinner table. Since Joe and I were classmates, we were seated next to each other. During lunch, Joe said that he had a problem with a passage in Luke. I told him that we could look at it after the evening meal. We were engaged in a two-man Bible study when the lieutenant junior grade in question walked into the room and asked what we were doing. Joe told the pilot that we were studying the Bible. In fifteen minutes, he was in the kingdom.

† The AD Skyraider, later known as the Douglas A-1 Skyraider, was an American propeller-driven attack aircraft. Although it was a single-engine plane, it could carry a heavier bomb than the four-engine B-17s of WWII.

When our Bible study attended an event conducted by the chaplain, I noticed another lieutenant junior grade with a Bible in one hand and a *Halley's Bible Handbook* in the other. I remember thinking, "How did we miss him?" After the event was over, I told him about our Bible study, and he joined it right away.

We were studying John 3. This fellow came out very strongly with, "You must be born again!" I was sure that we had stumbled across a solid Christian. I was thinking this when the Holy Spirit interrupted my thoughts. "What do you mean judging this man as a Christian? You have no idea whether he is one or isn't one."

I was convicted of this judgment. After the study, I asked him about assurance of salvation.

He said, "Salvation? What's that?" He had no idea what I was talking about.

I explained the gospel to him. It was the first time he had ever heard it. He received Christ. After the study was over, I said, "I have two questions to ask you. One, what do you mean walking around with a Bible in one hand and a *Halley's Bible Handbook* in the other hand?"

"I have been searching!" That made sense to me.

"Two, why were you so strong about, 'You must be born again?'"

"Oh," he said, "That's what the Bible said."

I had assumed he was a Christian—but he was just a ripe harvest.

The Bible study met in my room every night when the ship was at sea. Then I heard that I was going to get a roommate. I told this to the prayer meeting in the afternoon. We knew that a roommate might take a dim view of a Bible study being held in his room every night, so we prayed for a ripe-harvest roommate.

One afternoon when I came down from work, my new roommate was standing in the doorway. All I could see was one big wedge of muscle. He had his shirt off, which gave me a good view of his eighteen-inch biceps. My neck was only fifteen and a half inches. His name was Alex Aronis, and he had been runner up for Mr. California before he went to the Academy.

I looked at him and said silently, "Lord, you sent the wrong man." I knew I had to tell him about the Bible study, but I was scared. "He's going to pick me up and wipe the room with me," I thought. I told him about the study. I was nervous, so I just kept talking; I told Alex why we held the study, I told him my conversion, I told him my whole history, I told him the gospel.

When I finished, Alex said, "Do you know what I said when I came into this room today? I said, 'At last, a Bible.'"

Alex read the Gospel of Matthew through that night and the Gospel of John the next night. On Christmas Eve 1955, Joe asked him, "Alex, why don't you become a Christian?"

"Why should I?"

Joe told him.

"OK, Joe, what do I have to do?"

"I'll turn you over to Jim."

Alex Aronis received Christ. When we arrived in Yokosuka, Alex went to every other ship he had classmates on and led half a dozen of them to Christ.

On New Year's Eve, I came back on board from visiting Bessie, Douglas, and Evan at home in Yokohama. Alex was waiting to take me over to the USS Boxer, another aircraft carrier where he had a classmate. It was about midnight, and the sailors were coming back on board by the hundred. Alex's classmate was officer of the deck on the after gangway returning salutes to sailors as they came aboard. Alex and I told him the gospel while he was returning salutes. He said that he was ready to receive Christ. He stopped returning salutes as he bowed his head and called upon the Lord. The sailors had to wait for him to finish so he could return their salutes and give them permission to come aboard.

A few months later, the carrier came in to Manila Bay in the Philippines. While we was there, I met Russell and Dorothea Glazier from the Overseas Missionary Fellowship (formerly China Inland Mission). Mr. Glazier graciously invited me to speak Sunday evening at a Chinese youth group that he was ministering to.

On Sunday morning, Alex Aronis and I went to Grace Church because we heard that Joe Carroll was preaching there. When we arrived, the church was packed. We could not find seats together. Walking down the aisle, I saw one seat on the left next to Mr. and Mrs. Glazier. I told Alex he could keep looking; I would sit with the Glaziers.

Joe preached from Isaiah. During the sermon, I was greatly convicted of sin. When Joe gave the invitation, I had an argument with God. I did not want to walk down the aisle, for two reasons: 1) Mr. Glazier would see his speaker for that evening going down front to confess his sins. 2) Alex would see the person who had led him to Christ responding to the invitation. God was telling me to go, but my pride would not let me.

Then Mr. Glazier said, "Excuse us, Jim." They were responding to Joe's invitation.

"I'll lead the way," I replied.

When we got to the altar, Alex was already there!

Wednesday February 22nd

Dear Jim,

No mail for days—The news said B. Graham was speaking to 3000 Japanese pastors today.

Thursday 23rd—no letter as yet.... I've just come back from a drive with the children .... 5 years ago today you proposed—remember?

We had no responsibilities then but we have quickly accumulated some. 6 days & then March—how I long to see you again.

Your wife,
Bessie

During the months I was with CARDIV 5, I was on three different aircraft carriers—the *Hancock*, the *Kearsarge*, and the *Shangri-La*. Before I came aboard, I realized that I was going to be locked up in the same room with the sailors on my team for the next six months. I did not know who they would be. Someone else was handpicking them. I looked up the chief petty officer. I think his name was Jenkins. "Chief," I said, "I have been in the Navy for nine years and have heard four-letter words in every part of every sentence every day. I want you to let the men know that there will be no four-letter words in that room in the next six months." I never heard a word during those months.

I was on the *Hancock* (CV-19) from Thanksgiving to Easter. Then the flag moved to the *Kearsarge* (CVA-33) and finally to the *Shangri-La* (CV-38).

I came aboard the *Shangri-La* in early April 1956 via a bos'n's chair on a zip line in the East China Sea. It was right before lunch, so I went immediately to the wardroom. All the officers remained standing behind their chairs until the executive officer came in and sat down. The officers were still standing when I entered. I spotted a vacant chair and stood behind it. A lieutenant to my right turned to me and said, "That seat's saved." I stepped to my left and took that chair.

After we were seated, an ensign named Doten came in and took the saved chair. He turned to me and started to gripe about the communications officer, his boss. He told me in detail what a poor leader the communications officer was.

I began to ask him questions about his own relationships with the radiomen underneath him. His answers were awful. I said, "You're going to be the same type of leader your boss is."

Ensign Doten said, "I guess you're right. What's the solution?"

"Do you really want to know?"

"Yes!"

"Jesus Christ."

"Will you tell me about Him? I've always wanted to know Jesus. My parents are atheists and would not let me go to Sunday school."

I told him the good news over the next several weeks. When it came time for me to leave the ship, he was still not saved. I was leaving, and he knew he would not see me again. He came to me very concerned about what he would do without me.

"What do I do, what do I do?" he asked me.

"Go to Hell," I replied.

He received the Lord.

The months on Carrier Division 5 staff were decisive months for me in three major areas of my life: my wife, effective evangelism, and considering my future in evangelism.

Concerning Bessie: I had been on the opposite side of the Pacific during our engagement. I was on the opposite side of the Pacific when Douglas was born, and I was on the opposite side of the Pacific when Evan was born. Now I was at sea for the first six months of Bessie's third pregnancy.

In February, while on the *Kearsarge*, I had a dream. In the dream, two things happened. I dreamed that I lost Bessie, and I cried. Both of those shook me up. I haven't cried for real since eighth grade.

I had to consider my relationship to Bessie. I sent her money every payday. I prayed for her every day. I wrote to her every day. That dream of losing her caused me to look up Ephesians 5 to see if I was meeting my responsibility as a husband. I read, "Husbands, love your wives as Christ loved the church and gave Himself up for her" (Eph. 5:25). I thought, "That's easy; I am willing to give my life for my country. I can give it for my wife," and closed the Bible.

When I heard myself think, "That's easy," it stopped me. Was it *easy* for Christ to die for the Church? I thought I had better study about Christ dying for the Church before I said it was easy.

I made the study. It was life-changing.

Here are the results of my study: "And he was transfigured before them, and his face shone like the sun, and his clothes became white as light" (Matt. 17:2). Jesus was too glorious to look at.

> Just as there were many who were appalled at him—his appearance was so disfigured beyond that of any human being and his form marred beyond human likeness . . . . For he grew up before him like a young plant, and like a root out of dry ground; he had no form or majesty that we should look at him, and no beauty that we should desire him. He was despised and rejected by men; a man of sorrows, and acquainted with grief; and as one from whom men hide their faces he was despised, and we esteemed him not. (Isa. 52:14, 53:2–3)

His face was disfigured beyond that of any man, marred beyond human likeness. His face was hideous, and His body did not look human. No artist has ever painted a picture of the crucifixion this awful.

How did the brightness of the Transfiguration turn into an appalling sight? Isaiah 53:3–6 tells us. Every lie, rape, and murder past, present, and future, was nailed to the cross in the person of Jesus. When Jesus was sinless, He looked like it. When Jesus carried every sin in history, He looked like it. Not only did He carry every sin; He became sin itself. "For He made Him who knew no sin to be sin for us, that we might become the righteousness of God in Him" (2 Cor. 5:21, NKJV).

When Jesus died for the Church, He carried her sins. I knew that if I died, I would go to Heaven. That would be no sacrifice. Was I willing to die for Bessie's sins? That can't be done. But I am told to love her as Christ loved the Church. And I did not love her that much.

I wrote to Bessie on February 12 telling her that she was going to be loved like she had never been loved before. After I wrote the letter, I still did not love her as much as Christ loved the Church. But now I knew that I did not.

I do not have my letter, but I do have her answer.

February 24

My dearest,

Last night your wonderful letter of the 12th came, tonight I got 13th, 14th, 15th, 17th, and 18th all in a lot, and it is wonderful. I wish they could be spaced, but it can't be helped and so I rejoice. I will say the "love letter" was worth all the others you've written put together (not because they are unimportant but because it brought us together in a wonderful way). I have been yearning for you so much that to hear you love me as He loved us makes me marvel at His grace. I pray that He will keep you from seeing all the horrible things I see [in myself], and if He allows you to see them it will be so you can sanctify it by your prayers and exhortation. Keep loving me, Jim, like this, it puts a real glow in my life. I slept with your letter under my pillow just like any teenager. Maybe because I felt our love was becoming stodgy!

Monday, March 5, 8:15 p.m.

My dearest . . . .

I spoke at the Guild today on Mary and Martha in Luke 10 and as usual preached myself under conviction. I hope some of it brushed off on a few others . . . .

How I long for you and the days go by so very slowly. I wish I knew when I'd see you again. I'll try to be patient though.

All our love,
Bessie, Douglas, Evan, and ?

March 12/56

My dearest,

Yours of Mar. 1, 2, 3, 5, 6, 7 came today & rejoiced my heart. You have been wonderful about writing and I do appreciate it . . . .

Wed. I go to Yokohama for a prenatal check. I plan to buy lamps at the Oriental arcade D.V. The OCU will meet again at our place after this week . . . .

I had a letter from Mrs. Mother today. She has had the flu.

I feel a need for some meditation and prayer tonight. *It is so easy to teach others and become a castaway yourself.* I get some reading in but it is not very devotional in nature. I do need your prayers. I would love to have you pray over me for me tonight.

Funni* is bringing Evan up to bed now—Douglas is asleep already.

I'll close now with all my heart's love.

How I shall thrill at the sound of your voice on the 'phone! May it be before the end of April.

All my love
Bessie & boys

* The family's Japanese maid at the time

March 18th Sunday

My dearest,

Yesterday I was too tired to write and literally fell into bed as soon as I could . . . . Today has been full too but I knew you'd rejoice over the news of Mr. Pape speaking tonight at the Beach chapel . . . I got to the 7.30 mtg & there was a good attendance & Mr. Pape was excellent on the houses on 1. rock 2. sand "the world storm" etc . . . .

In speaking of your return, it seems too good to be true and until I can hug you tight I'll not believe it myself. I need you so, it is hard to be patient. The boys need you too, especially Douglas. He is talking more. Tonight I said for him to come to bed & he said to take Evan, so I said that Evan had had a nap already & he said he had [one] "yesterday." . . .

Now for bed—wish you were here dearest.

Goodnight
Bessie

3 April 1956
At Sea

Dearest Bessie,

It is late at night and I just finished work. I should go to bed but I want to wish you a very merry and happy anniversary. You will be at the conference on our anniversary so won't get this.

I want to tell you that you are more precious to me now than you were at our wedding and honeymoon and during the last four wonderful years. It seems so unreal that you belong to me. I could shower affection upon you Dearest Bessie.

I think of all of the places we have lived and how happy we have been. We have been and are wonderfully happy in each other and in the Lord.

Truly it has been "Days of Heaven upon the Earth."

I love you,

Jim

4 April 1956
At Sea
USS Shangri-La CVA-38

My Dearest,

Tomorrow we arrive in Hong Kong. The days have been working days with not much time for witnessing.

Yesterday I received a letter from Ross Olson. They seem to have an OCU Bible Study there in Coronado. Ross led another officer to the Lord. After I answer it, I will send it off to you.

Bessie, I've realized more every day how clumsy I have been in loving you. I've been like a blacksmith playing a Stradivarius with a hacksaw. I am praying that the Lord will teach me how to love you. You are such a wonderful creature. I want to bring out of you all the wonderful music that is in you. You must pray for me.

All of my love,

Jim

I miss the boys very much.

3 April 1956
at Sea

U.S.S. SHANGRI-LA CVA-38

Dearest Bessie,

It is late at night and I just finished work. I should go to bed but I want to wish you a very merry and happy anniversary. You will be at the conference on our anniversary so won't get this.

I want to tell you that you are more precious to me now than you were at our wedding and honeymoon and during the last four wonderful years. It seems so unreal that you belong to me. I could shower affection upon you. I love you Dearest Bessie.

I think of all of the places we have lived and how happy we have been. We have been and are wonderfully happy in each other and in the Lord.

Truly it has been days of Heaven upon the Earth. I love you
Jim.

5 April 1956
Hong Kong
USS Shangri-la CVA-38

My precious family,

I received three letters when I arrived back at the ship from you, also one from Joe Howard and one from General Harrison. The pictures were in one of the letters and they were so good. You are beautiful, Bessie. The pictures of you are so good. You look wonderful in your maternity outfit. I guess I just like you pregnant. I guess I just like you better every day regardless how you are.

It is almost midnight and I must get to bed. I will tell you about things later.

6 April

Yesterday I went shopping but my tastes seem to run too high. From there I went to the Peninsula Hotel to telephone you for our anniversary but you had already gone to the conference. I put in a reservation to call you Monday afternoon before I go to the OCU meeting. I telegraphed Jim Blocksom to get you an orchid for tomorrow for our wedding anniversary. I hope he got it in time. He should have it by now. I love you very much . . . .

Today I have spent the day in counseling the men individually. I only got to three today. I also conducted the noon devotion because the Chaplain was ashore. There is such a need for a Bible study on the ship.

I'm remembering the speakers for the conference.

I sure liked the pictures. One more month and I will see you and the boys as really are.

There is much to be done on the ship before then.

I love you dearly.

In His love,
Jim

Tuesday the 17th [of April]

My dearest . . . .

Our new *His* arrived and I was touched in heart by 2 articles on the lives of the 5 who gave all for Christ in Ecuador. You'll be blessed by them too. It reminds me how 3 Freds gave their lives in the Amazon valley & today Rosemary & Angus Cunningham are laboring among those same Indians. My heart was searched as I wondered if I could surrender you as those women did their men—I could more readily go myself. People might label it fantastic, but men give their lives for their country in daring ways—why not for their Lord? I feel so unworthy to be called His.

Yours ever
Bessie & boys

As for evangelism, those six months on the three carriers were the most effective evangelistic times of my life. It is where I practiced Acts 26:18 and the principles of war.[*]

Concerning my future in evangelism, my visions were:

- Establishing Christian military ministries in Japan, Korea, and Taiwan. (China was closed for another thirty years.) I thought I should be the one to do it. I wrote Bessie to tell her I was going to resign my commission to become a missionary to the militaries of those three nations.
- I had a great concern for establishing a full-time evangelist position to serve all of the U.S. military academies. I thought that

* See my book *Principles of War*.

he should be 1) an academy graduate, 2) an evangelist, and 3) out of the service. I was convinced that I knew the person to fill this position: Kermit Johnson, West Point '51, an evangelist to the military in Korea, and now a civilian. I wrote to Kermit and to several of our mutual friends about my guidance for him.

9 April 1956
Hong Kong
USS Shangri-la CVA-38

My Dearest,

Yesterday I had a wonderful time, most of it spent with Lutheran missionaries, but oh such a concern for souls.

Today I am going to call you on the telephone. I hope you are there. I trust the conference was fine. Even if there were less than 30 the Lord will have a purpose in each one that is there . . . .

When I have shared my burden regarding Kermit several people have suggested that I should be the man. I told them that it was the Lord's will that I stay in the service. In your last letter you said, "The Lord may lay His hand on you for a similar ministry—what then?"

I don't know "what then" but the possibility has been recurring in my mind more all of the time and yet I know that I could make no definite move unless the Lord clearly led the way.

1. I have such a burden for Chinese, Korean, and Japanese OCU.
2. I have a burden for the need for an evangelist and a teacher in personal evangelism.
3. With the Lord's help I could do the above.
4. I have a reputation in the OCU.
5. I am eligible for resignation in June.
6. I don't know of anyone else who has the burden and the capability.

7. In the service I couldn't do the above. This is not to say that I will
    not have a ministry in the Service, but to say it may have been
    preparation for a greatly increased ministry to the services.

No, I don't know we are going to Washington.
I know I have one month on this ship.

I love you very much,
Jim

10 April 1956
Hong Kong
USS Shangri-la CVA-38

Bessie,

If the Lord led us out of the Navy, we would not (possibly) have
as much money and since we have not accumulated any worldly be-
longings we would be starting with nothing . . . .

If the Lord leads me out of the Navy, I see no alternative but "full
time" Christian work living by faith. I don't think He would have me
get a job because that is what I have now. My first concern would be
to remain over here. Just thinking about it has panicked me into a
realization I know so little of the Gospel. I always use the same texts.

I have learned a lot about love for the people from the missionaries here. Being a visitor, almost every Filipino and Chinese tries to
cheat you, and it is hard not to take offense. In that sense they are not
lovable, but Christ loved us while we were just sinners . . . .

I am going to the Navigators for dinner tonight.

All my love,
Jim

11 April 1956
Hong Kong
USS Shangri-la CVA-38

My Dearest,

Tonight at the Emmanuel Church I met Lt. Harry Jaynton, the Executive Officer on the *Constant* on AM here in Hong Kong. He is a member of the OCU . . . After prayer meeting we came back together. He needed a shot in the arm. I am going to write to him also . . .

I have many things to do spiritually and physically during this next month. Pray for me.

The Lord is so good.

I must get saturated with the Word. I must let the peace of God rule in my heart. I have so many things before the Lord.

All yours in Him,
Jim

15 April 1956
At Sea
USS Shangri-La CVA-38

My Dearest,

I received two letters from you written since the conference and one from Kermit Johnson [about the OCU position] which I will enclose. I thought it very good. I just answered it.

Today has been a hard day spiritually speaking. John Mullen left the ship and I didn't get any more opportunities with him . . . .

[Concerning the OCU position], why does the Lord give me burdens for things that should be done and then not raise up the man to do them?

Do you think He wants me? I feel awfully confused. I really want to know.

I love you dearly,

Jim

Bessie did not think I should resign my commission to become a missionary to China, Japan, and Korea as I was planning. She wrote back and asked me, "Which language are you going to learn?"

Before her letter could arrive, I received a radiogram saying that my father had had a heart attack and was not expected to live.

20 April 1956

At Sea

My Precious Bessie,

Today I received a telegram that Dad [had] a second heart attack and that the Dr advises giving me leave in order to see him alive.

I'm not concerned because I know he is right with the Lord. I also know He has His hand in it and it will be for His own glory. If leave is granted, I will probably leave tomorrow and should see you shortly . . .

I love you dearly and long to see you and the boys . . .

Your own husband,

Jim

I flew off the carrier to Okinawa and then to Japan. I had one night with Bessie before flying to the States. She asked me if I had received her letter. Since I hadn't, she asked me in person what language I would learn.

I replied that that was a good question and that I would ask the Lord. Somewhere over the Pacific, I asked God. I was doing my regular reading in the Scripture. I was in Ezekiel 3 and came across verse 5: "For thou art not sent to a people of a strange speech and of an hard language, but to the house of Israel . . . ."

That shook me up. I did not believe in taking Scripture out of context and calling it guidance. Nevertheless, I wrote on the bottom of the page, "Wilson, remember this," and put the date next to it.

24 April 1956
Travis AFB

Dearest . . . .

Last night I started Ezekiel and got through 6 chapters. The Lord seemed to give me Ezekiel 3:5. It looks like guidance. I have it marked. The other night Bob Boardman gave me your verse Isaiah 58:11 with the emphasis on, "And the Lord shall *guide thee continually*."

26 April 1956
Home

Dearest Bessie and Boys . . . .

I caught a United Air Lines Air Coach to Omaha . . . . Floyd and Leonard were there. We drove home . . . . Harold came over and we went to the Hospital. Mom was there . . . . When I came in Dad broke down and cried. It's the first time I've ever seen him cry. I spent most of yesterday with him, read the Word, and last night before I left I laid my hands on him and prayed for him. I was with him again half the morning with Mom and read the Word to them. Last night I asked Dad if he wanted me to pray and he said yes.

There is a real need here.

30 April 1956
Mary Lanning Hospital

Dearest,

Yesterday morning I went to Sunday School with Harold and Marilyn to the Baptist church. The teacher was a deacon but didn't sound as if he knew the Lord. The sermon was good on salvation but without effect. In the evening I preached at the Baptist Church, and apparently without effect . . . I felt like I was preaching to a wall. However, afterward I met a few of the saints who really rejoiced in the message . . . .

Now about Dad. I've spent the whole day with him and he seems normal and gets better every day. Today has been the first day Mom has been back to school. Everyone else is in school or at work so I spend the whole day with Dad. They let me stay, visiting hours or not. We've talked about many things in the last few days and it has been a tremendous encouragement to him. His vocabulary has expanded and he writes very well . . . .

2 May 1956
Hospital

Dearest . . . .

I lay awake last night until 1:30 in the morning and spent most of it in prayer . . . . Today has been a wonderful day. I've talked a

Top: Jim's father and Bessie (1952)
Bottom: Jim's father, Jim's brother Ken, Jim, and Bessie (1954)

lot about witnessing to Dad. This afternoon while Dad was reading *Peace with God* and I was putting a ladder index on Marlyn's Bible, Miss Batten walked in. She is one of the Student nurses. She took Dad's temperature. When I showed Dad how I was doing on the index she wanted to know what I was doing. I won't go through the dialogue but within ten minutes she was a Christian. I've yet to see one so eager. She was like Lydia whose heart the Lord opened. It was wonderful. She has Friday evening off and we are going out to Stoddard's for Bible Study. We'll probably get some of the other Christians in the area.

Dad was really thrilled. We prayed tonight that the Lord would lead others into the room who want to know the Lord.

Buck is supposed to call me sometime today.

I plan to start back sometime Sunday.

The Lord is wonderful!

I miss you and the boys greatly.

Love,

Jim

While I was in Nebraska with my father, I called Cleo Buxton. The OCU Council had called "Buck" to be the General Secretary of the Officers' Christian Union in 1952. In his first year, Buck found about 300 additional Christian officers to join the OCU.

Buck asked me, "Where are you?"

"In Nebraska."

"I thought you were in the Far East. I am coming out to see you."

Harold and I met him in Grand Island, and we drove back to Hastings together. Trying to be smart, I said, "Buck, if you don't quit dragging your feet, I will get out of the Navy and run the OCU myself."

I was joking. But Buck replied that that was why he had come out to see me. He wanted me to resign my commission and be the OCU's East Coast staff member. He had read my letter to him about Kermit, only he thought God was speaking to me about *me*, not about Kermit.

I told him that if I got out of the Navy, it would be to become a foreign missionary. Even then, I thought I had just gotten guidance to stay *in* the Navy.

Buck asked me for the guidance I had received. I showed him Ezekiel 3:5. He read it and said, "That is not guidance to stay in the Navy. That is guidance to stay home." He thought it was God's leading for me to join the OCU.

My time on the carriers was up, so I returned to Kamiseya. Bessie was expecting the baby in August when I was due for a transfer to the Naval Security Group Headquarters in Washington, D.C. I had given up my plans for the Far East militaries. I requested a delay until October so that Bessie could travel.

Heather, circa 1957

In August 1956, our daughter, Heather, was born at the Navy Hospital in Yokosuka. Douglas turned three, and Evan was almost two. I had been at sea for Douglas and Evan's births. I was at the hospital for Heather's but had to stay in the waiting room.

The request to delay my transfer was granted. Sometime that summer, a personal letter (not official) came from Washington to our personnel officer at Kamiseya. In effect, it said, "You have a lieutenant at Kamiseya who asked to go to language school several years ago. Tell him he can now go. He can take any of the following ten languages,* and he has his choice of Syracuse University, Yale University, the Naval Intelligence School at Anacostia, or the Defense Language Institute Foreign Language Center in Monterey."

I was already a Naval Academy graduate, a Naval Postgraduate School graduate, and now this. I thought, "What a temptation!" As soon as I had that thought, a verse came into my head. "The Lord tempteth not any man."†

If this was a temptation from the devil, why? The answer was immediately apparent. If I took any of those two-year courses, I would be committed to the Navy for those two years and for four years afterward. That meant I would not be able to use the language I learned in missions work for another six years.

Then I remembered Ezekiel 3:5. Shortly afterward, I submitted my resignation to the Navy and accepted the position with the OCU.

* Two of the options were Korean and Chinese.
† James 1:13

EAST COAST STAFF MEMBER

> Likewise, you who are younger, be subject to the elders. Clothe
> yourselves, all of you, with humility toward one another, for "God
> opposes the proud but gives grace to the humble." (1 Pet. 5:5)

In November 1956, our little family sailed to the States on a personnel transport ship. Besides caring for Bessie, Douglas, Evan, and three-month-old Heather, I was in charge of the enlisted men who were also returning to the States.

I was discharged from the Navy on Treasure Island. We visited Ross and Betty Olson, Ed and Alexa Cottingham, and Dick and Dottie Mack. Then we flew to Denver. From there, I took a side trip to see Lorne Sanny (successor to Dawson Trotman) at Glenn Eyrie, the headquarters of the Navigators.‡

Shortly after we moved to Yokohama from Yokosuka, Bessie and I had started a Bible study in our home. The study included Dick and Arlene Francisco. Arlene had been brought up in an evangelical church in Albion, Nebraska, but had never received the Lord. Dick grew up in Christian Science, but had received Christ several years earlier. We were going through 1 John 1 in the Bible study. After Dick and Arlene went home that evening, Dick confessed sin, and Arlene received Christ. The change was wonderful. Although I was gone for the following six months, they grew in Christ in fellowship with Bessie and with Bill Pape's teaching.

---

‡ I had promised Bob Boardman in Okinawa that I would see Lorne on the subject of making leaders instead of followers.

In the early spring of 1956, Dick received orders to Norfolk, Virginia. He and Arlene drove across country and stopped in Albion to see Arlene's mother, Mrs. Broberg. She was a widow and could not drive. She had a 1954 Ford with ten thousand miles on it that she wanted to sell for $1,000. Dick and Arlene knew that we would need a car when we returned in the fall and that we did not have money. They decided to send us $1,000 to buy the car. Dick and Arlene continued to contribute financially to our ministry for the rest of their lives.

When I came home in April to see my Father in the hospital, Harold and I drove from Hastings to Albion to buy the car. In November, we flew to Nebraska to pick up the car and see all of the Wilson family. We then headed east to Windsor, Ontario, to see Bessie's brother Harvey's family, and then on to Washington, D.C.

We stayed with Ernestine Hersey and her three daughters, Joan, Ramona, and Patricia, until we found a house to live in. Ernestine had been close to Bessie in Japan, and her husband had been killed in the war. We were as close as a family.

We found a house, 614 Aspen Street, just off Piney Branch Road in Takoma Park, a D.C. suburb. The house was two blocks from Walter Reed Army Hospital and across the street from a Baptist church pastored by a Naval Academy graduate.

It was not long before Bessie was teaching a women's Bible class of about thirty women in our home. They sang hymns and read missionary biographies, and Bessie presented the gospel. The boys would sit in the back of the room next to the fan and listen in.

I spent my first five years out of the Navy (November 1956 to December 31, 1961) as the East Coast Staff member of the Officers' Christian Union with a major emphasis on ministry to the military academies. These included the U.S. Military Academy at West Point, the U.S. Naval Academy in Annapolis, Maryland, the U.S. Coast

Guard Academy in New London, Connecticut, the U.S. Maritime Academy in Kings Point, New York, the Virginia Military Institute in Lexington, Virginia, and the Citadel, the Military College of South Carolina. With the exception of VMI and Kings Point, I visited each of the academies several times a year.

Soon after arriving in D.C., I reported to the senior chaplain at the Naval Academy in Annapolis. This was to let him know that I would be working with the midshipmen representing the Officer's Christian Union. The chaplain was a liberal Congregationalist from Boston. He informed me that he hated Roman Catholics and evangelicals. He had changed the regulation book for midshipmen at the Naval Academy regarding religion to prohibit rosary prayer meetings and Bible studies in Bancroft Hall (the only residence hall for midshipmen). He also let me know that they would not be allowed to meet in the chapel.

I pointed out to him that if religion was not allowed in Bancroft Hall, it ought to be allowed in a chapel. He reluctantly agreed, and the OCU met weekly in St. Andrew's Chapel.

These restrictions went on for two years. In the spring of 1959, Ross Campbell, a first classman, told me that he had written his senior paper on the history of Navy Academy regulations concerning religion from 1845 to 1959. His conclusion was that religion had reached an all-time low in 1959. He showed the paper to his battalion officer before he turned it into the English professor.

I asked Ross to make copies of the regulations and give them to me. I sent a copy to Lt. Gen. William Harrison and Rear Admiral Robert Baughan in the Bureau of Naval Personnel. Concurrently, the executive department asked the English department for Ross's term paper. After it was all over, the paper was returned to Ross, and Ross gave it to me. I saw all of the endorsements written on it. The commandant had written a note to the superintendent of the Naval

Academy that he would take care of it. The superintendent replied that *he* would take care of it. At the same time, General Harrison wrote a letter to the superintendent to the effect that midshipmen were citizens of the United States, and, as citizens, they were free to proselytize or be proselytized anywhere at any time.

Admiral Baughan took the regulation to the Navy Chief of Chaplains. The result was that the senior chaplain and the superintendent were called to Washington. The chaplain was transferred, and the regulations were changed.

From 1956 to 1968, I held a weekly meeting at the Naval Academy where I taught the gospel and discipleship to midshipmen. Some midshipmen came to Christ, and many were built up in Christ. Initially, the meetings were held at St. Andrews Chapel between supper and study hall. Later they were held at 5:45 a.m. in the south end of Smoke Hall. The number of attendees varied over the years but averaged about sixty.

Time at the weekly meetings was limited, so there was not much opportunity for personal interaction with midshipmen, but many received Christ without personal attention from me. The same goes for the OCU Spring Leave conferences and conferences at White Sulphur Springs in Pennsylvania and Spring Canyon Lodge in Colorado, which I spoke at. I keep running across people that I do not remember. They remember, though.

Bruce Bickel was one of the first classmen. He had been injured in football, so he hadn't passed the physical, and he was in the Naval Hospital to get it fixed. Admiral Kauffman, the superintendent of the Naval Academy, went to the hospital to see Bruce. Bruce asked him if everything was right with him and the Lord. Bruce led the admiral to Christ.

One morning at the Naval Academy meeting, I was walking back and forth in front of the group when I saw a uniform with six rows of combat ribbons on it. I could not see any stars or bars, but I knew it had to be an admiral. It was Admiral Kauffman. The midshipmen had invited him.

After the meeting, the admiral invited me over to his house for a visit. When we got there, he said he had never met so many godly young men in the Navy in his life. He thought the second classmen (the juniors) were not as strong as the first classmen (the seniors). He wanted me to work them over so they would be as strong as the present seniors.

During those early years of the OCU, Clay Buckingham was company officer for A-1 at West Point. He was a captain at that time. I stayed with the Buckinghams whenever I went to speak at West Point. At a cadet meeting in their home, I spoke on the sheep and the goats from Matthew 25. One of the cadets told the junior chaplain.* He got very upset and wanted to see me. He accused me of undermining his work with the cadets. I asked him if he thought it legitimate for cadets to have access to evangelical teaching. He did not want to admit it but reluctantly agreed.

One day, Bessie told me that there were three sisters in her Bible study who attended Wallace Memorial, a famous Presbyterian church. Bessie told me that she thought one of them was not a Christian. I asked why. She replied that she did not have the fruit of a Christian. She was an alcoholic and a drug addict, and her children were not well-behaved.

I did not know the woman until she telephoned one day. She wanted to talk with Bessie, but Bessie was out shopping. It took me a while before I realized she was the woman Bessie had been talking about.

I asked her, "Helen,† do you mind if I read some Scripture to you?" She agreed. I read Galatians 5:19–21. " 'The acts of the flesh

* The chaplains for the corps of cadets are civilians.

† Not her real name

are obvious: sexual immorality, impurity and debauchery; idolatry and witchcraft; hatred, discord, jealousy, fits of rage, selfish ambition, dissensions, factions and envy; drunkenness, orgies, and the like. I warn you, as I did before, that those who live like this will not inherit the kingdom of God.' Helen, how many of those words describe you?"

She said, "About half of them."

Then I read Galatians 5:22–23. "But the fruit of the Spirit is love, joy, peace, forbearance, kindness, goodness, faithfulness, gentleness and self-control." I asked her, "How many of these words describe you?"

"None of them. I see I am not a Christian." Soon after, she received Christ, went to rehab, and began her Christian life.

Street view of 614 Aspen Street (Google Maps, accessed January 9, 2020)

OCU conference. From left: Arlene Francisco, Dick Francisco (holding Evan), Doyle Weathers, Alex Aronis (holding Douglas), Peggy Weathers, Bessie, Bill Pape

CHAPTER 30

WHAT SHALL WE EAT?

The grace of our Lord was poured out on me abundantly, along
with the faith and love that are in Christ Jesus. (1 Tim. 1:14)

When I was still on active duty, I had decided that if I ever got out
of the Navy I would go with a mission that did not require raising
support. That is not what happened in theory, but what happened
in fact. When I joined the staff of the Officers' Christian Union,
the position had a salary. That was the theory. The fact was that the
OCU did not have the money to pay it. For most of the five years
I was on staff, I was two months behind in pay. This allowed us to
trust God.

Soon after we arrived in D.C., I was called to see the senior chaplain at the Naval Academy. He was liberal and had difficulty with
what I was teaching the midshipmen. Although I was broke, I had
gas in the car, so I drove the thirty miles to Annapolis.

The drive was in a snowstorm. I parked the car, went in to see the
chaplain for an hour, and came back to find the car was dead. I had
driven in the snow with my lights on and neglected to turn them off.
I had one nickel in my possession. It cost a dime to use the telephone.

Apparently, I had forgotten the lesson I learned from my dead
car of January 1, 1954. I walked over to the math department to see
Dr. Findley Paydon, a Christian professor. He was home sick in bed.
I used a phone in the math building to call him and explain the situation. He told me to stay by the phone and someone would come
to me with $10. It happened. I called a tow truck to give me a jump,

then drove out to Findley's home. He insisted on loaning me an additional $15.

When I arrived home, Bessie said, "Jim, we are in trouble. Joe Carroll* and Sam Obetz are coming to the house, and I have nothing to feed them."

I told her I had $15. I went to the store to get the fixings for supper and also bought basics: four quarts of milk, a pound of cheese, eggs, and orange juice.

When Joe and Sam pulled in, they had the back seat full of groceries. Joe had cashed in an airplane ticket and gone to the store. He had duplicated everything I had bought with my borrowed $15, right down to getting the same brands. His stuff did not fit into the refrigerator. We put his milk, eggs, and cheese in the snow on the back porch.

I was miserable. Joe and I had been close in Manila and Yokohama. He could see that I was not rejoicing. I told him what the problem was: I prayed, and God answered, but God waited to the very last instant, so that when He answered I could not rejoice. I was bummed because God waited so long to answer.

Joe said, "Apparently you do not know Philippians 4:6–7."

I assured him I knew it, but I prayed with anxiety. "How am I supposed to be anxious for nothing?"

He said, "Back up to verse four. 'Rejoice in the Lord always, and again I say, rejoice.'"

"How do I rejoice always?"

"Read a book on joy—Philippians or 2 Corinthians."

Two days later, I had to go to West Point. I was still broke but was determined not to use any of the money I had borrowed from Findley for the trip. I had 50¢ of my own which I used to get to the

---

* An Australian missionary to the Far East

railroad station. I had a rail card for the train trip to Newark. There were no railroads to West Point, so I had no idea how I was going to get from Newark to there.

On the train, I read 2 Corinthians. When I got off the train, I was rejoicing in the Lord. I was scheduled to speak at a Christian Business Mens' luncheon at a hotel in Newark before going to West Point. I hoped the hotel was not on the other side of Newark. I walked out of the station and saw that it was right across the street.

Back in 1949 when I was still a midshipman, I had told Jack Wyrtzen that I thought I ought to pray for missionaries, but I did not know any. He suggested that I pray for Dick Hightower, a missionary to the Kikuyu people in Kenya. I knew nothing about Dick, but I began to pray for him regularly.

For the speech in Newark, I got a free lunch but no honorarium. I was able to speak in power. After the lunch, I was shaking hands with the businessmen and found a $20 bill in my hand. The man who gave it to me was Dick Hightower. I stayed overnight with friends and used the $20 to get to West Point and back home.

Years later, I told this story to Joe Bayly. He told me that at that time Dick was home from Kenya because members of his family had polio. Dick was dead broke, himself; but he was the one God called to give me the $20 I needed to get to West Point. That trip to the cadets was fruitful.

I remember one week in 1958 that taught me much about trusting God. It was Saturday, January 4. Bessie and I realized that we had no money and none of the children's basic food: milk, bread, and orange juice. We stood in the dining room and read Matthew 6:31–34 aloud to the Lord. "So do not worry, saying, 'What shall we eat?' or 'What shall we drink?' or 'What shall we wear?' For the pagans run after all these things, and your heavenly Father knows that you need them. But seek first his kingdom and his righteousness, and all these things will be given to you as well. Therefore do not worry about tomorrow, for tomorrow will worry about itself. Each day has enough trouble of its own."

Having read this, we told the Lord that we weren't anxious and that we were seeking first His kingdom and His righteousness, so it was up to Him. Then we thanked God.

The morning mail arrived. There was an envelope from Lancaster, Pennsylvania. It contained three $1 bills and a tract on the subject of Hell by Bishop J.C. Ryle. I had never been to Lancaster and knew no one there. We thanked God again. I went to Safeway and bought $2.96 worth of milk, bread, and orange juice.

On Tuesday, we were again out of the basics and still out of money. That evening, we explained to the children what the situation was and said we would ask God for the food. We stood in a circle in the living room. I did not have enough faith for the prayer, so I asked four-year-old Douglas if he would pray. In the name of the Lord Jesus Christ, he thanked God for milk and bread. We put Heather to bed with half of a baby bottle of milk, the last we had.

The next morning, I made pancakes with no milk and no eggs. After breakfast, I went to our room for study.

There was a knock on the door. Bessie and Douglas answered it. It was the milkman. He said, "I have four quarts of milk for you."

Bessie said, "You must have the wrong address. We did not order any milk."

He said, "I have the right address."

Bessie asked who sent the milk.

He replied, "Let's say Santa Claus sent it." (It was shortly after Christmas.)

Bessie replied, "Let's *not* say Santa Claus sent it. The Lord God sent it because this little boy prayed for it."

Four quarts arrived Wednesday morning, six quarts on Friday, and four on Monday every week for the next eleven months. It only quit then because we moved to Annapolis, and the dairy did not deliver that far. We never found out who sent it, although we have suspected it was Ernestine Hersey. God is good, and we praise Him for whoever it was. Whoever it was did not know the need because we did not let anyone know, but God knew and prepared the answer even before we prayed.

We put the milk on the floor of the entryway, stood in a circle around it, and held a little praise meeting. We thanked God for the milk and reminded Him that we had also asked Him for bread.

I went back upstairs to our room. Soon Bessie was running up the stairs with a $5 bill in her hand. She had been dusting the furniture in the living room and found it underneath a lamp on the end table.

We bought bread and some other basics with $4.50. We held another praise meeting and told God that we needed $24.50 that day: $9.50 for an insurance premium and $15 to get the car out of the mechanic's.

When the mail arrived, there was a $25 check from Alex Aronis in San Diego. We had another prayer meeting, thanked God, and told Him that I needed a new suit.

The day before, Scott Smith, a Navy dentist, had come to see me from Bethesda Naval Hospital. He was the one who had left us the $5. He thought he should pay me for the help I had given him, but he knew I would not accept it. He also thought we did not need the money, since we lived in a nice house. But he still felt compelled to give it, so he slid it under the lamp.

At the end of our conversation, I had told him that he should start a Bible study at Bethesda. I told him that there were at least two other officers there who wanted to study the Bible. He did not think there were any. I said, "Let's pray that God will lead you to officers who want to study the Bible." Scott thought that was a useless prayer.

When he got back to the BOQ at Bethesda, he went to the men's room. He still had his Bible with him. Lt. Jim Scribner saw the Bible and told him he had a friend who wanted to study it, and would Scott join them? On Wednesday morning, Scott called me and told me of the answered prayer and asked me to come to Bethesda that night to start the study.

On Wednesday evening, I went to Bethesda for the new Bible study. In addition to the three men, there was a Navy nurse, Commander Marjorie von Stein. She became a Christian either that night or soon afterward.

After the study, Jim Scribner asked me if I had been a Navy officer. I told him yes. He asked if I still had my uniforms. Again, I said yes. He said, "You are my size; I will give you $50 for a uniform." I accepted the offer, and he gave me $50.

The next morning, I went to J.C. Penney to look at suits. I browsed the racks but did not like any of the ones I saw.

The salesman came up to me. "You look like a thirty-nine extra-long. I am sorry, I only have one in the store in that size."

He took it off the rack. It was the only suit I liked. I asked, "How much?"

He said, "Fifty dollars," and then he corrected himself. "Fifty-one dollars. The extra dollar is for the state."

I had 50¢ left over from Scott's $5 and 50¢ left over from Alex's $25, so I gave him my $51 and left with the suit. I do not think I have been anxious about food or clothing since.

CHAPTER 31

METAMORPHOSIS IN THEOLOGY AND IN OVERCOMING SIN

For sin will have no dominion over you, since you are not under
law but under grace. (Rom. 6:14)

When I first became a Christian, I was interested in living the Christian life, as were my companions. I did not encounter theology or eschatology until my first class year. The dispensationalist view was held by Christians whom I respected, so I just assumed it was correct (although I did not know the word *dispensationalism*).

By that time, I was interested not only in the Christian life, but also in evangelism. I read a book on apologetics by a missionary to Korea and was impressed. I loved to argue and debate. However, on the downside, I found out that I could win arguments without winning people.

While in Hawaii in 1952, I realized while reading the Bible that the idea of a pre-tribulation rapture did not sound right. I read a couple books on eschatology and came to the view that people who were into eschatology (no matter which view they took) were focused on it too much. I was also focused on it for a few months. That focus did not make me godlier, nor did it hasten the Lord's return.

Here is my eschatology:

Brothers, we do not want you to be uninformed about those who sleep in death, so that you do not grieve like the rest of mankind, who have no hope. For we believe that Jesus died and rose again, and so we believe that God will bring with Jesus those who have fallen asleep in him. According to the Lord's word, we tell you that we who are still alive, who are left until the coming of the Lord, will certainly not precede those who have fallen asleep. For the Lord himself will come down from heaven, with a loud command, with the voice of the archangel and with the trumpet call of God, and the dead in Christ will rise first. After that, we who are still alive and are left will be caught up together with them in the clouds to meet the Lord in the air. And so we will be with the Lord forever. *Therefore encourage one another with these words.* (1 Thess. 4:13–18)

For the grace of God has appeared that offers salvation to all people. It teaches us to *say "No" to ungodliness and worldly passions, and to live self-controlled, upright and godly lives in this present age,* while we wait for the blessed hope—the appearing of the glory of our great God and Savior, *Jesus Christ, who gave himself for us to redeem us from all wickedness and to purify for himself a people that are his very own, eager to do what is good.* (Titus 2:11–14)

Dear friends, now we are children of God, and what we will be has not yet been made known. But we know that when Christ appears, we shall be like him, for we shall see him as he is. *All who have this hope in him purify themselves, just as he is pure.* (1 John 3:2–3)

In 1956, Bill Pape gave three talks at an OCU conference in Karuizawa. His subjects were what the Lord's return will mean to the lost, what the Lord's return will mean to the saved, and what the Lord's return will mean to the Lord. He did not dwell on the order of the events.

Although I could see that God was protecting me and using me from early on in my Christian life, I could also see that He was using me even when I was not walking in the light. It was apparent to me then and very apparent to me now as I recount my life.

In 1951, before I was married, I had begun to suspect that Christians do not have two natures.* The idea first came to me by Mabel Halverson and Doreen Shaw when I was helping them get an orphanage started in Sasebo. As I searched the Scriptures, it seemed to me to be true. I came to the conclusion from the Scriptures that when a person receives Christ, he receives a new nature, and the old nature is put off. In the circles I was in, it was a controversial position. At that time, most evangelicals believed that Christians have two natures at once, a good one and a bad one. It was a strong enough conviction for me that it changed my life in terms of obedience.†

I did not tell anyone else what I believed because it would have meant an argument. After Bessie and I were married, we argued about it for two years.

In 1955, we were in an adult Sunday School class in Yokosuka when one of the members of the class explained away some sin by saying, "That is just the old nature."

I remember thinking, "Should I take issue with him on this? If I do, Bessie will come out on the other side, and she and I will be arguing publicly on it."

I decided to chance it and spoke on the one nature of the believer. To my surprise, Bessie came out strongly in agreement with me. Later, I asked her why. She said that at that instant everything fell into place. "I realized that if I took the Scripture at face value, the single nature made sense." All of what she had held to before needed lengthy explaining to hold it together.

In early 1957, the OCU held a staff conference at Hudson House in Nyack, New York. One afternoon, General Secretary Cleo Buxton insisted that all of us take a nap. (This was so he could take a nap!)

* Read my book *Dead & Alive* for a complete discussion of this.
† I had already learned and was practicing confession of sin.

That made no sense to me. I was not tired, and I had never taken a nap in my life. I flaked out on a couch in the living room and used the time to meditate. My meditation took me to Romans 8:9: "But ye are not in the flesh, but in the Spirit, if so be that the Spirit of God dwell in you. Now if any man have not the Spirit of Christ, he is none of his." That meditation nailed it down. It was either/or. If the Spirit was in me, then I was in the Spirit, *not* in the flesh. If the Spirit was not in me, I was not a Christian. I wanted to shout! This confirmed what I had believed for the last six years.

I was so excited that I told Buck as soon as the nap was over. He was horrified. He thought I had just come up with some heresy. He asked me tell the OCU Council what I had found at their next meeting. The council unanimously agreed that it was heresy and forbade me to teach it to anyone while I was on the staff. I willingly obeyed them and did not teach it.

Why was I willing to follow the council's directive on this? I knew I was in the Lord's will as the Academy staff member, and I wanted to stay there. Believing this about the new nature was not what made it true. Teaching it to someone does not make it true. If it is true, then it is true of all believers, regardless of what they believe about it and regardless of what I teach. It did not need teaching. I willingly obeyed the council for this reason: teaching the one nature of the Christian did not make it happen. If it was true that we only have one nature and can't blame sin on the old nature, I did not need to teach it.

Sometime later, there was a Bible conference for the Royal Military College at Kingston, Ontario. My friend General William Harrison was the speaker. Cleo Buxton and I were present. After the conference, we all drove back to East Lansing, Michigan, together. While the general was in the restroom at a gas station, Buck said, "I told the general your heretical views on the nature of the believer. I asked him to straighten you out. You sit in the back with him."

The general and I went at it in the back seat. At the next rest stop, Buck said, "I don't want to hear you talking that way to a general." I think he thought the general wasn't winning the argument.

Four years went by. I was in a car with Buck and two other OCU staff members driving from East Lansing to the east coast. I asked Buck if I could be relieved of the injunction. I had proved that I could be trusted. If he kept the prohibition, it would be saying that he did not trust me as a staff member. The other staffers got on his case about it, and he cancelled the prohibition.

Although I did not study theology at all, I came across much of it in the next fifty years. I found out what people believed because they told me: Dispensational, Arminian, Wesleyan, Reformed, Pentecostal, or Lutheran. They told me their beliefs with varying degrees of dogmatism. They all had Scripture to uphold their positions and explanations for the Scriptures that were against them.

The chaplain on the *Brinkley Bass* had wanted to talk theology with me on a daily basis. He wanted to talk baptism, so he gave me a list of Scriptures, and I gave him a list of Scriptures. He said, "You win, but I am not going to change. I don't want to take any chances."

In another instance, while studying 1 Corinthians 12, 13, and 14 with a Pentecostal man, I got the same type of answer. He realized that the chapters did not teach what he believed, but he was not willing to change his belief to fit the Scriptures.

People have an emotional attachment to their culture and their beliefs. Most of these distinct beliefs have to be taught by someone else who has been taught them. An ordinary new Christian would not come up with any one of these doctrines by reading the Scriptures alone. What would he come across? Much on salvation, and much on holiness.

Should there be teachers? Yes, on salvation and holiness.

Here are a few texts which outline my theology.

But now apart from the law the righteousness of God has been made known, to which the Law and the Prophets testify. This righteousness is given through faith in Jesus Christ to all who believe. There is no difference between Jew and Gentile, for all have sinned and fall short of the glory of God, and all are justified freely by his grace through the redemption that came by Christ Jesus. God presented Christ as a sacrifice of atonement, through the shedding of his blood—to be received by faith. He did this to demonstrate his righteousness, because in his forbearance he had left the committed beforehand unpunished—he did it to demonstrate his righteousness at the present time, so as to be just and the one who justifies those who have faith in Jesus. (Rom. 3:21–26)

This is the message we have heard from him and declare to you: God is light; in him there is no darkness at all . . . But if we walk in the light, as he is in the light, we have fellowship with one another, and the blood of Jesus, his Son, purifies us from all sin . . . If we confess our sins, he is faithful and just and will forgive us our sins and purify us from all unrighteousness. (1 John 1:5, 7, 9)

His divine power has given us everything we need for life and godliness through our knowledge of him who called us by his own glory and goodness. Through these he has given us his very great and precious promises, so that through them you may participate in the divine nature and escape the corruption in the world caused by evil desires. For this very reason, make every effort to add to your faith goodness; and to goodness, knowledge. (2 Pet. 1:3–5)

Since, then, you have been raised with Christ, set your hearts on things above, where Christ is seated at the right hand of God. Set your minds on things above, not on earthly things. For you died, and your life is now hidden with Christ in God. When Christ, who is your life, appears, then you also will appear with him in glory. (Col. 3:1–4)

Your attitude should be the same as that of Christ Jesus: Who, being in very nature God, did not consider equality with God something to be grasped, but made himself nothing, taking the very nature of a servant, being made in human likeness. And being found in appearance as a man, he humbled himself and became obedient to death— even death on a cross! Therefore God exalted him to the highest place and gave him the name that is above every name, that at the name of Jesus every knee should bow, in heaven and on earth and under the earth, and every tongue confess that Jesus Christ is Lord, to the glory of God the Father. (Phil. 2:5–11)

I have been crucified with Christ and I no longer live, but Christ lives in me. The life I live in the body, I live by faith in the Son of God, who loved me and gave himself for me. I do not set aside the grace of God, for if righteousness could be gained through the law, Christ died for nothing! (Gal. 2:20–21)

CHAPTER 32

WHOEVER EXALTS HIMSELF

But he gives us more grace. That is why Scripture says: "God op-
poses the proud but shows favor to the humble." (James 4:6)

In the spring of 1957, the OCU held a staff conference at Tower
House in Mt. Vernon, Virginia. I had been on the OCU staff for
about six months. During that time, I saw a few things in the life of
the General Secretary Cleo W. Buxton (Buck) which I did not think
were honoring to the Lord. I planned on graciously bringing them to
his attention at the staff conference.

That did not happen, because Buck got to me first. He told me that
I was the most arrogant man he had ever met. He went on, "You are
twenty-nine years old. I have not met any man that old and this arrogant who has ever been able to change." He admitted that he had asked
me to resign my commission and come on staff because of my evangelism, even though he knew I had problems. He had thought my strong
points would make it worth having to put up with the arrogance. But
he was wrong. It was not worth it. He said that since he had asked me
to come, I could stay on staff for one year. "If you are not delivered
from that arrogance in one year, you will have to leave the staff. Just
plan on leaving in a year, because I do not believe you can change."

I was in shock. Before my conversion at age twenty, I was arrogant
because of my relative goodness. I did not smoke, drink, or use profanity, and I was not sexually immoral. I compared myself to everyone
I knew, and I came out morally better (I thought) than they did. I was
self-righteous, although I did not know the expression. However, I lied

many times in many ways. When I received Christ, I was set free from that. I no longer bragged about my morality. My new life in Christ took care of what I used to take care of by will power. I thought my arrogance had disappeared with my conversion. How could I be arrogant? I had memorized all those verses on humility!

Something had begun to happen to me that I did not recognize. Since I had become Christian, I had been giving my testimony—and people played up to me because I was a Naval officer and a Christian. I began to believe the good things they said about me. Then I had several miraculous deliverances in the Korean War, and I was even more played up to. Then I married a missionary, which *really* made me somebody. When I was asked to resign my commission to work with the OCU, I thought I was being asked to join the ministry because of my gifts. That was partly true. The other reason was that I had married Bessie Dodds. All of this had gradually made me more and more arrogant, and I was not aware of it at all.

I thought Buck was dead wrong, so I asked him for evidence. He took a letter from his pocket. It was from an officer whose home I had stayed in two weeks earlier in Massachusetts. The letter said, "If this man represents the Officers' Christian Union, consider this my resignation from the Officers' Christian Union." Buck had received several similar letters. He asked me if I wanted any more evidence.

I asked Buck for permission to leave the conference to go see Bessie. We were still living in Takoma Park, about thirty minutes away.

I went home and told Bessie. I was sure God had called me to work with the military academies. I was not prepared to leave in one year. Whether Bessie agreed with Buck I don't know, but she was very loyal and supportive.

We came up with 1 Thessalonians 5:12–13, "Now we ask you, brothers and sisters, to acknowledge those who work hard among you, who care for you in the Lord and who admonish you. Hold them in the highest regard in love because of their work. Live in peace with each other." This was for my relationship with the general secretary, especially when we thought he was wrong.

We came up with a plan. I did not know how I could change when I was convinced that there was nothing to change. We decided to pretend Buck was right and then correct this imaginary arrogance so that he would think I had changed, and I would not have to leave in one year.

In order to pretend to correct my "arrogance," I decided to make a study of the characteristics of arrogant people. When I began studying, I realized I had some of the symptoms. Arrogant people use the first-person pronoun very much in speaking and writing, and they especially tend to start their sentences with "I" (just like in this autobiography). I determined that in my reports to the main office, I would take great care not to use the word. In my first report, I found that it was *impossible* to write a single sentence that did not begin with "I." There was no other subject! The letter was sent with "I" at the beginning of every paragraph and every sentence.

Another part of the plan was to keep officers from writing to Buck criticizing me. How? Simple! I would ask all of my friends that if they saw anything that was not honoring to the Lord, would they be friend enough to tell me? On my next trip to the military bases, I asked this question. I started with officers who were very close friends of mine. I thought it would be safe to ask them.

The first person I ran into was Dick Francisco, who was driving me to the bus terminal in Norfolk. I presented my request to him. He said, "Do you really mean that?" When he realized I was serious, he immediately unloaded something on me. It was not on arrogance; it was something else, but it was very true, and I knew it.

My next stop was Charleston, where I stayed with Eric (USNA '51) and Claire Nelson. At my request, Eric also took the opportunity to tell me a few things, and Claire added some more.

A few answers later, I began to suspect that the general secretary might be right.

Six months went by. Buck and I were in the car driving south down the east coast from Bill and Doris Waldrop's wedding. I asked Buck, "How am I doing?"

He replied, "Jim, I have never seen so much improvement in one person in six months in my life, but I don't think you're going to make it."

I did make it. I stayed five years on the staff, from November 1956 to December 1961, then continued to work at the Naval Academy as a volunteer local representative from January 1962 until the summer of 1968. During those years, I humbled myself.

For whoever exalts himself will be humbled, and he who humbles himself will be exalted. (Luke 14:11)

I tell you, this man went down to his house justified rather than the other; for everyone who exalts himself will be humbled, and he who humbles himself will be exalted. (Luke 18:14)

But he who is greatest among you shall be your servant. And whoever exalts himself will be humbled, and he who humbles himself will be exalted. (Matt. 23:11–12)

CHAPTER 33

ONLY BY PRAYER

Just as sin reigned in death, so also grace might reign through
righteousness to bring eternal life through Jesus Christ our Lord.
(Rom. 5:21)

Army Major Mike Schnell was admitted to Walter Reed Army
Hospital with a diagnosis of myasthenia gravis. Mike and his wife
came to our home for Christian fellowship, and we prayed for him.
While he was still at Walter Reed, God gave me an assurance of his
healing. I was so sure that I told him about it. At the same time, the
medical team at Walter Reed told him that medicines could help in
eighty percent of the cases, but he was in the twenty percent. They
discharged him from the Army with full disability. He went home to
California, where he was expected to die. We got Christmas cards
from him for the next thirty years.

A few weeks after Mike was discharged, another army major arrived in D.C. Major Lowe and his wife, Betty, had an eleven-year-old
daughter named Holly. Holly was admitted to the psychiatric ward at
Walter Reed for observation because she had been acting strangely.
I only remember one of the symptoms—she would pull imaginary
threads out of her blanket. They finally decided her symptoms were
the result of an undiagnosed case of encephalitis of the brain. The
Army had no cure. The Lowes were told to find a psychiatric institution where Holly could live out the rest of her life.

One day in prayer, I was asking God to give me a word from Him
or faith so I could know that Holly would be healed as He had done

with Mike. I spent about forty minutes in prayer. During that time, I read Mark 9:14–29.

> When they came to the other disciples, they saw a large crowd around them and the teachers of the law arguing with them. As soon as all the people saw Jesus, they were overwhelmed with wonder and ran to greet him.
>
> "What are you arguing with them about?" he asked.
>
> A man in the crowd answered, "Teacher, I brought you my son, who is possessed by a spirit that has robbed him of speech. Whenever it seizes him, it throws him to the ground. He foams at the mouth, gnashes his teeth and becomes rigid. I asked your disciples to drive out the spirit, but they could not."
>
> "You unbelieving generation," Jesus replied, "how long shall I stay with you? How long shall I put up with you? Bring the boy to me."
>
> So they brought him. When the spirit saw Jesus, it immediately threw the boy into a convulsion. He fell to the ground and rolled around, foaming at the mouth.
>
> Jesus asked the boy's father, "How long has he been like this?"
>
> "From childhood," he answered. "It has often thrown him into fire or water to kill him. But if you can do anything, take pity on us and help us."
>
> "'If you can'?" said Jesus. "Everything is possible for one who believes."
>
> Immediately the boy's father exclaimed, "I do believe; help me overcome my unbelief!"
>
> When Jesus saw that a crowd was running to the scene, he rebuked the impure spirit. "You deaf and mute spirit," he said, "I command you, come out of him and never enter him again."
>
> The spirit shrieked, convulsed him violently and came out. The boy looked so much like a corpse that many said, "He's dead." But Jesus took him by the hand and lifted him to his feet, and he stood up.

After Jesus had gone indoors, his disciples asked him privately, "Why couldn't we drive it out?"

He replied, "This kind can come out only by prayer."

I found I had the faith that Holly would be healed. I got up and walked to Walter Reed. I found Betty in the hospital corridor. We sat down, and I told her that I knew Holly would be healed.

I did not tell her that I thought Holly was possessed by a demon; I did not know how to do that. A doctor came up and told Betty he wanted to see her. While she was gone, I prayed that God would let me know if I should tell her what I thought.

Betty came back and said, "Lord, I believe. Help thou my unbelief."

I said, "Betty, do you know where that is in the Bible? It is in only one place—in Mark 9, where a father says that about his demon-possessed son. I think that is the problem, but I will not bet on it. I will call your Christian friends, Colonels Kennedy, Sharpe, and Palm." I called them. They agreed with me, so I called a prayer meeting at our house that evening.

I went to see Holly the next day. She was still out of her mind. I was afraid to exorcise the demon. In the meantime, I encountered a Christian medical doctor (not a psychiatrist) at Walter Reed. He also thought that Holly was possessed. Shortly after that, an Air Force general's wife came to visit. She walked into Holly's room and told the demon in the name of Jesus to be gone, and the demon went. The psychiatrists insisted on keeping Holly for two more weeks in order to find out what happened. At the end of two weeks, she went home with her parents, in her right mind.

CHAPTER 34

DEAR ERNESTINE

4 June 1959

Dear Ernestine,[*]

First of all, my apologies for the delay in sending this.

Let me share with you a recent experience. Over last weekend and for several more days, Christine Steere and Betty Meader were with us. Maureen was also out for one night. We had the OCU Banquet and even had baby sitters, etc. Well, the drain on food and on money was more than normal, and we ran out (and we still had guests in the house). They (the guests) were still asleep when we called the children together into our bedroom for prayer, explaining the situation to them. Each of us prayed that God would provide, and in the morning mail was your check for $50.00. We were not looking to the OCU or to you, and we are glad we look to Him. We are thankful that you are so attentive to His guidance and know that you receive a greater blessing than we receive.

Bessie is at her Bible class. We received a letter from Marge Smith requesting a concordance like you have. I am sure she means a commentary, so that is what I am sending her.

We would like to see you, as we have some things to share with you for remembering in prayer. Our Lord is good.

Thanks again. Give our love to the girls.

Yours in His Joy,

Jim

---

[*] Ernestine Hersey, our good friend who also worked as my secretary when I first joined the OCU staff in 1956.

CHAPTER 35

THE CHRISTIAN BOOKSTORE, ANNAPOLIS

Concerning this salvation, the prophets who prophesied about the
grace that was to be yours searched and inquired carefully.
(1 Pet. 1:10)

When stationed in Japan, I became acquainted with Ray Oram, a Christian Literature Crusade missionary. From 1954 to 1956, I initiated spring and fall Bible conferences for the Officers' Christian Union in Japan. They were held at the Far Eastern Gospel Crusade headquarters, the Oiso Conference Center, and in Karuzawa. Ray Oram provided the book tables for each conference.

In 1955 and 1956, I ordered InterVarsity booklets by the hundreds and salted down the aircraft carriers with them. They got read. The combination of personal witness and books was very effective. I saw six cadets and midshipmen receive Christ in one year (1956–57) through the books I had given them. In the early 1950s, I received several boxes of Christian books addressed to the chaplain of the *USS Brinkley Bass*. I was the closest thing to a chaplain, so the books were delivered to me. Since sailors like to read (at least, they did at that time), I would go down the chow line and hand a book to every sailor.

For the first two years I was on the OCU staff, we lived in Washington, D.C. From there I travelled to military bases along the East Coast, and especially to the military academies. I carried a briefcase full of books on every trip. Each midshipman or cadet received a book. During the first year, I came across six cadets and midshipmen who had received Christ while alone with a book, the New Testament, or a tract. I realized I needed more books.

The advantages of books:

- The books held more information about more subjects than I could hold.
- The printed word speaks with more authority. Because of this, people give it more weight.
- Books continue to speak after I have gone. They can be read while I am asleep or hundreds of miles away.
- I can only be in one place at a time, but if I put hundreds of books in other hands, my message is multiplied many times.

Books multiply truth in quantity, quality, time, and authority.

It was not feasible to open a bookstore at West Point or the Coast Guard Academy, but the Naval Academy is close to downtown Annapolis. Both Gate 3 (the main gate at that time) and Gate 1 (currently the main gate) have immediate access to the business district. I presented the idea of opening a bookstore there to the OCU Council. It was voted down because I was a traveling staff member, and the council did not want me tied to a particular location.

A year went by. I presented the idea to Ed Steele*, a council member, and convinced him of the value of opening a bookstore outside the Naval Academy. This time the council was interested, provided I could find someone to run the store. Jean Vandenburgh, a friend of Bessie's who was on furlough from the West Indies Mission (now World Team), was staying with us for six months. She was responsible for literature in that mission. She said that she would gladly open

---

* Brother of Fran Steele, mentioned in Chapter 25. During WWII, Ed was a lieutenant commander in the Navy and was one of the earliest members of the OCU.

and run the store until she had to return. She insisted on writing a letter to the Council saying she was only good for a month or two.

At the council meeting, Cleo Buxton told the members that Jean would run the store so I could keep traveling.

Although I had been an OCU Council member, I had had to resign when I came on staff with OCU. As a staff member, I was not allowed to speak at a council meeting unless I was asked a question. I saw that the General Secretary was not going to read Jean's letter to the council. I slipped him a note: "Buck, read Jean's letter to the council."

He wrote back, "What for? It's passing, isn't it?"

The council voted in favor of opening the store under the impression that Jean was going to be permanent staff. If they had known that Jean was not staying, the resolution would not have passed. Although I was convinced that it was right to open the store, I was very uncomfortable with Buck's lack of communication to the board.

In November 1958, we moved to Annapolis, and the OCU opened the Christian Bookstore at 74 Maryland Avenue. I continued my work as the OCU East Coast Staff Member. When Jean left, I got two or three other temporary staff to run the bookstore in succession.

Early in 1959, a woman came in to the store to ask for a job. We had no job for her, but I asked about her background. She had left the Jehovah's Witnesses and had joined the Eastport Methodist Church. I asked her more questions about the gospel. She received Christ. When her nineteen-year-old daughter, Marie, came home, she asked her the same questions, and Marie received Christ. Marie called her friend Barbara and asked her the same questions. Barbara received Christ.

Another time, an ISI[†] staff member from Washington, D.C., came into the store. I noticed that she had a diamond on her finger. I asked her if her fiancé was a Christian. She said that he was an Episcopalian.

† International Students Inc., a ministry to international college students at campuses throughout the United States.

I pressed the issue. She assured me that he was a real Christian. How did she know? I asked. She was sure her fiancé was saved—he had been riding a train from New York City, sat next to a man named Jim Wilson, and became a Christian.

Not all train rides went that way. In 1957, I was en route to New York City to attend the Billy Graham Crusade in Madison Square Garden. On the way, I decided to have lunch in the dining car. It was crowded, so I was given a table with a young woman. Our conversation was rather pleasant. Then I asked her if she was going to hear Billy Graham. The conversation was no longer pleasant. She felt obligated to tell me her view of Mr. Graham. The description was long, negative, and evangelist-bashing. Then she asked me what I did. I told her I was an evangelist on my way to hear Billy Graham. She got up and left. She must have locked herself in a bathroom, because I looked for her in every seat on the train and couldn't find her.

One day in 1959, a midshipman walked into the Christian Bookstore in Annapolis and asked me if I knew any Christian girls. He and his friend were starved for female companionship. I gave him two names. He came in again, and I asked him how it had gone with the girls. It hadn't. He told me that one of them, Barbara, was engaged to be married.

Not long after that, Barbara came in. I saw that she had a diamond on her finger, so I asked about her fiancé. His name was Larry Moyer, and he was a trumpet player in the Naval Academy Band. I asked her if he was a Christian. She replied that he was. I asked how she knew. Her answer was that he went to the same church, and he sang in the choir with her.

"Barbara, how long have you been going to that church?"

"Three years."

"How long have you been a Christian?"

"Three months."

"What were you before that?"

"Just a church-goer."

"How do you know *he* is not just a church-goer?"

Her eyes got big. She said, "I'll send him in."

A few days later, he came. We went to my office. He did not seem friendly or open. I gave him the gospel, convinced that I was planting seed on hard ground. I also gave him some things to read, including *The Gift* by Father Chiniquy.

The next week, I was walking back from the post office and saw Larry walking toward me. He was looking at the ground and did not notice me. I decided not to speak to him because I thought he would be hostile. At the last moment, I did speak. He looked up and was very excited to see me. He had received Christ.*

After Larry's conversion, he had a strong witness to the other musicians in the Academy band, including Jim Hooper, the bass player. Jim played the bass horn in the marching band and the bass guitar in the orchestra. He was twenty-six years old and separated from his second wife. He hated her.

Jim was rebellious. One day when the band was playing a march in the Wednesday parade on Warden Field, Jim decided to play a different march at the same time. The band director did not hear it, but the band member next to Jim told the director. When Jim found out who had told, he punched him.

Larry brought Jim to the store for me to tell him the good news, but he was not converted. Then one Sunday evening, Jim was driving back from Baltimore where he had been to see a woman. On the way,

* Just before writing this, I received a note from Larry written on the outside of the envelope of a letter from Barbara. It says, "Jim, Thank you for sharing the good news in 1959 on Maryland Ave." Larry and Barbara Moyer have had over fifty years living for Christ. They have been missionaries in Guam for many years, some of that time with Christian Servicemen's centers. Barbara works in a Christian bookstore in Guam. Larry went to be with the Lord in early 2018.

he realized he was going to be dead before he got home, and, if so, he would go straight to Hell. He thought that if he were still alive when he got to Annapolis, he would come see me.

Jim did not know where I lived, so he went by Larry's house. The house was dark. He drove on and came across a roadblock. Someone had driven into a power pole, and the line was down. (That is why Larry's house was dark.) Jim drove to a drugstore on Rowe Boulevard, and then to another one, trying to find a phone. Both were closed. Finally, he found one open on West Street, but there was no phone book in the phone booth. He waited in line at the counter to get one. By this time, he was ready to give it up and go home and feed his dogs.

When he got the book, there were many James Wilsons listed. He called Larry to get my phone number. He called me and got no answer. By this time, he was really feeling desperate. He drove to our home on North Cherry Grove, parked on the wrong side of the street, and came and pounded on the door. I opened the door, and he almost fell in.*

He said, "I came out to get saved. I have one question to ask before that. I don't care what the answer is, but I would still like to know."

"What's the question?"

"If I become a Christian, do I have to take my wife back?"

I said, "I cannot tell you that, but I can tell you that God does not make deals. If you come to Him to be saved on the condition that you will not take her back, God will not save you."

He decided to get saved. When we had prayed together, he asked me what was next.

I said, "Get rid of your dirty magazines."

"OK. My roommates' magazines, too?" Then he said, "I don't think a Christian should smoke."

---

* I was six two, and he was several inches taller than me.

"You said it, I didn't. Give them to me."

He gave me the pack of cigarettes from his jacket, and we went to his car to get the carton.

A month later, Jim called wanting me to see his wife. I met the two of them in the bookstore, where she received Christ. In 1991, twenty-five years later, I was speaking in San Diego and looked him up. He had a very good report of his children and their walk with the Lord.

In 1959 or 1960, I met Jean Wentworth and Alice Crockett in the bookstore. Both were Christians from Severna Park, Maryland. They did not know each other, so I introduced them and suggested that they have a Bible study together.

Later, Alice came into the store with her husband, Frank. Frank said, "You got the women studying the Bible; when are you going to get the men studying?"

I said, "This Wednesday."

He said, "Where?"

"Your house."

It was a Bible study made up of professional hard hats. Frank was a B&O Railroad engineer. There was also a telephone lineman, a chief petty officer, etc. It was a great inductive Bible study. They really knew how to look at the text. They caught me if I ever mentioned a meaning.[†]

Years later, Frank attended a men's Bible study at the Evangelical Presbyterian Church of Annapolis with many Naval Academy professors. He wrote to me to tell me that these educated men did not know how to study the Bible for themselves. They had to use commentaries.

The Christian Bookstore was half a block from the State Capitol, two and a half blocks from the main gate of the Naval Academy, and one and a half blocks from St. Johns College. Next to the bookstore

---

† In inductive Bible study, you do not ask, "What does this verse *mean*?" You only look for what the text objectively says.

was an insurance office run by George Brungot, a Naval Academy graduate. I would visit him periodically, preach the gospel, and leave him a booklet or two. This went on for years with little or no effect.

Several more years went by, and I ran into George again. "I bet you think that I did not read any of those books you gave me. I read them all." George had become a Christian. His wife Jean had also come to the Lord through Bessie's Bible studies.

In 1959 or 1960, a Johnnie* came into the store on Maryland Ave. He was a Jew from New York City. His name was Stephen Sohmer. In the process of our conversation, I gave him a copy of *Prophecy and History in Relation to the Messiah* by Alfred Edersheim, a Viennese Jew who had become a Christian. Stephen came back into the store after reading the book. He was angry. I have seen people angrier than him, but not many. Later, another Christian at St. John's had a major influence on Stephen, and he received Christ. We used to have him babysit our children.

About 1960, Sadie Paydon invited me to speak to an adult Sunday school class at the Paydons' church. A member of the congregation named George Ferguson would bring his four-year-old to Sunday school, shove him into the class, cross the street to Read's Drug Store, and drink coffee until it was time to pick up his son. A friend of his said, "George, why do you spend 25¢ for coffee when you can drink it free in the adult Sunday school class?" That sounded fine to George. He came to the class that morning when I was teaching.

Three weeks later, George called me. "You don't know me, but three weeks ago I heard your teaching. That evening I was putting my son to bed. He's the kind who jumps out of bed as soon as I leave.

* A student from St. John's College in Annapolis

I was standing in the doorway to keep him in bed; I thought I would pray for him and did. When I prayed for him, something happened to me. I have gone to the same bar five nights a week for almost thirteen years. Now I only go one night a week, and I order Coca-Cola—and I love beer."

I said, "Anything else?"

"Yes, I have had a very foul mouth all the time. Now I go to work and can't stand everyone else's profanity. If I say something myself, I want to bite my tongue off."

"It sounds like you have been converted. Come on over to see me."

He came down to the bookstore at about noon. I said, "Let's go have lunch." We walked across the street to the Ann Arundel Coffee House. The owner of the shop was a man named Johnnie Johnston. When Johnnie saw George Ferguson walk in the door with Jim Wilson, he couldn't believe it. He didn't think those two guys would ever be seen together. We sat down in a booth. Although he was very busy with the lunchtime rush, Johnnie came and sat with us. After about twenty minutes, he said, "George, I have listened for twenty minutes, and you have not said one bad word."

Two doors away from the bookstore was a mom-and-pop grocery store called the Busy Bee. The owners were a Mr. and Mrs. Dammeyer. Every day for about two years, I would go into the store and buy a Grimes Golden apple and a 5¢ Hershey bar to add to my lunch.

Although I had been in his store many times, Mr. Dammeyer had never been in ours. So one day at lunch I took a copy of *Through Gates of Splendor*, by Elisabeth Elliot, and went to see him. "Mr. Dammeyer, I know you are wondering what in the world we are doing in our store. In addition to selling books, we also loan them. I brought one up to loan to you." He was grateful.

A few days later he came in to return the book. He was in shock. He had no idea that there were Indians like that in this world and had no idea that there were Christians like that, either. He was given another book about the same people. He read all five books written about the missionaries who were martyred by the Auca Indians. When he came to return the last one, I was unpacking books in the back room. He had been deeply touched by what he read.

I said, "Mr. Dammeyer, have you ever read anything by Billy Graham?"

He eagerly said, "No, No." I gave him a copy of *Peace with God*.

That evening, I read in the newspaper that Billy Graham was going to be on Channel 5. We had no TV. I called Mr. Dammeyer to tell him that Billy Graham was going to be on in five minutes. He said Diane would turn it on. Diane was his high-school daughter who had already received Christ reading *By Searching* by Isobel Kuhn.

While I still had him on the phone I said, "Mr. Dammeyer, you and I have never talked about God." He said he would like to do that and invited me to his home the next night.

The next morning, I was walking by The Busy Bee. He saw me through the window and came running out of the store. "Remember, you are coming to my house tonight." Then he said, "I have the afternoon off." I told him to come with me. He came with me back to the bookstore and called on the name of the Lord.

In 1961, a saleswoman from a local radio station began coming into the bookstore every day, although I never bought any advertising. For about forty-five minutes a day, she told me the soap opera of her life. She continued it for weeks with no repetitions in the story. I could see that she was on the edge of losing her mind.

After this, I said to her, "Ginny, I think I know the solution to your problem."

She got up and said, "I see you do not understand the situation," and stomped out.

Ginny had a seventeen-year-old son named David. One day when I was away in Virginia and called home, Bessie said that she thought that Ginny needed to go to an institution and, if so, she was willing to take David in to our home.

When I got home, it became apparent that Ginny was crazy. I convinced her to see two doctors,* and they committed her to an institution. David and I rode with her in the back of the ambulance. On the way there, she said awful things to her son; she told him that if she had a knife, she would kill him.

When we got back to Annapolis, I moved David into our home. It was raining, and he refused to move his stuff in the rain. I told him I would pray that the rain would stop. It did stop, and we shifted our three children around to make a room for him and moved his things in. He stayed with us until he graduated high school the following spring. He would stay out until two a.m. Bessie would wait up for him; I went to bed. He was having difficulty at school; Bessie insisted that we take different parts and read Macbeth together to help him. David received Christ sometime during the year.

One night, everyone but me had the flu. Bessie was sick in bed. In the middle of the night, I heard noises in the hallway. I went to the bedroom door to see what it was. David was coming out of his room, headed for the bathroom. Heather was coming out of her room with the same destination. Douglas was coming down the hall. The three of them met outside the bathroom. They all bent over and vomited at the same time. Guess who had to clean it up?

One day in 1960, Bessie sent me to Safeway to buy a few things. I took four-year-old Heather with me. I only had $3.03. As I went through the store, I threw things into the basket without adding up the

* In Maryland it takes the signatures of two medical doctors to commit someone to a psychiatric hospital.

price in my head. When we got to the line at the cash register, Heather asked me for a penny for the gumball machine, and I gave her one.

Immediately behind me in line was Huddy Shields. Huddy was in one of Bessie's Bible studies. She was married to a wealthy man. Her basket was stacked high with expensive items. It suddenly occurred to me that I might not have enough money to pay for the few items in my basket. I didn't want to be embarrassed in front of Huddy, but it was too late to get out of the line—the clerk was already ringing up my items.

I prayed, "God, don't let this happen in front of Huddy Shields."

The clerk ringing up the items in the basket. "That will be $3.02."

I gave her my $3 and my two pennies and left with Heather chewing her gum.

Our friend Peggy Panetti was teaching a Bible class for preschoolers in the church we attended. She wanted to be part of an adult class, so she quit teaching the kids' study and joined Bessie's Bible class. In the first session, she found out she wasn't saved.

Peggy needed to talk to someone about this. The Panettis lived two blocks from us. Peggy walked up and down our street with her two little girls, hoping Bessie would come out for a walk. She had given up and turned around to walk home when Bessie finally came out. Peggy ran toward her.

"I'm not a Christian, I'm not a Christian!" she cried.

Bessie tried to reassure her. "Yes, you are."

But she wasn't. They all walked over to Peggy's house, and Peggy received Christ in the garden.

"Well, when are you going to go after Fred?" she asked me later. Fred was her husband.

I talked with Fred several times. Then someone gave me a back-board with a hoop on it for my boys to shoot baskets, but I didn't have a pole to mount it on. I happened to mention this to Fred. "I've got a pole," he told me. "I'll help you put it in, if you'll do it on Sunday," he said, thinking I wouldn't!

I said, "Yes, I'd be glad to."

So Fred helped me put the pole in the ground, and we mounted the backboard on it.

Fred was ready to become a Christian, but he had a problem. He was a member of the Elks Club. Fred said, "I go to the Elks Club every Wednesday night to drink beer. I'm not going to quit that." He wanted to know if he got saved, could he still drink beer? I told him yes.

Fred was an insurance salesman, and he collected premiums door to door. There were a lot of Christians on his route, so he told them all he'd been saved. He also told them, "And Jim Wilson said I could drink beer!"

Soon I got a telephone call from Betty Greenville.* "Fred says he got saved. Is that so?"

"Yes."

"He also said you told him he could drink beer and be a Christian. You didn't say that, did you?"

"Yes, I said it."

"But a *real* Christian wouldn't drink beer," Betty said.

"Tell me, Betty, are you a Southern Baptist?" I asked her.

"Yes."

"Do you believe that a person is once saved, always saved?"

"Yes."

I said, "Have a beer."

---

* Betty's last name escapes my memory, so this may be an invented name!

CHAPTER 36

RUNNING THE BOOKSTORE

For all have sinned and fall short of the glory of God, and all are
justified freely by his grace through the redemption that came by
Christ Jesus. (Rom. 3:23–24)

When we first opened the Christian Bookstore in Annapolis, my
boss insisted on giving a twenty percent discount to all midshipmen.
Our profit margin on book sales was fifteen percent; a twenty percent discount would put us five percent in the red every time we sold
a book. I objected. He insisted. He said that the OCU would make up
the difference. They were not able to do it, and, over the next three
years, that decision put the store $3,000 in the red.*

By the fall of 1961, the OCU had $17,000 in overdue bills, $3,000
of which was owed by the Annapolis bookstore. The OCU Council
made two major decisions in the fall of 1961, both of which affect-
ed us. The first decision was to close the bookstore. We had had an
amazing ministry there for those three years, so I encouraged the
council to give the store to me rather than close it. They agreed, and
we formed a local nonprofit corporation called Christian Books in
Annapolis. I was still the OCU east coast staff member, but I took
over the bookstore and its $3,000 debt.

I did not want to leave the OCU work for the bookstore. Instead of
continuing as the staff member for the entire east coast, my plan was
to stay on as the OCU Naval Academy local representative and run
the bookstore on the side. The other decision of the OCU Council

* That would be roughly equivalent to $25,000 in 2020.

changed that. It had been the policy of the OCU to pay staff before paying bills. I had no objection to that. But then I found out that January staff salaries were paid before January bills, February staff salaries were paid before January bills, and March staff salaries were paid before January bills. I objected to that. I might be two months behind in salary, but I was still being paid before bills that were behind much further.

The general secretary said that he would obey his own conscience as to when and whom he paid first. When I received my next paycheck, I cashed it and used the money to pay some of the bookstore's bills. The general secretary took the matter to the OCU Council. In September, the council voted to pay staff regardless of other bills.

After the meeting, the general secretary said to me, "You heard the decision of the council. Are you going to stand by your decision?"

I told Buck that I would not receive any salary until the entire $20,000 of OCU's debt was paid. The next time I got a paycheck, I again used it all to pay bookstore bills.

I had no intention of leaving the OCU staff. I knew I had been led by God for the work at the military academies. God wonderfully provided for our needs with no salary during the last three months of 1961.

For example, I took a job substitute teaching at the junior high. I only worked two days, but it helped. There were many times when we went without. God always answered, but it was sometimes at the last moment. I got very unhappy with God that He would wait so long.

Many times, I trusted that God would provide. Other times, I worried and worried right up until the provision came. One time, we were overdue in rent about two weeks. Bessie said, "Jim, where is your faith?"

I asked Bessie, "What do you mean?"

"Your faith is like Eeyore's tail. It's either there or it isn't there, and yours isn't."

After three months without salary, I was in a quandary. The general secretary had made what I regarded as several unethical decisions concerning finances which the council did not know about. I realized that he was not going to change his approach to such things. I did not see how I could work under his leadership, and yet I was called to the ministry and did not want to leave my position as the OCU representative at the Naval Academy.

The problem was solved by my realizing that there was no one to take my place on the staff. That meant that I could resign from the regular staff and remain as the local OCU representative at the Naval Academy. I resigned effective December 31, 1961 and volunteered as the substitute OCU representative.

The OCU told the membership that I had left their staff in order to run the bookstore, which was not true. I left the staff because of the financial irresponsibility of the general secretary and because the council had condoned that portion of the irresponsibility which was known to them.

From January 1, 1962, until the summer of 1968, I continued my ministry as local representative of the OCU at the Naval Academy, but not as a paid staff member. I worked with Christian Books in Annapolis and continued traveling to speaking engagements. My travels did not focus on military bases anymore, but on universities. I spoke by invitation to Christian groups and conferences at colleges and universities in Maryland, Pennsylvania, and Virginia: the University of Maryland, Goucher College, Towson State, Penn State, the University of Pennsylvania, the University of Virginia, Harrisonburg, Lehigh, Drexel, and William and Mary. The Lord was working in our personal lives, correcting us, and touching other lives through us at the same time.

When we inherited the store from OCU, we also inherited the $3,000 debt. We prayed and worried about it for several weeks. Then one Monday morning in the shower, I prayed a prayer of faith and knew we had the $3,000. When I got out of the shower, I told Bessie we had the money. She believed me. I went down to the store and told our treasurer, Findley Paydon, that we had did not have to pray for the money any longer; our prayers had been answered.

At noon, I received a call from a stockbroker in New Jersey. He told me that a client of his had instructed him to sell $3,000 worth of stock and send a check to me. He was calling to find out how to make out the check and what address to mail it to. The check arrived the next day.

This sort of thing did not happen often, but it happened often enough for me to not be surprised when it did.

After Cleo Buxton resigned, Paul Pettijohn took over the position of general secretary of the OCU. Later, the position was vacant again. Art Athens, a friend of mine, was a Marine major who had been the brigade commander when he was a midshipman, then a White House Fellow, before becoming a successful Marine. I called him and suggested that he apply. He said he wasn't qualified. I asked him what his gifts were.

He said, "Leadership and teaching."

I told him that those were the qualities they were looking for.

Art resigned from the Marines with no assurance that he would get the OCU job. When his resignation came to Marine Headquarters, General Krulak (future commandant of the Marine Corps) called to ask him why he was leaving the Corps. Art told him it was to run the OCU. Krulak said if that happened, he would rejoin OCU.

Art got the job, and the OCU turned around. After several years, he became the commandant of Merchant Marine midshipmen at Kings Point, New York, then the director of the Vice Admiral James B. Stockdale Center for Ethical Leadership at the Naval Academy.

CHAPTER 37

CORRIE

James, Cephas and John, those esteemed as pillars, gave me and
Barnabas the right hand of fellowship when they recognized the
grace given to me. They agreed that we should go to the Gentiles,
and they to the circumcised. (Gal. 2:9)

After Corrie ten Boom spent the last day of our honeymoon with
us, we did not see her for about four years. She came to visit us and
to minister in Annapolis at least twice. Corrie was not well-known
at the time, so people would not come *en masse* to hear her speak.
On one of her visits, I drove her around to seventeen different Bible
studies during the week. When I was taking her to the plane, she
said, "Jim, I cannot understand it. In Australia, many people received
Christ. Here in the U.S., very few have received Christ. Do you think
God has taken away from me the gift of evangelism?"

I said, "No, Corrie, the gifts and calling of God are without repentance. The reason is this: I have heard you speak seventeen times this
week, and not once have you spoken the gospel. The closest you got
was when you mentioned the nail prints in His hands."

I had given a copy of *A Prisoner and Yet* to Mrs. Greengold, a
Jewish woman who lived on the same block as us. She was so impressed that she wanted Corrie ten Boom to speak to her synagogue.
On Corrie's next visit to Annapolis, we planned a meeting for them.
It was held in the Jewish Community Center, and the place was
packed out. Corrie and I were the only non-Jews present. As I sat
there listening to her, I thought, "If Corrie says, 'Jesus Christ' one
more time, we're not going to get out of here alive." But we did.

On another visit, Corrie was staying at a home with two parents and their fifteen-year-old daughter. The mother wore very heavy makeup. Corrie, of course, wore none, and she wore flat shoes. Bessie also wore no makeup. The mother spoke to Corrie. "Corrie, please tell Bessie to wear some makeup. It would greatly improve her testimony." Corrie did tell Bessie, and they both laughed over it.

We did not see Corrie again until we visited her on our way to Evan's wedding in El Centro, California, many years later, shortly before the stroke that took away her ability to speak. She was retired and living in Orange County, California. Bessie wanted her to pray for our children Heather and Gordon, which she did.

Back row: Herb Sprague, ?, Doug Powell, John Knubel, A.J. Egerton, Jim
Front row: Cal Dunlap, Bessie, Corrie

CHAPTER 38

A.J.

Now Stephen, a man full of God's grace and power, performed
great wonders and signs among the people. (Acts 6:8)

In 1959, I gave a copy of *The Dynamic of Service*, a book on personal
evangelism by A. Paget Wilkes, to a young "Christian" midshipman
named A.J. Egerton who was starting his plebe year at the U.S. Naval
Academy. A.J. was from Texas. He was an athlete and had come to
the Academy to play football. He had an infectious personality. His
summer cruise that year was to be part of the opening of the St.
Lawrence Seaway. I hoped the book would help him in evangelism
as it had helped me.

A.J. became a very effective evangelist. It was not until 1963 that
I found out that he himself had been converted reading the book on
that summer cruise. On his senior cruise, A.J. led a midshipman of
the class of '64 to Christ; he in turn led midshipmen to Christ up to
the class of '68.

When A.J. was commissioned in 1962, he was assigned to a ship
in the Mediterranean. It may not be their way today, but sailors used
to keep paperback books in their back pockets to pass the time. In
the Mediterranean, A.J. put thirty-five copies of Billy Graham's *Peace
with God* in the back pockets of the sailors on his ship.

During his summer tour in 1963, A.J. fell on the bridge of his
ship in the Mediterranean. The doctor thought he had been overcome by stress and sent him to the psych ward of the Philadelphia
Naval Hospital. The doctors there discovered that A.J. had a massive

malignant brain tumor. They operated, but the surgeon was unable remove the entire tumor. The surgeon did not tell A.J. that he still had brain cancer and that his condition was terminal.

Somehow, I found out about it. I was at an OCU family conference at Camp Wabanna when I made the decision to go to Philadelphia to tell A.J. about his cancer. Hal Guffey, USNA '55, accompanied me, and we left immediately.

We arrived at the hospital around noon. We knew we would have to see the surgeon first but did not know how to go about it. We had lunch in the cafeteria and prayed for guidance.

After lunch, Hal and I were walking down a corridor when a doctor in a white coat came around the corner, and we ran into each other. We both apologized, and he started to go on his way. I realized he looked familiar. I stopped and called, "Doctor!" He turned around. It was Joe Winston. His father-in-law, David Morken, had officiated at my wedding eleven years earlier in Yokohama, and I had been of some help to Joe and his wife when he was in medical school at Emery University.

Joe recognized me and said, "I know why you are here." He had been doing residency in the psych ward when A.J. was there. He said that he would go with us to see the surgeon. After a lengthy discussion, the surgeon agreed to tell A.J. that he had terminal cancer.

A.J. met with the four of us, but the surgeon did not tell him about the cancer. He beat around the bush. Hal and I went back with A.J. to his room, and I delivered the news. I said, "If you want the elders to pray for you, I will round them up in Philadelphia and come back here with them."

A.J. asked for time to pray about it. We came back later, and he told us that he did not want the elders to pray for him. He would rather go to be with Jesus. I thought he was dead wrong. He was only twenty-three years old. I argued with him until he finally consented to the prayer. I was wrong. I should not have pressured him.

A.J. was retired from the Navy with full disability. Instead of going home to Texas, he came to live with us on North Cherry Grove in Annapolis and was a witness with me to the town.

I remember one incident when a woman came into the bookstore to see me. We were in the large room upstairs. I reached into my pocket for my New Testament. It wasn't there. While I was wondering where it was, I looked up, and there was a New Testament in the middle of the air coming toward me. A.J. had thrown it to me.

A.J. went to Texas for Christmas and died there on January 23, 1964.

CHAPTER 39

A HOUSE

But we see him who for a little while was made lower than the
angels, namely Jesus, crowned with glory and honor because of the
suffering of death, so that by the grace of God he might taste death
for everyone. (Heb. 2:9)

We had lived on North Cherry Grove in Annapolis for four and a
half years. The house had no closets, and we had four children. I
started looking for another house to rent that we could afford. Jim
Meredith, a real estate agent, was helping me. We looked at many
houses and could not find anything. In desperation, he said, "Jim,
why don't you *buy* a house?"

The reason we did not buy was that we had no money. Instead of
telling Jim that, I said, "Ok, if we buy one, we would have a lot more
requirements: not so new that it is pretentious and expensive, not
so old that we have to nail it together, within walking distance of
Germantown Elementary School,* four bedrooms, two bathrooms,
lots of closets, a dry basement, storm windows, a fireplace, and a
hallway around the living room so the kids can find their way to the
kitchen without interrupting any counseling that might be happening in the living room."

I thought, "That will keep him busy."

Two weeks later, Jim Meredith called and said he had found the
house. I asked how and where. He said that he had not been able to

* Germantown was a nongraded school, i.e., it did not have distinct grade levels. It
had been great for our children.

find any four-bedroom houses in the Germantown school district, so he called a friend of his in real estate who lived in the district and asked him if he knew of any. His friend replied that there were not, but then said, "I will sell you mine."

"Is it for sale?"

"It wasn't, but it is now."

Jim wanted me to see the house. So I went. It was the last house on a dead-end street and was situated on three lots. It was five years old but made of pieces of other houses that had been dismantled. The only new things in it were the windows, the roof, and the plaster. It had everything on my list. The price was $17,500.

Jim Meredith knew he had the right house for us. We walked out, and he wanted to talk money. I didn't know what to do. I knew it was the right house, too, but I had no money. To get rid of him, I told him I would pray about it. Jim left.

Just then, a professor friend of mine drove up in his VW Bug. I asked him what he was doing driving up a dead-end street. Graham said that he was looking for me. He asked if he could see the house. I said he could if the lady would let us back in.

When we came out, Graham asked me if I thought it was the right house. I assured him it was. He asked the price. It was $17,500.

He said, "Twenty percent of that is $3,500, and $800 for closing costs makes $4,300. I will have a check for you tomorrow for $4,300."

His wife had been talking with Bessie, and Bessie had told her where I had gone and why. She told her husband, and he came looking for me right away. Six months earlier, they had determined that if Jim and Bessie ever decided to buy a house instead of renting, they would make the down payment. The next day, I took the money to Jim Meredith. Later, we were given another gift that paid for the rest of the house.

Several years later, a friend named Bob Poskett called to tell me that a fellow he knew had told him that was going into the Episcopal seminary. Bob asked him how he had been converted. He said that a man named Jim Wilson said he was going to pray for money, and the next day he walked in with $4,300. That convinced him of the gospel. That man was Jim Meredith.*

---

* He later found out that they did not believe in God at that seminary, so he left and went to British Guinea as a missionary.

CHAPTER 40

GORDONS

The grace of our Lord Jesus Christ be with your spirit, brothers.
Amen. (Gal. 6:18)

One day I received a letter from an ensign in San Diego asking what to do with an officer in his Bible study who was a member of the Reorganized Church of Latter Day Saints. The officer was disrupting the study. I told the ensign I would correspond with the Mormon.

After a while, the correspondence was taking up too much of my time, so I sent him *Is Mormonism Christian?* by Gordon Fraser. Gordon was a missionary to the different tribes of Native Americans in the West. He founded the Indian Bible Institute in Flagstaff, Arizona. He had gotten interested in Mormonism because at that time the Mormons believed that Native Americans had dark skin because they had been cursed by God, and that if anyone was converted to the Latter Day Saints their skin would turn white.

The officer liked Gordon Fraser's book and wrote me a response. Instead of answering his letter, I sent it to Moody Press and asked them to forward it to Gordon Fraser to take up the correspondence. I had no idea who Gordon Fraser was, but I no longer had to be concerned with this Mormon.

In the winter of 1961, I received a phone call. The man on the other end identified himself as Gordon Fraser. I had no idea to whom I was talking; the name did not ring a bell. He sounded as if we knew each other.

"Where are you?" I asked.

"On the edge of Annapolis."

"Where are you staying?"

"I will get a hotel room."

"No, you stay with us." I gave him directions to the store. I still had no idea who I was talking to. I thought I would figure it out eventually.

When I got off the phone, I checked my two-thousand-card Rolodex file. There was no Gordon Fraser in there. I called Bessie to let her know we had a guest for supper and overnight. Then I told her I had no idea who it was I had invited.

Bessie was expecting our youngest child. She replied that she had had a headache all day and was not feeling well. She would feed the guest, then excuse herself and go to bed. It would be up to me to entertain him.

When Gordon arrived at the bookstore, I discovered who he was. Bessie had a great supper prepared. She had such a good time that she did not excuse herself and go to bed; she stayed up late talking with us.

Gordon, 1965

Gordon's visit was a very great blessing to Bessie. She considered it a fulfillment of Hebrews 13:2: "Do not forget to entertain strangers, for by so doing some people have entertained angels without knowing it."

Our son Gordon was born in April 1961. We named him after Gordon Diehl, Mrs. Mother's son.[*]

---

[*] The mother of Bessie's best friend. Since Bessie's mother had died, Bessie called her friend's mom "Mrs. Mother."

JUNIOR HIGH BIBLE STUDY

For it is all for your sake, so that as grace extends to more and more
people it may increase thanksgiving, to the glory of God.

(2 Cor. 4:15)

Bessie taught a weekly Bible class for the kids in our neighborhood
on both North Cherry Grove and Genesee Street in Annapolis starting when Douglas was in first grade. When he entered junior high,
Bessie encouraged me to start a junior high Bible study. I did not see
how I could do it, because I was too busy already, and I did not know
anything about junior high kids.

I thought that would settle it, but Bessie was persistent. She kept
insisting, and I finally said I would do it.

I thought about what junior high kids like. I concluded that they
liked to mess around, and they liked to eat. I planned the study for
after school Wednesday. It consisted of thirty minutes of touch football, Frisbee, or buck-buck, then thirty minutes of eating, followed
by an hour of inductive Bible study. We ended up teaching about
twenty kids at a time for two years. I think they all received Christ.

Sometime during those years in Annapolis, we sponsored a Billy
Graham film at the Circle Theater. One of the results of this was the
conversion of an entire family, Dick and Beverly Cullers and their
three daughters and one son. Shortly after the film, we started holding the junior-high Bible study at the Cullers' home.

CHAPTER 42
DESEGREGATION

But on some points I have written to you very boldly by way of
reminder, because of the grace given me by God. (Rom. 15:15)

We lived in Annapolis from November of 1958 to July of 1968. Back
in the 1950s and '60s, the restaurants there were segregated. I was
unaware of this at first; I grew up in Nebraska where there were no
black people, so when I went to a restaurant, it did not occur to me
that it was odd that there were no black people present. I did not
realize that they were not *allowed* there.

Back in 1935, my mother sent Lorraine and me to take lunch to
my father, who was working within walking distance of our house.
She told us that Dad's partner was black, and he was a very nice man.
She was preparing us because she knew that we had never seen a
black person before.

Even in the Navy, there was only one black sailor on board with
me, a quartermaster on the *Brinkley Bass*. Before that time, black
men had been stewards' mates, there to make the beds of the officers.

Around the time I started running the Christian Bookstore in
Annapolis, I found out that black people were wanting to eat in the
restaurants that were all-white. They were demanding to be let in.

I had a decision to make. What should I do as a Christian? Should
I hold a placard outside the local restaurant with the black people
and demand that they be let in, or should I get inside the restaurant
with Mr. Barnes and help him throw them out? Neither one seemed
right to me: to support an unfriendly, belligerent protest, or support

an unfriendly, antagonistic restaurant owner. I prayed about it and determined that neither was a good, Christian option. But a third alternative of doing nothing was *also* wrong.

My solution was to step up the evangelism to both blacks and whites. I asked God to open the doors for me. I knew what I was doing at the Naval Academy and at the bookstore and speaking at colleges, but I did not know how to do evangelism in the black community.

My prayer got answered quickly. We were living in the Germantown School District, so Heather was enrolled in Germantown Elementary for fifth grade. Germantown was a non-graded public school. It was also an all-white school. It had been a great experience both for Douglas and Evan, and we wanted to stay in that district.

We had lived there for two years when the federal government ordered all schools to be desegregated. The Annapolis school districts were rezoned, and we suddenly found ourselves in the Adams Park School District.

Adams Park had been an all-black school. Our home was the last house on a dead-end street. Past the dead end, there was a solid block of trees. On the other side was Adams Park School and the black neighborhood of Annapolis. The theory was that by putting a white neighborhood in the district, the school would be desegregated. Instead, most of the white parents put their kids into private schools at that time, in what was called "white flight."

Douglas and Evan were in junior high, and Heather was going into fifth grade. Gordon was five years old. Germantown had no kindergarten, so he would not have gone to school for another year, anyway. However, Adams Park had a federally funded kindergarten program because most of the black children were not ready for first grade.

Gordon was ready for first grade, and we assumed he would not be accepted into kindergarten because of that. When he was accepted, I did not know why. Later I found out that he was accepted because he was white; the school could not get the federal money if the kindergarten was all black. They needed Gordon in order to meet the desegregation requirements. He came home from school the first day and said, "There is only one other kid with a face like mine."

Heather was one of two white girls in the fifth grade, and the following year she was the only white girl in the sixth. All of her teachers were black. It seemed that Heather was the favorite with the principal, Mr. Noel; the fifth-grade teacher, Miss Duval; the music teacher, Mr. Clemens; and the librarian. It appeared to us that it was because she was not self-conscious about being white in an all-black school.

For years, a $25 U.S. Savings Bond was given to the sixth-grade student who was the best in English, determined by the highest score on a standardized test. Heather and one of the black girls tied for the high score, and each received $25.

Then in April 1968, Martin Luther King, Jr. was killed. One of Heather's classmates greeted her the next morning as she was ascending the flight of stairs with a fist to the stomach saying, "You killed Doctor King!" Heather was picked on by her classmates for a while after this. Then one day the bullying just stopped. I asked Heather what had happened. She told me, "I asked God to make it stop." And it did.

I became an active member of the PTA and sponsored a book fair at the school. The kids bought books (not Christian ones, just regular children's books), and we showed a cartoon film and several Moody Science Films.

About this time, a tall, blonde white woman named Irene Johnson came to see me. After getting divorced, she had received Christ and joined a Southern Baptist Church in Baltimore. Shortly after that, the pastor made a pass at her. She was so disillusioned that she left Christianity and met and married a black medical doctor. He was the president of the NAACP in Anne Arundel County. He had a practice in Annapolis and was not a Christian. She thought that she was his second wife but later found out she was his third wife. After they were married, she also discovered that he was addicted to prescription drugs.

Irene realized she needed help, so she went back to one of the Baptist churches. The pastor was eager to help until he found out whom she had married. Her husband was black *and* the president of the local NAACP. The pastor could see that the Johnsons might want to join his church if he helped them, and he did not want that. His church was not ready to receive a black doctor married to a white woman. Irene got this response from at least two pastors.

Then one of the pastors sent her to me because I did not have a church to integrate. I told her I was willing to reach out to her husband. I went to his office and sat in a long line of patients waiting to be seen. Periodically, he would come out of his consulting room. Each time he came out, he looked at me. Later he told me that he thought I was there because I had a venereal disease and did not want to face a white doctor.

At last, it was my turn. When we were alone, I said, "Doctor, I am not sick. I need more time than you can give me here, so I came to ask for a special appointment." He wanted me to give him a brief on what I would say if he gave me the appointment, so I gave a brief of the gospel.

Dr. Johnson set a time, but when I showed up, he was not there. His second wife had taken him to court for failing to provide support. When I got in touch with him, he said he could see me at eleven a.m. Sunday. I told him I was busy at that time, so we settled on Sunday evening.

I went to his house. He was wide open and received Christ at about six in the evening. His life was marvelously changed. He was delivered from the drug addiction and other worldly things. When Dr. Johnson had his next birthday party, Bessie and I were the only ones invited.

One morning, Irene called me at home. She was in hysterics. I had to hold the phone away from my ear. I asked her what the problem was. She said that her husband had been with another woman, and she was going to shoot him when he came home. I asked why she was calling me. She said she thought I might think of some reason for her not to shoot him. She could not think of a reason not to kill him as soon as he came home.

"How do you know he is having an affair?" I asked her.

"I found someone else's comb in the car."

"Irene, for all I know, he could be unfaithful to you, but he was not in this instance."

"How do you know?"

"I know the devil very well. The one time he would have you shoot your husband is the time when he was innocent. Put the comb back in the car and forget about it."

She put it back, but she was steaming all day. In the afternoon, she decided to take a hot bath to cook the anger out of herself. While she was in the bath, her thirteen-year-old daughter came home from school and yelled up the stairs, "Mom, have you seen my new comb?"

"Look in the car," she replied.

Dr. Johnson died of an aneurism while we were still in Annapolis. I attended the funeral. It was a gospel meeting with great preaching, along with testimonies of his short Christian life. I inherited all of his suits. We were both tall, but he was bigger. They had to be adjusted to fit me. I definitely needed the clothes, although some of them were a little too loud for me.

In 1965, Christy Wilson* visited us, and I took him to some of the black churches to preach. Christy had been the only missionary in Afghanistan for twenty years.

Doug and Evan had two close black friends (brothers) who lived two blocks from us. They came to our junior high Bible study. Their mother, a Mrs. Holland, was a fourth-grade teacher at Germantown Elementary and active in Asbury Methodist Church. I ended up preaching there one Sunday morning. Mrs. Holland asked Heather to join a special Saturday group called P.A.C.E. to improve race relations.

When Heather and Gordon attended Adams Park Elementary School, I walked them to school each morning, then I walked through the black district to the bookstore. I would meet all of the kids from the district on their way to school. They would line up to get the gospel tracts I gave to each of them. One day, I did not take the walk until later, so I did not meet any of the children. I did see two men on the opposite side of the street. They yelled to me. They asked if I was the man who gave tracts to the kids. I said I was. They wanted to know if I had any for them.

When I first opened the bookstore in November 1958, it was with the primary objective of reaching midshipmen from the Academy. What I hadn't thought about beforehand was that the midshipmen are not allowed outside the Academy grounds except on Saturdays and Sundays. I was so focused on witnessing to midshipmen that I did not want to waste my time selling books to little old church ladies and the black townspeople—the only customers who were actually coming in to the store.

Frank McGowan was one of those people. Frank was a black janitor and had two jobs, one at the Academy and another at the

* J. Christy Wilson Jr. (1921–99) inspired students to consider missions by helping launch the Urbana Missions Conference. He is credited with coining the term *tentmaking* to describe bivocational missions work. A 1997 lecture by John Piper on Wilson is available at desiringgod.org.

hospital. He came in regularly to buy 39¢ paperbacks published by Moody Press. One day, he said, "Mr. Wilson, I understand that you start Bible studies. I have four friends who would like to study the Bible. Would you teach us how?"

I said I would be glad to. We had a little round coffee table and chairs in the store. Frank and I sat down, and I launched into the basics of Bible study.

After a bit, I noticed that Frank was not paying attention. I was beginning to get impatient when he said, "Do you know why we want to study the Bible? We want to find out how to be born again."

At that moment, I saw Bessie driving up in front of the store to take me home. I waved her to keep going and preached the gospel to Frank. At the end, I asked him to receive the Lord. He was very convicted of sin but would not call upon the Lord. I finally found the reason. He had another woman besides his wife, and he could see difficulties coming. He struggled for a bit and finally surrendered to Christ.

Frank was a good and effective witness to the rest of the black community. He went on to lead many other janitors and barbers to the Lord. Those barbers in turn witnessed to the midshipmen who sat in their chairs. The people who came into the bookstore were not the ones I had been eager to witness to—but the midshipmen I wanted to reach for Christ were reached indirectly, through my witnessing to the people God put in front of me.*

God abundantly answered my prayer for access of the gospel to the black community.

---

* Many years later, I went back to Annapolis on a ministry trip. I went over to Frank's house and met his daughter, who looked about twenty years old. She had been born after her father became a Christian. She told me that he was at the grocery store. When I arrived at the store, he was there in the checkout line. When he saw me, he left the line to run and hug me. I can remember only one other man who hugged me, and that was for the same reason. They both had become Christians.

CHAPTER 43
BOOKSTORES AS COLLEGE MINISTRY

Grace to you and peace from God our Father and the Lord Jesus
Christ. (Phil. 1:3)

While visiting Pennsylvania State University to speak at InterVarsity
Fellowship on one of my road trips for the OCU, I noticed that there
was no Christian bookstore in the area. Penn State is located in State
College, a town in the middle of the Pennsylvania mountains. There
are twenty thousand students there with no place to go. I came home
convinced that there should be a literature witness in State College. I
wondered about other university towns. I checked all the college towns
I knew of against the list of bookstores in the Christian Booksellers
Association and drew a blank. With the exception of our store in
Annapolis, there were *no* Christian bookstores in college towns.

Shortly after that, the Christian Bookstore sponsored a faculty
conference for the mid-Atlantic states with Carl Henry[†] as the main
speaker. During the conference, I spoke on the dearth of bookstores
in college towns and shared my concern for Penn State.

John Sanford, a PhD candidate at the University of Maryland in
College Park, came up to me afterward. "Why talk only about state
colleges? There's a vacant bookstore one block from the University of
Maryland. It still says 'Books' on the window."

Christian Books in Annapolis had no money, but we did have
books. I signed a lease for the vacant store, split the Christian

† Carl F.H. Henry (1913–2003) was an American theologian and the founder of the
National Association of Evangelicals and *Christianity Today.*

Bookstore inventory, and took half of it to College Park. We needed a man to run the new store. We prayed.

Don Hudson had just graduated from Dallas Seminary. He was playing racquetball with a student who had graduated from the Naval Academy. The student asked Don what he was going to do next. Don replied that he felt called to work with college students in the Baltimore-Washington, D.C., area. He did not know with whom, but not Campus Crusade or InterVarsity. His friend suggested me, and Don came to Baltimore to spy out the land.

On Sunday, Don went to church at a Brethren Assembly. The speaker was Carl Armerding.* Carl also suggested he check in with me. He did and found out that he was answered prayer. In 1963, we opened the Lamplighter Bookstore one block from the University of Maryland.

In order to give Don a day off, I would come to College Park to cover for him once a week. It was normally on Monday. One day, a hippie named Hardy Cook came in. When he realized that he was in a Christian store, he felt obligated to tell me why he was not a Christian. I had heard the same story many times before. His reasons for rejecting Christianity were the Conquistadors, the Crusades, the Inquisition, and hypocrites.

When he finished, I asked him these questions.

"Are hypocrites Christians?"

"No!"

"Were the Crusaders Christians?"

"No!"

"Were the Conquistadors Christians?"

"No!"

"Were the Inquisitors Christians?"

"No!"

* Carl E. Armerding (1936–) is professor emeritus of Old Testament at Regent College and also served as the college's second president.

"Hardy, you just told me that you are not a Christian because of all these *non-Christians*. That doesn't make any sense at all."

I told him that I had been asked to speak at the InterVarsity Fellowship that evening in the Student Union Building and gave him the time and the room number.

It was a long room with a long table down the middle. There were about seventy-five students there. The room was so crowded that when I stood up to speak, I stood in the corner. I noticed that Hardy was standing in the corner to my right.

When I finished, two girls right in front of me had questions. When I was done answering them, I looked up to find that Hardy Cook had left. I was annoyed with the two girls for detaining me. I said I had missed the guy I had invited to the meeting.

I continued to talk with students until finally I made it out into the hallway. I looked up, and there was Hardy. "Hardy, I thought you left!"

"I got out of there as fast as I could. I was down at the other end of the Student Union when two girls walked by. One of them said to the other, 'Too bad that fellow Mr. Wilson invited to the meeting left.' I figured they were talking about me, so I came back."

"Hardy, if you want to talk, I will listen."

"No. You talk, and I will listen."

We went back into the room and sat at the table with some of the Christian guys, and I explained the gospel to him.

Pretty soon, Hardy was physically shaking. I knew he was convicted of sin, so I suggested that he receive the Lord.

He responded, "No, no. Mind your own business! This is a personal thing."

"OK. When you receive the Lord, go down to the Lamplighter and tell them you got saved. Good night."

"What do you mean, 'Good night'?"

"I am going home to bed. It is a personal thing, so you go home and take care of it." I shooed him out the door.

The parking lot for the Student Union Building was at the bottom of a steep hill. The Christian guys were walking with me to my car when we heard someone running down the hill behind us yelling, "Mr. Wilson, Mr. Wilson!" It was Hardy Cook. "I couldn't wait until I got back to my dorm. I have to accept Christ now." And he did.

One day, a hippie student came into the store in College Park. It did not take long for her to find out she was in the wrong kind of bookstore. I watched her walking around the store, getting more and more turned off by the Christian books she saw. She started to head for the door. I cut her off by standing between her and the doorway. I smiled at her and said, "The books aren't that bad!"

"Like what?" she retorted.

I started with the *The Chronicles of Narnia* series, telling her about the various books. She wasn't listening. She was just waiting for a chance to get past me and out the door. Then I said, "We have some wonderful missionary biographies."

She blew up at that. "What do you mean, going out there and putting clothes on all those innocent natives?"

I prayed for wisdom. Right next to me was a copy of *The Savage My Kinsman*, a picture book of the Waorani Indians written by Elisabeth Elliott. In the back was a full-page photograph of one of the Indians walking away into the bush, holding hands with little Valerie Elliott. Neither of them had a stitch of clothing on. I flipped the book open to that page and handed it to her. "It looks like the natives are taking the clothes off the missionaries."

She took a look at the photo. "Give me that book!" she said. She sat down and read it. When she was done, I gave her another book. She stayed for four hours and received the Lord around four that afternoon.

The Christian Booksellers Association board was up to running two bookstores in Maryland, but they were unable to commit to stores outside the state. The former director of InterVarsity stopped in the Lamplighter, and I shared my burden with him. Later, John Alexander, the national director of InterVarsity, was speaking at College Park. I went to hear him and asked for five minutes. It seemed to me that InterVarsity should get into this ministry. They had a large publishing house and staff members at every university. John gave me permission to write to him on the subject of literature ministry, and I did. Here is the letter I wrote him laying out my thoughts:

Dear John,

Since our conversation on Thursday I have had time for meditation and some prayer. First let me give you a brief history of the work here.

In October 1956, I resigned my commission in the regular Navy in order to become the East Coast Staff Member for the Officers' Christian Union . . . . I traveled out of Washington, D.C., with a briefcase pregnant with books and I.V. booklets. After a few months, I had come across six people who had received Christ while they were alone as a result of reading the New Testament or books or tracts. This made me realize that my personal ministry was greatly extended in quality and quantity and time by the use of literature. I needed more literature.

In November of 1958, the OCU opened a bookstore 2.5 blocks from the main gate of the Naval Academy. I continued to travel for three more years as Academy staff member as well as run the bookstore.

The ministry of the bookstore was immediately evident to us. It took me a while longer to recognize that anyone who bought a book in a college town had some access to students. When we opened the store, we had students in mind, and it annoyed me when people asked for Christian books which were not related to the University mind. But because we were a public store, we reluctantly gave way to demands, only to find out that our ministry to midshipmen [actually] increased. For instance, a negro* janitor at the Naval Academy received Christ in the store. He has since led a Bible study with some of the barbers in the Naval Academy who talk to midshipmen about the Lord.

We did not open the store with enough capital, and the monthly capital input required to keep the store running was not available through the OCU, so the OCU voted to close the store as of 31 December 1961. By this time, it had a wide outreach to Annapolitans as well as to the Naval Academy. Prof. J.F. Paydon of the math department, who had been on the OCU Council when the store opened, did not think we could spiritually afford to let the store close. He took the leadership in forming a committee and then a corporation which was established before the end of the year. Enough money was raised to buy the store from the OCU. Christian Books in Annapolis, Inc., opened the store 1 January 1962. Almost concurrently, I left the OCU staff to assume the responsibility of the leadership of this new literature ministry. The purpose of CBA is as follows: To be a positive witness for Jesus Christ beginning in Annapolis and Anne Arundel County. To this end we intend to operate: 1. Bookstores, 2. Lending libraries, 3. Distribute Christian Literature, and 4. Anything else that propagates the Christian faith.

By 1964 the bookstore in Annapolis was paying for itself under the management of Mr. Richard Waters. Most of my time was spent in the personal ministry and group ministry of the store. As a non-profit corporation, we have encouraged the starting and continuance of many inductive Bible study groups: elementary school, junior high, high school, midshipmen, professors, officers, and many neighborhood women's groups and evening couples' studies.

---

* This was the most polite term at the time.

The bookstore became a combat information center as well as a place for personal and literature contacts. We have sponsored two local faculty conferences and several other special events or people for evangelism or edification. In the spring of 1967, it occurred to me that our witness to the Naval Academy (combined with the inside witness of the OCU) had been effective in spite of the limitations of a small student body with a very limited egress to the town of Annapolis (essentially Saturday afternoon). Suppose the limitation was not there? Would we be more effective to more people if we were located at Penn State with 20,000 students [who had] unlimited access to the town of State College and no place else to go?

With the thought that this was likely, I looked in the directory of the Christian Booksellers Assoc. to see if there was a Christian bookshop in State College. There was none. My curiosity was aroused, so I looked up the names of other college and university towns. Unless it was a town like Wheaton or a city like Philadelphia, I drew a blank. At that time, I think there were 800 Christian bookstores in the country, and they were not in college towns. I remember looking up Ann Arbor and counting the number of Christian bookstores listed in Michigan. There were between 40 and 50 such stores in Michigan and none of them were in Ann Arbor.

In thinking about this, I came to some conclusions which might not be valid because I did not have definite data. Most Christian bookshops in the U.S. are, first, free enterprise attempts to make a living and, second, opportunities to serve the Lord. The book business is a marginal business. The Christian book business is even more limited. The vast majority of Christian books are written for Christians. Of the 6,000 evangelical titles in English, most of these are for the saints. Therefore, if a Christian bookshop owner has a stock of these titles and intends on selling enough of them to make a living, his store must be in an evangelical community and a community with extra money.

Christian books are not in the same category as food and clothing. The college student population is not an evangelical community, nor does it have extra money for items not essential. This is why Christian bookshops are not in college towns. The stores which have opened in college towns have had to close.

Bookstores overseas are not free enterprise. They are mission stations. To make the bookstore pay for itself is a secondary objective, not the primary one. The first place a mission bookstore will open up is on the doorstep of the university because students are 1. literate and 2. looking for answers . . . .

As you know, we have had interest from graduate students, faculty members, and other interested Christians for stores near other campuses.

Four main needs: a local, motivated committee; the right man (mature—willing and able to counsel, listen, advise, evangelize, and [do] the humdrum work of running a bookstore); the right location; and enough money . . . .

There have been hundreds of experiences which have kept us going. The biggest is that of the snowball effect on the Christian witness in the community and university and academies. It gets bigger and bigger, and all of the time the bookstore is an unassuming innocent source. It is difficult for the enemy to take shots at the bookstore, which is a legitimate business and serves all of the churches. The bookstore doesn't generate loyalty to itself, and therefore it is harder to choose up sides.

Our hesitancy to start a bookstore someplace else is that we do not wish to increase the number of ministries which are effective but only marginally so. We believe an awakening will start here, and we do not want to get side-tracked in duplicating the witness we have here until this snowball here takes the whole town, academy, and St. Johns College.

This does not mean that there isn't a need at other universities. It only means we want to move in the Lord's time the Lord's way and with His provision.

Let me suggest why this is a legitimate field for InterVarsity . . . . InterVarsity has the best publication program for university students in the world and a very inadequate means of distribution . . . . If you had your own outlet near the university, you would move many thousands of books for the edification of the believer and for the winning of the lost. Our first year at College Park we sold less than $4,000, our second year close to $16,000, and it will increase this year.

According to the Pratt Library*, 2,250,000,000 books were sold in 1965. Our problem in Christian literature is not inadequate publishing but inadequate distribution.

The bookstore is a place where isolated Christians, freshmen, and others will come only to find out that they are not alone. It is a place of evangelism [which is] normal and unpushy.

People with problems are looking for answers in a book. In describing what he wants in a book, the customer is really telling the clerk what's bothering him. If the clerk is alert and willing to listen, he will be able to provide the right book but may also lead the person to Christ or establish a continued witness. Don and I are both overwhelmed with this kind of business.

We have a lending library that gets a heavy business, [and] we give away books, mostly IV booklets, to interested people with whom we have had a conversation in the store. This really pays off.

If you think that this might turn into something, and if you think I can be of any help, I would be glad to seek the Lord about coming to Chicago for a short visit.

* The Enoch Pratt Free Library is the public library system of Baltimore City.

If InterVarsity is not interested, then we may try to fill the need. If so, we will probably have a booth at Urbana at the next convention.

Sincerely in Christ,
Jim Wilson

InterVarsity decided to go with it in Ann Arbor, Michigan. Keith Hunt and Jim Nyquist of InterVarsity Press came to see me in Annapolis, and I was invited to Urbana '67 in order to recruit staff for the prospective store in Ann Arbor. I chartered a bus from Maryland and loaded it with students who wanted to attend the Urbana conference in Urbana, Illinois.

Urbana is held every three years between Christmas and New Year's when students are on break and have time to attend. When our bus arrived, it was about five degrees outside, with a foot of snow on the ground.

My friend George Verwer* was one of the speakers that year. He had come straight from his mission work in India. I had written a book on evangelism called *Principles of War*, and George and British InterVarsity were interested in publishing it in India. As soon as his talk was over, I went up to George's hotel room to talk with him about the book. He answered the door in his pajamas.

I said, "George, how did you get into your pajamas so fast?"

"I never took them off!" He was so cold that he had given his talks with the pajamas on under his suit.

At Urbana, I met a young man named Jim Carlson who was running all the after-meetings. I invited him to come on staff at the Ann Arbor store, which we planned to call Logos Books. It was the prototype for the eighty similar InterVarsity stores which followed.

* George Verwer (1938–) is an evangelist, author, and the founder of Operation Mobilisation.

In the winter of 1968, I was invited to Keith Hunt's home in Michigan to present the principles and problems behind running a Christian bookstore.

1. It could not be a free enterprise, for-profit bookstore.

    a. At that time, a Christian bookstore could not succeed as a free-enterprise event unless there were at least sixty thousand people in the market area. That would garner enough sales to support one man.[†] The population would need to be much bigger if the town were liberal. If there were fewer than sixty thousand people in the area, there would need to be an unusually high percentage of Christians in the population. (N.B.: A large college in a small town does not meet these requirements.)

    b. A viable business and an effective ministry do not easily go together. From each book we sold for $10, we would take $6 to repurchase the book. Another $3.50 would go for the rent, lights, heat, and salaries. That would leave a 50¢ profit per book.[‡] We wanted to give books to students. If we gave a book to someone, we have just given away the $6 to repurchase the book. We also gave away the lights, the heat, the rent, the salaries, and the profit. In order to make this up, I would have to sell twelve $10 books at 50¢ profit each to gain back the $6 to repurchase the book. I would have to sell twenty books to regain the whole $10 I gave away.

---

† Fifteen percent of gross sales was needed for salaries. If you sold a $100,000 worth in one year, the hired man would get $15,000. If you had two people on staff, each would get $7,500.

‡ Assuming we actually reached the minimum sales of $100,000 a year

2. In order to have an effective ministry, the store should have a minimum of two full-time employees—one responsible for the business, the other for the ministry.

3. The person in charge of ministry should be the person in charge of the store. The businessman should not be in charge. If the businessman is senior, he will never allow the other to give away a book. Both services cannot be primary, and the ministry must take precedence.

In late winter, Jim Carlson said that he wanted to be part of the new ministry in Ann Arbor. I told him that they still needed another man. Then early in the year, Jim Nyquist asked me to be the ministering half of the two-man team. I had not considered leaving Annapolis before. Now I had to seek the will of God.

The Ann Arbor location would be the first of many stores, and I would be getting in on the ground floor. It looked to me like it was the right move, but I did not want to run ahead of Bessie, so I did not seriously discuss it with her.

At spring break, I took a book table to the OCU Spring Leave Conference at Willow Grove. I prayed that if it were God's will for us to move, Bessie would be a hundred percent on board. Bessie had five women's Bible studies in Annapolis each week, some of them with thirty women. It was a fruitful ministry, one that I was not sure she would want to leave. My ministry there had been fruitful as well.

When I got home from Willow Grove, Bessie said, "I think we should go with InterVarsity." I gave them an affirmative answer.

CHAPTER 44

ANN ARBOR

The grace of the Lord Jesus be with you. (1 Cor. 16:23)

713 Genessee Street

Annapolis, Md. 21401

April 25, 1968

Dear Friends,

We are moving to Ann Arbor, Michigan, as soon as possible after school is out this June.

Yes, we are surprised too and will be grateful for your prayers in the transition stage, for after almost ten years in Annapolis, our roots have gone fairly deep. The move is in answer to a request from InterVarsity Christian Fellowship for Jim to set up a book store ministry pattern beginning in Ann Arbor at the University of Michigan where there are some 30,000 students . . . .

We are convinced of the effectiveness of a bookstore located close to a university campus, especially since the Lamplighter opened near the University of Maryland. Our store here in Annapolis has had more of an indirect effect on the United States Naval Academy because midshipmen cannot be in town as freely as other college students can; and it has been rather the combined effect of faculty members and townspeople who, in being helped, have been an influence for Christ at the Academy . . . .

Before we moved to Annapolis, Jim prayed for the conversion of hundreds of midshipmen. Through the years we have had the

JOY of seeing many come to Christ, most of whom have continued in the way. This year has seen a remarkable increase in the witness among the midshipmen, with the mids themselves leading others to Christ. In a recent visit made by the Campus Crusade singing group, "The New Folk," some 116 made professions of faith and 145 asked for further help in counselling. We rejoice at this answered prayer . . .

We trust our next letter will be from Michigan with rejoicing over God's good hand upon us (Nehemiah 2:8, 18).

In His love,
Jim and Bessie Wilson

In June, I spoke at an InterVarsity conference at Hudson House in Nyack, New York. While there, I made a large initial order from all the Christian publishers so that the books would arrive in Ann Arbor when we moved there in July.

The ministry started off strong. We opened Logos Books on Church Street in July 1968. I was surprised that Jim Carlson (the businessman) was going to be in charge, not I (the ministry staffer). I had assumed it would be the other way around. It was contrary to what I had taught because it would limit the ministry, but I accepted it, thinking that it would be no problem.

We had been open a month when I noticed a small woman in her late twenties walking toward the door, hiding behind bookcases. I had watched her as she wandered through the store. Someplace in the wander, she realized she was in the *wrong* kind of bookstore. She was trying to make her escape without being seen.

I cut her off before she got to the door and greeted her. She was a little woman, not very feminine, an in-your-face Jewish atheist. Her name was Barbara Friedman. We went at it head-to-head for an hour. She was not timid at all—she argued loudly, aggressively, pointing her fingers.

A few days later, I was in the store alone with no customers, so I called Barbara and said, "Barbara, come on down to Logos, and we'll go a few rounds." Down she came. This started what has so far been a fifty-year friendship.

1706 Jackson Avenue
Ann Arbor, Michigan 48103

Dear Friends:

Four months ago, we left Annapolis. At that time, we knew it was the will of God to leave Annapolis, but we were not sure how we were to be used in Ann Arbor. The news of God's working in Annapolis has been a great encouragement to us. Now we would like to share with you news of God's hand upon us here.

We are living in a six-bedroom house about two miles from the Logos Bookstore and are confident that we are in the right place. The children have rooms of their own, and we still have a guest room.

Logos Bookstore opened on July 15, 1968. We have had many customers, hours of student conversations, and have sold $5,000 worth of books . . . . There is great ignorance of the good news of the love of Christ. We are convinced there will be many who will receive Christ in the months to come. We must do much planting and watering for that to happen, and we need your prayers . . . . We are more than ever convinced of the strategy of reaching into the student world in this way, making ourselves accessible to those who are seeking answers and who are so open to the printed message of any kind . . . .

With great appreciation for love in Christ,
Jim and Bessie Wilson

Another time, a young woman came into the store. She was dressed in tweed and very classy. When she realized it was a Christian store, she decided to tell me why she was not a Christian. Her objections to Christianity included the Conquistadors, the Crusades, the Inquisition, and hypocrites.

I had heard these reasons before. I replied, "That is amazing! I agree with you about all of them. I'm a Christian. I do not see the connection."

She looked at me as if I wasn't all there.

"I will tell you why I'm a Christian. Twenty-three years ago, I had an encounter with God. It was like having a bath on the inside, and I have been happy ever since. I am sorry you are not a Christian." I turned and started to walk away.

She grabbed me by the arm. "Wait—aren't you going to tell me how this happened?!"

"Well, we do not believe in holding customers against their will."

"I have all the time in the world."

We went into my office. This time I gave her my testimony with the Good News in it. She stayed for a long time. I gave her several InterVarsity booklets. I have not seen her since, but I know this: she got plowed and planted in good ground. I believe she has since become a Christian.

Sometime later, a young man came into the store and asked me if I knew anything about publishers. I replied that I knew a little and asked him why he wanted to know. His name was William Walter Scott III.

"I've written a book," Bill said.

"What's it about?"

"You wouldn't like it."

"You don't know I wouldn't like it. What's it about?"

"It's about riots."

"What does it say about riots?

"You wouldn't like it."

I told him he should not judge me. He gave me the manuscript. He was right! I did not like it. The book that Bill had written was about the Detroit Riot of 1967 that had resulted in the burning of a large portion of the city. The riot erupted during the aftermath of a police raid on an illegal after-hours club run by William Scott, Bill's father. After the police arrested the eighty-five people who were inside the club, Bill provided beer for the crowd. He threw the first bottle through a drugstore window, starting the riot. Barbara Friedman's father owned a men's clothing store on 12th Street. It was burned down.

Bill lived across the street from the bookstore. I saw him regularly and preached the gospel to him.

CHAPTER 45

CONCORDIA COLLEGE

In love he predestined us for adoption to sonship through Jesus
Christ, in accordance with his pleasure and will—to the praise of
his glorious grace, which he has freely given us in the One he loves.
(Eph. 1:5–6)

After my initial order, Jim Carlson did the ordering for the bookstore. To my chagrin, he began stocking non-Christian books—
not dictionaries or other such innocuous things, but titles like *The
Tibetan Book of the Dead*, works by Nietzsche, by Paul Tillich (whose
view of Jesus as savior was the same as one drunk helping another
drunk out of the gutter, and that Jesus was only better in that he
helped more people than most of us), and various immoral secular
novels. Jim said he did this to build bridges to the university. I said
that we should build bridges by loving people, not by distributing
false doctrine to the students. These authors would not have been
allowed to speak at an InterVarsity meeting. Why should they be
allowed to speak through the bookstore?

I was not able to convince Jim, so I took my objection to the local committee. They backed him. I then appealed their decision to
the national board of InterVarsity. They asked me to write a policy
statement for all future bookstores, which I did. They accepted my
written statement, *except* for the sentence that excluded these kinds
of books.

I did not know what to do. I took a thirty-day break to pray about
it. At the end of the thirty days, I was still in turmoil. At one point,

Bessie thought I was going to break out in tears. She ran out of the room so she would not see something like *that* happen. It didn't happen, but it was close. I was very confused.

The night before I went back to work, I made a list of pros and cons. When I finished, there were thirteen pros for staying with the bookstore and thirteen cons. I was even more confused than before.

The next day, I had to run a book table at a conference in Mill Lake, twenty miles away. On the way, I said to myself, "Wilson, for years people have come to you for wisdom in these kinds of problems, and you always have an answer. Suppose you came to yourself with this problem. What would you say to you?"

I answered quickly, "If what you want to do is contrary to what the Bible teaches, then what you want to do is wrong."

I listened to this bit of wisdom and with it looked at my list of pros and cons. (I was driving, so I looked at them in my head. I knew them by heart.) To my surprise, all the pros were what *I* wanted, and all of the cons were biblical. I got to Mill Lake, called Bessie, and told her that we were leaving InterVarsity. She had known it was the right thing to do before I had and was losing respect for me because of my hesitancy to make the decision.

We went to Windsor to visit Bessie's brother, Harvey. While there, I got hives all over my body. At the time, I thought it was something I ate, but in retrospect I think it was the result of making a right decision contrary to my desires. Apparently, I had a great emotional attachment to that ministry. I carried some bitterness for a few weeks afterward about having to leave it.

When we returned from Windsor, I started looking for a job. I applied for one unloading furniture and gave a short résumé. They did not believe that I had graduated from the Naval Academy. They asked to see my diploma. I got it for them. Then they wanted to know why I wanted to unload furniture when I had a degree from the U.S.

Naval Academy. I told them I needed to feed my family. They gave me the job; I was to start the next afternoon.

When I got home, Bessie told me she had seen an advertisement for a bookstore manager at Concordia College. I told her I didn't want to run a Lutheran bookstore. She said I might as well do that as unload furniture, so I called the number.

A few weeks earlier, I had spoken at a Christian Business Men's luncheon on the subject of literature evangelism. Paul Herpolsheimer, the business manager at Concordia College and a recent convert, was at that luncheon. When he realized it was me on the phone, he offered me a three-year contract for the job.

I went to see Paul. I did not want the position permanently, but I told him that I would do it for the two or three remaining months before summer vacation. I thought I would have guidance from God as to where I should be by that time. However, I gave Paul one condition. I needed money to get some decent books for the store. He said that he did not want to have money tied up in dead stock all summer. I told him that was my condition. He came up with $500. The money was turned over three times in those few months.

1706 Jackson Avenue
Ann Arbor, Mich. 48103
May 15, 1969

Dear Friends,

There are things in this life that we (Bessie and I) desire very much. They are legitimate desires. They are more than desires on our part; they are promises on God's part. Desires or promises, they are listed in a beautiful way in Isaiah 58:11: "And the Lord will guide you continually, and satisfy your desire with good things, and make your bones strong; and you shall be like a watered garden, like a spring of water, whose waters fail not."

There is a hitch to this promise of continual guidance and spiritual refreshment. It is an "iffy" promise. Here are the "ifs" from verses 9 and 10:

- "If you take away from the midst of you the yoke (slavery)

- the pointing of the finger (accusation)

- and speaking wickedness (*vanity* KJV, boasting?)

- If you pour yourself out for the hungry, and satisfy the desire of the afflicted

- Then shall your light rise in the darkness and your gloom be as the noonday."

Earlier in the chapter, we find that God will answer when we call, that our righteousness will go before us, and His glory will come behind us and "your light break forth like the dawn, and your healing shall spring up speedily" (verse 8).

How could we ask for more? It is a promise of exuberant life, some of that more abundance Jesus promised, Light that breaks and Health that springs!

What are the conditions?

- Setting men free from evil

- Removing their heavy burdens

- Delivering men from oppression

- Feeding the hungry from our own supply

- Bringing the poor and afflicted to our own house

- Clothing the naked

- Taking care of our own family. (verses 6 and 7)

The promises are spiritual and physical, but so are the conditions. If you are interested in the conditions which are not acceptable, they are listed in verses 1–5.

A year ago, we were guided to leave Annapolis with the promise, "My presence shall go with thee and I will give thee rest" (Exodus 33:14). We were asked to join Inter-Varsity Christian Fellowship in the opening of a bookstore in Ann Arbor, and our last letter informed you of the tremendous blessing and outreach of the store. We rejoice in God's faithfulness.

When InterVarsity Press opened Logos Bookstore, we found that there was a desire to carry [some books] which on some points were contrary to the gospel of Christ in order to build bridges to people who would not understand or who would be offended if the store did not stock or order the books (such as Tillich). We held that however open our strategy of access was, it could not include distributing the teaching of false teachers even at a minimum on a special-order basis. This we based on New Testament teaching regarding false teachers.

There has been no disagreement on basic doctrine in theory. What InterVarsity believes is a legitimate strategy of access to people, we believe to be a violation of basic doctrine. After months of discussion, InterVarsity Press came out with a guideline which was permissive on stocking and ordering such books. We have waited on the Lord for the last month, seeking His mind whether we could continue to minister in Logos under these guidelines established by InterVarsity. We have made this decision to resign as of May 1st.

We are counting on the promises of Isaiah 58 for His continual guidance and refreshing. At this instant, we do not know what God has in mind for us for our future service. We anticipate that we should stay in Ann Arbor until school is out. Almost

concurrent with my resignation, an advertisement for bookstore manager at Concordia Lutheran Junior College (Missouri
Synod) appeared in the newspaper. I answered and agreed to
take the position until the end of May. I have been there one
week and have been very impressed with the spiritual character
of the faculty and students. This is a college of 500 students. The
school has asked me to take the responsibility of the bookstore
for next year. We are open to go anyplace where He leads us and
we ask for your prayers.

There is no break in fellowship with Jim Carlson [or the]
InterVarsity staff. We would describe our feeling toward them in
terms of I Thess. 5:13: "and to esteem them very highly in love for
their work's sake" . . . .

In His Love,
Jim & Bessie

When the school year ended, I still did not have a call to ministry
elsewhere, so I agreed to stay at Concordia a month at a time.

Across from the cash register there was a high wall of concrete
blocks. Behind that was a vacant room which had been the post office. I told Paul I would like to expand the bookstore into that room.
He said that it would cost money to have the wall removed.

"You are already paying me for the summer; I will do it myself."

"You'll need help."

"I will get my kids."

He said, "I can't afford to pay your children."

"I will pay them in books."

We moved twenty tons of concrete. The baseball coach took some
of the blocks for a dugout at the ballfield. I paid Doug and Evan
a book a day and Heather a stuffed animal a day. We painted and

stocked the expanded store before summer was over, and I stayed
another year at Concordia. It was a great year of ministry.

When I had been at Concordia College for only a few days, the
president of the college came into the store. He told me to lock the
door. I was on the phone. I locked the door and went back to the
phone. When I got off the phone, Dr. Zimmerman said, "Your books
are alright. Do not let anyone tell you they are not." He had had faculty
members tell him that the new bookstore manager had non-Lutheran
books in the store, *and* he was a Baptist, *and* he was counseling students! "We can't have you counseling students, though," he told me.

"I do not have to work here, either."

"Why can't you just manage the bookstore?"

"Because I am called to minister to students, not to sell books.
However, if a student wants to talk about baptism or the Lord's
Supper, I can send him to someone else. This is a Lutheran college,
so I will not talk about Lutheran subjects since I am not Lutheran. If,
however, someone thinks he is a Christian just because he has been
baptized, I will consider him not a Christian. If someone thinks he
is saved because of baptism instead of the death and resurrection of
Jesus Christ, he is not a Christian."

He responded, "Go right ahead."

During one order for the store, I included sixteen copies of *I Loved
a Girl* by Walter Trobisch. After classes one day, I put one copy on the
president's desk, one on the vice president's desk, one on the dean of
men's desk, one on the dean of women's desk, six copies in the women's
dorm, and six copies in the men's dorm. The president came to the
bookstore to pay for his copy and said it was the best book he had read
on the subject. I sold eighty more copies at the college.

One evening back in the summer of '68, when I was still working
at the Logos store, a student named Andy had come in. He was high
on marijuana. He sat down at a table, and we had a long talk about

the gospel. It was my practice to record the gist of these conversations on four-by-six cards and file them; then in future days I would use the cards to pray for the people.

On a morning several weeks later, I was praying through the card file and realized I hadn't seen Andy for a while. I asked God to bring him into the store. About noon that day, Andy came in and said, "I thought I would come in."

I said, "I am glad you did." We had a good conversation.

Several more months went by. By this time, I was at Concordia College. I was driving from home and had not yet figured out the shortest way to get to the store. I was driving one direction and realized I was taking the long way, so I turned left to get over to the road that was shorter. While I was between the two ways, I saw Andy on a bicycle. I pulled over.

"What are you doing?"

"I'm joining the circus tomorrow," he said.

"Oh. Good! Come to the college in the morning, and I'll drive you out to the circus."

He came to meet me in the morning, received the Lord, and did not join the circus.

I realized that the move to Concordia meant I would not see Bill Scott anymore. One Sunday evening on the way to church, I stopped by his room on Church Street. He invited me in. A female student named Sandy Smith was there with him. I continued the gospel where I had left off. Sandy did not like it. Trying get rid of me, she said to Bill, "Let's go over to my apartment." Bill agreed. I said, "Let's go" and tagged along to Sandy's apartment, where I continued to tell Bill the good news.

The next Sunday, I stopped by again. Sandy was there. Bill said, "Jim, why do you come so late? You should come when everyone is here. Sandy is just left over from the crowd."

"What do you mean, 'everyone'?"

"I teach a university-accredited undergraduate class called Sensitivity Session. Come to the class."

Sandy said, "Jim, if you're coming to the class, don't come dressed like an FBI agent." They were hippies, and I always wore a suit and tie.

The next Sunday, I came to the class at three p.m. (in my suit) and sat in a circle with about twenty students. The method for the class was to have students say insulting things to each other with gross words to see how sensitive the others were. The students did quite a thorough job.

I had attended twice when Bill told me that I could conduct the class the following week. I agreed.

The following Sunday, I got the class's attention and began to preach the gospel. Sandy tapped Bill and took him out in the hall. They came back in a minute later. Bill said, "Jim, Sandy objects to you speaking, and she wants to read a paper she has written."

I yielded. Sandy read her paper, after which the students ripped into her for what a stupid paper she had written and ragged her for stopping me.

One Sunday, Bill decided to give a monologue as if he were a homosexual. He used effeminate speech and mannerisms. At the end of the speech, he turned to the person on his left and asked him if he accepted him. He asked this to everyone in the circle. They all gave strong affirmatives instead of their normal imprecations. I was the last person in the circle. He asked the same question of me.

"Bill, you know that I love you. But after all of the natural reasons for homosexuality (no father, lack of love, slum-dwelling), God still says it is sin!"

Sandy piped up. "Jim, you have been invited here. Everyone can give his opinion. You can give your opinion, but don't sit there and say it is God's opinion."

That broke up the meeting. Bill got in my face and called me all kinds of things (not nice things). Sandy cheered him on.

On November 15, 1969, there was a massive march on Washington, D.C., demanding an end to the war in Vietnam. The regular Sunday meeting was cancelled so the class could join the march. That gave me a day off. Bessie and I invited two Chinese students from Concordia College to our home for Sunday dinner. In the middle of the afternoon, the telephone rang.

"Is this the Jim Wilson that goes to Bill Scott's group?"

"Yes."

"This is Sandy Smith. I went to the march on Washington, but I didn't like it, so I came home. I want to see you."

There was no way I was going to see Sandy Smith alone. I told her that I would take the Chinese students back to the college, then Heather and I would pick her up. (Heather was in eighth grade.) We picked up Sandy and brought her to our house. She received Christ and stayed overnight at our home.*

I have not been able to find Bill Scott since.†

Keith and Rusty Hunt also moved to Ann Arbor around the same time as we did. Their son Mark was going into his senior year at

---

* Sandy later went on a short-term mission to Denmark and married Mark Karls, the president of the InterVarsity chapter at Michigan University. Mark went to Trinity Evangelical Divinity School and has been pastoring Methodist churches in Michigan ever since. Their children are walking in the light.

† His family has not seen him in decades, either. According to a 2016 article, Scott went into "a downward spiral marked by drug addiction, mental illness, and homelessness," moved to Daytona in the late 1990s, and "disappeared somewhere in coastal Florida." (Bill McGraw, "He started the Detroit riot. His son wrestles with the carnage," *Bridge Magazine*, December 19, 2016.)

Pioneer High School. Mark asked his mother to pray that he would find a friend there. He came home after the first day of school with a new friend who lived on the same block. The friend spent a lot of time at their home and received Christ as a result. The friend's mother was so impressed with the change in her son that she came to see Rusty and received Christ herself.

This new Christian mother had a next-door neighbor with a twenty-five-year-old married daughter. The daughter had high blood pressure. The University Hospital had recommended that one of her kidneys be removed to lower her blood pressure. It was done, but it did not lower her blood pressure, so the other kidney was removed, too. She was then informed that the hospital did not have a dialysis machine. They found one for her at an osteopathic hospital in Garden City, thirty miles away. Somewhere in the midst of all this, her husband said that he couldn't take it anymore and divorced her.

The mother called Rusty for help for her daughter. Rusty told her that she couldn't help her because she and Keith were on their way to Cedar Campus in the Upper Peninsula where Keith would be directing camp all summer. Instead, Rusty sent me the story and told me that I had the responsibility for the young woman.

I found the osteopathic hospital and went to her room. I told her who I was.

She said, "I'm going to die."

"I'm glad you said that. Are you afraid to die?"

She was afraid. I told her I could help her to not be afraid.

She received the good news and called upon the Lord. She said, "Now I know what my brother was talking about when he was in the Air Force." She made me promise to tell the good news to her father, stepmother, and mother. I did, and they all responded positively to the gospel.

I visited her regularly. She got weaker and weaker. I would sit by her side and read Scripture and lean over her bed and sing, "What a Friend We Have in Jesus." She died later that summer, unafraid and joyful.

Sometime later, her stepmother called and asked if we could have a Bible study. We started one at the Hunts' home.

I invited Barbara Friedman to join us for the study. One evening a few weeks later, she Barbara walked in the door, aimed her finger at us, and said, "Listen, you guys! I am *not* going to become a Christian." Bessie and I both laughed. We laughed because we knew that when someone says they are not going to become a Christian, this means that they have been thinking about it.

Sometime later, a Chinese friend offered to cook our family a big Chinese dinner. Since she was going to cook a lot of food, I asked Mr. Saunders, an old missionary to China, if he knew anyone who liked to eat Chinese. Mr. Saunders said, "Ralph Toliver." Ralph was a PhD student in mathematics. He was the son of China Inland missionaries, but he was an atheist. He had rejected God because he had been sent to the States to a CIM* home to attend school while his parents stayed in China. Ralph loved to eat. We invited him and Barbara Friedman to the Chinese dinner.

We wound up inviting both of them to Sunday dinner every week for a year. During that time, we talked to Barbara a lot about Jesus, but I never said a word to Ralph about God. After the meal, Barbara, Ralph, Douglas, Evan, Heather, Gordon, and I would walk to the city park a block away and play Frisbee, touch football, or other activities. In the winter, we would work on jigsaw puzzles.

One noon, Ralph came riding up to the house on his motorcycle. Evan turned to me and said, "Dad, can I have a motorcycle?"

* China Inland Mission, now OMF International

Ralph said to himself, "Can I have a dad like Evan's?"

At the end of that year, Bessie and I took our family, Ralph, and Barbara to the University of Michigan to see a performance of Gilbert and Sullivan's *HMS Pinafore*. After the play, Ralph came home with us. He wanted to talk about God. He received Christ and grew in the faith rapidly. Later, Bessie fixed him up with a nurse, and they were married.*

In August 1970, Ben Hyde was visiting me from Detroit when Barbara came over. Ben and I both talked with her, encouraging her to receive Christ. We did this for some time, and she did not argue with us. We were puzzled about this until she finally told us, to our amazement, that she had been a Christian for two weeks![†]

One day, a freshman girl came into the Concordia Bookstore. She was a Christian and was very sweet and innocent, but she was depressed and was not willing to talk about it. I asked God for help. As soon as I prayed, I somehow knew that she had been sexually molested by her father. If this was common then, I certainly was not aware it. Such things were unknown to me.

---

* Ralph and Marilyn Toliver joined Wycliffe Bible Translators and as of 2018 had just finished translating the New Testament into Ambo-Pasco, a Quechua dialect in Peru.

† In 1971, we moved to Moscow and opened Crossroads Bookstore. In 1973, Barbara asked us if she could come out and join the work. She managed both Crossroads Bookstore in Moscow and One Way Books in Pullman at different times. She took time off to get her master's degree in mathematics then came back full-time with us as an evangelist. She worked with the Chinese Christian group in Pullman for many years. She has knocked on every door in Moscow to give away copies of *How to Be Free from Bitterness*. In 2016, she retired due to memory issues and returned to Ann Arbor to live with her two sisters. Since her conversion her attitude has always been up.

"What do I do?" I thought. "Do I say anything to her? Suppose it is not true and I am accusing a godly father?"

But I knew that it was true, and so I told her. It was true, and God gave me wisdom to help her.‡

During the fall semester in 1970, another student came into the Concordia College store to see me. She was depressed and did not know why. I asked her a lot of questions. I could not figure out what the problem was. "Are you sure you don't know why you are depressed?" I asked her.

She said maybe she knew. At Christmas, she had received a fraternity pin from a student at another college. At spring break, she had expected to receive an engagement ring. Instead, he asked for his pin back and told her he was engaged to someone else. He had since married the other woman.

"I think that is why I am depressed. "

"I don't think that is the problem. Do you want to tell me what it is, or do you want me to tell you?"

She said, "Neither."

I said, "Then you tell God right now."

She did, and returned to her room rejoicing. The next day, her roommate came in. "My roommate tells me that you can help people, and they don't have to tell you what's wrong."

I said, "That's true.

She also went back to her room rejoicing. Another one of their roommates came down the next day, and *she* went back to her room rejoicing.

A month or so had gone by when the fourth one came in to see me. She said, "My roommates tell me that you can help people, and

‡ My son Douglas asked me if I put incidents like this into a charismatic category. The answer is "No." I put them under answered prayer and the faithfulness of God.

they don't have to tell you what the problem is. I don't have a problem; I just want to know how you do it."

I said, "Well, it's simple. Besides problems with parents, there are only three types of problems college students typically have. They are lying, cheating, and sex." Then I said, "Which is yours?"

She was caught off guard. She then said, "Lying. I had a term paper due, but I didn't write one. I told my professor I had done it and put it on the stack of term papers on his desk, and he must have misplaced it. I told my parents and my roommate that I had written the paper."

I said, "Let's confess the sin right now." She did. Then I said, "I will give you thirty minutes to tell your professor." She left and called a few minutes later to tell me that he was not on campus. I told her to tell him on Monday.

On Monday, I ran into her professor and asked him what he had done about it. He said, "I gave her until Friday to write it."

CHAPTER 46
A DECISIVE POINT

The God of peace will soon crush Satan under your feet. The grace
of our Lord Jesus Christ be with you. (Rom. 16:20)

In 1971, after two years at Concordia College, I realized that we
should be moving on. I had published my first book, *Principles of
War*, in 1964. (It was first published chapter by chapter in *Command*
magazine in the late 1950s.) The sequels, *Weapons and Tactics* and
Taking Men Alive, were written (in my head) in the mid-1960s. I had
studied the principles of war ten years earlier in a course on strategy
and tactics at the Naval War College. After taking that course, I began to practice the principles of war tactically in evangelism.

There is one strategic warfare concept I could not practice while
I was in the Navy. It is called the *decisive point*. A decisive point is
a location where if a battle was fought and won, the victorious side
would not just win the battle, they would win the entire war. That
point is simultaneously strategic and feasible. Feasible means that
you can take it, and strategic means that it matters if you take it.

Annapolis was a decisive point for taking the U.S. Navy. I had
known it was a decisive point before we moved there. I had already
rejected West Point and the Coast Guard Academy, not because they
were not important, but because there was no location near either
of them where I could have a bookstore as a command post. When
cadets got permission to leave the West Point campus, they did
not stick around; they went off to New York City. Thus, I selected
Annapolis for our OCU command post.

By capturing the Naval Academy for Jesus Christ, I would have a major influence on the whole Navy. When I was still on the OCU staff, my plan had been to spend two years in Annapolis, then move on to the U.S. Navy Postgraduate School in Monterey for two years, then two years at the Army Command and Staff School in Leavenworth, Kansas, and two at the Air University in Montgomery, Alabama.

I spent two years in D.C. and two in Annapolis before I left the OCU staff. Once I was no longer travelling for OCU, I simply concentrated on Annapolis and was there for another seven and a half years. During this time, we had several Billy Graham films and sponsored faculty conferences and author lecture series, with speakers like Elisabeth Elliot, Dick Halverson*, Corrie ten Boom, and Art Glasser†.

In 1968, we moved to Ann Arbor. This was a shift away from the military community. Now that I was in the civilian world, I did not know where the decisive points were.

As mentioned above, the two ingredients that determine whether a point is decisive are its importance in relation to the whole and its feasibility, i.e., whether it can be taken with the forces available.

When I left Annapolis, I started considering the important places. New York City is definitely important. If we take New York City for Jesus Christ, we have just taken the country. The problem? New York City is not feasible, and therefore not decisive. The other major cities in the country—Chicago, Los Angeles, Seattle, New Orleans, etc.—had the same problem. They were all important, but too large for us to take. After two and half years in Ann Arbor, I realized that although our ministry there was effective, it was not a decisive point. Ann Arbor was also important but not feasible.

---

* The Rev. Richard C. Halverson (1916–95) was a pastor and served as the U.S. Senate chaplain.

† Arthur Glasser (1914–2009) served as a missionary in China, home director of OMF, and dean of the Fuller Seminary's School of World Missions.

I finally decided to break my evaluation down by state. What are the most important places in any given state? Answer: the largest cities, the state capitals, and the state universities. After much study, I came to the conclusion that the decisive point in any given state is where there is a major university in a small town. The university makes it important; the small town makes it feasible.

So in the winter of 1970–71, I started checking on such places. One day, I received two letters. One was a $25 gift from Ray Clemons in Boise, Idaho. As mentioned in an earlier chapter, Ray had become a Christian seventeen years earlier in Yokosuka, Japan. The other was a letter from Elmer Hiebert in Pullman, Washington. I had been corresponding with Elmer for almost two years. He wanted to get a Christian book ministry started in Pullman. I had been giving him advice, but nothing had happened.

But those two letters caused me to look at those two states in particular. I noticed that the University of Idaho was in Moscow, Idaho, nine miles east of Pullman, Washington, the home of Washington State University. Here were two major universities in two small towns in two different states, and that were very close together. I could fight the battle in one place and take two states.

This was not enough guidance by itself. I realized that we would need to spy out the land together in order to see how Bessie could handle the location. I did not say anything to her the next morning about what I was thinking because I thought she might put on the brakes, thinking that her wild husband was about to do something outside the will of God. I prayed that God would make things clear.

That evening, Bessie said, "Jim, do you think God is saying something to us about Idaho?"

"I don't know, but we should check it out."

We had spent an even three years in Ann Arbor. The first year was with Logos bookstore, and the next two with Concordia College

Bookstore. Although we thought our stay in Ann Arbor might be permanent, it turned out to be an interim ministry between two long-term ministries: twelve years with the military academies (1956 to 1968) and forty-eight years and counting in the Pacific Northwest, all of it literature-centered.

The years in Ann Arbor had been effective. It was a time of much growing in wisdom and preparation for decades of more complete, extended ministry than all the years before.

During those three years, atheists, students, and hippies came to Christ, and others had their faith in the Lord strengthened. Doug and Evan had a great witness at Pioneer High School. We increased our home hospitality over what we had been able to do in Annapolis when our growing children had been our focus. In Ann Arbor, they started to become part of the ministry. In Moscow, they would be a major part.

Bessie had very serious sinus infections for our twelve years on the East Coast and for the three years in Michigan. Our first year in Michigan she had a nose operation called a sub-mucous resection. It did not seem to help much. Our two main considerations for a move away from Ann Arbor were the right place for ministry, and a healthy climate for Bessie.

I have never seen everything fall into place like the events leading up to our move to Moscow. We had no money for a trip to investigate the location. We prayed for it. My mother sent us $100. She had never done that before. Mrs. Meredith sent Bessie $100 from Florida. Our prayers were answered, and so in February 1971 we had two tickets. (Bessie was going to take a side trip to her home in Edmonton.)

The night before we were to leave, we realized that we had our tickets, but we had no money to take with us or to leave with the kids. (Doug, Evan, and Heather were in high school and planned to stay in Ann Arbor while we traveled to scope out the land.)

Bessie's suggestion was to cash in her ticket and have me go alone. I said, "You need to go along to see if the weather is right for you."

"How are we going to do it?"

"I don't know, but I cannot take time to figure it out tonight, even though we are leaving tomorrow."

Remember that a year earlier, a young woman had come to Christ in the osteopathic hospital, and her mother, father, and stepmother had all received Christ. The stepmother had just had a hysterectomy. Normally I would not visit a woman the same day as her hysterectomy, but I needed to visit her, and we were leaving the next day.

So I went to the hospital. Her husband and I sang hymns to her. She interrupted us. "Jim, would you think we were trying to buy your friendship if we gave you some money?"

I said, "No, I would not think that."

She nodded to her husband, and he gave me a $50 bill. As we were leaving later, he pulled out his billfold and said, "That wasn't enough," and gave me $50 more.

Dave Pratt met us at the airport in Spokane, Washington. He had been a Mormon and a Marine officer stationed at the Naval Academy. He was the crew coach of the Navy lightweight crew. The cox'n of the crew in '61 and '62 was Larry Yandell, and the stroke oar was Bob Greenman. Bob had received Christ in the bookstore during his second-class year, and Dave received Christ as a result of a Bible study. Dave was now the assistant dean of engineering at Washington State University in Pullman. He was the one who had prompted Elmer Hiebert to write to me about bookstores. Bessie and I stayed with Dave and his wife Marilyn.

Elmer Hiebert took us to meet Larry Johnston in the physics department at the University of Idaho. Then he took me to a television studio in Pullman and introduced me to Jim Hardie.

Elmer said, "Jim Wilson used to be with the Navigators."

I said, "That was twenty years ago."

Hardie said, "That's when I was with the Navs. Jim Wilson . . . Were you a naval officer? From Nebraska?"

I replied in the affirmative.

Jim Hardie was the man Dawson Trotman had sent to Nebraska to follow up on the thirty-some new Christians I had left there (including my brothers and my father) in the three weeks after my commissioning.

Bessie had no sinus problems on our visit to Idaho, and we returned to Ann Arbor convinced that it was the will of God for us to move there.

1706 Jackson Avenue

Ann Arbor, Michigan 48103

Dear Friends,

"And this is the confidence that we have in Him, that if we ask anything according to His will, He heareth us: and if we know that He hear us, whatsoever we ask, we know that we have the petitions that we desired of Him" ([1] John 5:14–15 [KJV])

In the past, the teaching of these verses came to us mainly in the form that in prayer the important thing was to determine the will of God by the means suggested in the Scripture. These means would be seeking by prayer to bring our will into line with the will of God, carefully evaluating the day-by-day circumstances, heeding any checks in our spirits by His Spirit, and looking into the Word of God for the light on our path that He has promised (Psalm 119:105). This is wonderfully true, but recently a fresh blessing came from these verses relating to the word confidence.

It was in relation to our proposed trip to the Pullman/Moscow area. We were becoming convinced that it was the will of God for us both to fly to the area, but there was the matter of financing the trip. This is where the "confidence" took on new meaning. In prayer we experienced a confidence (stronger than ever before) that if this trip was the will of God for us, the money would be provided. In the space of ten days, the amount needed came from five different sources. Perhaps it is another way of saying what Hudson Taylor said, "God's work done in God's way will not lack God's supply," or words to that effect. Perhaps we would not need to spend so much time pleading for things if we became more convinced of the will of God. We would have confidence about the petitions; we would not have to pray for confidence. It would be there. Also, we would not be busy making plans and asking God to underwrite the expenses. We want to continue to learn in this area . . .

Our decision is to move to Moscow, Idaho, this summer . . . . Our son Douglas graduates from high school in June and has been pursuing an appointment to the Naval Academy . . . . As we go to Idaho, Evan will be a senior in High School and Heather, a sophomore. Gordon will be in the 5th grade and increasing his knowledge of dinosaurs. (He finds his mother very ignorant on this subject in spite of his efforts to teach her from his little models!) . . . .

We ask your prayers for conversions and restorations among the students at Concordia College up to the last day and for the wisdom in the choice of Jim's successor as manager. [We] believe that the course of many lives has been radically changed and that the Lutheran Church (Missouri Synod) will feel the influence of these changed lives in the days ahead.

Confidently, in Him,
Jim and Bessie

We made the move in July. Two Chinese students in Ann Arbor needed $50, so I bought their '54 Ford for that amount. Doug and Evan drove the Ford.

The other four of us came in a 1969 Ford LTD station wagon with air conditioning. A few days before we left, Bessie was making iced tea with boiling water. The pitcher shattered. She had third-degree burns on both thighs. She was in great pain and utterly helpless for the move. That's why I bought the LTD with air conditioning, so it would be comfortable for her.

The two cars traveled together until we got to the Franciscos' house near Chicago. We stayed for a visit and sent Douglas and Evan on ahead to my mother's trailer in Nebraska. Her trailer was next door to the country schoolhouse where she was still teaching.

My father had died four years earlier while we were visiting. In January 1967, he had asked me to come home for a visit. I was not able to come right away, but we made plans to visit in July.

In the spring, I was invited to speak at the InterVarsity chapter at Penn State University in State College, Pennsylvania. I was given hospitality at a professor's home. Right before I was to speak, I became very sick with a high fever. I did not know what was wrong. I was able to speak, but afterward I went to bed and had a high fever and chills all night.

The next morning, I found out I could not see a doctor until eight a.m. It was still very early. I realized that I could be halfway home by eight. Rather than wait around for the doctor, I got in the car. It was a beautiful day, the kind of glorious weather that is normally wonderful for a drive through the mountains. Instead, it was awful. I felt so sick every minute of it; I thought I was going to die. In July, I was to drive all the way down to Nebraska to see my father. At the time, I could not imagine being able to do that drive.

I finally got home. Bessie had taken the kids to the OCU family conference at Camp Wabanna. I got myself to a doctor. I spent one night in the hospital, several weeks in bed, and several months on an antibiotic.

At the time, I had no idea who J.R.R. Tolkien was. While I was at home recovering, I had checked out *The Two Towers* from the library and was reading it in bed. During that time, I had the worst nightmare I have ever had. It did not occur to me that the nightmare was the result of the fever. I thought it was *The Two Towers*. It kept me from reading Tolkien for years!

Every year, we held a June Week banquet for the Christian midshipmen at the Naval Academy. My father had become a Christian in 1950 three weeks after visiting me at the Naval Academy for my graduation and attending this banquet. I normally planned the banquet each year. Now, seventeen years after my graduation, I was too sick to put on a banquet. Instead, we had a picnic at North Severn (a naval base on the north side of the Severn River).

In July, we drove straight through from Annapolis to Nebraska. On Wednesday afternoon, we arrived at the one-room schoolhouse where my mother taught. My parents were living in a trailer on the school grounds. We spent all day Thursday with them. The last words my father said to Mom before he went to sleep on Thursday night were, "Doesn't Jim have great kids?"

The next morning, my mother woke me up to tell me that she thought my father was dead. He had died in his sleep. He had been ill for many months; I think that he had stayed alive by willpower until I got home.

When I flew home on emergency leave after his heart attack in 1956, I had taught my father how to memorize Scripture. Later he told me that he circled every verse that he had memorized with India ink. When we stopped to visit Mom on the way to Idaho, I looked through Dad's Bible to see which verses he had memorized. I could not find any verses circled. I was wondering if Dad had lied to me. Then I realized that he had circled whole chapters and whole books.

After a few days with my mother, we headed for the Black Hills, Mt. Rushmore, Crazy Horse, and Yellowstone Park. We stopped at a restaurant in Wyoming named Crossroads. I decided that the store we would open in Moscow would be called Crossroads.

On a long grade after Cody, Wyoming, Douglas decided to save gas by putting the '54 Ford out of gear and coasting downhill. He had to ride the brakes. When we arrived in Pullman, we discovered that the brakes had been sawn in two.

We stopped to see Ray and Larry Ann Clemons in Boise, then headed north. Coming up the White Bird switchback, the car overheated, and so we had to stop. It was still overheated when we got to Cottonwood, Idaho. We took another switchback at Lewiston, Idaho, where there is a two-thousand-foot climb from the Clearwater River to the hills of the Palouse.

In Moscow, we checked in with Elmer Hiebert. Elmer had registered the ministry he was hoping to start as a nonprofit under the

View from Lewiston Hill Overlook. (Photo by Daniel Foucachon)

name Inland Christian Laymen. That would be the corporation under which we would open our bookstores.*

For the first six weeks we were in the Moscow-Pullman area, we
house-sat for a WSU professor in Pullman who was on sabbatical.

Back in February, when we were still in Ann Arbor, I had been
invited to speak at a ski weekend for midshipmen in Pennsylvania.
Ben Hyde (from Annapolis) said that he would like to go, and he
would drive me there in his Volkswagen.

The drive to Pennsylvania should have taken eight hours, but we
ran into a blizzard going east, and it took us fourteen. On the drive,
Ben asked to join our bookstore venture in Moscow. He came west
at the same time as we did and stopped at the Christian Booksellers
Association in Denver. With his help, we opened One Way Books
next to the Audian Theater on Main Street in Pullman in August.

Doug, Evan, and Heather heard that there was a Young Life event
in East City Park in Moscow and went to it. Later in the evening
they returned with several Christian girls in tow: Julie Olsen (now
Garfield), Grace, Gloria, and Debbie Larson, Signe Cox, and Sandy
Benson. They were members of Emmanuel Lutheran Church in
Moscow. Martin Larson, the Larson girls' father, was the pastor and
a member of the committee we had put together to open Crossroads
Bookstore in Moscow.

---

* In 1977, we changed the name to Community Christian Ministries.

CHAPTER 47

MOSCOW, IDAHO

Therefore, preparing your minds for action, and being sober-mind-
ed, set your hope fully on the grace that will be brought to you at
the revelation of Jesus Christ. (1 Pet. 1:13)

We moved from Pullman to Moscow the week before Labor Day,
1971. That week, I had been driving around Moscow with Martin
Larson, looking for a house to live in. We were driving north on
Jefferson Street, around the corner from the high school, when Mr.
Larson said, "That house is for rent."

"How do you know?"

"Donny Olson was saving it in case we got an assistant pastor, but
we are not going to get one."

He took me to see Donny. Donny said, "The house has four bedrooms, two baths; cost is a $150 a month, no lease, and you can move
in tomorrow." He insisted that we see the house first.

I said, "I'll take it."

"Don't you want to see it?"

"I don't need to see it." I was going to be busy opening a bookstore
on Main Street in Moscow. I had found a place next to Hodgins Drug
Store that was perfect.

I did go see the house, though. When we got there, a group of high
school kids were out by the garage, smoking. I asked Donny what
that was all about. He informed me that the kids were not allowed to
smoke on the school grounds, so they stepped off the grounds into
the backyard of this house.

We moved in that weekend. On the north side of the house was a city parking lot. The house's two-car garage was at the back of the lot, facing into the parking lot. Immediately behind the garage was a high bank of earth. On top of the bank were the Moscow High School grounds.

My first thought was to open the bookstore in the garage. I checked with the city to see if I could do it. The answer was no; it was not zoned for commercial use. I told my kids that they could have the garage and do what they wanted with it.

On Sunday evening a week later, Douglas, Evan, Heather, and Gordon invited their mother and me to the garage. We went out to see it. The inside was decorated in a blatant "Jesus People" style. Bessie and I had always been lovingly direct with the gospel, but this was not something we would have thought to do. There were two portraits of Jesus made on the grain of the wood wall. The paint just outlined the grain. There was a half-size picture of a hippy carrying a sign saying, "God is dead," and a big blue hand coming down from a cloud to pull the sign out of his hand. Lettering across the back wall read, "Jesus is coming soon. You ready?"

Douglas had driven to Spokane and come back with a stack of Jesus People newspapers. On Monday morning before school started, he went to the garage to hand out the Jesus People papers to the crowd of school kids. The rest of us were busy enjoying breakfast when Heather said, "Dad, there is a police car out by the garage."

I went out to see what was happening. Some of the high school kids were smoking outside our garage. The exchange went something like this:

Officer: "Kids, there have been too many complaints from too many neighbors for too many years. This is because there has been too much noise and too much debris. Please make my job easy and split."

I said: "Officer, the kids can smoke in my garage if they want to."

Officer: "It's your garage."

They all ran into the garage. Then the first bell rang at the school, and they all ran off to class. Doug and I looked at each other and realized we had landed on our feet.

The garage was insulated with sawdust boarded up inside the studs. It had an attic. We looked into it and found a dozen kitchen chairs. There was an oil stove in the main room. I called the oil company to put up a tank and attach the stove. Doug and I went to GTE* and picked up several cable spools for tables, and a friend shortened them for us. We flagged down a Pepsi truck and told them to install a Pepsi machine. We got automobile hub caps to hold cigarette butts, and we were in business.

The high school kids called the place God's Garage. (The area had previously been known as Doper's Ditch.) For the next eight months, we had about eighty different kids a day in the garage from eight a.m. to eleven p.m. Doug was there with his guitar during those hours singing everything from "Bottle of Wine" to "I've Been Redeemed."

During the first month in Moscow, I was busy getting the bookstore ready. We opened in November. The Pullman store had opened in August.

After he graduated from high school back in Ann Arbor, Doug had enlisted in the Navy on the condition that he would not be called to active duty until after we were settled in Idaho. Before he left, I told him I could still whip him in wrestling. He was up for it. Bessie said, "Don't. Somebody will get hurt." We went at it any way. At one point, I was on top, but my left arm was underneath him. I heard a snap like a twig breaking. I whispered to Doug that we had better stop. We got up and found that the knuckle of the third finger of my left hand was hanging downward. It would not straighten up. I

* GTE, then known as General Telephone & Electronics Corporation, was the largest independent U.S. telephone company at the time.

did not want to tell Bessie that I had broken my finger. When I was around her, I would keep my left hand on the table, palm down; that pushed the last part of my finger back where it should be. I did tell Heather about it. (I may have told Bessie after the finger healed.)

Doug left for the Navy in November 1971. That meant I had two bookstores and God's Garage on my hands. I left Elmer Hiebert with One Way Books in Pullman and Ben Hyde in Moscow with Crossroads and spent most of my time at God's Garage with Wally McDowell, a grad student who helped out there.

The high school kids' nickname for me was Rooster, or Roost for short. Bessie was Mrs. Rooster. Gordon was in fifth grade. One day, he told me, "Dad, don't let Mom come out to the garage."

"Why not?"

"She has never heard words like this before."

We ran God's Garage for eight months and closed it in the spring of 1972 after a boy had to get eight stitches because of a beer bottle that was thrown into the garage and shattered. But over the course of that short ministry, a number of kids came to the Lord.

In the winter of 1971–72, I was invited to take part in a panel responding to Gordon Lathrop, who was speaking in the CUB ballroom at Washington State University. Gordon was a Lutheran theologian and the chaplain of Pacific Lutheran College in Tacoma. I think I was selected because of my effectiveness in reaching high school kids in God's Garage. The other panel members were Mr. Bowman, the United Church of Christ pastor, King Rockhill, the Methodist pastor, and professor Paul Brians, founder of the WSU Society for the Propagation of Militant Atheism. The panel members were not allowed to debate with each other, and were only to speak about Gordon Lathrup's comments.

The ballroom was packed. Gordon started by making fun of Jesus people. After doing that for a while, he said, "Let's talk about Jesus." He said that there was not much known about Jesus. Only two things were certain: he was baptized by a man named John, and he had fellowship with the down-and-outers.

I took notes on everything Gordon said. When he finished, the panel members were allowed to speak. The United Church of Christ pastor said he wished he could differ with Gordon, but he had to concur with everything he had said. King Rockhill said the same thing.

After that, the atheist said, "I came here to fight with Christians, and I agree with everything Mr. Lathrop said. Why doesn't he be honest and admit he's an atheist?"

Then it was my turn. I started by admitting that I was a "Jesus People." Then I commented that if Gordon was a Lutheran clergyman, he must serve communion on Sunday morning. How could he do that if Jesus hadn't died for the sins of the people? I continued by giving the gospel.

When I stopped, there was a standing ovation. I was new in town. I thought, "Either this place is filled with Christians, or these people are sick and tired of their pastors not believing anything."

The next day, the pastor of the United Church of Christ called me. He seemed angry. He had heard that I'd said that Gordon Lathrop was not a Christian. I assured him that I had not said that. (I hadn't.) He calmed down.

Once he was calm, I said, "I did not say it, but I could have."

He got excited again and wanted to know why.

"He told everyone himself," I said. "He told us all that he did not believe in the deity of Jesus or His death and resurrection. If there is a minimum of truth that defines a Christian, that is it. Gordon does not hold to the minimum. He is not a Christian."

A similar event had happened in Annapolis in the mid-sixties. The president of the YWCA called me on the carpet in her office on State Circle. She had heard that I had said that Bill Hudnut, pastor of the Presbyterian church in Annapolis, was not a Christian.

I had not said that, but I assured her that I could have. I had told Bill that I held to the Gospel as presented in 1 Corinthians 15 and asked him where he stood on the same text.

> Now I make known to you, brethren, the gospel which I preached to you, which also you received, in which also you stand, by which also you are saved, if you hold fast the word which I preached to you, unless you believed in vain. For I delivered to you as of first importance what I also received, that Christ died for our sins according to the Scriptures, and that He was buried, and that He was raised on the third day according to the Scriptures, and that He appeared to Cephas, then to the twelve. (1 Cor. 15:1–5 NASB)

Bill avoided the deity, death, and burial of Jesus and said that that was just one view of Christianity. On the resurrection, he said, "I could tell you I believe it, I could tell you that I do not believe, or I could tell you I don't know. I will tell you I don't know if the resurrection happened, and what's more I don't think it is important."

I passed this information on to the YWCA president. I was not bothered that Bill Hudnut was agnostic about the resurrection. But if he did not believe in it, he was certainly in no position to determine its importance. If he did not know if Jesus had been raised from the dead, then he did not know that he was saved. "Moreover we are even found to be false witnesses of God, because we testified against God that He raised Christ, whom He did not raise, if in fact the dead are not raised" (1 Cor. 15:15 NASB). If Bill himself did not know that he was saved, then I certainly did not know that he was saved.

Julian Byrd had received Christ in God's Garage through Doug before Doug went on active duty. Julian asked me to teach him the Bible every day because he was sure to get into trouble over the summer without daily help. Every noon at Crossroads Bookstore, we had time in the Word.

Julian's father, Bill, a communications professor at the University of Idaho, asked me to do the same at the Student Union Building (SUB) every day for more people. I got extra teachers, and we began holding noon Bible studies on campus. Then the director of the Campus Christian Center asked if we would move the studies there. We did, and for a number of years we had two classes a day, 11:30–12:30 and 12:30–1:30, five days a week. They ranged from twenty to eighty students each and included PhDs as well as University of Idaho students. Then we duplicated this at the K-House* on the WSU campus. Bessie and I also each taught a weekly Bible class at both universities.

---

* Short for Koinonia House, a facility used by various campus ministry groups.

CHAPTER 48
CROSSROADS BOOKSTORE

Grace to you and peace from God our Father and the Lord Jesus
Christ. (2 Cor. 1:2)

Two months after we opened Crossroads, three freshmen girls from
UI came in. I recognized one of them as Lois Johnston. Her father,
Larry, was the first Christian we had met when we had come to spy
out the land the previous February. Her mother was a member of the
committee that opened the store, and I knew that Lois was a Christian.

The other two, Muffy and Penny, were ecstatic about the books
they saw. They were talking about InterVarsity Christian Fellowship.

I thought, "Boy, three Christian freshman girls!"

When I thought that, the Holy Spirit convicted me. "What do you
mean, judging these girls to be Christian? You do not know that."

I was so convicted I blurted out, "Are you girls Christian?"

Muffy and Penny replied, "No we're not Christians."

"Why are you so interested in Christian books?"

"We have been looking for answers."

I said, "Come with me."

They came upstairs to my office, and both Penny and Muffy received Christ.

Muffy was worried about it. What would her boyfriend Sam
think? He was a student at WSU and a hippie. Muffy's father and
Sam's father had been classmates at West Point, class of '51. Their
fathers had another classmate, Kermit Johnson, who was an Army
chaplain in Germany. Muffy had left Germany for UI in order to be
near Sam at WSU. Kermit told her to look up InterVarsity while she

was there. I knew Kermit and had corresponded with him in 1956 when he was in Korea and I was in the East China Sea.*

Some weeks later, a longhaired student came into the store looking for a Bible. For some reason, I was certain that this was Muffy's boyfriend. I sold him a Bible and gave him *Basic Christianity* and *Mere Christianity*.

There were several God-caused reasons that brought Sam to the Lord. I learned later that he was impressed that someone with short hair and a necktie would give a hippie like him anything. Sam is now a tenured professor in biochemistry at the University of Idaho and happily married to Muffy. (Penny married Dave Honsinger. Theirs was the second wedding I officiated.)

Evan also joined the Navy. Before he left in the fall of 1972, he painted large murals from *The Chronicles of Narnia* in the lower room of Crossroads, a half-floor down in the back of the store. We called it the Narnia Chamber. It had Eustace as a dragon with the gold armband squeezing his arm. Trumpkin the dwarf was there, and Susan shooting her bow.

One day a UI freshman studying piano performance came to see me in the Narnia Chamber. She wanted to tell me that she had decided not to be a Christian. She said, "If Jesus was like the Lion [Aslan], I would become a Christian right now." I told her that Jesus was more like the Lion than the Lion was and explained why. She received Christ.

Another time, two young hippies came in to see the Narnia Chamber. I showed them around. They were unfamiliar with Narnia and asked me about the pictures, so I told both girls the Narnia story

---

* Kermit was the man I had thought should be the OCF East Coast Staff Member before I realized the Lord was leading me to leave the Navy and take the position myself.

and also told them the gospel. They responded and came to the Father through Jesus Christ.

I asked if they were students. They said that they lived on a seven-acre farm seven miles east of town on Moscow Mountain. I asked, "You two girls are working seven acres?"

"We are living with our boyfriends; they are doing the farming." I did not ask what they were growing. (It was marijuana.)

A few days later, one of the two came in again and announced that she was moving back to Bakersfield, California. She was not getting along with her boyfriend since she had gotten the "Jesus thing."

We went to the Narnia room to talk. I asked her how long she had lived with Craig. She said two years. Then I taught her the biblical definition of marriage. I explained that marriage was made up of two things, vows and cohabitation. I told her, "If you have vowed, then you may not divorce him just because he is not a believer. If you have not vowed, then you *must* leave him. If you are not married, I will find some Christians in Bakersfield for you to check in with."

Soon after, a young hippie came in to see if we had more of the Bible. I asked him what he meant by "more." More copies? More languages? More versions?

"No, more of it."

"How much do you have already?"

He showed me a copy of the *Good News for Modern Man* translation.

"How much of that have you read?"

"All of it."

I said, "There ain't no more."

This was Craig, the boyfriend. He had been saved. I sold him a few Christian books. Later, I took both of them to lunch at A&W, and they asked me if I would marry them.

I had not performed a marriage before. I called the county courthouse and told them I had not been ordained, licensed by any denomination, or been to seminary or Bible school. I was pastoring a home church, but it had no official membership, and no incorporation. I told them I had been asked to officiate at a marriage and inquired what the rules were. The clerk said to come on up to the courthouse and sign my name.

I went to the courthouse. She gave me a blank sheet of paper and told me to sign my name at the top. That made me official! I have been performing marriages ever since.

The wedding took place in a mountain meadow. All the hippie guests sat in a circle on the ground. (Bessie and I were the only non-hippies there.) When I pronounced them "man and wife," the groom did a backward somersault and yelled, "Hallelujah!"*

After we had been in Moscow a few months, an old retired Nazarene minister named Mr. Waterman started coming into the store once a week for me to pray with him about a wayward daughter. We prayed faithfully for her every week. Then Mr. Waterman died.

A year later, in 1973, a woman came into Crossroads wanting some Christian books. She told me she had just been saved. I asked her about it. She had gone to see *Jesus Christ, Superstar* and had gotten saved during the movie, although the movie was made to be against Jesus. She was Mr. Waterman's daughter.

When we first opened Crossroads Store in November 1971, a man named Leo Boron used to come in. He was a math instructor at UI. Leo was eccentric. He wore hats—many different kinds of hats:

---

* Unfortunately, the marriage did not last; Craig later left her for someone else.

cowboy hats, African pith helmets, Russian fur hats, and more. He had several different buttons pinned to his suit jacket. One of them said, "Homework causes brain damage." The first time he walked into the store, he announced in a loud voice, "Let's us Christians all go shoot some gooks in Vietnam!" He came in every morning and every afternoon with something offensive to say. "Let's us Christians all go hang some niggers in Mississippi!" "Let's us Christians all go crucify some Jews!" He did this for years.

One day, he walked a little farther into the store than usual. I handed Heather the keys and whispered, "Go lock the front door." We had him locked in.

I got to him gradually. He would not take any books, so I got creative. Leo lived in a single room in the Egan Apartments. Over the door of each room was a transom, a small vent window, that was normally open. One afternoon when Leo was at class, I went over to the Egan Apartments and threw booklets on the four gospels through the transom into his apartment. When he was in the store again another day, I offered him one of the booklets. He said, "I've read that." He had been reading the booklets I slipped through his window.

One day I followed Leo out of the store and walked up Main Street with him. He told me that every college president in the country had an Anglo-Saxon name, first, middle, and last, and every elected member of the U.S. House and Senate had an Anglo-Saxon name. (This is not true anymore, but he was more right than wrong at the time.) He hated people with Anglo-Saxon names. To my misfortune, I was named James Wilson, and my associate was Benjamin Hyde.

Our stock with Leo went up in 1973 when Barbara Friedman came to work with us. Leo was very fond of Barbara and would bring her flowers.

Then Leo had a heart attack. I went to see him in the hospital in Spokane afterward. I had a hard time recognizing him because I had never seen him without one of his hats. To my knowledge, he did not respond to the gospel before he died, but he did know that we loved him.

We brought a Billy Graham evangelistic film to Moscow and showed it in the Nuart Theatre. I was responsible for training counselors and taking care of the people who responded to the invitation. Our three oldest children served as counselors. Heather was in high school and asked me to pair her up with a little girl when the invitation was given. No little girl came forward. Heather spotted someone tall with long black hair. She went up beside her, only to find out that "she" was an Indian man. Her convert was not a little girl! The man was in town singing with Up with People*. He became a Christian.

In 1974, a young hermit ventured into Moscow to buy some murder mysteries. He went first to BookPeople, a bookstore on Main Street. It was closed, so he came up the street to Crossroads. Barbara gave him two books, *The Cross and the Switchblade* and *Basic Christianity*.

The next time he came in, I was busy with someone upstairs. I left the person I was with because the phone rang. After I got off the phone, the hermit announced, "I've come to return these books." Barbara was talking to someone, Luke (another worker) was talking to someone, and I had someone waiting for me upstairs—so no one

---

* Up with People was a subsidiary of the Moral Re-Armament, a motivational singing movement. In order to join the group, you had to confess to your parents all the moral sins you had committed in college. It was liberal group and not associated with the gospel.

paid any attention to him. He put the books on the counter near the door but did not leave.

I walked up to the counter to see what the books were and asked him what he thought of them. He said, "*The Cross and the Switchblade* wasn't much, but *Basic Christianity* was great."

Nancy Greensides,[†] a young Christian, was the only one not busy. I told Nancy, "Take this fellow down to the Narnia Room and lead him to Christ." She did.

Through Crossroads, I got to know a Christian woman who lived in a small town fourteen miles away. One day she called to tell me that her fourteen-year-old daughter had locked herself in the bathroom and was screaming, and she wanted to know if I could help. I got in the car and drove out to her house.

The daughter was still in the bathroom screaming when I got there. I sat on the floor outside to talk her down. Once she had calmed down, she agreed to continue the talk only if I sat on the floor behind a big chair and she sat on the floor behind the couch. We continued our "conversation" that way.

Finally, I gave her a challenge. "I'll beat you in a quarter-mile race." She jumped to her feet. "You can't!"

We went outside to a straight road. I must have been crazy. I was sixty-five at the time! I think I beat her by about a foot. Whatever the problem was, it was solved.

Another Christian woman from the same town called me. I also knew her only from meeting in Crossroads. She said, "I need to see a counselor. Do you know any Christian counselors?"

† Now Nancy Wilson, my daughter-in-law, married to Douglas.

I told her that I knew half a dozen professional counselors. "I know another half dozen who could give better counsel cheaper. You can start with me." We made an appointment.

Her story was the worst I had ever heard. (I have heard worse since, but not at that time.) I saw her twice. Later she transcribed many of my talks and edited the original edition of my book *On Being a Christian* in 2001.

In the early '70s, I became friends with a particular UI student who was a customer at Crossroads. We would meet to talk in the Student Union Building and in the bookstore. One of those times, I asked him why he did not like Christians.

He said, "They all have a holier-than-thou attitude."

I replied that I knew many Christians, and none of them had a holier-than-thou attitude. I asked him to name one of these Christians. He named another student that I knew. I reflected on that Christian and replied, "He does not have a holier-than-thou attitude. He is doing his best just to keep his own head above water. He doesn't have time to look down on anyone else."

He believed me. "Well," he asked, "Then why does it *seem* like he has a holier-than-thou attitude?"

"Oh," I replied, "He *is* holier than thou."

When Douglas returned from active duty, he enrolled at the University of Idaho. When he and Evan were both undergraduates, they took classes from a man named Dr. Seaman, a philosophy professor and militant atheist. One day Dr. Seaman was walking down

Main Street with me. He said that Douglas had told him that he had never heard his father and mother fight. I assured him that was true.

"How could that be?"

That was easy—we did not fight. If Bessie and I had a difference of opinion, we did not have that difference in front of the children. When we were expecting our first child, Bessie and I made the decision that we would not differ out loud in front of our kids. When one parent corrected a child, the other parent would not alter the discipline of the first parent, even if they disagreed strongly.

I knew that my sons disagreed with Dr. Seaman. I asked him if they were respectful in class. He said that they were very respectful. "How did you do it? My sons are losers." His son was a follower of a Black Panther leader named Eldridge Cleaver. Cleaver had written a book called *Soul on Ice*. Later, Cleaver received Christ and wrote another book called *Soul on Fire*. I sold a copy to Dr. Seaman.

Inland Christian Laymen Newsletter

February 16, 1974
514 East "C" Street
Moscow, ID 83843

Dear Friends:

Jim is very busy with the Billy Graham film *Time to Run*, and will be until next Wednesday; so I am going to try to write the entire letter before the postal rates go up in March.

As well as the film, this past week saw the opening up of a small outlet for books on campus called Cair Paravel. We rent a small room downstairs in the Campus Christian Center. Our daily Bible study lectures continue upstairs with good attendance. Christian students will be manning this store all day and in the first week have reported good conversations.

So much could be written of the past year. Hieberts have moved to Tempe, Arizona, and opened up a store called Quo Vadis with a local committee but still under ICL. Jim is hoping for a visit there soon. Ben Hyde has left to study at Multnomah Bible School, and is using his other gifts in rehabilitation efforts with Youth for Christ. Barbara Friedman joined us in the summer and, to our joy and hers, has seen seeking hearts come to the Saviour as she witnesses to His power and reality . . . .

We look on these stores as a training ground not only for book store management, but training in witness as well. The staff meet every Thursday morning before work for prayer and fellowship and they are joined for part of the time by staff from various churches and organizations. Jim says a very good spirit of fellowship prevails and has led to some joint efforts by evangelicals in the community. We continue to hear of others who wish to open up stores, so we envision training others from time to time, and, who knows, the time may come when a training course can be offered for bookstore enthusiasts! Pray with us, please.

Next summer, July 7–13, Jim will be speaking for the Officers' Christian Fellowship at Spring Canyon Lodge in Colorado. We'd love to see some of our old friends there and make some new ones too . . . Some of you have received our ICL paper *Roots By the River*. If others wish to do so, please send us a card asking to be put on the list. It has a message, a book review, and ICL news.

Family news next. Doug is now on a nuclear sub out of Norfolk, the *USS Ray*, quite a change from the diesel sub he was on before. Evan is at El Centro at the Naval Aerospace Recovery Facility, and we understand that he photographs parachutes. What rejoices our hearts is the desire they both have to witness for Jesus Christ and their desire for good Christian reading. They seem to gravitate in their thinking to bookstore ministry in the future, but our concern is that they be faithful in the place God has put them in the present. Heather graduates from high school in May, and Evan hopes to get home for it. Gordon is in his first year of junior high and attends a study Jim conducts weekly. We are praying that some of the *Time to Run* contacts will be encouraged to come to it.

"We have this treasure in earthen vessels," Paul tells us in 2 Corinthians 4:7. Looking at the passage before this, we see he has likened the light of the gospel coming into the heart to the light of creation. "For it is the God who said 'Let light shine out of darkness' who has shone in our hearts to give the light of the knowledge of the glory of God in the face of Christ." It is light with a purpose. The face of Christ is illumined to us, not in visions necessarily, but in our coming to recognize that the Christ of the Gospels is indeed the Son of God, our Lord and Saviour. This then is our treasure, the personal knowledge of Jesus Christ as He comes to make His home in our hearts.

Paul says "earthen vessels," and this represents our bodies, or more specifically our whole lives. When I was in Japan, I was amazed at the talent of the Japanese with their flower arrangements or *ikebana* as it is called. What I noticed was that the perfection of the flowers was not obscured by a garish, highly-painted vase. Generally, the pottery was nondescript in color and low in comparison to the arrangement.

Paul further says "that the transcendent power belongs to God and not to us," which gives the purpose of the earthen vessel. The question comes to each of us then, "Is my life showing or obscuring my treasure?"

In recent years among evangelicals (influenced by the secular world), there has been a rising desire for maturity in ourselves and in our relationships with others. Christians are being helped in conferences, through books, and by counselors to accept themselves and others. In women's circles, "fulfillment" is sought and taught . . . But my question is a warning: Is there not a danger of over-preoccupation with the *vessel*? Is God going to be glorified by my "actualizing my potential" or by my humbly, gratefully displaying my treasure? Whether we seek positive improvements in our personalities or elimination of bad habits in ourselves, let our motives be *that Christ will be seen* increasingly in our lives.

Thank you for your prayers.

Our love in Him,
Jim and Bessie Wilson & family.

CHAPTER 49

THE CHURCHES

Of this gospel I was made a minister according to the gift of God's grace, which was given me by the working of his power. (Eph. 3:7)

When we were getting in the car to leave Ann Arbor, I told Bessie that even if we found the best evangelical church in America in Moscow, Idaho, we would not join it. She wanted to know why. We had joined churches in San Diego, Monterey, Washington, D.C., Annapolis, and Ann Arbor. My answer was, "When we join such a church, once they discover that you know more than the average church member, they put you to work in the church doing something that does not save sinners, edify believers, or glorify the Lord. We are in the business of saving, edifying, and glorifying, so we are not going to join."

When we arrived in Moscow after those first six weeks in Pullman, we immediately started a home church. It met on Sunday afternoons. In the mornings, Doug and Evan went to Emmanuel Lutheran while I taught Heather and Gordon in Sunday school at home.

I also visited different churches. Lalia Boone invited me to teach an adult class at the Methodist Church. Most of the people in the class were new Christians who had been saved in February when a lay witness mission had visited the church. These people did not know that they had been saved. They only knew that instead of just being Methodists, they were now happy, singing Methodists.

The rest of the class were liberal Methodists, two of whom were Fred and Mertie Kohl. The Kohls and their three children all received Christ. After the first class, a fifty-nine-year-old man followed me home and received Christ. Later his wife, daughter, and daughter's husband received Christ as well. They are all with the Lord now.

In October 1971, the Evangelical Free Church at the Grange asked me to preach until they found a permanent pastor. Elmer Hiebert had been their pastor, but he was moving to Tempe, Arizona, to start the Quo Vadis Bookstore next to Arizona State University. So I preached at E-Free and still had Sunday school at home for Heather and Gordon. In addition, Douglas and Evan and Heather went to the Emmanuel Lutheran Church youth group and joined a choral group there called Salt Unlimited. It was led by a woman named Marva—now the retired Lutheran theologian Marva Dawn. She was the one who arranged for Douglas to preach his first sermon in a small Lutheran church in the Moscow area.

The E-Free church never did call a pastor. I met with the deacons and said, "If we ever get a hundred people in attendance, let's divide into two churches of fifty people each." That did not make sense to them. Maybe they thought that they would not get a hundred people in the congregation, or maybe they just thought that was crazy. In any case, it ended the conversation.

The church at the Grange continued to grow. Because I was doing more conference speaking out of town on weekends, the church called Lowell Carlson to share the preaching duty. From 1972–74, I had received no salary for preaching. When Lowell joined in 1974, the church decided to give us each $100 a month.

In 1973, we had about sixty people; in 1974, we had a hundred, and in 1975 about four hundred. When we reached four hundred people, I asked the deacons if they wanted to build a building. They were emphatic in their *no*.

I said, "Then we divide the church."

We did it geographically. On 15 September 1975, we sent about thirty people to Moscow to start a church there with my son Doug and Lowell Carlson preaching while I stayed on at the Grange. (Doug had gotten out of the Navy that August and started studying at UI that same month.) The new church initially called itself Faith Fellowship. Because there was a Pentecostal church in Pullman called Living Faith Fellowship, they changed their name soon after to Community Evangelical Fellowship. CEF met in Greene's Body and Paint Shop. Bill and Shirley Greene had gotten right with the Lord in a Bible study that Bessie and I held in their home.

At the same time, we kept our afternoon home church going for five years. It had started as a place for our family to have church. Episcopalians, Presbyterians, Methodists, and college kids starting coming to the home church in addition to their morning service. Soon the house was filled, so we divided it into two homes. I preached in the morning at E-Free (at the Grange) and at the two home churches in the afternoon and evening.

When I started preaching at the Grange, I had to quit doing the morning Sunday school for Gordon. I told him he could go to Sunday school at the Grange. That was not good enough for him. He said that he did not learn anything in Sunday school there. He only learned when I taught him. I said, "OK, I will teach your class at the Grange." That meant I was teaching four times every Sunday.

The church at the Grange continued to grow and moved to two services. In 1976, we started a student church on the WSU campus with about seventy-five students. We had an 8:30 service at the Grange, a 9:45 service at WSU, an 11:00 second service at the Grange, and two home-church services. (Doug Busby taught the adult Sunday school class at the Grange while I preached on campus.) Now I was teaching *five* times on Sunday.

In 1977, we closed the home churches so they would not compete with the new E-Free church (CEF) in Moscow, which Douglas was now pastoring.* Around the same time, we started holding a hymn sing in our home on Sunday evenings to get new believers familiar with hymns faster than they would by singing them just once a week on Sunday morning.

In 1978, I realized I should not be shuttling back and forth on Sunday morning. We decided to divide the Grange congregation into two churches. Doug Busby would stay with the main E-Free church at the Grange, and I would take the other half of the church and meet elsewhere. We thought that the church would divide down the middle with an equal number of families and students in each. It divided evenly in numbers (about 250 in each group), but all of the families stayed at the Grange, and most of the students came with me. The new student church met at Edison School in Pullman. Edison was demolished later that year, and we moved to Franklin School.

In the meantime, the main E-Free church with Doug Busby grew out of the Grange and began meeting at Gladish School. A small group left to start another church back at the Grange. Denny Rigstad and a graduate student named Robert Littlejohn pastored it.

In the fall of 1979, Bessie and I left the student church for a four-month sabbatical. We visited Bessie's family in Edmonton and Mrs. Mother in Calgary, then went to Vancouver, B.C., to rest. While in Vancouver, I team-taught a class at Regent together with J.I. Packer. We returned to Moscow just before Christmas.

In 1980, Denny Rigstad and Robert Littlejohn both left. The main E-Free church asked me to pastor both the student church and the new little Grange church. I did that for several months and realized I should not do both. I left the student church with Nils Swanson and

* CEF later changed its name to Christ Church.

continued with the little Grange church. Nils's student church later became Cornerstone Evangelical Free Church.

The original Grange church had grown from thirty to four hundred in the first three years I was there. Now I was again in the Grange with only thirty people. Over the next three years, instead of growing as it had before, it went from thirty people to twenty, because we were now competing with two successful churches in town. We did not want to compete.

At a prayer meeting in September 1985, we realized that our little church had seen a Dutch woman, a Nigerian man, two Chinese, and an Indian receive Christ. A month later, we started the International Church with English classes, babysitting, and transportation. On the first Sunday, we had thirty-five international adults and sixteen children in attendance.

The church grew to about eighty, mostly Korean. About a dozen of them received Christ. Then a Korean pastor came to town, and they started a Korean church. Most of the Koreans went to the new church, but the Koreans who had received Christ did not go. They stayed with us because they did not like the culture of Korean churches.

The church grew again to about eighty, this time mostly Chinese. Then they started the Pullman Chinese Christian Church; I preached there once a month for many years.

For several years, we held effective English classes at the International Church. We could not transport all the internationals in our cars, so we bought a school bus. Then we bought a second bus. Then we had an International Church service at the Grange in Pullman in the morning and another one in the afternoon at Logos School in Moscow.

Because the international students had no money, we soon could not afford the rent at the Grange, even though it was cheap. We moved both international churches to our two bookstores for a while. Finally, we recombined the two churches into one which met in the Moscow bookstore. It was still an effective outreach for several years after this; then our core attendance of Americans moved away, and we were left with a few Christians who were not given to outreach. Later, it became an outreach church again, although not one with an international congregation. In 2015, we changed our name to Word of Life Church. The church stayed small and was closed by a vote when I retired from preaching in 2017.

Jim, circa 1980s.

CHAPTER 50

114 SOUTH HOWARD STREET

For you know the grace of our Lord Jesus Christ, that though he
was rich, yet for your sakes he became poor, so that you by his
poverty might become rich. (2 Cor. 8:9)

For our first two years in Moscow, we lived on Jefferson Street immediately across from the post office and next to the high school. For
the winter of 1973–74, we lived on C Street until we found a permanent home at 114 South Howard Street. Vicky Bureau first drew our
attention to this house. She had taken care of the previous owner, a
Mrs. Thompson, before she died. The house had two bedrooms, a
bathroom, living room, kitchen, and a dormitory bedroom upstairs
as well as an attached studio apartment.

The asking price for the house was $22,800. We had no money.
Vivian Canode, the realtor, asked me if I had the G.I. Bill for a house.
I had no idea. I had been out of the Navy for eighteen years and had
never paid any attention to the G.I. Bill. I had the form, but I had
no idea where it was. Vivian got me a new one. On this paper, I was
guaranteed a $25,000 federal loan for my eleven years of active duty.
We bought the house with no down payment and moved in in the
spring of 1974.

There was only one problem with the house. The dining room was
in the living room, the piano was in the living room, the television was
there, the record player was there, the Bible studies were there, and
all of Heather and Gordon's friends were there. Consequently, some
counseling had to take place in the kitchen or one of the bedrooms.

In 1973, Wayne Stevenson moved to Moscow from Detroit to get his family away from the big city. A man named Glen Edwards led Wayne to the Lord at his workplace. Barbara had introduced Glen to the Lord. Wayne invited me to his home, where his wife received Christ.

I was talking to Wayne about my small house problems. He suggested I add on to the house. I told him I had no money. He said, "If you ever get $200, let me know, and I will tell you where to dig for the footings. If you don't get any more money, you can call it a dog pen." Wayne poured the foundation for us. It took a year, but we added a back porch, a fourteen-by-sixteen-foot dining room, and a nine-by-fourteen-foot study.

The neighbors on the corner owned the house just north of us. There was a short fence between our properties. The neighbors told me that every year old Mrs. Thompson would move the fence a few inches into the yard next door. I removed the fence so the original property line was once again intact.

When Wayne was working on the addition, he told me that he was greatly concerned for how his brother-in-law was doing spiritually. The problem was the brother-in-law lived in Wales, Wisconsin. Could I help him?

"Wayne, I am flying to Wales on Monday." I was going to visit my brother who lived eight miles from Wales. My sister-in-law Glenda met me at the Milwaukee airport. I asked Glenda for her car and drove to the brother-in-law's house. He was very open to the gospel. We talked for most of an hour.

Around this time, one of Gordon's friends became a Christian, followed by his mother, his father, and an older brother. The mother came to see me. She had a coworker who was in great trouble and appeared suicidal. I agreed to see the woman. She came to our home and told me some awful stories. I told her I would take care of the stories one at a time. I also told her firmly that I would not see her a second time unless she put into effect what I told her the first time. It was amazing how fast those sins disappeared.

One time when I was with her, I realized she was a thief. That was not one of the sins she had talked about. I cannot remember whether I got this knowledge by some kind of revelation or whether I picked up from her materialistic conversation. (No one could have been as materialistic as she was without stealing.) It may have been a combination of the two. In any case, I was very certain she had stolen quite a lot.

I told her I wanted her to give me a list of all the places she had stolen from and a dollar estimate of how much from each. It told her to make her estimate high, then add twenty percent to it and bring me the list the following week.

She resisted. She wasn't a thief! Well, she might have taken some drawing paper or something from the office once or twice.

I said, "Don't give me that excuse. I want the list."

She brought it to me. It was between fifteen and twenty stores with a total value of $800 worth of stolen items. It included Crossroads Bookstore (where we were talking in the office), where she had stolen all her stocking stuffers the previous Christmas.

I told her I wanted the money the following week. She came with $400 and the rest the week after. I took the money and the list and paid the stores back. I did not give her name to the stores.

For the seven years of her PhD work, a Jewish girl named Marny, who had become a Christian, spent all her time at our house from early morning to late at night. She wouldn't stay overnight, but she was there almost every moment that she was not teaching or sleeping.

Marny was a very disciplined woman. She would get up early in the morning, do eighty sit-ups, run a mile and a half, and then have her quiet time.

One day, I said, "Marny, I'd like you to quit having your quiet time."

"Quit having my quiet time? How does a Christian survive without quiet time?"

I said, "You are not doing very well *with* it."

Being a Christian who is walking in the light means reading the Scripture regularly, but *not* because you are required to. Marny was doing her quiet time as a legalistic practice. She wasn't meeting with the Lord Jesus. It had become part of her daily discipline, like the eighty sit-ups. She was just doing what she was supposed to. It probably still yielded some benefit, but she was not walking in the light. I told her, "Marny, you can start having your quiet time again when you *want* to meet with the Lord Jesus." It was great, both when she didn't have her quiet time for a while, and when she got back into having it.

The yellow house on Howard Street
(Photo by Jim's great-granddaughter Jemima Merkle)

CHAPTER 51

THE SCHOOL OF
PRACTICAL CHRISTIANITY

Devout converts followed Paul and Barnabas, who, as they spoke
with them, urged them to continue in the grace of God.
(Acts 13:43)

One day in 1976, I was reading in Acts and came across this description of the Apostle Paul in Ephesus: "Paul entered the synagogue and spoke boldly there for three months, arguing persuasively about the kingdom of God. But some of them became obstinate; they refused to believe and publicly maligned the Way. So Paul left them. He took the disciples with him and had discussions daily in the lecture hall of Tyrannus. This went on for two years, so that all the Jews and Greeks who lived in the province of Asia heard the word of the Lord" (Acts 19:8–10).

While reading this passage, I realized that Paul had taught daily in the same place for two years. The result was that everyone in Asia heard the word of the Lord Jesus. I assume that the seven churches of Asia came from these people he taught.

I wanted everyone who lived in Idaho and Washington to hear the word of the Lord Jesus. This prompted me to start my own Bible school called the School of Practical Christianity.

I knew I would need help with this. I called Doug Busby, then a senior at Trinity Evangelical Divinity School. I had known Doug during his last two years at the Naval Academy and saw him again in New London, Connecticut, when I spoke at the Coast Guard

Academy.* I asked Doug Busby if he would like to be the principal of the School of Practical Christianity. I told him that if he took that job, he could also be pastoring a church within the year.

Doug wondered about supporting his family. I had no idea what to do about money. I said that I would trust the Lord with him for $6,000 a year. We did not make it to that amount, but he managed to live on what came in.

The school was a success in quality and numbers. It had no entrance requirements, no tuition, no assignments, no exams, no grades, and no credit.

We held the school summer and winter, three hours a day, five days a week, for a number of years. In the summers of 1980 and 1981, we rented two fraternity houses, one at UI, and one at WSU. There were about forty students in each of the summer schools, plus house parents and cooks.

Later we took the school on the road for two-week sessions. We held it in Spokane,† Bellevue, Bremerton, Annapolis, and San Diego. No one gave us an invitation to hold these schools except in San Diego, where Major General John Grinalds invited us to the Marine Corps Recruit Depot. We invited ourselves to all the other locations. How we paid for it I have no idea. Normally, we took four teachers: Doug Busby, Nils Swanson, my son Douglas, and myself. Bessie came with us to the Annapolis school. Douglas and I were the only ones in San Diego.

We continued to hold the school in Moscow regularly until 2008.

---

* In 1972, my son Douglas was stationed across the river from New London in Groton on the *USS Tusk*, a diesel-powered submarine, and I had gone there to visit him as well as to speak at the Academy.

† This was a one-month school.

CHAPTER 52
LIFE BETWEEN THE SEXES

As each has received a gift, use it to serve one another, as good
stewards of God's varied grace. (1 Pet. 4:10)

In 1973, a group of male students from WSU came to me and com-
plained that women had access to instruction about relationships
with the opposite sex, but nothing was available for men. In response,
we set up a weekly class for men called Life Between the Sexes that
ran for a semester at a time. I had about forty men in the class that
first semester. Then the women came to me and said, "What about
us?" so we started a women's class at the K-House. At one point,
Bessie had seventy women in her class.

The second semester, I had just finished teaching the first class
at UI when a freshman girl asked me a question. I knew her family
because she had gone to Moscow High. This was her question: "I
have known this guy for five years, ever since junior high. We have
been best friends. We started going out in September. We are not
best friends anymore. Why is that?"

"It is hard to be friends when you are making out all of the time."
She seemed affronted. I asked, "When are you going to get married?"

"Married? We can't get married. I'm a freshman. He is still in
high school."

"When are you going to get married?"

"I told you, we can't get married. Why can't we go together for
four years and then get married?"

"You tell me. How fast has the physical relationship progressed since September?"

"Pretty fast."

"Project that progress for the next four years at the same rate of increase."

Her eyes widened. "Oh. We are not going to make it."

"In the next six months, you have three options: One, get married."

"I told you, we can't get married!"

"I know, but that is one of the options. Two, go to bed with him."

"We're Christians; we can't do that!"

"Three, break it off."

"No way!"

"I'm sorry—those are your only three choices. Tell me, will it be harder to break it off in six months than to break it off now?"

"Much harder."

"Then cool it now!"

She broke it off.

Two guys at UI came to me to sign up for their third time through the class. They said, "The first time we took the class, we did not believe a word you said. The second time, it made some sense. Now we are coming to learn this time."

A WSU girl once asked me, "I have taken this class four times. If I take it the fifth time, do I get a man?" She is now a pastor's wife in California.

Early on in the Life Between the Sexes classes, we threw a Christmas party for the attendees. I asked the following questions to the seventy-five or so students at the party: How many would be going to one of the spring conferences sponsored by the different campus groups, InterVarsity, Navs, etc.? To my surprise, the total was under fifteen. Then I asked how many would like a spring conference for the non-affiliated students. The answer was an overwhelming affirmation. We had our first Advance (not a retreat!) that spring at Camp Sanders with Gene Thomas as the speaker and 150 students in attendance. From then on, we held Advances every spring and fall.

At the same time as we were getting these classes going, Sam Adams, one of the WSU professors, began starting up college Young Life groups for kids who had been in Young Life in high school. As a high school student, Sam had been part of the first Young Life group in the country. At the first WSU meeting, Sam had about five hundred kids. He trained seventy-five of them to be leaders for the Young Life high school clubs in the surrounding towns.

How did that affect us? The kids who joined the college Young Life started coming to the E-Free Church at the Grange. We held baptisms in the Palouse River and the Snake River in the spring and the fall. We would have about thirty candidates each time. When they gave their testimonies, the overwhelming majority said they had been saved at Malibu, the Young Life Camp.

CHAPTER 53
LEAVING & CLEAVING

In order that the promise may rest on grace and be guaranteed to
all his offspring—not only to the adherent of the law but also to the
one who shares the faith of Abraham, who is the father of us all.
(Rom. 4:16)

Doug got out of the Navy in August 1975 and started as a freshman at UI at the age of twenty-two. He asked me what he should major in. I advised him that math and the hard sciences were the safest. In these subjects you would be dealing with God's facts. In all other subjects—sociology, anthropology, biology, and even history and English—you are taught a lot of falsehood. Doug didn't go the "safe" way. He tested out of over forty credits and majored in philosophy. He married Nancy Greensides on December 31, 1975. He finished his bachelor's and master's degrees in the same four years. During those four years, he sang in a band*, began to pastor the Moscow church, and he and Nancy had two children.

Evan left for the Navy in the fall of 1972 and got out in 1976. He enrolled at UI and began his studies in art, but later changed to history. He had been back in Moscow for a year when Leslie Rye came up from California to study at UI. Evan had been stationed in her hometown of El Centro for most of his time in the Navy. Evan and Leslie were married in 1978.

* Mountain Angel Band released one album, *Angel Food*, in 1978. You can find some of the tracks on YouTube.

114 South Howard Street

Moscow, Idaho 83843

December 1978

Dear Friends,

We are never more conscious of the blessing of friends as we are at Christmas. Contrary to some, I still enjoy the "catching up on news" from letters, mimeographed, printed, or the few lines on a card. Thank you for keeping in touch.

The personal high light of 1978 was in the nature of a double blessing. On August 12th, Evan and Leslie were married in hot, hot El Centro. That same evening, Nancy, Douglas, and Rebekah Lee welcomed in Moscow, Idaho, Nathan David. Our cup was full. A new home established in one case, a new life to guide to eternal life in the other.

The Lord had graciously provided a super-saver air trip to L.A. for Jim and me, Heather, and Gordon. We hired a car for the week in California. To our joy and delight, we had a precious hour with Corrie ten Boom, all the more precious because of her stroke that same month. We understand she is improving and regaining her speech.

We had an excellent group of students for our summer session of the school of practical Christianity. Now we have a fine but smaller group studying with us. Pray with us for God's direction in this.

Douglas will have his master's degree in philosophy shortly, and we ask your prayers for him and Nancy. They have a desire to study this summer at Regent College up in Vancouver, B.C., and are looking to the Lord for His direction. Doug pastors Faith Fellowship in Moscow, a growing and alive fellowship.

Evan will be going into his junior year in the art program at UI in '79 and continues to use his ability in the Lord's work. He has done cartoons for the evangelical pro-life group which have drawn much comment. Leslie will be graduating in education in the spring.

Heather will be graduating in history and would like to do graduate work, preferably in Scotland. She is enquiring into this now . . . .

Gordon will graduate [high school] in May, and he is considering what Heather did, stay out of school for a year to get his bearings before continuing his schooling.

We had a lovely visit with Jim's mother in October, and she met her two granddaughters-in-law and her two great-grandchildren.

I do not know how to ask you to pray for us, nor what our prayers for you should be. Amy Carmichael, in one of her poems, said something for all of us:

> Give me the love that leads the way,
> The faith that nothing can dismay,
> The hope no disappointments tire,
> The passion that will burn like fire,
> Let me not sink to be a clod:
> Make me Thy fuel, Flame of God.

Yours in Him,
Jim & Bessie

Doug and Nancy, 1975

Evan and Leslie, 1978

Heather, 1979

Gordon, 1979

CHAPTER 54

COMING TO THE LORD
OR COMING TO THE TEXT

Working together with him, we appeal to you not to receive the
grace of God in vain. (2 Cor. 6:1)

In the late seventies, I got to know a young married couple who
worked at Washington State University. Their marriage was in bad
shape. The wife was very smart and very organized. She went to
multiple people for counseling, attended our school of practical
Christianity, and read several marriage books. I met with them both
a couple times and with her more times. She knew all the right answers but did not seem able to put them into effect in her life.

She came to see me and asked if I had five minutes. I did not have five
minutes, but I also knew that she probably meant thirty-five minutes.

I said, "Isn't the Lord available?"

I should not have said that. She turned around and walked out. I
thought that she would not come around again soon.

However, shortly after that, she was at our front door at home.
Bessie met her and sent her to the backyard to sit in one of the chairs
under the apple tree while Bessie went to find me.

At that moment, I was reading a book by Watchman Nee. I had
just read the paragraph where Nee said, "Two men can hear the same
text preached at the same time. 'I am the way the truth and the life,
no man cometh to the Father but by me.' One of the two will be so
impressed that he will come to the Father by Jesus Christ. The other
will be so impressed by the words that he will come to the text."

Having just read that paragraph, I quoted it to the young wom-an under the apple tree. She said, "What's the difference between the two?"

I said, "The first has love, joy, and peace, and the other has a plaque on the wall."

The next day she called to tell me that she was not a Christian. I replied that I did not think she was, either. She got upset with me because I agreed with her.

I told her that I would not tell her how to become a Christian. Her head was filled with the gospel already. If I told her how to do it, she would go through the motions just like she had done with the counseling and the marriage books and not be any more saved after-ward. I said, "After you have some tiny understanding of the holiness of God, and after you have some tiny understanding of how sinful you are in the light of that holiness, and after you have some tiny understanding of how much love God has for you in your sinfulness, then I will tell you the good news."

I did not hear from her for several weeks. Then she called and asked, "How could the Father love the Son and send Him to the cross?"

I replied, "The text says, 'For God so loved the *world.*' That tells us not how much He loves the Son, but how much He loves the world." I realized that she probably had that "tiny understanding" and decid-ed to tell her the gospel.

I wanted to speak to her heart. Her head was already filled with truth, but it had not sunk in. So I gave her the gospel in song and poetry instead of prose. Over the phone, I sang her hymns like *The Love of God*, *The Deep, Deep Love of Jesus*, and *At Calvary.*

Sometime later, she was working a job cleaning apartments. As she pushed the vacuum around, she was singing, "He is Lord, He is Lord, He has risen from the dead, and He is Lord." She was converted while singing that chorus.

RESTITUTION

What shall we say then? Are we to continue in sin that grace may
abound? (Rom. 6:1)

In 1980, I was preaching to the E-Free student congregation at Franklin
School. I knew students did not get to be eighteen years old without
stealing. So once a year I would preach on restitution (taking stolen items
back, or paying for them plus twenty percent). At the close of the meeting, a student came with his wife and baby and said he wanted to see me
right away. I told him to come to my house at two o'clock that afternoon.

They showed up, and I asked him what the subject was. He said,
"What you preached about this morning."

I asked him, "Wasn't it clear?"

"Yes."

"Then take action on it."

"I still want to tell you about it." He said, "I have a leather fringe
coat I do not feel like wearing anymore. I have a pair of gym shoes I
found on the beach at the boat races in the Tri-Cities*. I had seventy
rock music tapes that cost $6.99 per tape. I don't like that kind of
music anymore, so I threw them away. I took a bicycle from a house
in Spokane ten years ago."

"What's your problem?" I asked. "You know what to do."

"I don't have any money."

"What are you and your wife living on?"

"The money I made last summer. I budgeted it out for the rest of
the school year."

* Kennewick, Pasco, and Richland in eastern Washington

"*Oh*," I said, "You *do* have the money!" I told him that the money he had saved up was not his; it belonged first to the people he had stolen from.

He drove to Spokane and found the house he had stolen the bicycle from. There was a party going on. He walked up and knocked on the front door. The husband answered, and he asked him if they had lost a bike ten years ago. The husband did not know, so he called his wife. She confirmed that they had lost a bike. He gave her $100. She went over in a corner and counted it.

Another student had dropped out of school to work as a heavy-equipment operator for a construction firm. In the spring, he decided to come back to WSU in the fall to finish college. He went to his boss to give him three months' notice. The boss said, "Since you are not coming to work in the fall, don't bother coming to work tomorrow."

He was so angry at being fired that he took a lot of tools home with him that night. He thought the company owed it to him for letting him go with no notice when he had been trying to give them three months' notice.

Then he came back to college and heard me teach on restitution. He went home for Christmas, collected the tools he had taken, and put them in his car to take back to the company.

On the way there, he was listening to Christian radio. The teacher said, "If you are thinking about returning things you have taken in the past, don't do it. That is Old Testament. We are in the New Testament, under grace. It is not necessary."

The student thanked God, turned around, and took the tools home. This time he engraved his initials on them.

He came back to WSU after Christmas and heard another message from me on restitution. The next time he went home, he returned the tools—with his initials on them.

CHAPTER 56

DISCIPLESHIP

To Titus, my true child in a common faith: Grace and peace from
God the Father and Christ Jesus our Lord. (Titus 1:4)

Over the years, many people have asked me to disciple them. I always
said *no*, although I knew Christians are commanded to disciple. I refused
because I knew what those people were really saying was, "I want to be a
little Jim Wilson, and I want an inordinate amount of your time to help
me get there." I would just be making Xerox copies of myself. I did not
think that that was right, but I also felt guilty for turning people down.

Then in 1980 I went to an interdenominational conference for
pastors on Vancouver Island. There were elders present from all of
western Canada and the western United States. One of the speakers
was Vince Stryges, an elder from the Church of the Redeemer in
Mesa, Arizona. During his talk, Vince said, "Many people have asked
me to disciple them, and I have always said, 'No.'"

I sat up and paid attention.

He said, "One time I decided to say, 'Yes.' I asked the fellow who
asked me to disciple him what the key passage on discipleship was.

"He came up with Matthew 28:18–19: 'All authority in heaven
and on earth has been given to me. Therefore go and make disciples
of all nations, baptizing them . . . and teaching them to obey everything I have commanded you.'

"I said, 'Are you a Christian? Have you received Christ?'

"The young man said, 'Yes.'

"'Have you been baptized in the name of the Father, the Son, and
the Holy Spirit?'

"The young man said, 'Yes.'

"'Well, there's only one thing left for me to do—teach you to obey everything that Jesus commanded. Now, everything is a lot, so you will have to cooperate. I would like you to read the New Testament and mark every command. If you have obeyed it, mark it green. If you have not obeyed it, mark it yellow. Once you've marked it yellow, go obey it. After you have obeyed it, mark it blue; that will turn it green. You can come to me if there is something you do not understand. But if you understand it, just obey it. When your New Testament is green, come back and see me.'"

I thought that was wonderful, but I was too chicken to try it. Then a senior from Washington State University named Mike McFarland came to see me. "Jim, I'm in the Campus Crusade Discipleship Program. I've done it all, but there must be more. Will you teach me the *more*?"

I said, "Yes," and I gave him the green New Testament assignment I learned from Vince. "Come back and see me if you don't understand it. If you do understand it, just obey it." He never came back.

Sometime later, I was counseling a student at One Way Books in Pullman, Washington. After we finished, I asked him what he was doing with his life.

"I'm in the Campus Crusade Discipleship Program." How did he like it? "Oh, it's the best thing ever." I asked if anyone ever dropped out of the program, and he said, "Yes."

I said, "What do you do with the dropouts?"

"Well, they must be backsliding since they are quitting the program, so we give them a hard time for dropping out."

I asked if he knew Mike McFarland who had come to me for discipling. He said that Mike was his roommate. I asked if he was in the program.

"He used to be, but he dropped out."

"Are you giving him a bad time?"

"Oh yeah, we're giving him a bad time."

"How is he doing?"

"He's way ahead of us."

The average discipleship program is only a partial program. The apostles were told to teach their converts to obey *everything* Jesus commanded. Each of those converts was also to teach his own followers to obey everything. According to the Great Commission, every Christian is responsible for teaching every convert to obey all the commands. There is no escape hatch. It makes no difference whether you are called to be an elder or an engineer. The requirement for making disciples is still there. But the main thing is to obey everything that Jesus commanded you.

CHAPTER 57

A COMMUNIST SPY?

For the grace of God has appeared, bringing salvation for all
people. (Titus 2:11)

In the early eighties, many Chinese graduate students began to arrive in Moscow. China's Cultural Revolution had ended in 1976. The
Chinese universities were reopened, and five years later we saw the
first young Chinese in the U.S. (Before that, we had visiting scholars,
but not graduate students.) Bessie and I opened up our house for
English conversation classes. Different classes were being held simultaneously in almost every room in our home. When the students
thought that their English was good enough, they quit attending.

We had been doing this for several years when I received a call
from one of the students. He asked if I would come teach his wife to
read English using the Bible. I said I would and asked him why he
wanted me to use the Bible to teach her English.

He said that his wife had just come from Shanghai. She had become a Christian on her own in China while he was here in the States,
and she wanted to learn English and the Bible. When she arrived in
the U.S., this young man found out that his wife was a wonderful
new woman.

I taught them both together, and he received Christ. He wanted me to promise that I would not tell any of his friends that he
was a Christian. He said that one of them was a communist spy and
would get him in much trouble back in China. I asked which of his
friends was the spy. He said, "Li Tong." This new Christian left for

PhD studies at the University of Illinois in Urbana; I visited them there during Urbana '93.

One day, I went to see a visiting scholar I had been witnessing to. I spotted him on the balcony outside his room, and he invited me up.

When I went into the room, I was dismayed. There were ten other Chinese there. I did not see how I could talk to him about Christ with all of them around, so I did not say a word.

Then a visiting scholar seated across the table from me said, "I know a verse of Scripture. 'The wages of sin is death, but the gift of God is eternal life in Jesus Christ our Lord.'"

I asked him how and when he had become a Christian. It was through a friend of ours. That opened up the door for conversation, so I went around the room asking each person if he was a Christian. Most of them were not. There was only one woman there. She said that she was not a Christian but that her husband was, and he kept encouraging her to become one. I asked what her husband's name was. She said, "Li Tong." He wasn't a communist spy after all! He was a Christian himself.

CHAPTER 58
SABBATICAL

You then, my child, be strengthened by the grace that is in Christ Jesus. (2 Tim. 2:1)

In the first seven years of living in Moscow, I jogged about one and half miles every weekday, sometimes at the gym on the indoor track, and sometimes on the outdoor track. I could do a six-and-a-half-minute mile, but it was normally a seven-and-a-half-minute mile.

On days I jogged, I would sleep six and a half hours a night. If I went to bed at midnight, I would wake at six thirty a.m. If I had not jogged, I would go to bed at midnight and get up at seven thirty.

During the days, I was working very, very hard. I did not realize it until two things happened in 1979.

I was teaching a class for the School of Practical Christianity at the Campus Christian Center at UI. There was a certain phrase that I wanted to use for emphasis. When it came to the point in my lecture where I wanted to say it, I said it. Immediately, I forgot I had said it, and I said the phrase again . . . and again immediately forgot I had said it. I said it again. And again, I forgot I had said it. This happened six or eight times. I had no idea that I was standing there repeating myself over and over until suddenly the class broke out laughing. I had no idea why. When the students told me of my repetitions, I realized I needed a rest.

The other event happened as I was driving back from St. John, Washington. I was speaking at a Methodist Church there every night. St. John is fifty miles from Moscow. On U.S. 195, there is a turnoff to Pullman, Washington. There are many lights indicating this turnoff. I took the turn, then took an immediate right to go down the long hill into downtown Pullman. After I took the right, I noticed a farmhouse and a barn on top of a hill to my left. The problem was that there was no farmhouse and barn in that location, and I knew it. While I was thinking about that, I came upon the Wawawai Road grade. I had *not* taken the turn to Pullman at the lights. I had apparently driven right past them and turned off at Wawawai Road. The problem was that there was no barn or farmhouse like that on Wawawai Road, either.

The next night, I took Ray Roan with me to check for barns and farmhouses. There were none. My only understanding of this was I had gone to sleep driving and had dreamed up the farmhouse. When I have driven on that road since that time, I have still thought about it.

It was time for a break. In deciding where to take a sabbatical, we looked for a place in a city because Bessie did not like cabins in the country. We also wanted a place where we did not know anyone. We came up with Vancouver, B.C.

I got all the bases covered, and we left for a sabbatical in Canada. Dave Tong managed Crossroads while I was gone, and I left the students in charge of the student church. There were about 225 attending. When we came back, the student church was still there, but the attendance had dropped to seventy-five.

On our way to Vancouver, we stopped in Edmonton to visit Bessie's brother Jim and his family as well as Bessie's sister Molly. Our first month there, I slept eleven hours a night, the second month ten hours a night, and the third month nine hours a night. When we returned in December, I was sleeping eight hours a night. Looking back on those years, I think there had to have been sin in my previous workload. That was over thirty years ago. I have not had the problem of exhaustion since.*

---

* I am back to sleeping eleven hours a night now, but I am ninety-two years old.

Bessie and I had a lot of free time on sabbatical. We both went on a diet. We didn't have a scale in Canada. When we arrived back in Moscow, we had lost so much weight that we had to have our clothes altered to fit us. I also ran about thirty-five miles a week. Running that much ended up hurting my knees and my heels, so much that I could hardly walk. My heels got better, but my knees never did, and I had to quit jogging.

Although we didn't know many people in Vancouver, I did know a man named Carl Armerding[†] who was there. He was the president of Regent College, a graduate school for theology at the University of British Columbia. I had known Carl since he was an ensign in the U.S. Navy in Maryland. I called him to see if we could audit any classes at Regent. He said, "Yes, if you will teach a semester course on the evangelistic mission of the church." I agreed and sent him an outline of the course and a bibliography. He wanted to give credit for the course, and I did not have any advanced degrees, so he decided to have J.I. Packer teach the first three two-hour sessions on the Lausanne Covenant.

I made an appointment with J.I. Packer. I knew he was Reformed, and I wasn't. I thought we should have an agreement so we did not confuse the class. He saw no problem. He had seen his book *Evangelism and the Sovereignty of God* on my bibliography, so he thought I must agree with him. I pointed out that I also had A. Paget Wilkes's *Dynamic of Service* in the bibliography, which was a book that was not in the Reformed stream of theology.

During those six hours which he taught, even though he was asked very pointed questions about predestination, Packer did not give decidedly Reformed answers. I realized that he was making a big adjustment because the class was primarily mine.

Carl required me to give grades for the class. I had every student write a tract or a personal letter of at least 1,500 words with the

† See chapter 43.

gospel in it, with a note attached to the paper saying who the letter was for: 1) someone with his eyes closed, 2) someone with his eyes open, or 3) someone ready to receive Christ. They would not get a grade unless they actually gave the tract to an unbeliever or sent the letter. One student wrote a three-thousand-word letter to his father. The first half of the letter was great; the second half was awful. I told the student that if he sent the first half of his letter to his father, I would give him an A. If he sent the whole letter, I would give him a D. That made sense to him.

Regent College was designed as a graduate school for professionals who were not in ministry. Its aim was to educate physicists, doctors, lawyers, and engineers so that their theology would be up to par with their other learning.

But there was a disconnect in communicating this. The professionals came to Regent College to become godly, only to be hit with academic requirements that made PhD studies in physics look like a piece of cake. How do I know this? I ended up counseling many of the students. Because of the stringent academic requirements, they were actually becoming *less* godly. They were depressed, out of fellowship, and disillusioned. All of the faculty members were godly men, but they were scholars, not pastors. It was not their job to teach godliness, and they did not know how to do it.

At the end of the semester, in December 1979, I insisted on having all the faculty together so I could tell them my observations. I recommended that they do four things:

- Lay off some of their requirements.
- Be willing to pastor their own students.
- Call in pastors from the city to meet the spiritual needs of the students.
- Hire a full-time chaplain.

The advice was received warmly. I have no idea whether it was implemented.

Spring 1980

Dear Friends and Family,

The Lord replied, "My Presence will go with you, and I will give you rest." Then Moses said to Him, "If your Presence does not go with us, do not send us up from here. How will anyone know that you are pleased with me and your people unless you go with us? What else will distinguish me and your people from all the other people on the face of the Earth?" Exodus 34:14–15 NIV

The Lord's presence went with us and He did give us rest.

Our time in Vancouver, Canada, seems like a dream to us now. Coming back as we did a few days before Christmas meant that we plunged into activity and it continues. This has made it difficult to write personal letters, so here we are again with some family news and prayer requests for future ministry.

Our big news is that because of Heather and Marny's visitation activities with foreign student wives plus our long-time interest in the International Students Inc. (headed by friends Hal and Betsy Guffey), an invitation was presented to Heather to spend 8–12 months in Egypt. She would work with Lydia Matta and be exposed to a Moslem culture . . . . Her parents are very happy for her and only wish they could go too! . . . .

Jim, Heather, and Marny will drive to Colorado for an evangelical conference for International Students at Star Ranch, May 17 to 24. It will give Jim the opportunity to visit the CCM store in Laramie, Wyoming, plus the proposed new store at Provo, Utah. God's hand

seems to be at work in the initial stages of a new work at Provo.
Chris Vlachos is God's man for this venture, and he is a grandson in
the faith (Barb Friedman introduced him to Christ in 1974 and Jim
led Barb to our Lord in Ann Arbor in 1970) . . .

In His Love,
Jim & Bessie

CHAPTER 59
AROUND THE WORLD
IN EIGHTY DAYS

Through whom we have received grace and apostleship
to bring about the obedience of faith for the sake of his name
among all nations. (Rom. 1:5)

Our daughter Heather lived at home during her university days, and she had an active ministry to international students. When she graduated, Hal Guffey, the president of International Students Inc., asked her to go to Egypt to reach out to international students in Cairo. Since she did not want to raise support, Heather earned money for the trip by working for a year in the College of Mines at UI doing secretarial work and typing out a book on mine ventilation for one of the professors. In the meantime, people had promised to support her without being asked.

Heather was gone to Egypt from fall 1980 through spring 1981. Many of the people she worked with were refugees from communist Ethiopia.

Heather had gone to Cairo under the sponsorship of Bethel-Emmanuel, an evangelism and discipleship ministry founded by Lydia Matta that ministered to young people in the Egyptian capital. During Heather's time there, she had a friendly witness on the train into the city center to a Muslim brother and sister. They invited her to their home. She told her sponsor about it. Her sponsor said that if Heather went to their home, she would drop her sponsorship, and Heather would be all on her own. She was concerned that they might get kicked out of the country if they witnessed to Muslims.

Heather reported this to me and Hal Guffey. Why had she come if not to witness? Hal decided to send me to Egypt to talk Heather's sponsor and told Heather to hunker down until then.

I found a ticket with Northwest Airlines for $1,500. It was a special called "Around the World in Eighty Days." I had to spend at least four days in four different locations.

A freshman named Kelly Dillon heard that I was going and asked to come with me. I told him he could on the condition that he had his parents' permission, that he could get visas for all of the countries (Japan, Korea, the Philippines, Thailand, Pakistan, Egypt, Germany, and France), and that he could get flights parallel to mine. He did it. We planned that if for some reason I lost him anyplace on the trip, he was to fly directly home. I lost him in Paris near the end of the trip, and he flew home.

We went to Japan first. Starting on Sunday, I taught for one week at the church Jim Blocksom pastored in Tokyo. The meetings were in the morning and in the evening. After the Tuesday morning meeting, I saw a woman talking to Jim in Japanese. I had no means of knowing, but I was sure that she wanted to talk with me. On top of that, I knew the subject. She had been molested by her father. This knowledge was so sure that I rebelled against God in suppressing it. There was no way I was going to bring up that subject! For all I knew, her father could have been the godliest man in Japan. Also, to my knowledge that problem did not even occur in Japan. I was determined not to touch it.

Sure enough, she wanted to talk with me. Jim acted as our interpreter. We had been talking for about twenty minutes when Jim told me that she had just told him that her father had molested her. I was not surprised. I told Jim that I had known it for twenty minutes already. He told her. He came back and said, "She doesn't believe you." There was no reason why she should.

After another hour, I knew that she was a thief, and that she had stolen very much. I responded to God that I would not let it pass this time. I told Jim that she had to return everything she had stolen or pay for it plus twenty percent. Jim told her, and she broke down. She was a thief.

Two days later, I saw the same woman talking with Becky, Jim's daughter. I asked Becky if the woman wanted to talk with me. She responded strongly, "No, no! He knows all about me!"

However, we did visit, and she received Christ. Several weeks later, after I had returned home, I received a call from Portland, Oregon. It was the Japanese woman's husband. He was in the U.S. for his import-export business. He wanted me to know that he had seen such a change in his wife that he had become a Christian, too.

After that week of meetings, Kelly and I flew to Korea to see Ben Hyde and some Koreans I had taught English to at UI. A Korean English professor had the three of us over for lunch. It was memorable. Another professor of English was there. He had been orphaned in the Korean War, and an Alabama Infantry Regiment had adopted him. He could speak English Alabama-style.

Since I was the honored guest, I got the hot seat—literally. Korean homes are heated with a fire under the floor. You could tell because the varnish was turned black. I had to sit on the hot floor. There was a screen behind me that I could lean against.

The wife and daughter brought out four delicious Korean dishes. I ate my fill, only to find out that there were more courses. They brought out four more different dishes, then four more, then four more, then two more: eighteen dishes for five men. I thought I was going to die.

It was four o'clock in the afternoon. I thought I had an hour to die before I went to the U.S. Army post to speak. But my Korean host came back to Ben's apartment with Kelly and me, and I could not lie down like I wanted to.

As soon as he left, it was time for us to go to the Lt. Colonel's home. His wife said, "I know you are homesick for American food, so I cooked you some southern fried chicken." I excused myself, but Ben and Kelly ate it.

Ben took us to the military chapel near Taijan where I was to speak. A missionary acted as the chaplain. There were very few people present.

While I was speaking, I noticed that one soldier had tears in his eyes. At supper, I mentioned it to Ben. We found the soldier. His jeep had been blown up in Vietnam. While he was in the hospital recovering, his wife and child were killed in a car accident in the States, and he was left alone. He responded to the gospel.

The previous Christmas, I had given Bessie a beautiful new NIV Bible. Bessie did not want me to go on this round-the-world trip with my beat-up Bible, so she insisted that I take hers. Here was this new Christian with no Bible. I gave him Bessie's.[*]

We returned to Japan for another four days then went on to Manila. I spoke to missionary kids at Faith Academy where we stayed with Russ and Ramona Simons. I had opportunities at the Servicemen's Center at Olongapo (Subic Bay), Clark AFB, and with Alex and Carol Aronis.

We stayed overnight in Bangkok with a WSU graduate. We were standing on the sidewalk outside a restaurant when a pimp interrupted our conversation to give us his card.

---

[*] He got out of the Army and took a job as cook on an oil rig in the Gulf. Then he joined the Navy and was sent to be the cook on a newly commissioned destroyer out of Bath, Maine. The skipper of the destroyer was Scott Redd, who had come to Christ as a midshipman fifteen years earlier.

Then we went to Karachi to stay with missionaries for one night before flying on to Cairo to spend two weeks with Heather, where I helped her sort out the trouble with her sponsor.

One evening, I was to speak at the Bethel-Emmanuel youth group at seven p.m. Heather and I arrived just in time for the meeting. No one was there. We went to the library and found a joke book. We read jokes to each other until the young people showed up at nine. We were not mistaken about the time of the meeting; it was the cultural norm to arrive two hours late.

While walking through Cairo, we ran into Ginger Johnston. Her father, Larry, was a professor of physics at the University of Idaho and the first Christian I met in Moscow. Her mother Millie was on our bookstore committee for years.

Hal Guffey had signed me up to speak at several churches, including a Brethren Assembly and a Free Methodist Church. I remember the congregational singing. It was in Arabic. I did not understand the words, but the singing was all nasal.

There was a wall down the center of the sanctuary at the Free Methodist Church. The men sat on the right side of the wall, and the women sat on the left. As the speaker, I could see both the men and the women. I told the congregation that their Muslim neighbors who had lived near them for so long had admired them so long that they were waiting for the Christians to tell them the Good News. If they did tell their Muslim neighbors the gospel, there would be an immediate increase in the number of Christians, and next week there would be many new attendees at the church, most of them named Mohammed.

Heather had an Ethiopian refugee friend in Cairo named Abraham Belay. He knew at least five languages. As we were walking away from the church, Abraham said, "The interpreter did not translate a word you said. He said something else entirely."

Heather took us to see an Ethiopian family. They were refugees from the communists who were ruling Ethiopia. I was talking with one of the men before dinner and asked him if he thought the United States was Christian. He replied in the affirmative. I asked him what he knew about the United States and how he knew it. He knew it from movies, newspapers, and television. What did he know? He knew that the United States was sexually immoral, with many divorces and murders.

I assured him that Christians were not like that, and therefore the United States was not a Christian nation. I explained that many Americans said that they were Christians when they really were not. They were Christian in name only. Then there were the real Christians. They had a different character.

He brightened up. He said, "We are the same. We have Muslims in name and real Muslims."

I said we were not the same. He did not understand why we were not. "In America, when a nominal Christian becomes a real Christian, he becomes like Heather—loving and kind. In Islam, when a nominal Muslim becomes a real Muslim, he becomes angry and hateful."

He said, "You're right; look at Uncle Ahmed!"

Dinner was a stew comprised of large pieces of chicken and whole boiled eggs. My plate was full. I was full. I thought I could not eat any more. I managed to clean my plate. The hostess came up on my left to offer me some more. I said, "No, thank you." As I was saying that, she was filling my plate over my right shoulder. A clean plate was the cultural way of indicating that I was still hungry. Saying "No, thank you," was just a polite phrase; the hostess assumed I did not mean it.

January 1982

Dear Friends:

Do we want to please God in these very troubled days? Do you personally want to please Him?

"Without *faith* it is impossible to please God." (Heb. 11:6)

"This is the victory that has overcome the world, even our *faith*. Who is it that overcomes the world? Only he who believes that Jesus is the Son of God." (1 John 5:4–5)

How crowded our lives get! How unnecessary do the things which clutter our lives finally appear to us when we think of the importance of faith as seen above. Salvation from sin is ours by faith. Day by day protection from sin is ours by faith. A future assured us in His eternal presence is ours by faith. Heb. 11:6 also says God rewards those who diligently seek Him.

For some family news now . . . . We received Heather home from Egypt June 1st, and it took most of June to get her feeling better. Cairo was not a health spa for her, but she came back with some terrific pictures she had taken. Jim had been able to follow through on some of her Ethiopian refugee contacts while he was there, and several became Christians. We are hoping for two or three of them to come and study here. We request prayer for them. Heather is undecided about the future but sees herself in some foreign place, so keep her before the Lord in your prayers, please. She is presently serving as secretary for the Christian day school here, helping teach English to foreign wives, and forming a closer tie with a young Saudi Arabian wife by the name of Fatima . . . .

What shall I say about Jim except that he is busy, busy. He had a nine-week trip around the world, spending two weeks with Heather in Egypt. He has had many conferences, mostly for the Officers Christian Fellowship. He is lined up for more this year. The Lord willing, he will be on the East Coast for four weeks in February. He pastors a "mostly student" church in Pullman, and the students have blessed his heart as he meets with them on Tuesday to prepare and pray for Sunday meeting . . . .

On Christmas day we had for dinner guests two graduate students from mainland China, one from Taiwan, one from Japan, and two from Korea.* The two from Korea and the one from Taiwan all received Christ since they have been in this country. The Japanese was a Christian when he came here. The two from mainland China are interested.

The personal ministry is always expanding. Some of you are very close friends. The new needs keep us from being in close touch with old friends. Please continue to pray for us.

In His love,
Jim and Bessie Wilson

---

* For many years, I went out each Thanksgiving and Christmas morning to the university dorms, knocking on doors and inviting students (mostly international, because the others went home for the holidays) to dinner. Bessie told me each time how many people to bring home, and I would keep knocking on doors until I had collected that many. "But when you give a banquet, invite the poor, the crippled, the lame, the blind, and you will be blessed. Although they cannot repay you, you will be repaid at the resurrection of the righteous" (Luke 14:13–14).

CHAPTER 60

BOOKSTORES

He has been appointed by the churches to travel with us as we
carry out this act of grace that is being ministered by us, for the
glory of the Lord himself and to show our good will. (2 Cor. 8:19)

One of the driving forces in my decision-making over the years was
a combination of two historical considerations—the use of literature in world evangelism and the principles of war applied to world
evangelism.

The first has been around since the apostles were writing letters
and biographies. The second has been around just as long, but not
recognized as such. Our first bookstore in Annapolis put both into
effect for ten years, from 1958 to 1968. The Christian Bookstore was
a place of personal contact and selling, loaning, and giving away
books on the gospel and obedience. It was also a command post for
many evangelistic opportunities outside the store. Annapolis was
more than just a decisive point. There we were able to use principles
of war such as concentration, the offensive, surprise, pursuit, and
others. The store was not planned to be a moneymaking business but
rather a "people" store.

After we moved to Ann Arbor, the two stores in Maryland became
free-enterprise businesses. They moved away from the Academy and
the University of Maryland to business districts. Both sold hundreds
of thousands of dollars annually and for years were effective as businesses, but evangelism was no longer their *raison d'etre*. Both eventually went bankrupt, with the Lamplighter going first.

From the beginning, Logos Books in Ann Arbor did not have evangelism as its priority. After nearly a year there, when I found that InterVarsity's primary objective for the store was not to take the city, the university, and the state for Christ (as evidenced by the books they were willing to carry), I left. Leaving Logos Books was the closest thing to heartbreak I have ever experienced. However, it was the right thing to do.

Logos became the prototype for eighty similar InterVarsity stores, most of them near colleges. They had the same objectives as the Ann Arbor store (i.e., they were not evangelistic). Their emphasis was business, not ministry. They sold non-Christian books and even anti-Christian books. They were not effective in either business or evangelism. The overwhelming majority of the stores went under in a very few years.

After two years spent regrouping at Concordia College in Ann Arbor, I was ready for another try in Pullman, Washington, and Moscow, Idaho. For the next twenty years, we fought the battle effectively from a single location with the goal of taking both states for Christ. We had the right location, we had a command post in each town (One Way Books and Crossroads Bookstore), and we had the right staff, both in quantity and quality.

In the first six years after Community Christian Ministries opened One Way Books in Pullman and Crossroads Bookstore in Moscow in 1971, we saw a very effective evangelistic outreach. It was so effective that we started to look at other major universities in small towns. Our first consideration was Laramie, Wyoming.

While we were thinking about this, a friend told us of a young man named Rich Henderson in Deerfield, Illinois, who said the Lord had called him to open up a Christian bookstore in Laramie.

Every year, I would go to the Christian Booksellers Association annual conference. One year, it was held in Atlantic City. I met Brian

Woomert there and recruited him to run a bookstore. He came out to Moscow around the time that we heard about Rich Henderson.

Rich and Brian opened the Watering Hole bookstore in downtown Laramie in 1978, along with a young woman named Toni Strzebala.

Three years later, I visited Laramie and found five vacant stores across the street from the university dorms. The lease at our place was nearly up. Before I left, I told Rich and Brian to move into one of those stores when our lease expired. I returned to Moscow and found out the Laramie committee had resigned the lease for the downtown store. I was sick about it, but realized there was nothing I could do.

That winter, I was to speak at a Coast Guard Academy ski retreat in Vermont. I had another meeting in Burlington, Vermont, with Bob Pyke. During the meeting, my son Douglas called to say that the roof at the Watering Hole had fallen in. There was so much snow on the roof that it had caved it in and carried the second floor with it. Toni Strzebala was alone in the store at the time. She dove under a table to escape injury. The books were ruined. The new lease was cancelled, and we moved to the location across from the dorms.

In the 1940s, there was a restaurant owner in Chicago who was friends with Al Capone. During World War II, he worked as a cook at a Navy boot camp in Northern Idaho. About the time we opened The Watering Hole, his son, Chris Vlachos, came to Moscow to attend the University of Idaho because his mother was from Idaho.

Chris had been stoned all through high school and was stoned at UI. As an assignment for one of his classes, he decided to write a paper on the Genesis flood. His professor suggested that he look for reference material at Crossroads. He came in, and Barbara led him to Christ.

Chris spent Christmas at our house. He was leaving at the end of Christmas break to go back to Chicago. I did not see how he could survive as a Christian there. However, that summer, I received a card from him from Schloss Mittersill, the location of the InterVarsity student mission event in Austria. The next summer, he was in the Philippines helping missionaries. After that, I did not hear from him for a while.

Then a UI professor returning from a sabbatical at the University of Utah in Salt Lake City called to ask me how to get a mission to Mormons started in Moscow. I asked why he was interested. He told me that while he was at the University of Utah, he and his wife had a student living with them who led Mormons to Christ in their living room. It was Chris Vlachos. Chris called me to tell me that he had witnessed to Spencer Kimball's niece after she returned from her mission. (Kimball was a member of the Council of the Twelve Apostles, one of the highest governing bodies of the Mormon Church.)

In the fall of 1979 when Bessie and I were on sabbatical in Vancouver, Chris visited Moscow. He asked Douglas if he could open a bookstore in Provo, Utah, so he could give books to people like we had given books to him. A friend of Chris's from Chicago gave us $3,500 to get it up and running, and in June 1980 we opened His Place in Provo.

In the early eighties, we also received an invitation from a group in Logan, Utah, to open a bookstore near Utah State University. I met with a committee and told them we would do it if we found the right man.

Tom McClenahan, Larry and Millie Johnston's son-in-law, told me he would like to open a store at Cheney, Washington, for Eastern Washington University. I investigated and discovered that a Christian bookstore had just opened there, so I suggested Logan. He moved there and opened Oasis Books.

In the meantime, InterVarsity had decided to close down their official presence in Utah, Idaho, and Eastern Washington. Eldon Peterson was their staff member at Utah State. He did not want to leave his ministry at the university, so he came on our staff at Oasis Books.

Brad Scheelke had a master's degree in engineering from Washington State University. He had planned on going to Jordan as a tentmaking missionary, and he had a friend there who was going to fix it up for him. Brad volunteered to help in our Utah store until things were ready in Jordan. He is still at Oasis Books thirty years later.

My son Gordon's lab instructor at the University of Idaho was a PhD candidate in botany named John Sowell. Gordon invited him for a cookout in our backyard on Memorial Day, and he received Christ there. John later married Nancy Abbott, my secretary at Community Christian Ministries. After several years of teaching in Moscow, he was called to Western State College in Gunnison, Colorado. Nancy got in touch with me about starting a bookstore/coffee shop there. A large gift was given to us to buy a building. The Brushfire Coffeehouse is still a major witness in Gunnison.

By 1984, His Place in Provo was in great financial trouble. The store was a very effective outreach, so the CCM board did not want to close it and ordered me to bail it out. In order to do that, none of the staff at any of our stores got paid for several months. (Our policy at that time was that the staff did not get paid if the bookstore was in the red.)

When Doug got out of the Navy, he lived in our attached studio apartment until he got married in December 1975. When Evan got out of the Navy, he lived in that same apartment until he got married in August 1978. Then Gordon lived in it until he got married in December 1983. After that, I gutted it, thinking I would make a master bedroom and bath with the study being part of it. However, it stayed gutted for a year. (Again, no money.)

Doug and Evan were both on the CCM staff with families to support when we all went into "no pay" mode for several months. I took out a $10,000 second mortgage on the house. I used $5,000 to add the master suite and $5,000 to keep the three Wilson families eating. We were able to pay it off early.

Also in 1984, Julian Byrd told the CCM board that he wanted to go to Boise and open a store at Boise State University. The board said, "No, Boise does not fit the parameters for our strategic ministry." It is a large city.

Julian said he was going anyway, whether or not the board agreed. The board backed down. Steve Barry, who had been working with Julian at the Johnson Sunday school,* went with him. We opened Cornerstone Books in half of a retail store space. A few months later, Julian decided to go to Regent College. Over the next twenty years, Cornerstone was closed several times for many months each time for lack of a location. We finally gave the store to a local ministry.

In Laramie, Wyoming, Rich Henderson and Brian Woomert both left the Watering Hole. It fell on Toni Stryzebala to run the store. She made it pay for itself, but it ceased to have an evangelistic ministry. On one of my trips to Laramie, I told Toni that we had to have an evangelist, and that if we did not get one, we would need to close the store. We gave her the option of moving to Oasis Books in Logan. She moved, and we used the bookshelves from the Watering Hole for our new store in Gunnison. After several years, the store in Provo also closed because of lack of staff.

One of our most effective locations was One Way Books in Pullman. Although we had a good location on campus and great stock, it began to languish after many years, and finally we only had one staff member. In 2009, we reluctantly closed the store after more than thirty years of operation because it was no longer an effective place of evangelism.

I convinced the OCU, InterVarsity, Christian Books in Annapolis, and Community Christian Ministries in Moscow to open a total of about ninety bookstores. We knew that none of these stores could

---

* An independent Sunday school in Johnson, a small town south of Pullman, WA.

support themselves, because they were not designed to. They were designed to be places to meet and minister to people, not to be successful businesses. The combination of personal witness and books was very effective.

Over our many years of service, I was unable to impart this peculiar vision to others or to impart the principles whereby these places of ministry could operate as a ministry and still remain as a business. I was not able to teach people how to read books, sell books, or evangelize. That was my failure. All but two of the bookstores are now closed because, without a strong evangelist to run them, they were not effective at evangelism or as businesses.[†]

In order to be effective, we had to have at least two staff members at each store. We started out that way. Our stores were in the right places, but we could not, or did not, concentrate our forces. Laramie and Provo got down to one staff member in each store, and in both cases that person was not into evangelism. Our staff also dwindled to one each in Boise, Moscow, and Pullman, and the locations became ineffective in both business and evangelism.

When we had more than one staff member at each store, the stores were very effective. Instead of increasing staff to have a concentrated force at each decisive point, as the original staff left, they were not replaced, and the ministries weakened. We kept each one going ineffectively for several years. In doing this, we were violating our own principles. We should have provided the necessary concentration of staff or closed the stores. Closing meant firing or transferring the workers, and I was reluctant to do that.

This happened at five different stores. They ate up time and money. Several of them just died, without us closing them. I accept the

---

[†] Oasis Books in Logan, Utah, and the Brushfire in Gunnison, Colorado, are still running as effective ministry locations.

responsibility of not providing the concentration of force in trained staff to take over these cities for Christ.

I was convinced that the bookstores were a good idea because each Christian bookstore I had been with personally was effective as both a business and a place of evangelism. However, most of CCM's stores did not have an evangelist on staff. Those that did died when the evangelist left. I had mistakenly thought the *store* itself was the means of effective evangelism; but it was the evangelist in the store.

Bookstores are a very good place to do ministry, because all kinds of people come into bookstores. But the *person* in the store is what makes it a ministry, not the store itself. Whoever is in the store has to learn how to be an evangelist and a counselor, and it has to be someone who loves people.

Giving books away is the most effective method of literature evangelism, for several reasons. People are reluctant to part with money to get a book that they should have. When you lend books, people forget to return them. But when I give a book to someone, I get to determine what they read. They might not read it right away. The books are like time bombs, sitting on the shelf, waiting to explode.

Many years ago, a senior midshipman came into Christian Books in Annapolis with great joy. I asked him what it was all about.

He said, "Do you remember the booklets you gave me my sophomore year?"

"Yes."

"I read them."

Where do I get the money for the books I give away? Gifts from all over. None of it is requested. Some of the books that we give away are wasted. Many are not. Lives are changed.

His Place Books, Provo, Utah

Jim at Crossroads, Moscow, Idaho, 1970s

Oasis Books, Logan, Utah

The Brushfire, Gunnison, Colorado

CHAPTER 61

GETTING AHEAD OF THE LORD

For by the grace given to me I say to everyone among you not to think of himself more highly than he ought to think, but to think with sober judgment, each according to the measure of faith that God has assigned. (Rom. 12:3)

One thing that has led to sin in my life is my vision on how to evangelize. Several times I have run ahead and acted on my vision only to find out it was not the will of God. I have spent hours, weeks, months, and money on things that were not right. But it was not just *my* time and money. I had convinced other Christians it was the will of God, and it spent their time and money as well.

Here is one such case. After we moved to Michigan, Christian Books moved to Parole, a shopping district far away from the Academy. Years later, from Moscow, I took action to open up a store near the Academy again. We found a place, but it was a poor location. We found a young Christian couple to run it, and we found some money. It took several years to get the store open. The Beacon Bookstore had no customers of any kind, and we did not have the money to support the couple. It closed after just a few weeks.

I realized I had run ahead of the Lord by pushing my vision of evangelizing midshipmen. It had Jim Wilson's fingerprints all over it. It was not of the Lord.

Over the years, I have convinced many people to come on CCM staff as evangelists. A few stayed, but most did not. Some who stayed should not have. Again, it was Jim Wilson trying to do God's work for Him.

I am grateful that many times He led me in perfect ways. Those occasions were not a waste of time or money. Major instances of God's guidance include the decision to resign my commission in 1956, our move to Annapolis in 1958, the move to Michigan in 1968, and the move to Moscow in 1971.

At the time, Bessie thought the first two were wrong decisions. It was hard to override her view, but God gave me the grace to do it. Afterward, Bessie saw that both decisions were right, and we had a great ministry in both D.C. and Annapolis.

CHAPTER 62

CONFERENCES

> But I do not account my life of any value nor as precious to
> myself, if only I may finish my course and the ministry that I
> received from the Lord Jesus, to testify to the gospel of the grace
> of God. (Acts 20:24)

From 1957–2000, I spoke at conferences for Officers' Christian
Fellowship. This overlapped with conference-speaking for
InterVarsity, International Students Incorporated, and the Christian
Businessmen's Connection. For many years, a typical month of
speaking engagements looked something like this:

October 1990

Dear Friends,

"He was a good man, full of the Holy Spirit and faith, and a great
number of people were brought to the Lord" (Acts 11:24). This is
speaking of Barnabas. The preceding verse tells us that "he was glad
and encouraged them all." In chapter four we find his name means
"son of encouragement." We also find that he "sold a field he owned
and brought the money and put it at the apostles' feet." When he was
with Paul he was not the chief speaker (Acts 14:12), although in Acts
14:1 we see, "There they spoke so effectively that a great number of
Jews and Gentiles believed."

Barnabas was good, full of the Holy Spirit, full of faith, glad,
encouraging, generous and unashamed to speak the gospel. The
result was that great numbers were brought to the Lord. If we are

not seeing great numbers turning to the Lord it may be that we are lacking the other characteristics which were in Barnabas' life . . . .

During this month I will be conducting four seminars at the National Convention of CBMC* in Portland, Oregon (October 3–6). On October 21–24, I will be the speaker at Fellowship Baptist Church in Moorestown, New Jersey. From October 25–28 I will be at my 40th class reunion for the class of 1950 of the U.S. Naval Academy. I will be there to witness to classmates, some of whom I witnessed to over 40 years ago. On the 29th I will be speaking to midshipmen of the Officers' Christian Fellowship at the Naval Academy. On the 30th I will be attending the prayer meeting for Christian Literature Crusade Headquarters in Fort Washington, Pennsylvania. Please pray for me . . .

Thank you for your giving and prayers.

In our Lord Jesus Christ,
Jim Wilson

In 1966, Bill York invited me to be the speaker at a regional InterVarsity conference in Virginia. He asked me to talk on *Principles of War*, which had been published in 1964. The last chapter of the book is on obedience to God as opposed to volunteering in response to a challenge.† Jesus did not challenge people. He *commanded*. Jesus did not say, "If you love me, volunteer." He said, "If you love Me, *obey* Me."

This was my subject on the last evening of the conference. At the end of my session, a young woman asked to see me privately. She told me that she was a Wycliffe Bible Translator in Papua, New Guinea, and she was the next speaker. She said I had just ruined her talk. She had come to the conference to challenge the students to become Wycliffe Bible Translators.

* Christian Business Men's Connection
† See Appendix C for more on this.

I said, "Since you are a translator, there is much Scripture you could teach on."

She replied, "You still do not understand. I don't know why I went to New Guinea, and I don't want to go back."

"And you came here to get these students to make the same dumb mistake you made?"

I asked her if she had ever been forgiven for lying. She said yes. I told her that God would forgive her the same way for going to the mission field as He would for lying. "Let's confess it right now." She confessed.

The next morning, I was walking across the campground and saw a student from Cyprus with a big smile on his face. He looked like he would be pleasant to talk with. I walked up to him and asked how he liked the conference.

He replied, "Do you really want to know?"

I told him I did.

He said, "Your talks were the most boring talks I have ever heard, and last night's was the *worst*. It was so bad that I almost decided to pack my bag and go back to school. But then that wonderful missionary from New Guinea spoke, and I went back to my room and received Christ."

The missionary would not have given the talk she had if she had not heard my talk on obedience versus challenge and changed her topic. That student came to Christ as a result. I was never so glad to have been boring in all my life!

In the summer of 1968, I was the teacher for the second week of a two-week InterVarsity Student Leadership conference at Hudson House in Nyack, New York. The teacher for the first week was a nationally known Christian. I realized I was in a difficult position. The students had been together for a week, and they had been listening to a powerhouse the entire time. I, on the other hand, knew no one there, and no one knew me.

On Sunday afternoon, there was a picnic on the beach of the Hudson River. The students did not know it, but I used the time to memorize everyone's name by repetition, spelling, and association. I worked hard. If two girls were the same height and same hair color, I would walk around so I could see them together and record the differences in the shape of their heads or faces. That evening after I was introduced for my first talk, I introduced each of them by name. They thought I was a genius.

It was a working evangelism conference. In addition to evangelism lessons, we went as a group to Maryknoll Seminary to tell the gospel to the nuns in the convent and the men in the seminary. We had a banquet that night at Hudson House and invited them to it. Several came. I preached the gospel at dinner.

We also made an evangelistic trip to the headquarters of the ACLU in Nyack and another trip to the training camp for Up with People on an island near Manhattan.

In May 1969, I was speaking on the love of God the Father at an InterVarsity conference near Akron, Ohio. I said that when we pray, we should pray to the Father; that is the way Jesus taught us to pray. One student was shaken up. He had always prayed to Jesus. He couldn't even say the word *Father*. He couldn't get it out of his mouth. He felt it was wrong to say it. He got over it by praying, "Daddy, Daddy."

Bessie and I spoke together at an International Students Inc. staff conference at Star Ranch in Colorado Springs. I gave six talks on evangelism. Much of my book *Taking Men Alive* was written from these talks.

While at a CBMC regional conference in Missouri around 1987, I realized that Dick Daykin, my roommate from my youngster year at the Naval Academy, lived in St. Louis. He was the chief highway engineer for St. Louis County. He had been the first person I had witnessed to after I received Christ. I did not know if I would be welcome, but I thought I would try. I had tried to contact him several years earlier and had reached his father, who told me that Dick was chief highway engineer for St. Louis County.

It turned out I was welcome. After the conference, I stayed overnight at Dick's home. He and his wife took me out for a prime rib dinner, and as soon as we sat down at the restaurant, he said, "Jim, would you tell my wife the same story you told me forty years ago?"* Other Christians had been witnessing to him. He died shortly after that.

When I was just beginning full-time Christian work and travelling to conferences, one time I stayed with a Christian family I knew in Norfolk. Later they moved to Annapolis. I got to know their oldest daughter when she was three. I watched her grow up and get married. It was a difficult marriage. I helped to make it less difficult. I wrote letters and telephoned, I visited their home in New Jersey, and she and her husband came to Moscow to attend our School of Practical Christianity. Nothing seemed to work. This went on for years.

One year, I was speaking at a Midshipmen's Labor Day Conference at White Sulphur Springs.† Afterward, I had to go down to Annapolis. The couple was living there, so I called to tell her I would be in town.

She said, "Go to my husband's office, and I will bring lunch."

* See chapter 10.
† OCF's conference center in Pennsylvania

After lunch, I read them Galatians 5:19–21: "The acts of the flesh are obvious: sexual immorality, impurity and debauchery; idolatry and witchcraft; hatred, discord, jealousy, fits of rage, selfish ambition, dissensions, factions and envy; drunkenness, orgies, and the like. I warn you, as I did before, that those who live like this will not inherit the kingdom of God." I asked her how many of those words described her.

She said, "All of them."

I asked how long this description had been true.

She said, "All my life."

"If that is true, you are not now, nor ever have been, a Christian."

Her husband jumped up. "I didn't come here to find out my wife isn't a Christian!" He stopped and then said, "But I believe you."

I told her that I was not going to tell her how to be saved, because all the words of salvation were hollow to her. God, Jesus, grace, faith, repentance—when she heard these, she automatically translated them into "work." I told her not to read her Bible or go to church and said I would see her sometime in the future.

A year later, I was speaking at the same conference at the same place. After the conference, I called her. They were living in eastern Pennsylvania. A Marine officer volunteered to drive me to their house.

When we arrived, she ran out to the car saying, "I'm a Christian, I'm a Christian. Nobody is going to tell me I'm not! I believe all of it in my head, and none of it in my heart."

I said, "Susie, you said it. I didn't."*

That evening, I read her many paragraphs of Scripture. She kept saying, "Is that what it says?" It was like it she was hearing it all for the first time.

I was to go on to Princeton the next day. I could not find public transportation to get there. Susie said she would drive me halfway if

* Her name has been changed.

my friends could meet us. Fred Miller said he could. We got in her pickup. She drove, and I started reading Scripture out loud.

I read 2 Timothy 2:23–26: "Don't have anything to do with foolish and stupid arguments, because you know they produce quarrels. And the Lord's servant must not be quarrelsome but must be kind to everyone, able to teach, not resentful. Opponents must be gently instructed, in the hope that God will grant them repentance leading them to a knowledge of the truth, and that they will come to their senses and escape from the trap of the devil, who has taken them captive to do his will."

When I finished, I said, "I read this paragraph because it tells of four 'wills' that have to do with salvation: God's will, the Christian's will, the non-Christian's will, and the devil's will. The key will is the Christian's. God tells him how to speak and how not to speak. I want you to know that I have talked to you gently and patiently."

She said, "The trouble with me is that I am just a strong-willed woman."

I replied, "I don't think so."

"What do you mean?"

"I think you are a weak-willed woman."

She wheeled on me. "What did you say?" She was angry.

I did not answer her question. I just read the next paragraph from 2 Timothy. "But mark this: There will be terrible times in the last days. People will be lovers of themselves, lovers of money, boastful, proud, abusive, disobedient to their parents, ungrateful, unholy, without love, unforgiving, slanderous, without self-control, brutal, not lovers of the good, treacherous, rash, conceited, lovers of pleasure rather than lovers of God—having a form of godliness but denying its power. Have nothing to do with such people."[†]

† 2 Timothy 3:1–5

When I finished, she said, "I am guilty of every one of those."

I looked over the list. "No, Susie, you're not treacherous."

She said, "Yes, I am."

I decided to keep reading. "For among them are those who enter into households and captivate *weak women* weighed down with sins, led on by various impulses."*

She said, "Is that what it says?"

"That's what it says."

"I am going to become a Christian before you get out of the truck."

In early 2011, I returned to the East Coast and saw Susie again. She dates her Christian life from that trip in the truck many years ago.

In the mid 1980s, I had been speaking at a week-long OCF† conference at Spring Canyon Lodge near Buena Vista, Colorado, and was to teach next at an International Students, Inc. conference at Star Ranch near Colorado Springs. I was driving east down a mountain on US 24. At the bottom, there was a Y in the road. The left is US 285 to Denver. US 24 goes straight on to Colorado Springs.

Several hundred yards ahead, I could see a man in a white robe with a sash for a belt. I was driving the speed limit. Behind me was a car, and behind him was a very big truck with a derrick. I decided to pick up the "robey," but knew I was going too fast to stop where he was, so I slowed down and pulled over about a hundred yards beyond him.

The car behind me passed, then the truck. As the truck went by, it laid about a hundred feet of rubber on the road. I thought, "Was I responsible for that?"

* 2 Timothy 3:6

† OCU had changed its name to Officers' Christian Fellowship in 1972.

The robey was walking barefoot on the asphalt. He got into the car. He did not say, "Thank you." Instead, he unrolled a scroll and began to read. "The emancipation proclamation of Jesus Christ Lightning Amen!"‡

He continued reading. I found out that Jesus Christ Lightening Amen was opposed to killing any animal. That is why the robey did not wear leather shoes or a leather belt. I told him that there was a Bible on the seat behind me. I asked him to grab it and read chapter 3 of Genesis. When he finished the chapter, I said, "It looks like the first clothes in this world were made out of leather."

He said, "Wait till I show the brothers this!"

He went on with the proclamation, and I learned that Jesus Christ Lightening Amen was opposed to all sex, including within marriage. I pointed him to some legitimate sex in the Bible.

He said, "Wait till I show the brothers this!"

This sort of thing continued all the way to Manitou Springs, where I pulled up at a red light. To my right was the big truck. The driver looked out the window, recognized my car, and shouted that I was responsible for almost killing several people. He said this with anger and four-letter words and threatened to break my windshield.

I was being very polite when the light turned green. I thought it the better part of wisdom to step on it, so I did. As I pulled away, the robey rolled down his window, looked up at the truck driver, and said, "God loves you!"

I asked the robey where he wanted to go. He said a Methodist church would be fine; they would be good for some food. I told him he could come with me to Star Ranch instead, and they would feed him there.

‡ A man named Charles Franklin McHugh had legally changed his name to Lightening Amen, claimed to be Jesus Christ, and started a cult called Christ Family. He was convicted on drug charges in 1987 and stated that the sect had disbanded two years earlier.

The robey was only eighteen. He had been in Colorado Springs to go to court for a driving offense he had committed before he joined the cult.

We arrived at Star Ranch for the international student conference and went in to eat. Because of his dress, the other students just assumed the robey was another foreign student from some Middle Eastern or Asian country. He received Christ and got deprogrammed. Max Kershaw gave him some shoes, and I gave him a sweatshirt. He joined a Baptist church and later enlisted in the Army.

In the summer of 1989, I had an engagement to speak at a retreat in Sun Valley, Idaho. From there, I planned to drive to our ministry in Logan, Utah, then on to Nebraska to see my mother. I left Moscow fairly early in the morning. I had not gone far when I realized I had not had enough breakfast, so I stopped in Lewiston, Idaho, (thirty miles from home) and bought a pint of chocolate milk. I set it down in the cup holder and headed out on US 95.

I had not gone far when I saw a scruffy little man standing on the side of the road and pulled over to pick him up. He was very thankful. He was going to Grangeville to find a cheap trailer for his mother to live in. They were too expensive in Portland, Oregon, where he was from. I asked him more questions. He was twenty-one years old. He told me his best friend had run off with his wife and little boy. Then he took a bottle out of his pack and put drops in his eyes. He had glaucoma. I asked him about his father. His father had left when he was a baby. If he ever found him, he was going to sit him down, buy him a beer, and ask him why he had left. If his father came up with an adequate explanation, he would forgive him. I could tell that he did not expect to find him or get a satisfactory explanation.

I asked him if he had ever gone to church.

"Yes, I went to church once, and they did not talk about money."

"That's the kind of church I am in."

"Really?" He pulled a $1 bill out of a pocket. "When we stop, I am going to buy a pop, and you can have the change."

I realized that he had been traveling all night from Portland and had had nothing to eat. I said, "If you are hungry, you may have that chocolate milk."

He drank it down very fast and said, "You can have the whole dollar."

I asked him if he ever read the Bible. He reached into his backpack and pulled out a little red Gospel of John published by Moody Press in 1928. I asked him if he read it.

He replied, "Some."

I asked if he believed that Jesus was the Son of God. He said yes. I asked if he believed that Jesus died on the cross for our sins. Again, he said yes. I asked if he believed that Jesus rose from the dead.

He looked at me. "No. No. I never heard that one!"

"You have the Gospel of John. Please read the last three chapters."

He laboriously read them silently. He looked up and said, "That's amazing. That's amazing."

We stopped in Craigmont, where I bought him breakfast. At Grangeville, I left him and went on to Sun Valley.

Two weeks later, after I returned home, I was cleaning out the car and found the "whole dollar" stuffed into a crack in the front seat.

I was squeezed into a seat in the back of the plane en route from Dallas to Salt Lake City after speaking at a conference in East Texas in the early 2000s. I asked the attendant if there was a seat available in an exit row. She said all seats were taken, but soon she came back with a tiny woman who did not care where she sat. She was willing to trade seats with me. I got her window seat in an exit row.

Next to me was a man who looked like a cowboy. He was glued to a paperback. In the aisle seat was a man I judged to be a good ol' boy Texan. After a bit, the cowboy got up and left. I have no idea where he went because there were no other seats on the plane, but he never came back.

I sat there and read my Bible. Soon the man on the aisle took out a new Bible and waved it around to get my attention. I responded. He had thought I was a Mormon reading the book of Mormon.

It turned out that he was an engineer going to Boise on business. He had grown up a Southern Baptist. He was now a Methodist and had been a Christian for about a week. He was to give his testimony in church the following Sunday and did not know what to say.

I taught him Scripture all the way to Salt Lake City. He got off the plane ahead of me and waited. He said that he had never prayed out loud in his life, but he wanted to pray for me, which he did.

As we parted company, I said, "See you in glory." That overwhelmed him.

He sent me a tape of his talk. Shortly after that, his wife contacted me to tell me that he had died, but that he had left instructions for her to tell me that he would see me in glory.

CHAPTER 63
LOGOS SCHOOL

According to the grace of God given to me, like a skilled master
builder I laid a foundation, and someone else is building upon it.
Let each one take care how he builds upon it. (1 Cor. 3:10)

Douglas and Nancy a few other parents wanted their children to attend a Christian school instead of public school, but there were none in the area. So they started their own school. Logos School held its first classes in 1981 when my granddaughter Bekah was just ready for kindergarten. They had about nineteen students across the grades. Heather, who had just returned from Egypt, became the Logos School secretary.

On the return from a family reunion in Nebraska in the summer of 1975, we stopped at Yellowstone Park because our Triumph 650 motorcycle, which Evan was riding, had broken down. Evan was on leave from the Navy. Doug had been unable to attend but got out of the Navy around the time the reunion broke up.

Dave Tong had a summer job in Yellowstone Park. We looked him up. Back in Moscow, Dave and Doug put together a band. They were on vocals and guitar. Evan was also on guitar, and Tom Garfield was on drums. A woman named Diane Gillespie came down from Coeur d'Alene to be their female vocalist. Dave Tong married her. I conducted their wedding at Emmanuel Lutheran Church. Diane's sister Meredith came out from the East Coast to attend the wedding.

When we were starting up the first School of Practical Christianity, Meredith called from Florida and asked to come. She then moved to Moscow and became the kindergarten teacher for Logos School.

Meredith and my son Gordon were married in December 1983 in the middle of Gordon's senior year at the University of Idaho.

Tom Garfield, who had just graduated from UI, became the Logos principal. When we first arrived in Ann Arbor, Michigan, we went looking for a church. We found Huron Hills Baptist Church, part of the Baptist General Conference. There we became friends with Bob and Lois Garfield. Their son, Thomas, was a classmate of Evan's, and they became close friends. I taught the high school Sunday class which included Doug, Evan, Tom, Mark Hunt, and the pastor's daughter, Charlene Johnson.

A year after we moved to Moscow, Idaho, Tom and Evan enlisted in the Navy together on the buddy system. After boot camp in San Diego, Tom was sent to a ship in the Atlantic fleet. In the meantime, Tom's older sister Judy came to Moscow and worked in Crossroads Bookstore for a few years. The older Garfields retired to Oregon. Tom got out of the Navy and moved to Moscow in 1976 to attend the University of Idaho. He was the Logos School principal from his graduation in 1981 until his retirement in 2017.

After Logos had been going a few years, I realized that although the students were receiving a good Christian academic education, it was short on practical application. I encouraged Tom Garfield to let me teach a two-hour-a-week practical Christianity elective to the high school students. Subjects included obedience, confession of sin, bitterness, relationships with parents, evangelism, and life between the sexes. I taught that class there for five years.

When Bekah finished twelfth grade, Doug started New Saint Andrews College. His three children (Bekah, Nathan, and Rachel) and Gordon's four children (Brooke, Dane, Mallory, and Heather) all graduated from NSA. Bekah's two oldest children are currently students at NSA.

CHAPTER 64

EVAN, LESLIE & THE BIG HAUS

Grace to you and peace from God our Father and the Lord Jesus
Christ. (Gal. 1:3)

Evan was born in the Naval Hospital in Oakland, California, on
October 8, 1954. He came to Christ with some resistance at the age
of eight, but his resistance only served to make him more confident
of what the Lord had done. His gifts growing up were artistic (paint-
ing, cartooning, and graphic design). After a stint in the U.S. Navy
as a photographer's mate (1973–77), he enrolled at the University of
Idaho with a fine arts/painting major.

While in the Navy, Evan was stationed at the National Parachute
Test Range in El Centro, California. He led a very active Bible study
on the base there. Another sailor who had come to Christ through
the study brought along his girlfriend whom he had met at a Baptist
church in town. After they broke up, this girl, Leslie Rye, continued
attending the Bible studies, and she and Evan began dating.

When Evan's enlistment was up in 1977, I went down to California
to help him move home and ended up cleaning his apartment with
Leslie while Evan filled out forms on the base. As Evan and I drove his
VW van up Interstate 5 the next day, I let him know that I wouldn't
mind having Leslie as a daughter-in-law. It took him another month
to figure that out for himself.

Leslie switched schools to move up to Idaho that summer, and
they were engaged in November. They married in August 1978 and
immediately started opening their home to people. Leslie is a remarkable cook, and Evan likes to talk. It was a good combination at

a level that caused them to begin thinking about arranging a formal ministry around it.

After two years of marriage, when they thought they were unable to have children, Evan and Leslie found a large (eight thousand square feet) arts and crafts mansion for sale. Evan was going to school on the GI Bill, and Leslie worked part-time as a secretary. They had no money and were in no position to qualify for a loan.

Realizing that they could not afford this huge purchase, they approached Community Christian Ministries to see if we wanted to buy the house for them to run as a hospitality ministry. CCM was not interested in making the purchase, but we had a real estate agent take us up to the house to meet the owners, Lloyd and Helen Skramstad. They were wonderful Christian people who had run an old folks' home there, but their own age was making it impossible to continue. Evan and Leslie explained what they wished to do with the home and how they could not afford the asking price.

A few days later, the Skramstads called. They had prayed about it and were convinced that the Lord wanted this ministry to happen. They didn't want to rent the house out, and they didn't even want it to go to another Christian ministry they supported that was interested in using it. They explained that since Evan and Leslie could not get a loan, they would sell it to them with no down payment, and they would carry the contract themselves. Even though their lawyer tried to talk them out of it, the contract was drawn up (with Bessie and me cosigning), and Evan and Leslie moved in at the end of August 1980 and opened The Big Haus boarding house with their first nine residents. Over the years, hundreds of young singles have grown in their Christian walk there. Evan and Leslie have even had Haus "grandchildren" live with them when couples who met at the Big Haus sent their college-age children to live there decades later.

Within a year of buying the Big Haus, the supposed barrenness was reversed, and my grandson Davis was born. He was followed by Michal Angela, Graeme, and Evan Gunn Wilson.

Evan's artistic side has been amply used through the years as well. He worked as a designer and press operator for CCM for a few years, then did advertising design for the local newspaper. Feeling the need to be more available for ministry contacts, he left the paper and formed his own graphic design business which he kept for twenty years, quitting only as the Big Haus ministry grew and demanded more time. Evan also taught at both Logos School and Montrose Academy for as long as their children were enrolled there.

The Big Haus ministry* is now serving the Kingdom into their fourth decade with Bible studies, readings, and seminars, coupled with the living situation that allows Evan and Leslie to serve and counsel the wide variety of Christians that move through the Haus. Their most popular seminars are The Mojo Oracles (for young single men), The Tao of Eve (for the women), Fire and Reign (on marriage), and Bloodline (on rearing children). Their life of hospitality has seen those topics and others tried, tested, and proved since 1980.

Evan has also been pastoring All Souls Christian Church since 1990, a small congregation with a commitment to Richard Baxter's idea of "mere Christianity." Always thinking about new ways to draw people into discussions on Christianity, Evan and Leslie grow and change the ministry to give others an experience of all the good things of beauty, thought, and spirituality that they have been given.

* www.thebighaus.com

CHAPTER 65
BULL FROGS & DARTH VADER

See to it that no one fails to obtain the grace of God; that no
"root of bitterness" springs up and causes trouble, and by it
many become defiled. (Heb. 12:15)

In 1988, Bessie and I visited Heather in Istanbul, where she was working with Worldwide Evangelization Crusade. While we were there, I was invited to speak at an American military Christian conference near a lake in the countryside fifty miles from Ankara. I was met at the Ankara train station. We all piled into buses to drive the fifty miles. When we arrived, the men began pitching tents. I asked the colonel where I was to sleep. He yelled to everyone to see where they were sleeping.

One of the airmen said, "I am the only one in my tent. You can sleep with me." I told him that I had a reputation for snoring. He replied, "I'm your perfect tent mate. I ran a jack hammer at Offutt AFB in Omaha. I am completely deaf in one ear. I had an infection in the other ear and have to wear a hearing aid in it, but I take that out at night. Your snoring will not bother me."

After supper and the evening meeting, all the guys were telling stories in a tent about seventy yards away from my tent. I decided to go to bed. As I was trying to fall asleep, the bull frogs around the lake were making an awful lot of noise.

The next morning, the colonel asked me how I had slept.

I replied that I had to get up once from heartburn because of eating too many chili dogs.

The deaf airman retorted, "It didn't keep you from snoring." The night before, when everyone else was finally ready for bed, he had told the men in the bull session, "You guys spear the frogs, and I will shoot Mr. Wilson."

Ten years earlier, I had been the speaker at a Methodist conference at Camp Grizzly, the Boy Scout Camp near Moscow. Something was wrong with the rooms in the lodge, so everyone had to sleep on the floor in the large meeting room. I woke up with several shoes on my sleeping bag. Even getting hit with them in the night hadn't woken me up and stopped the snoring.

A few years had gone by when I saw one of the women from the Colfax Methodist Church who had been at the conference. Just to start a conversation, I asked her if she remembered the subject of the conference. She replied, "That's not what I remember!"

In the mid-1990s, a sleep study discovered that I had sleep apnea. I was put on a CPAP machine. Bessie greatly appreciated the difference, except that she did not like me to face her in bed. Apparently, I looked like Darth Vader.[*]

---

[*] I no longer have sleep apnea and haven't used the CPAP since the summer of 2015.

CHAPTER 66
MORE MOSCOW MINISTRY

In him we have redemption through his blood, the forgiveness of
our trespasses, according to the riches of his grace. (Eph. 1:7)

We had been in Moscow for twenty years. There was an annual
march against Roe v. Wade. I normally participate, but Doug was
very active in the movement.

There was only one doctor left in Moscow who still performed
abortions. The local right to life group decided to march in front of
his home. They were also going to put pro-life signs up in his yard.
Doug was part of the group. He persuaded them not to put up the
signs until his father talked to the doctor about the gospel. I think I
said, "Thanks a lot."

Periodically, people would come into Crossroads Bookstore and
ask if I had seen Dr. Britzman yet. I kept putting it off. One day, I
called him up and told him who I was. "Dr. Britzman, we have both
been in the same town for a long time. It's time we got together."

He said, "What took you so long? If you want to talk about abor-
tion, the answer is no!"

I replied that I did not want to talk about it, even if he did.

We went out to lunch once a week for many months. One week,
he asked Dr. John Grauke (my personal doctor of many years and a
strong Christian) to join us. John asked him why he had lunch with
me. Dr. Britzman said, "He tells me wonderful stories, and he gives
me books."

After he retired, his wife would not let me come see him. I did get
out there the day he died, but he had died before I arrived, and the

family would not let me into the house. I have no idea whether he ever called upon the Lord. He did tell me that he had quit performing abortions after we began meeting together.

Bessie and I had driven a series of old Fords and a '69 Chevy. We had no idea what a new car looked like. At Christmas 1991, Sam Minnich presented us with an '89 Mercury Sable.

Sometime after that, I was invited to speak at a Young Life ski weekend at White Pass in the Cascades. Since I had to drive that far anyway, I thought I would drive to Bremerton first to follow up on the Christians there, then return to White Pass for the weekend.

I climbed into the new Sable. It was snowing hard when I left home. When I got to Pullman (nine miles west of Moscow), I realized that I needed chains on my tires. I put chains on and drove fifteen more miles to Colfax, where I stopped and took off the chains. I drove to Dusty, where the highway turned into six inches of slush. I drove slowly at thirty-five miles per hour to avoid having to put the chains back on. I realized that at that rate, I would not get to Bremerton in time for anything.

At right about that time, I lost control of the car. It spun around and went backward into the ditch on the right-hand side of the highway. I got out of the car and found that the left rear wheel was at a forty-five-degree angle to the ground. Two college kids stopped to tell me a tow truck was pulling a car out of the ditch a mile away. They went to get it for me.

The tow truck towed my new car back to Greene's Body Shop in Moscow. Bill Greene said I was foolish for driving in the snow with all-weather tires. He gave me a set of snow tires to put on the '69 Chevy.

I had asked Barbara to take care of Crossroads Bookstore in the mall while I was gone.* I cancelled the Bremerton meeting and called Barbara to tell her she did not have to take care of the store. I would manage it that evening. On the way there, the Chevy began to wobble. I pulled into a parking lot to find that I had a blowout on one of the snow tires. I walked the rest of the way to the mall, then called Young Life and cancelled my teaching for the White Pass ski weekend. This story is told to show that there is more than one way to discern the will of God.

While we were in California visiting Heather for Thanksgiving in 2002, Bessie broke her hip. We were not able to return home until January. I knew she could not get in and out of a low car, so I bought a bright blue 2000 Oldsmobile minivan.

Ten years later, a young man asked to borrow the van overnight, saying he would return it at seven thirty the next morning. I knew he was a thief. He had stolen from me twice, from the bookstore more than once, and from another store and several churches. He had spent time in jail for these burglaries. I gave him the keys anyway, suspecting that I might not see the van again. In the middle of the night, I woke up and knew it was gone. It was found in a junk yard in Reno two years later, completely trashed.† He was later arrested again in Portland for other crimes and sent to a prison in southern Idaho.

---

* After a number of years on Main Street, the bookstore had moved into an available space in the mall.

† The character of Marty in the movie *The River Thief* is based on this incident. That movie was produced and directed by my grandson Nathan. Moreover, it was filmed in my house while I was recovering in California from my broken hip.

Why did I lend him the car? Matthew 5:42: "Give to the one who begs from you, and do not refuse the one who would borrow from you"; his father had been the manager of Crossroads Bookstore years before; I had performed his parents' wedding; and his mother stayed in our home for many months.

It is normal for me to be in contact with non-Christians every day. I also interact with people who are evil in the eyes of the law: murderers, alcoholics, drug addicts, registered sex offenders. I have known six murderers who were wonderfully saved, one of whom is still serving a sixty-five-year sentence without parole.

Many years ago, I read in the newspaper of a drug-related murder in Pullman. Nancy, my daughter-in-law, called to tell me how burdened she was for the man who had committed the murder. I encouraged her in this burden. She said that I did not understand: she was burdened that *I* go see him. I asked her what his name was and where he was incarcerated. She did not know.

A few weeks went by. I had to meet a man named Bob Pyke at the Spokane airport. I stopped at the Whitman County Jail in Colfax on the way to ask if they had a man implicated in a drug-related murder from a few weeks earlier.

The officer said, "You must mean Mr. Dinehart."

I asked if I could see him. He said *yes*, and I told him that I would be back in two hours. I went to Spokane, picked up Bob, and returned to the jail.

The interview was on a telephone through a window. Jim Dinehart looked awful. He had cysts all over his face and ears. He looked physically guilty. He asked me who I was and why I had come to see him. I told him I came because my daughter-in-law had insisted. Did he know her? No. Pretty soon, he figured out I was religious and began to back off. I told him I would return in two weeks and would leave him some things to read in the meantime.

When I came back, they let me see him in person. The first thing he said was, "I didn't know that Jesus was like that." He was wide open for the gospel. The third time I saw him, he was clearly saved. His countenance was greatly changed.

The prosecutor did not think he could win his case against Jim Dinehart because it had been clearly self-defense. The defense did not think they could win their case because it was a death in a drug-related incident. Both sides wanted a plea agreement, and so the judge signed off on it.

The father of the dead man (who had not seen his son since he was born) came up from California and objected to the plea agreement. The judge recused himself from the case, and a new judge was brought in from Spokane for the sentencing.

The police had videotaped Jim's confession *after* he had been saved. He looked so different. I went to the sentencing. They played the tape. The new judge gave Jim an even lighter sentence than the plea agreement because he could not believe this joyful man deserved even that. Jim spent his sentence in the county jail then moved back to Alaska. He came back to Moscow for his wedding so that I could officiate it.

The man who is still serving sixty-five years was so changed when he was saved in the county jail that the jailor and the other prisoners could not believe that such a wonderful man could have committed a double murder.

I went to *his* sentencing. The judge was a black woman. She asked the defendant to recount the murder. He did. He did not justify himself at all. When he finished, she said that she was giving him sixty-five years without parole because he had shown no remorse when recounting the murder. He was so forgiven by God and so rejoicing in the Lord that he would have had to fake remorse. Remorse is worldly sorrow. "For the sorrow that is according to the will of God produces a repentance without regret, leading to salvation, but the sorrow of the world produces death" (2 Cor. 7:10). He really did have godly sorrow.

I also met a murderer in Maryland who was an evangelist on the Eastern Shore. He had also been saved in prison. He was so changed that the prison did not believe that he could have murdered anyone and called in a psychiatrist to figure him out. The psychiatrist concluded that a man with this character could not have possibly committed a murder without being temporarily insane, so they set him free.

December 29, 2005

Dear Dorothy,

It is a Sunday afternoon. Bessie is reading across the table from me. Chicken is in the oven. It is quiet in the house.

Last winter, from December to May, I was recovering from heart surgery. You sent a very caring note to me. Bessie may have answered it, but I did not. Please forgive me this delay.

I want to thank you also for [your daughter] Leslie. She is a good wife, mother, daughter-in-law, cook, seamstress, pianist, singer. Thank you also for helping the family get to Leslie's 30th reunion. The boys had a wonderful time . . . .

Because I am now 78, have had heart surgery, and slowed down physically, I am more conscious of my mortality and that of my friends, classmates, and relatives. It seems that weekly I get news that one of my classmates has died. My older brother died at 67; my next younger brother died at 67, and recently a sister-in-law died at 68. It would be foolish for me to think that I am going to live much longer. Now you have lost your twin sister. It is time for serious meditation.

Today, almost two weeks later, we have just returned from a Thanksgiving dinner and half a day at Evan and Leslie's. As usual the food was great. Gordon, Meredith and their four were there also, plus a few other guests. It was a pleasant time.

It is another Sunday afternoon. There is six inches of snow outside and every tiny branch of every tree in town is white with inches of snow.

As a Christian, I believe the Bible seriously and have been reading it for 60 years and believing it for 58 years. Most people I have talked with over these years think that they will go to Heaven, or hope that they will go to Heaven, but are not absolutely certain that they will go to Heaven. They think that it is not possible to be absolutely certain. It is. Please read the Gospel of John, the fourth book in the New Testament. You will find it very exciting reading.

Bessie sends her love.

With love and respect,
Jim Wilson

CHAPTER 67
DESCENDANTS

The grace of our Lord Jesus Christ be with you all. (2 Thess. 3:18)

When Heather came back from Egypt, she worked as the volunteer part-time secretary for Logos School their first year. Then in 1982, she worked at the Worldwide Evangelization Crusade headquarters in Fort Washington, Pennsylvania, for six or seven months. Heather was accepted as a candidate with the mission but was required to go to Pasadena, California, to study at the Zwemer Institute, which she did for the 1983–1984 school year. She took classes on Islam at Fuller Seminary's School of World Mission, and then she spent a couple months at home before heading to Turkey in the fall.

Heather lived in Turkey for five years. Bessie and I visited her twice in Istanbul; the second time was for her wedding in 1989. She married Ararat Torosyan, now the vice president of operations for Enertech, a power plant equipment supplier in Brea, California. They live in Altadena where Heather has been a housewife, homeschool teacher, and women's Bible teacher. Two of their three children are now married and have children of their own.

In the summer of 1988, Gordon and Meredith's second child, Alexa Grace, was born, but not breathing. The medical team could not get her to breathe for four minutes. Alexa was airlifted to Spokane, Washington.

I was in Salt Lake City with further speaking engagements scheduled in Boise and Portland. I drove to both, left the car in Portland, and flew to Spokane to be with Gordon and Meredith. The doctors told them that Alexa would only live for twenty minutes if they took her off life support. After praying about it, they decided to remove that life support. They sang to her and prayed. She did not die. Alexa was sent home, where she needed round-the-clock help. The doctors taught Gordon and Meredith how to care for her. Alexa lived for fifteen months on and off hospice care and died one evening in Gordon's arms.

In March 1994, their family was living in Lynchburg, Virginia, where Gordon was teaching at Liberty University. Meredith was pregnant with her youngest child, Heather, and wanted Bessie to be with her the birth.

Bessie and I drove to the airport in Spokane. We waited for hours for our plane to Chicago. O'Hare was snowed in. Finally, we were able to get on a plane for San Francisco, where we had several hours' wait for the red-eye flight to Washington, D.C. Bessie tried to sleep in the airport.

We arrived in Lynchburg right after an ice storm. There was no power and no heat. Even the wood for the fireplace was covered with ice. The next morning, Bessie had her coffee, toast (cooked over the fire), and marmalade in front of the fireplace. Heather's birth was a home birth with a midwife. Another ice storm came through afterward, and Bessie and I moved to a motel.

Gordon earned his PhD in environmental science and public policy from George Mason University in 2003. He is now the senior fellow of natural history at New Saint Andrew's College and is also an expert on intelligent design.

All of our children's children are faithful Christians serving the kingdom. Twenty-seven of my thirty-four great-grandchildren live in Moscow. All are walking in the light, and I am trusting God for the ones who are still on the young side. God has promised, "Know therefore that the LORD your God is God; he is the faithful God, keeping his covenant of love to a thousand generations of those who love him and keep his commandments" (Deut. 7:9). God has blessed us with four generations. We only have nine hundred and ninety-six more to go.

Jim and Bessie with Evan, Doug, Heather, and Gordon, 1963

Jim with Gordon, Doug, Heather, and Evan, 2017

Jim with Doug's children——Bekah, Rachel, and Nate (2014)

Doug and Nancy with their grandchildren (2015)

Evan and Leslie with their children——Michal Angela, Graeme, Gunn, and Lincoln——
plus spouses and one grandchild (2017)

Heather and Ararat with their children——Yeran, Sevan, and Masis——
plus spouses and one grandchild (2018)

Gordon and Meredith with their children——Mallory, Brooke, Dane, and Heather——
plus spouses and two grandchildren (2014)

Great-grands

CHAPTER 68
BESSIE

And now I commend you to God and to the word of his grace,
which is able to build you up and to give you the inheritance
among all those who are sanctified. (Acts 20:32)

It seems that most of my life was spent with people outside my family. However, Bessie and our four children have been most important to me. My years with Bessie were wonderful. She was committed to me in my ministry as well as continuing a Bible teaching ministry of her own. In Annapolis, she taught Bible classes to three groups of about thirty women each. She had a women's Bible study in Moscow and taught noon Bible studies to students at UI and WSU for a number of years, in addition to teaching Life Between the Sexes classes with me. She was not a natural hostess, but she was committed to hospitality all of the time.

Bessie was a wonderful mother to all four of our children. She was a "single mom" for many months while I was at sea and also for many days, weeks, and weekends for the next forty years while I spoke at conferences and visited distant bookstores.

In all of these trips, Bessie objected to my leaving only a few times. Once was on our fifth wedding anniversary. The other was our sixteenth anniversary. The first time, it was the will of God. I am not sure about the second. One of those times we got out of fellowship with God and with each other. We both had to confess our sins.

Another time my boss told me to come to the main office in East Lansing, Michigan. Bessie thought I should not go. She had no reason. I assured her that I had no option; I had to do what the general secretary

Elizabeth Schaefer Dodds with daughters Molly and Bessie, circa 1923

wanted. She replied that she would pray that I would not go.

When it came time for me to leave, the entire east coast was snowed in by a massive blizzard. All airports were closed. I told Bessie that she did not have to shut down the whole coast to keep me from going to Michigan!

Then there was the time I was going to take Tom McClenahan to Logan to introduce him to the committee before we opened Oasis Books. Bessie was sure I should not go. I called Tom and asked if he would mind going by himself. He did not mind; I did not go.

Otherwise, Bessie knew that God used me on those trips, and she was always willing for me to go.

One morning, Bessie said, "I think you should go see Louise." (Louise was part of our weekly inductive Bible study.) She had no particular reason; she just thought I should do it.

I said, "Bessie, I have many priorities ahead of Louise."

Pretty soon Bessie said again, "I think you should go see Louise."

"Bessie, I told you that she is not high on my list of things to do."

"I think you should go see Louise."

I thought maybe Bessie knew something I didn't. I put Louise on the top of my list and went to see her.

I knocked, and Louise opened the door. "Jim, how did you know?" Bessie was right!

Bessie began to get weak early in 2010. In May, she turned ninety-one. For the last seven months of her life, I quit everything else I was doing—preaching, counseling, visiting family—and stayed home to be with her. Nancy, Leslie, and Meredith provided the meals. I would do my work and exercise in one of the front bedrooms and gave her a referee's whistle to call me with.

During those months, I read four chapters of the New Testament to her every day. We went through the New Testament four and a half times and the book of Isaiah once.

Bessie did not want hospice. She wanted Heather to come up from California to be with her when she died. Heather came up in the summer and stayed for two weeks, but Bessie did not die.

Our doctor again wanted to have hospice care for Bessie. She refused; she wanted me. Finally, I called hospice on a Tuesday in September. They were a great blessing.

Bessie and Jim on her ninety-first birthday, 2010

On Thursday, I told the hospice nurse to let me know when I should call Heather. She said I should tell her to come right away. Evan and Leslie picked Heather up at the airport the next day, and she arrived home around eleven p.m. Bessie was asleep. We sang to her. In the morning, we sang to her again; she was still asleep. She died before eight in the morning that Saturday, September 18. She was not sick. She was on no medications. She was ninety-one and a half years old, and she just wore out.

Bessie's favorite verses were Isaiah 58 and 2 Corinthians 4:6-7. Two of my favorite verses are 2 Corinthians 4:4-5. The 2 Corinthians verses are on her headstone:

The god of this age has blinded the minds of unbelievers, so that they cannot see the light of the gospel that displays the glory of Christ, who is the image of God. For what we preach is not ourselves, but Jesus Christ as Lord, and ourselves as your servants for Jesus' sake. For God, who said, 'Let light shine out of darkness,' made his light shine in our hearts to give us the light of the knowledge of God's glory displayed in the face of Christ. But we have this treasure in jars of clay to show that this all-surpassing power is from God and not from us.

We had a graveside service for the family. The memorial service was held a month later in the Nazarene Church. Many people were there. Bessie had a very wide ministry in Moscow and Pullman for the thirty-nine years she was here. Our four children and Marny Lemmel testified at the service, and I preached. It was a glorious, rejoicing time. People wondered at the lack of sadness. I will be pleased (if that is possible) if there is as much joy at my memorial.

Of all the wonderful Christian women in my life, Bessie was number one. We were married for fifty-eight and a half years. She was a wonderful wife, mother, grandmother, and great-grandmother.

Bessie and Jim in front of the Howard Street house

CHAPTER 69

CONTINUING THE MINISTRY

To all in Rome who are loved by God and called to be his holy
people: Grace and peace to you from God our Father and from the
Lord Jesus Christ. (Rom. 1:7)

In 2012, I wrote to Community Christian Ministries' donors about
my desire to have a warehouse of free books. We do not have an ac-
tual warehouse, but the free distribution has greatly increased since
then. The books are kept in my home and given out from there. The
book flow has been very good. The real measurement will be in the
lives which are changed. There will not be an accurate measurement
of that on this side of glory.

However, we are seeing changes in more and more people. When
I first began writing this biography, I had three young men in their
late twenties living with me. Two of them had been long-time alcoholics. One of them was clearly saved. The other was clearly not,
although he thought he was.

The third was Luke Mays, the grandson of close friends Graham
and Libby Gutsche. After Bessie died, I planned a trip to the East
Coast to visit friends. Wendy Mays, the Gutsches' daughter, grew up
with our kids in Annapolis. I asked her about her children. One of
her sons was married and living in California. The other was Luke,
who was still at home. I asked if he might be willing to drive me up
and down the East Coast. She said that she would ask him. I did
not know that he was backslidden. And I insisted on singing hymns
while we drove. He is now a growing Christian.

After that trip was over, I asked Luke if he would drive me to our bookstore in Utah. While we were there, he went whitewater rafting, then drove home to get his dog and moved into my upstairs. He also drove me to Oregon, then down to California to visit Heather.

Luke lived with me from 2011–12. While he was with me, he transformed my backyard into a garden with herbs, flowers, strawberries, blueberries, raspberries, gooseberries, red and white currants, rhubarb, cherry trees, three raised vegetable beds, a river rock stream, a pond, and a hive of honey bees.

In September 2011, Luke and I traveled to Logan and visited the Utah State University campus with Brad Scheelke and Eli Brayley, our two men on the Oasis staff at that time. We set up a long table of free books. Eli preached while Brad sat at the table in conversation with students. Luke, Lauren Wilson (my great-niece), and I passed out booklets. It was an exciting seven-hours-a-day for three days.

In March 2014, I had the opportunity to do the same in Red Square at the University of Washington. It was for only three hours with a team from Calvary Chapel. During dead week and finals week, we had a table at the University of Idaho. Luke Mays, Phil Carr, and I talked with believers, Mormons, Muslims, and atheists from many different countries. We passed out about seven hundred copies of *How to Be Free from Bitterness* and several hundred dollars' worth of books and Bibles in various languages.

CHAPTER 70

EVA

For if, because of one man's trespass, death reigned through that
one man, much more will those who receive the abundance of
grace and the free gift of righteousness reign in life through the one
man Jesus Christ. (Rom. 5:17)

At Thanksgiving 2012, I travelled to Nebraska and Missouri to see my three surviving brothers and their families. My granddaughter Mallory went with me as my travelling companion. It was a wonderful time.

On the way back, I realized that I did not fit into coach seats anymore, either fore and aft or port and starboard. At Christmas, I was going to fly to California to visit Heather's family. I wanted to fly first class, but I did not have the money for it. I prayed that I could fly first class.

Shortly after that, I received a letter from a former Wycliffe missionary to Papua New Guinea. I had met him about three times, all of them a long time in the past. I had known his wife when she was a student at WSU. The letter enclosed a $1,000 check with a note that said, "Do not use this for ministry. Use it for yourself."

I could recognize answered prayer. I thanked God and bought a first class ticket.

On the return trip, the plane had to leave LAX at some awful time in the morning. Heather and my granddaughter Yeran took me to the airport. On the way, I said, "I hope God allows sinners to travel first class." We asked God to provide someone to sit next to me who was ready to receive Christ.

I had a window seat on the port side. I sat down and began my daily Bible reading. Soon a woman came on board and took the aisle seat next to me. She did not say anything but opened her laptop and began to work. After a bit, she said, "I only had fifteen minutes of sleep last night," closed the laptop, and went to sleep.

When breakfast arrived, the flight attendant woke her up. She saw my book and asked what I was reading. I told her it was the Bible and that I had been reading it since I became a Christian. She said, "A born-again Christian?"

I said, "Yes, but that is the only kind of Christian there is."

She told me that her grandfather was a Christian, and he read his Bible all the time.

I thought this was the answer to my prayer and started to tell her the good news.

She stopped me, holding up both her hands. "Wait a minute! My grandfather went to Wheaton College, and he married the president's daughter. He was a famous missionary to Japan and a magician. His name is Phil Foxwell." I recognized the name. She continued to talk. "He isn't really my grandfather; he is my adopted grandfather. Although he really isn't my adopted grandfather, either; I adopted him because I never had a grandfather. He is ninety-six years old and in a nursing home. I see him once a week."

I began to tell her the gospel. She had grown up Roman Catholic. Before we landed in Seattle, she received Christ. I told her to read Luke, John, Acts, and Romans. She said she would like a Bible like mine. I had one in my briefcase, so I gave it to her. She started to read Luke 1. I stopped her and told her to read chapter 15. She read the parable of the lost sheep and said, "That's wonderful."

I said, "Keep reading."

She read the parable of the lost coin and the story of the prodigal son.

I said, "It looks like God is into parties. There is a birthday party right now in Heaven because you are a sinner who has repented."

We landed at SEATAC. I realized I didn't even know her name. I asked if she was staying in Seattle or flying on. She said she was flying to Spokane. I told her I was flying to Moscow.

She said, "I'm driving down to Moscow from Spokane."

"What are you doing in Moscow?"

"I'm the referee for the UI women's basketball game against Hawaii. I will give you free tickets." Eva* gave me her name and told me how to get the tickets.

I got home at noon and checked with the family to see if they wanted to go to the game. They were all busy. I asked the Wintzes next door. They were busy, but after dinner Valerie Wintz called to say that Maddie, her ten-year-old daughter, wanted to go to the game. It was halftime when we arrived, so we got in free anyway.

I could see Eva in her striped referee's shirt on the other side of the court. I went down to the desk and told the man to tell her that Jim Wilson was there. I gave him an envelope full of Christian literature to give to her. He told me that if I could wait for her after the game, she would meet me.

When the game was over, I asked Eva if she had to get back to Spokane right away or if she had some time. She said, "Let's go to Applebee's." She asked the two male refs if they would like to come along. The five of us went to Applebee's. I picked up a few extra New Testaments for them, and we got a large booth in the restaurant.

The first thing Eva said to the other refs was, "Today is my birthday." Then she read to them from my booklet *How to Maintain Joy*. I have seen her two or three times since then in California and here in Moscow. The next time I was in California, I visited Phil Foxworth in the nursing home. I mentioned various missionaries I knew in Japan. He knew them as well.

* Name has been changed.

CHAPTER 71
CALIFORNIA, SUMMER 2014

But he said to me, "My grace is sufficient for you, for my power
is made perfect in weakness." Therefore I will boast all the more
gladly of my weaknesses, so that the power of Christ may rest upon
me. (2 Cor. 12:9)

July 23–30, 2014

I am in room 4119 in the rehab wing of Huntington Hospital in Pasadena, California. On the 26th of June, our youngest son, Gordon, and I flew from Spokane to LAX to visit Heather and her family. Yeran, their oldest daughter, was going to marry Chris Terzian on the 13th of July. After a few days, Gordon flew on to Bandong, Java, to teach the faculty of a Christian school on Creation Science for ten days.

The two weeks with Heather's family was spent reading, counseling, and teaching. Gordon arrived back from Bandong on Friday, July 11. The rehearsal was on the 12th, followed by a rehearsal dinner at Ararat and Heather's home.

About nine thirty p.m. the day before the wedding, Gordon took me up to my room and then left. As I reached up to remove my glasses with my right hand, I fell over to my left. Gordon heard the fall and came back in to help me up. I could stand, so I assumed nothing was broken.

The wedding was at 4:30 on Sunday in a Japanese garden. I was hurting badly, so I was wheeled to my position in a wheelchair. Chris's pastor, Aren Bahadourian, conducted the first half of the wedding.

When he finished, I spoke, sitting on my walker. My text was Luke 1:74–75, where John the Baptist's father prophesied about the

Lord Jesus six months before Jesus was born. To the congregation, I spoke on the righteousness that comes from God (salvation). To Chris and Yeran, I spoke on holiness, because they had already received God's salvation. They were pronounced husband and wife, followed by dinner and dancing until 10:30 p.m. (I did not dance.)

I was to fly home with Gordon the next morning. Gordon's daughter Mallory was to marry Caleb Barendregt in Moscow the following Saturday. I knew I could not make it onto the plane; I was in too much pain. Gordon flew home alone, and Heather took me to the emergency room at Huntington Hospital, where I found out that my left femur had broken just below the ball. I had been walking on the broken hip all day Sunday.

Surgery was performed on Wednesday. On Friday, I was transferred to the rehab section of the hospital. It is now Saturday, July 26. I have been here eight days. Bessie spent time in the same hospital after breaking her hip in 2000. Apparently our family thinks California is for breaking hips in.

August 3, 2014, Altadena, California

From the day I arrived here on the 26th of June until the 12th of July, the mockingbirds were making music all day long. I spent the last two weeks in the hospital (July 14–August 1). On returning to Heather's house, the mockingbirds had quit singing—not a peep. Then yesterday afternoon one of them sang for a few hours. Nothing today. Every few days, a big flock of wild parrots flies over squawking, and then the same number of crows crowing. I see a few hummingbirds and a few bats. It is very quiet here now.

This morning at the United Armenian Congregational Church, a Turkish pastor, a former Muslim, spoke in Turkish, confessing the

Turkish massacre of Armenians in 1915. Heather and Ararat understood the Turkish. I got a little bit of it translated into English. Then the assistant pastor spoke on the last part of Matthew 15 on forgiveness. It was very good.

The moon is almost at its first quarter in a very clear sky.

August 7, 2014

I am sitting at a table at Heather's home. Before Yeran's wedding, I would sit on the back deck and listen to the mockingbirds all day long. This morning I saw a flock of sixteen parrots. They also made a lot of unpleasant noise.

I cannot tell of all encounters I have had with unbelievers and believers during these years. I have forgotten many of them. Recently, I had correspondence and a visit from a family with eight children. I had apparently taught and counseled the wife before their marriage and presented the gospel at the wedding. I have no recollection of it. I was very chagrinned about that.

Today I heard of another man, an unbeliever. Apparently, I told the woman he wanted to marry not to marry him. He came to see me and received Christ. They have been married for thirty-five years. I have no memory of any of that either. I suspect there have been more of these events.

August 16, 2014

This is Heather's fifty-eighth birthday. Today her son Masis gave a diamond to Araz Der-Tavitian. She is a godly young woman. On the 5th of August, Yeran and Chris left for Granada where he will attend medical school. On the 6th of August, Heather and Ararat celebrated their twenty-fifth wedding anniversary.

September 1, 2014

Since I came to California, I bought a new Bible at Archives Bookstore in Pasadena. The large print and the bright sunshine have been two extra blessings in reading the Word.

My reading this morning was Psalms 40 and 41. On a Saturday night in Baltimore at a Youth for Christ meeting in October 1947, I heard the first five verses of the 40th Psalm read and preached by Gregorio Tingson. It hit me hard. After the meeting, with help from Pete Peterson, I called upon the Lord, and He put a new song in my heart.

Six years later, while in grad school in Monterey, at a church in Pacific Grove, I taught the first ten verses of Psalm 40, starting with verse 10 and going back to verse one. Ten years later, in our bookstore in Annapolis, Maryland, I received a letter from a man in Pacific Grove who asked, "Are you the same Jim Wilson that taught ten verses of Psalm 40 in Pacific Grove in 1953?" Years later, while teaching for InterVarsity in Stillwater, Oklahoma, I received the same response from teaching Psalm 40. In my regular reading, it gets read twice a year. If you have not ready it recently, stop right now and read it.

The two weeks I spent in the hospital in California gave me many opportunities to present the gospel and to make about $1,200 worth of books available to the staff and patients. I spent a month at

Heather's house. After six weeks, I was allowed to put weight on my left foot. I returned home on the second of September. My left leg is now about three-quarters of an inch shorter than my right leg. If I stand on my right leg, I can swing the left one, and it will not touch the floor.

In the years since Yeran's wedding, I have been reduced to not driving and not traveling long distances. With the combination of little strength in my legs, pain in my hands, a broken left hip, and a weak shoulder, I stay at my desk, and my ministry is left to correspondence, telephone counseling, and the people who come to see me.

In good weather, I sit on the back porch to read and write. Doug and Nancy live with me. In the summer, Nancy finds big white peonies and tulips in the garden, which she cuts and puts in the house. She also brought in the irises which now adorn my desk.

CHAPTER 72
BOOKS

Let us then with confidence draw near to the throne of grace, that
we may receive mercy and find grace to help in time of need. (Heb.
4:16)

My first acquaintance with Christian books was during my first class
year at the Naval Academy in 1950, when Corrie ten Boom gave me
her book *A Prisoner and Yet*. Other books that had a major effect in
my life include *The Calvary Road* by Roy Hession in 1951; *Continuous
Revival* by Norman Grubb in 1956; *Behind the Ranges*, a biography
of James Fraser, in 1957; and *C.T. Studd* by Norman Grubb in 1951.

When I was a senior at the Naval Academy and had been a
Christian a little over two years, I read a book on apologetics. I loved
it. I set about debating with classmates using apologetics.

It did not take me long to realize that this apologetic approach
was a problem. I could win arguments but not win people. In fact,
I might alienate people. In addition to this, I got into the argument
in such a way that I would sin, not with my facts or reasoning, but
with my attitude. With a very few exceptions, I gave up apologetics
and arguing from that point on. I may give an apologetics book to
someone, but I will not talk apologetics.

Later, I learned 2 Timothy 2:23–26: "Don't have anything to do
with foolish and stupid arguments, because you know they produce
quarrels. And the Lord's servant must not be quarrelsome but must
be kind to everyone, able to teach, not resentful. Opponents must be
gently instructed, in the hope that God will grant them repentance

473

leading them to a knowledge of the truth, and that they will come to their senses and escape from the trap of the devil, who has taken them captive to do his will."

I learned how to avoid foolish questions. Knowing the answer to such a question is not a good enough reason to give it. The other person does not want an answer. He wants to quarrel, and "the servant of the Lord must not quarrel." We are to teach with kindness and gentleness.

I used to like reading Dickens. I could open one of his books at random and enjoy any page. But I had a problem. I wanted to jump into the book and evangelize! I did not want to read about kids in trouble when I was ministering to kids in trouble all week. Why entertain myself with more tragedy when I was living with it daily? I stopped reading *David Copperfield* and *Great Expectations*. I also stopped reading Dostoyevsky.

The same happened with military history. I learned from history, but I had to read about men dying by the hundreds and thousands because of poor leadership. Why read about dying in war when I had been next to dying men in the Korean War? As a Christian, I not only saw men dying; I saw them dying without Christ.

When I was at sea off and on for six years, I read my Bible. Early in that time, I decided that if I found a command in the Bible that to my knowledge no one had ever obeyed, by grace I would obey it. When I got back to home port, I found I was out of step with the Christians because of this desire for obedience.

I have read some systematic theology (all kinds). I found that these systems were all partly right, but dogmatically wrong also. Instead of reading theology, I read biographies. I imitate the good things and avoid the bad things. I read books on evangelism and holiness (not the doctrine of holiness, but holiness in fact).

My book *How to be Free from Bitterness* was first printed in Annapolis in a mimeographed newspaper which we called *The*

Nameless News. For the next twenty-five years, I included that topic in many lectures. In 1990, Douglas had one of my lectures transcribed and printed a thousand copies in a booklet format. Since then, we have printed ten to fifteen thousand copies of *How to Be Free from Bitterness* each year, and it has been translated into over twenty different languages.

CHAPTER 73

GIFTS AND THE FRUIT OF THE SPIRIT

> For by grace you have been saved through faith. And this is not
> your own doing; it is the gift of God. (Eph. 2:8)

The gifts of the Spirit are listed in 1 Corinthians 12 and Romans 12.
I think I have a few of these. From 1 Corinthians 12, I can identify
one gift—faith. "To one there is given through the Spirit a message
of wisdom, to another a message of knowledge by means of the same
Spirit, to another faith by the same Spirit, to another gifts of healing
by that one Spirit . . . " (1 Cor. 12:8–9). From the list in Romans 12,
I have the gifts of teaching, exhortation, and giving. Other qualities I
may have are not gifts; they are simply commands that I have obeyed.

"So Christ himself gave the apostles, the prophets, the evangelists,
the pastors and teachers" (Eph. 4:1). I am not an apostle, nor a proph-
et. Evangelist, pastor, and teacher all describe me. I pastored a church
for forty-five years. It was not my primary ministry—just a responsibility. In those same years, I ran bookstores and taught at conferences,
Schools of Practical Christianity at home and abroad, for InterVarsity,
ISI, OCF, CBMC, and many churches that invited me.

At the end of 1 Corinthians 12 there is a wonderful statement:
"And I will show you a more excellent way." What is that way? Love.
Love is more important than all of the gifts of the Spirit. Romans
12:9–12 makes a similar statement: "Love must be sincere. Hate
what is evil; cling to what is good. Be devoted to one another in love.
Honor one another above yourselves. Never be lacking in zeal, but
keep your spiritual fervor, serving the Lord. Be joyful in hope, patient in affliction, faithful in prayer."

The gifts of the Spirit are functional. They are not all given to everyone but are distributed among the saints for the benefit of all.

The fruit of the Spirit is qualitative. All of the fruit of the Spirit is for every believer all the time.

> But the fruit of the Spirit is love, joy, peace, forbearance, kindness, goodness, faithfulness, gentleness and self-control. Against such things there is no law. Those who belong to Christ Jesus have crucified the flesh with its passions and desires (Gal. 5:22–24).

> Love is patient, love is kind. It does not envy, it does not boast, it is not proud. It does not dishonor others, it is not self-seeking, it is not easily angered, it keeps no record of wrongs. Love does not delight in evil but rejoices with the truth. It always protects, always trusts, always hopes, always perseveres. Love never fails. But where there are prophecies, they will cease; where there are tongues, they will be stilled; where there is knowledge, it will pass away (1 Cor. 13:4–8).

It took me a few years to realize that I needed to have all of the fruit of the Spirit all of the time.

"Do not get drunk on wine, which leads to debauchery. Instead, be filled with the Spirit, speaking to one another with psalms, hymns, and songs from the Spirit. Sing and make music from your heart to the Lord, always giving thanks to God the Father for everything, in the name of our Lord Jesus Christ. Submit to one another out of reverence for Christ" (Eph. 5:18–21). If this is true, I will always have the fruit of the Spirit; and if I am filled with the Spirit, I will also have boldness to speak the gospel. If I am filled with the Spirit, I can obey all of the commands in the gospels and epistles without effort originating with me. This means that obedience from the heart is normal.

In talking with many believers, I find that in every case there is some area where they now are effortlessly obedient, where it had been impossible for them to obey at all before their conversion. The area was different for each person. They may have been very profane before their conversion, and now they are not at all profane. They may have been habitual liars, thieves, or promiscuous, and now they are that way no longer.

"Or do you not know that wrongdoers will not inherit the kingdom of God? Do not be deceived: Neither the sexually immoral nor idolaters nor adulterers nor men who have sex with men nor thieves nor the greedy nor drunkards nor slanderers nor swindlers will inherit the kingdom of God. And that is what some of you were. But you were washed, you were sanctified, you were justified in the name of the Lord Jesus Christ and by the Spirit of our God" (1 Cor. 6:9–11). "And that is what some of you were." This new obedience was not conscious. It just happened.

This kind of obedience is available for believers *all* of the time for *every* command. Have you not experienced this yourself? Experience is not what determines truth.

I learned very much Scripture the first several years of my Christian life. That knowledge did not give me the power to obey. However, I did *have* the power to obey. I just was not experiencing it.

> His divine power has given us everything we need for a godly life through our knowledge of him who called us by his own glory and goodness. (2 Pet. 1:3)

> For if you possess these qualities in increasing measure, they will keep you from being ineffective and unproductive in your knowledge of our Lord Jesus Christ. (2 Pet. 1:8)

Two truths that made a great difference in my life are 1) having all of the fruit of the Spirit in my heart all of the time and 2) having the commands in the New Testament in my heart. Previously, these truths had only been in my head. "I have hidden your word in my *heart* that I might not sin against you" (Psalm 119:11).

It took a long time to hide these truths in my heart, but it should not have. I was still getting impatient and sometimes angry after we moved to Moscow in 1971, and I had a bout of bitterness in the mid-seventies that lasted several days. But by having all of the fruit of the Spirit in my heart and the commands also there, I found that obedience is normal. The commands are not just in my head; they are part of me. I am not saying that I do not sin. I am saying that when I obey God, it is not by my own effort or trying, but by grace.

"So then, just as you received Christ Jesus as Lord, continue to live your lives in him . . . " (Col. 2:6). When I received Christ, it was not by effort. It was by grace through faith. I walk exactly the same way as I received Christ, by grace through faith.

"This is the message we have heard from him and declare to you: God is light; in him there is no darkness at all . . . . But if we walk in the light, as he is in the light, we have fellowship with one another, and the blood of Jesus, his Son, purifies us from all sin" (1 John 1:5, 7). This walk is the right kind of effortless.

"Whoever claims to live in him must live as Jesus did" (1 John 2:6). I am an evangelist, but not because I have the gift of evangelism. I do it by obeying the command to disciple the nations by grace through faith. It is by the fruit of the Spirit, especially love and joy, and by knowing and speaking the Good News to unbelievers.

CHAPTER 74

PRINCIPLES TO LIVE BY

> For our boast is this, the testimony of our conscience, that we
> behaved in the world with simplicity and godly sincerity, not by
> earthly wisdom but by the grace of God, and supremely so toward
> you. (2 Cor. 1:12)

I am a slow learner. It took me ten years to understand grace and respond to it at age twenty. Here are a few other principles to live by and the approximate times I understood them and began to apply them in my life:

- Pay attention to what the Bible says, not to what you think it means (age twenty-two).
- My decision to obey God is independent of the evangelical culture around me. If I find a Scripture that to my knowledge no one had obeyed since the day it was written, I will obey it (at sea, probably age twenty-four).
- The necessity of keeping short accounts with God, daily and hourly, from 1 John 1:5, 7, and 9 (Sea of Japan, 1951, and Japan, 1955).
- Head knowledge of the Scripture is not the same as heart knowledge, Psalm 119:9–11 (Sea of Japan, 1952).
- An arrogant person is not aware of his own arrogance (Washington, D.C., 1957–58).
- Bitterness can be identified and gotten rid of (Annapolis, 1960s).
- The *be* commands in the Bible are more important than the *do* commands (1980s).

- Obedience is more associated with grace, love, and faith in the Bible than it is with works, Colossians 2:6 (1980s).
- The harvest is plentiful and ripe (Japan and East China Sea, 1955–56).
- What the Bible teaches takes precedence over the desires of the heart (Ann Arbor, 1969).

C H A P T E R 7 5
CONCLUSION

But grow in the grace and knowledge of our Lord and Savior Jesus
Christ. To him be the glory both now and to the day of eternity.
Amen. (2 Pet. 3:18)

There have been too many events in my life to write them all here.
The ones I record are meant to be instructive. The ones I leave out are
not omitted because I do not think that they are important; most of
my encounters have been God-caused and are therefore important.

The grace of God has been evident in my life and in the lives of
Bessie and our children, grandchildren, and great-grandchildren. I
cannot adequately tell of His grace in the lives of all of our descendants, but they all know our Lord, and to my knowledge they are all
walking in the light.

The adjectives that describe grace in the New Testament are quan-
titative and superlative. God's grace is plentiful, bountiful, overflow-
ing. He giveth more grace, grace upon grace, more abundant grace.

God has lavished His grace upon me all my life. He gave me
wonderful parents and five brothers. In infancy, I had scarlet fever,
smallpox, and diphtheria, and I recovered completely from all of
them. He helped in my education: elementary school, high school,
the Navy as an enlisted sailor, the Naval Academy, and the Naval
Postgraduate School. I am grateful for physical protection in the
Korean War, meeting and marrying Bessie, evangelism in the Navy,
and meeting and being helped by many godly men and women in
the Navy and afterward. God has given me much grace over more
than seventy years of teaching, preaching, and admonishing. He has

given me grace in several hospitalizations: heart surgery, gall bladder surgery, two hip surgeries. He gave me grace in giving me Bessie for fifty-eight and a half years. He has given grace in our four children.

Bessie was given much grace. When she was a child of five, her mother died. She was the youngest of seven, with five brothers and one sister. Two of her brothers were killed in WWII. One brother and her only sister died of alcoholism. The two remaining brothers loved their little sister. Bessie received Christ when she was fifteen. Her father received Christ on his deathbed when Bessie was twenty-five.

Bessie attended Prairie Bible Institute for three years. She was a missionary to homestead country in Alberta, Canada. Then she worked with high school kids in Toronto with Inter-School Christian Fellowship in 1944. In 1945, she started an ISCF group in Calgary, Alberta. In 1946, she attended the first InterVarsity Student Missionary Convention in Toronto (now called Urbana) and committed herself to foreign missions. She applied to the Women's Union Missionary Society, intending to go to India. They instead wanted her to go to Japan to reopen the Women's Bible College in Yokohama that had been closed during WWII. Bessie sailed for Japan in December 1948. She studied the Japanese language for fourteen months in Tokyo and moved to Yokohama to reopen the college in 1950.

God gave Bessie much grace during our times of separation. We were apart for all of our engagement. Then I was in San Diego for six months while she was in Japan and had two additional months in the Sea of Japan while she was in Yokohama. Douglas was born in San Diego while I was in the Sea of Japan. Evan was born in Oakland when I was stationed in Japan. I was in the East China Sea for five months while Bessie was pregnant with Heather in Yokohama. During my time with OCU and for many years afterward, I travelled extensively to teach and preach.

Through all of this, we could see God's hand of grace upon us. It has been wonderful.

He giveth more grace when the burdens grow greater,
He sendeth more strength when the labors increase;
To added afflictions He addeth His mercy,
To multiplied trials, His multiplied peace.

His love has no limits, His grace has no measure,
His power no boundary known unto men;
For out of His infinite riches in Jesus
He giveth, and giveth, and giveth again.

—Annie Johnson Flint

THE GOSPEL

Having read this book, you may realize that you are not a Christian. If you are not a Christian, you have many sins and a nature that is prone to sin. In order to get rid of your sin, you need a new nature, and you need to get rid of your old nature. You cannot do this yourself. It can be done only by God.

Here is your part:

1. You need to want to be set free from the guilt and judgement for your sins and from the power of sin.
2. You need to know that you are helpless in this want.
3. You need to know that being good and not being bad will not set you free, nor will any other means of self-effort.
4. You need to know that God has already accomplished this deliverance by sending the Lord Jesus to earth to die for the ungodly. "You see, at just the right time, when we were still powerless, Christ died for the ungodly" (Rom. 5:6).
5. Three days after this death for our sins, the Lord Jesus rose from the dead in order to make us righteous. "He was delivered over to death for our sins and was raised to life for our justification" (Rom. 4:25).
6. The Holy Spirit is now drawing you to turn from your sin, to call upon the Lord Jesus, trusting Him, His death, and His resurrection.

That if you confess with your mouth, "Jesus is Lord," and believe in your heart that God raised him from the dead, you will be saved. For it is with your heart that you believe and are justified, and it is with your mouth that you confess and are saved. (Rom. 10:9–10)

Now, brothers, I want to remind you of the gospel I preached to you, which you received and on which you have taken your stand. By this gospel you are saved, if you hold firmly to the word I preached to you. Otherwise, you have believed in vain. For what I received I passed on to you as of first importance: that Christ died for our sins according to the Scriptures, that he was buried, that he was raised on the third day according to the Scriptures, and that he appeared to Peter, and then to the Twelve. (1 Cor. 15:1–5)

Now that you have called upon the Lord Jesus, thank Him for bringing you to the Father, for forgiving your sin, and for giving you everlasting life.

Now, in your joy of your forgiveness, tell someone what God has done for you.

PEOPLE WHO HAVE
INFLUENCED ME SPIRITUALLY

The people and books that had the most influence on me were people who drew attention to the text of the Bible itself, not to the interpretation.

The Naval Academy is a sheltered place; so is a destroyer at sea, especially in war. They are not good places for social meetings. However, of the people I met in my last year at the Academy and my first two years at sea, several were close friends until they went to be with the Lord, and many others had a great influence on me spiritually. There are natural explanations for these people entering my life, but it is still amazing to me.

Midshipmen—There are three men from the class of '49 that I owe much to: Willard "Pete" Peterson, John Bajus, and Jim Inskeep were with me when I received Christ on that Saturday night in October 1947. They were a great encouragement to me and were my mentors for the next two academic years. The day the *USS Brush* hit a mine, the *USS Worcester* came to the rescue. John Bajus was on the *Worcester*.

Roy Grayson was another member of the class of '49. We became close in Monterey. Eric Nelson, class of '51, I looked to several times for wisdom my last year at the Academy.

Classmates (USNA Class of 1950)—Caryll Whipple was a Christian before I was. He invited me to the pre-reveille Bible study led by Pete. I was also close to my classmates John Kirk and Morris Riddle, both Christians.

I know several other classmates who received Christ. Frank Young became a Christian in the spring of 1950 through Gene

Scheele's witness in Memorial Hall. Jim Wilkins received Christ through the ministry of a Presbyterian Church in Walnut Creek, California, in 1953 or '54. Joe Howard was saved in his stateroom on the Sunday morning before Thanksgiving, 1955, on the aircraft carrier *USS Hancock*; Dave Cook in the winter 1954–55 on the *USS Boxer*; and Lee Bendell when he was a battalion officer in the Brigade of Midshipmen at the Naval Academy in the mid-sixties.

Older Christians who helped me while I was still a midshipman included Findley Paydon and his wife Sadie. We met in their home once a week for Bible study. Findley was a math professor, and Sadie had been on the InterVarsity staff. She was the one who later gave me Bessie's address in Japan and asked me to look her up.

In my senior year at the Academy, I met Joe Bayly of InterVarsity, who taught me inductive study of the Bible; Bessie and I led weekly inductive Bible studies most of our married life. Corrie ten Boom taught me forgiveness. Lt. General William K. Harrison taught me integrity, evangelism, and leadership as a Christian in the military. Gene Scheele taught me personal evangelism, and Dawson Trotman taught me how to memorize Scripture. Jack Wyrtzen of Word of Life taught me more about evangelism in 1949. Cleo Buxton drew my attention to my arrogance and earlier had invited me to be the East Coast Staff member for OCU. I only knew Gene Scheele from Saturday to Monday in the winter of 1950. The others were lifetime friends.

After the Academy, these people helped me in my Christian life.

- Willis Bishop from Washington Bible College
- Miss Irene Webster-Smith (everyone called her Sensei), who helped many war crimes prisoners receive Christ. She took me to meet Bessie in November 1950.

- Bessie Dodds, headmistress of a Bible school for women. We were married in Yokohama. She was my closest friend.
- Mabel Halverson and Doreen Shaw taught me the one nature of the believer and how to walk in the light in 1951.
- Three missionaries in Hong Kong who had spent forty years in China taught me the reality of demon possession. They were Mr. Olsen of the Lutheran Free Church, Archdeacon Vyvyan Donnithorne of the Anglican Church in West China, and Dr. Vaughan Rees of the China Inland Mission.
- David Morken, missionary to cannibals in Sumatra before the war, taught me evangelism. After the war, he conducted citywide campaigns with the gospel in every major city in China. He then spent fourteen months under house arrest under the Communists in Shanghai. He officiated at our wedding in Yokohama in 1952.
- Lou Zamperini, whom I met in Tokyo when he returned to Japan to forgive the Japanese guards for how they had treated him in prison
- Bill Pape, author of *The Lordship of Jesus Christ* and rector of the Chinese Church in Tokyo. He was with CIM in southwest China before and during the War. He was pastor of the Chinese Church in Tokyo after the war and later teacher at a Bible school in Germany and pastor of a church for the deaf in St. Catherine's, Ontario. I met him in Tokyo in 1955, and he taught me Bible exposition from 1955 to 1965.
- W. Robert Smith, professor of philosophy at Bethel College in St. Paul. Dr. Bob spoke at many OCU conferences.
- Joe Carroll, whom I met in 1956, taught me how to walk in the light and how to speak publicly. He kept missionaries in fellowship with God and with each other in India, the Philippines, and Japan. He founded the Evangelical Institute

in Greenville, South Carolina, and the Great Commission
Mission. Joe helped me in Manila, Tokyo, Washington, D.C.,
and Idaho.

- A missionary whose name I cannot recall taught me personal
  evangelism from Acts 8, 9, and 10 in 1955.

All of these contacts I met while I was on active duty in the Navy.

APPENDIX C

MY LIFE IN THE WORD

When I first received Christ my second year at the Academy, I had no Bible, and I could not afford to buy one. My roommate did not read the Bible, so I borrowed his. It was a Scofield Reference Bible. My last year at the Academy, I used a Gideon Bible. (There was a shelf full of white Gideon Bibles in the chaplain's office.) There were maps in the Sunday school papers, and I pasted one in the back of the Gideon Bible.

Most of the Christians I knew were dispensational. They recommended that I buy a Scofield Reference Bible. Soon after I was commissioned, I bought one. Sometime in the first year, I read the notes at the bottom of the page and knew that they were not right. I quit reading the notes, then I quit reading that Bible. I bought a KJV text-only Bible and used it for many years.

In 1953, Koichi Yamamoto came to the States to study at a Nazarene college in Kansas. He and his wife Nana stopped by Monterey to visit us. Koichi had no English Bible, so I gave him the Scofield. He had given me his five-hundred-year-old Samurai sword in Japan. I gave it back to him after we moved to Moscow.

After Dawson Trotman came to the Academy in 1950, I started to memorize Scripture regularly. Dawson taught us how to memorize Scripture so we would not forget it. I bought into it. I started with the "B rations," three verses at a time, and completed the Navigators' Topical Memory System in the next fourteen months. That was 108 verses. In San Diego, I started to memorize three verses a week for the next year. The following year, I memorized five verses a week. I was arrogant about how much Bible I knew. Later I figured out that memorizing Scripture was not hiding the Word of God in my heart. It was only in my head. In the many years since, I have been meditating on the same Scriptures. Many of them are now in my heart.

Five months after Bessie and I were married, while we were in Bremerton, Washington, I started to read all of the Bible. I read two chapters of the KJV New Testament every morning and four chapters in the Old Testament every evening. In the next nine months, I read the OT once and the NT two and a half times. I have been reading the Bible all the way through every year since then.

In 1968, I switched to the Revised Standard Version. In 1978, I switched to the New International Version. Then in 2014, I switched to the New American Standard Bible. Now I read through a different translation each year. Since I do not know the biblical languages, I read different English versions. So far, I have read the ones already mentioned as well as three Roman Catholic translations (the Knox Bible, the Jerusalem Bible, and the Douay-Rheims Bible), a Jewish Old Testament, the New English Bible, the Living Bible, the New King James Version, the Good News Translation, and the English Standard Version.

Until the last ten years, I did not keep a record of my Bible reading. Then I started to use Robert Murray M'Cheyne's Bible reading schedule. It is simple. On January 1, you read Genesis 1, Ezra 1, Matthew 1, and Acts 1, then read the next chapter of each the next day. Doing this, you read the Old Testament once a year, the New Testament twice a year, and the Psalms twice a year. Because my day gets filled up with counseling, it is easy for my Bible reading to get squeezed out. If I skip a day, I make myself catch up the next day.

APPENDIX D

OBEDIENCE

"Behold, to obey is better than sacrifice" (1 Sam. 15:22).

King Saul has just won a battle of annihilation, and now, because of disobedience, Samuel pronounces: "The Lord hath rejected thee from being king" (15:26).

Those are hard lines with which to meet a triumphant, victorious king. It was a hollow victory and an empty triumph. Saul had tried to improve upon the commandment of God. We do the same today, only in more subtle ways.

There are certain words that command respect. They speak of something held in high regard. Few people hold a negative view of these words. One of them is *volunteer*! The sound of the word may cause shivers to run through a person. It is used where ideals are at stake, where danger and death are the reward, where sacrifice is necessary. It has the sound of someone above the crowd—the exception—someone of a free will doing something with the consequences clearly in mind. The word occurs in time of war, and it also applies to the spiritual war, especially in the foreign missions enterprise, as in the Student *Volunteer* Movement of the early part of the twentieth century.

In recent months I have been asking groups of Christians a simple question: "Would you rather volunteer or would you rather obey?" With very few exceptions, every group has responded overwhelmingly to volunteer.

The first time I asked this question was at a junior-high Bible study group. Everybody wanted to volunteer. When asked why they would rather volunteer, the answer was clear. They got credit for volunteering and no credit at all for doing what they were told. One boy added some further insight into the problem. He was thinking about volunteering to clean the basement and was feeling rather fine about it, when his mother cut his musing short with an order for him to clean the basement. She ruined it all! Suddenly, he did not want to clean the basement.

This question was prompted by the passage we were studying:

> Suppose one of you has a servant ploughing or minding sheep. When he comes back from the fields, will the master say, "Come along at once and sit down"? Will he not rather say, "Prepare my supper, fasten your belt, and then wait on me while I have my meal; you can have yours afterwards"? Is he grateful to the servant for carrying out his orders? So with you: when you have carried out all your orders, you should say, "We are servants and deserve no credit; we have only done our duty." (Luke 17:7–10, NEB)

A word that occurs today with great frequency is the word *challenge*. Although it is not a synonym for *volunteer*, there is a close relationship between these words. If *challenge* is used as a synonym for *encourage* or *exhort*, no harm is done. But the word in today's vocabulary connotes the concept of the defiant challenger flinging down the gauntlet; this sort of challenge involves the application of subtle pressures on a man to attempt that which he previously has been either unwilling or unable to do. Often we hear Christian speakers portraying the difficulties and hazards of particular tasks in such a way as to provoke in the minds of their hearers a human pride that makes them eager to volunteer and do that which needs to be done.

The dictionary definition of "challenge" has a close resemblance to the word as we use it today, with one exception: we challenge our own team. According to *Webster's New World Dictionary*, and according to tradition and history, a challenge comes from the enemy, the adversary, the sentry, the opposition.* A challenge should not come from our team. It is defiance, a dare.

Now with this definition, we see the challenge occurring in Scripture. It first occurred subtly, challenging God's authority, when the serpent said to the woman, "You shall not surely die." Other examples include these:

- Satan's challenge to God to let him have access to Job (Job 1:9–11, 2:4–5)
- Goliath's defiance of the armies of Israel (1 Samuel 17:10)
- Elijah's challenge to the prophets of Baal on Mount Carmel (1 Kings 18:21–27)
- The Rabshakeh's famous challenge to the people on the wall to surrender (2 Kings 18:27–37)

When the challenge comes from the enemy, it may come as a threat, a lie, or a promise. In any case, it is an attempt to get us to respond on the enemy's conditions. The very nature of a challenge is to lay out conditions determined by the challenger that the challenged must accept. If he is wise, the challenged will never respond to a challenge on the challenger's conditions.

There is a wonderful example in the New Testament of the enemy's challenge and the proper response: Acts 4:17–31. The apostles' response was *first* according to *God's* directive. "But Peter and John answered them: You yourselves judge which is right in God's sight, to obey you or to obey God. For we cannot stop speaking of what we ourselves have seen and heard" (vv. 19–20, GNT).

They were then threatened again. The apostles' response to this second threatening was to present this challenge from the enemy

* *Webster's New World Dictionary of the American Language*, College Edition (1953), s.v. "challenge."

to the Lord: "'And now, Lord, take notice of the threats they have made, and allow us, your servants, to speak your message with all boldness . . . .' When they finished praying, the place where they were meeting was shaken. They were all filled with the Holy Spirit and began to speak God's message with boldness" (vv. 29, 31, GNT). The apostles did not respond to the challenge in the flesh; they obeyed God and gained His power to be obedient.

Obedience is a willing or an unwilling carrying out of an order or a command. Most of our own experience from childhood up has been of the unwilling kind of obedience. This is one of the reasons *volunteer* has a better reputation than *obey*. In our experience volunteering always means being willing. Obedience always means to be unwilling. If, however, we had known something of willing obedience, then volunteering would be out completely. God does not ask for volunteers, nor does He challenge His own children. When Jesus called His disciples, He did the choosing. He said, "Follow me." It was a simple imperative. There were also a great many volunteers who followed Jesus. The volunteers did not last.

Perhaps you think that volunteering is a greater expression of love than obedience. What is your basis? Jesus said, "If you love me you will obey my commands," and "The man who has received my commands and obeys them—he it is who loves me" (John 14:15, 21, NEB). He made simple, absolute, and authoritative statements. These were not challenges seeking volunteers, nor were they goals or landmarks to stretch our reach, to make us try harder. They were imperatives of an absolute nature. Not to obey them was sin. Every imperative from God since has had an absoluteness in its character that defies improvement of the commandment or satisfaction if one falls short of the requirement.

In order to get men into the armed forces, they put out recruiting posters. "Be all that you can be," "Aim High," "The few, the proud, the

Marines." These are challenges to appeal to the pride of men so that they will volunteer and join the army. However, once the man volunteers, the whole system changes. He is no longer appealed to. He is commanded, and he obeys. The army could not command him into the army, so they used the challenge in order to get him to volunteer. Once he is in, it is a different story. Enlisting is the beginning of a command-obedience relationship.

There is also an upper limit to this obedience, not as clearly defined as the enlistment at the beginning. In fact, it is always defined after the fact. For instance, an Army captain calls for his own position to be bombed with napalm in order to destroy the enemy who has his company outnumbered and is overrunning his position. He receives the Silver Star and is recommended for the Congressional Medal of Honor for "danger above and beyond the call of duty." In the Army, there is a beginning to obedience, and there is a place above and beyond obedience. Between the lower limit and the upper limit the relationship is command-obedience.

Is there a lower limit to obedience in our relationship with God? There may be a lower limit in our ability to obey, but not a lower limit in the requirement to obey. This ability begins when we know Jesus Christ. In 1 John 2:3 we are told, "If we obey God's commands, then we are sure that we know him" (GNT). But before we knew Jesus Christ, we were under the command of God. And 1 Timothy 1:9 says, "It must be remembered, of course, that laws are made, not for good people, but for lawbreakers and criminals, for the godless and sinful, for those who are not religious or spiritual, for men who kill their fathers or mothers" (GNT). Even our repentance unto life was commanded by God. In fact, it is a command to all men. Here it is in Paul's declaration at the University of Athens: "God has overlooked the times when men did not know, but now he commands all men everywhere to turn away from their evil ways" (Acts 17:30, GNT).

No, God does not have a lower limit to obedience. He does not challenge us to volunteer for Christ. He commands all people everywhere to repent.

Is there an upper limit to obedience in the Christian life? Is there a "danger above and beyond the call of duty"? Can we volunteer beyond the highest command of God? What is the greatest command? Jesus said: "And thou shalt love the Lord thy God with all thy heart, and with all thy soul, and with all thy mind, and with all thy strength: this is the first commandment" (Mark 12:30). Now look at it again and see if by volunteering we can go beyond it. The superlatives are all there. God requires all of each of our faculties to love Him.

In Christian churches today it is normal to hear challenges to greater heights than ever before, but less of the commands. Because the commandments of God are way beyond us—ideals that are not very realistic for the present—we make a graded scale and challenge Christians to follow the graded scale one step at a time. This is because we do not believe God provides the power and love and wisdom to obey His superlative commands as they are given. And since He does not provide, we decide we will dispense with the obedience, which is frustrating, and do it our way: challenge-volunteer. If we volunteer for less than the commandment requires, we are disobedient, even if we gain our objective.

There are many Christian works that are using the challenge today to get Christians supposedly to obey God in everything from Bible reading to the Great Commission. They are using it because it seems to work. Christians are proud, too proud to obey. They will go to foreign mission fields because of a challenge presented in a dynamic way describing the lostness of the people, the dangers, and the hardships, whereas they will not go in obedience to a simple command given by Jesus Christ. A challenge is an appeal to the pride, to human ego. The challenge is doubly wrong:

- It puts people on the foreign field who should be there, but it gets them there with a wrong motive.
- It puts people there who should not be there.

There are men who have gone to the field in response to a challenge only to find it was obedience that could keep them there.

If we are not to challenge and we are not to volunteer and our only experience of obedience has been reluctant, recalcitrant obedience, how do we get so that we willingly obey? It all has to do with our view of the Commander. Do we worship Him, stand in awe of Him, love Him, fear Him, long to be with Him? Or are we buddy-buddy with Him? Do we think it is a fifty-fifty relationship? The latter is not love and will never get instant obedience. All of our obedience will be qualified, and therefore disobedience.

> Now the end of the commandment is charity [love] out of a pure heart, and of a good conscience, and of faith unfeigned. (1 Tim. 1:5, KJV)

> If ye be willing and obedient, ye shall eat the good of the land. (Isa. 1:19, KJV)*

---

* Originally published as Chapter 11 of my book *Principles of War: A Handbook on Strategic Evangelism.* The sixth edition was co-published by Community Christian Ministries and Canon Press in 2017.